THE
AFROCENTRIC
PARADIGM

EDITED BY

AMA MAZAMA

Africa World Press, Inc.

P.O. Box 1892

Trenton, NJ 08607

P.O. Box 48

Asmara, ERITREA

Africa World Press, Inc.

P.O. Box 1892
Trenton, NJ 08607

P.O. Box 48
Asmara, ERITREA

Book Design: Getahun Seyoum Alemayehu
Cover Design: Ashraful Haque

Library of Congress Cataloging-in-Publication Data

The Afrocentric paradigm / Ama Mazama, editor.
p. cm
Includes bibliographical references and index.
ISBN 1-59221-016-3 (hard cover) -- ISBN 1-59221-017-1 (pbk.)
1. Afrocentrism. I. Mazama, Ama, 1961-
DT15 .A365 2002

2002010372

CONTENTS

Acknowledgements

Asante Sana

To God, to the Loa, to the Ancestors and to the Elders who have walked with me, and showed me the path, I give infinite praise and thanks.

Several people have helped, in many different ways, in the completion of this book. Although it would be impossible to list them all, I must nonetheless first and foremost acknowledge Adisa Alkebulan's most precious, dedicated and relentless technical assistance and moral support; Molefi Asante, my friend and colleague, who always encouraged me, and made himself available when clarification was needed; P. Yaa Asantewaa Reed's kind words and deeds of support; Zainabu Jones's fighting and generous spirit; Ibo Changa, who took me to the river and did for me more than either of us knows; as well as many of my students, graduate and undergraduate, for whom I ultimately edited this book, hoping that it will inspire them to keep the flame alive.

To Kassahun Chekole, who has done more than any to provide a safe space for Afrocentric scholarship and immediately accepted to publish this book, I owe much gratitude.

Finally, I wish to thank my life-partner and husband, Garvey, and our beautiful and beloved children. This book is for them.

INTRODUCTION

The Afrocentric Paradigm

Ama Mazama

The publication of *Afrocentricity: The Theory of Social Change* (1980), by Molefi Asante, along with that of *The Afrocentric Idea* (1987), and *Kemet, Afrocentricity and Knowledge* (1990) introduced fundamental referential changes in the African community. Today, Afrocentricity has become a formidable Pan-African development, which must be reckoned with, as it is present in the United States of course, but also in Africa, Europe, South and Central America, and the Caribbean, where it is widely discussed. The reason for its appeal lies both in the disturbing conditions of African people, and the remedy that Afrocentricity offers.

Although most Africans, on the Continent as well as in the Diaspora, have, at least in theory, put an end to the colonial rule to which we were subjected for many years, we nonetheless still find ourselves in a state of mental subjugation that has gravely interfered with our ability to recover our integrity and truly decolonize ourselves. The reason for this is that colonization was not simply an enterprise of economic exploitation and political control, as it was commonly held, but also an on-going enterprise of conceptual distortion and invasion, leading to widespread confusion, and ultimately, "mental incarceration." In fact, the economic and political dimension of colonization must be analyzed within the broader context of the European cultural ethos that generated the economic exploitation and political suppression of African people, and co-opted our struggles for emancipation from colonial domination by controlling our conceptual/cultural space through the imposition of the European cultural mode as universal. The mental/conceptual aspect of colonization has never stopped. It has simply taken on new names, from civilizing mission in the nineteenth century, to modernization, development, democracy, globalization, and free market, nowadays.

The ontological *reduction* of colonized people that is a necessary part of colonialism has been well understood and described, thanks in particular to Albert Memmi (1991) and Frantz Fanon (1952; 1968). Those two authors exposed quite brilliantly the dialectical relationship that colonialism creates between a hyper-valorized colonial culture and a systematically denigrated colonized culture. Animality and puerility are the two major metaphors around which the reductive discourse on the colonized is organized. Conversely, the colonizer, who is supposed to have reached a higher level in the evolutionary ladder, is made to symbolize the perfection that maturity and wisdom bring. The conclusion is self-evident: only through a careful imitation of Europeans can colonized people hope to improve their lot, and move out of animality and childhood into full humanity and adulthood. This imitation process corresponds to what Mudimbe (1988) has referred to as the *conversion* process.

This other, yet critical, aspect of colonization has generally not been as well understood as the reduction process mentioned above. The reason for this is probably that the critiques of the colonial enterprise still functioned within a fundamentally European conceptual framework. Frantz Fanon, for example, was a Marxist, and as such, adhered to evolutionary thinking As a result, he seemed to agree with the Europeans that the "African masses" were in need of "development." The same analysis applies to Aime Cesaire's famous *Discourse on Colonialism* (1989), in which Cesaire attacked and condemned European colonialism. However, Cesaire still did not question some fundamental European values, such as progress, and the linear and Universalist position that generated it. In other words, what was being critiqued was not Western modernity, but its abusive practices, as if the two could be separated. Europe's tacit advancement of its own culture as some "no man's cultural land," its implicit claims to cultural neutrality were never seriously challenged for they were not construed as problematic.

Such an approach, which was to be expected given the time, could not allow one to understand European colonization as the systematic imposition of the European world view, whereas ways of being, doing, seeing, feeling, knowing, etc. were being devalued, discarded, and replaced with supposedly better, i.e., European ones, resulting in Europe's occupation of quasi-all human space.

Afrocentricity, however, contends that our main problem is precisely our, usually unconscious, adoption of the Western worldview and perspective and their attendant conceptual framework. The list of those ideas and theories that have invaded our lives as 'normal', 'natural', or even worse, 'ideal', is infinite. How many of us have really paused to seriously examine and challenge such ideas as 'the need for democracy', 'planning', 'progress', 'the nation-state as the best form of political and social organization', to name only a few? Our failure to recognize the roots of such ideas in the European cultural ethos has led us, willingly or unwillingly, to agree to footnote status in the White Man's Book.

4

We thus find ourselves relegated to the "periphery," the "margin" of the European experience to use Molefi Asante's terms, spectators of a show that defines us from without. In other words, and to use Afrocentric terminology again, we do not exist on our own terms, but on borrowed, European ones. We are dislocated, and having lost sight of ourselves in the midst of European decadence and madness, it becomes increasingly difficult for us to orient our lives in a positive and constructive manner, hence the plight that is ours.

The challenge is monumental: our liberation, Afrocentricity contends, rests upon our ability to systematically displace European ways of thinking, being, feeling, etc., and consciously replace them with ways that are germane to our own African cultural experience. They key idea here is *epistemological centeredness*: Afrocentricity, Molefi Asante tells us, establishes

> A frame of reference wherein phenomena are viewed from the perspective of the African person ... it centers on placing people of African origin in control of their lives and attitudes about the world. This means that we examine every aspect of the dislocation of African people; culture, economics, psychology, health and religion ... As an intellectual theory, Afrocentricity is the study of the ideas and events from the standpoint of Africans as the key players rather than victims. This theory becomes, by virtue of an authentic relationship to the centrality of our own reality, a fundamentally empirical project ... it is Africa asserting itself intellectually and psychologically, breaking the bonds of Western domination in the mind as an analogue for breaking those bonds in every other field. (1991: 172)

To the extent that it places the African experience at the heart of African lives, it is only fair to state that Asante's main category of thought is culture, defined as "shared perceptions, attitudes, and predispositions that allow people to organize experiences in certain ways." (Asante, 1990: 9).

The Afrocentric idea is a powerful one. Kwame Nantambu even suggests that it represents "the most potent challenge to the European power structure (European nationalism) in the past 100 years." (1996: 47) The Afrocentric idea rests on the assertion of the primacy of the African experience for African people. Its aim is to give us our African, victorious, consciousness back. In the process, it also means viewing the European voice as just one among many, and not necessarily the wisest one.

There is still, however, considerable misunderstanding, in the academic world and as a result, in the community at large, about what exactly Afrocentricity entails. The definitions of Afrocentricity are multiple, most scholars giving their own working and free version of the original one elaborated by Molefi Asante, often choosing to emphasize particular aspects of the paradigm to suit their own purposes.

Others seem to take for granted that the term Afrocentric is self-explanatory, and as a result, do not bother to define Afrocentricity. Kinfe

Abraham's study of Black Nationalism (1991) comprises a section entitled "Afro-centric and Pan-African Strategies" which unfortunately does not include a definition of Afrocentricity. Another case in point is Janice Hamlet's recently edited *Afrocentric Visions* (1998), which quite curiously does not even contain an introduction, let alone a definition of Afrocentricity by the editor.

Finally, there are also those who clearly misunderstand Afrocentricity altogether. Such is the case, for example, of Patricia Hill Collins who argues that what makes one Afrocentric is the participation in "a core African value system" coupled with the experience of oppression (1991: 206). However, to be African is not to be necessarily Afrocentric, as shall be discussed below. In addition, Afrocentricity stresses the importance of cultivating a consciousness of victory, as opposed to dwelling on oppression. Another striking example of total misunderstanding of Afrocentricity is provided by Russell Adams (1993). According to Adams, "the purest form of Afrocentrism places Africa at its center as the source of the world's people and its most fundamental ideas and inventions" (1993: 34). Afrocentrism places Africa at the center of African people's world, while stressing all people's entitlement to practice and celebrate their own culture, as long as it does not interfere with the collective well-being: "All people have a perspective which stems from their centers. (...) While Eurocentrism imposes itself as universal, Afrocentrism demonstrates that it is only one way to view the world" (Asante, 1988: 87-9). Furthermore, Adams suggests the following classification of Afrocentrists: the "Nile Valley" Afrocentrists (the "hard-liners" identified as espousing "pure Afrocentrism," and gathered around Molefi Asante); the Continental Afrocentrists, who do not pay any special attention to Kemet; the Afrocentric Infusionists, primarily concerned with making the African cultural and social experience a part of the curriculum; and the Social Afrocentrists, for whom "Africa per se is more of a target of interest than of inspiration" (1993: 35), and whom, upon examination, seem to favor integration into white society. Such intellectual bric-a-brac, dumped under the label Afrocentricity, is bound to dilute the meaning and the power of the Afrocentric idea as well as to create a great deal of confusion.

Our contention is that there is confusion in large part because scholars have often failed to approach Afrocentricity in a systematic manner. We must, therefore, be particularly grateful to Danjuma Modupe (this volume) for identifying the seven following basic and interrelated components of the Afrocentric theory: the Afrocentric objective; the consciousness matrix for definition; the formal academic framework; the condition complex; theoretical constructs; the structural gluon; and victorious consciousness. Generally speaking, the source of Afrocentricity, Modupe contends, is the African collective cognitive will to cultural and psychic liberation, while the ultimate objective of Afrocentricity is African development, i.e., African existence on African terms. What will allow the Afrocentric goal to be reached is what Modupe calls a consciousness matrix, informed by Afrocentric consciousness, a fundamentally dynamic process. Concerning the academic manifestation of Afrocentricity, the focus of this author, Modupe suggests that the Afrocentric academic framework is made up of three pyramidal elements: *grounding* in the

African historical and cultural experiences (i.e., epistemology); *orientation*, i.e., having and developing interest in Africa and her people. This component, which is essentially psycho-intellectual, corresponds to the axiological dimension; while *perspective*, the third component, is a self-conscious way of looking at, and interacting with the world, and as such may be said to correspond to the ontological and cosmological dimensions. This pyramid culminates with the attainment of consciousness of victory. As Modupe rightly explains, all three components are necessary in order for one to be able to refer to an Afrocentric framework. For example, while one may be well grounded in African culture and history, one is not necessarily Afrocentric. Indeed, it is critical that Afrocentricity be correctly understood as a perspective, not as a worldview, as some mistakenly do. In that respect, the term 'African-centeredness' is clouded with confusion, and would need to be defined by the many who use it, especially in free distribution with the term Afrocentricity.

As we seek to bring further clarification to what Afrocentricity entails from an academic standpoint, we would like to suggest, as a first step, that Afrocentricity, within the academic context, will best be understood as a *paradigm*.

The concept of 'paradigm' is undoubtedly ambiguous. It has received multiple definitions since its very inception, in 1962 (Kuhn, 1962). Margaret Masterman (1970: 61) reports no less than twenty-one definitions by Kuhn himself (1962) of a paradigm!

Kuhn borrowed the term 'paradigm' from Linguistics, where a paradigm refers to a class of linguistic items, either lexical or grammatical, which are in complementary distribution. His intention, as a philosopher of science, was to show how a particular mode of scientific thought and practice becomes established as an accepted and/or dominant mode, thus being labeled 'normal science', and may be subsequently displaced by a new mode competing for 'normalcy' or disciplinary recognition (1962; 1970). While Kuhn's model was primarily intended for the natural sciences, it has been widely applied to the studies of human life as well. One of the chief accomplishments of the concept of paradigm, as developed by Kuhn, is to make explicit the existence of premises upon which all intellectual inquiries are necessarily based, thus rendering the idea of scientific neutrality and universality untenable.

There are two central aspects to a paradigm as defined by Kuhn: the cognitive aspect and the structural aspect (Eckberg & Hill, 1980: 117-8). As far as the cognitive aspect is concerned, Masterman (1970), suggests the existence of three different levels: a) *metaphysical*, i.e., an organizing principle, a set of beliefs; b) *sociological*, i.e., a set of scientific habits, "a disciplinary matrix" (Kuhn, 1970: 182), "the shared commitments of any disciplinary community," (Eckberg & Hill, 1980: 118), be it in terms of methods, conceptual apparatus, techniques, etc.; and c) *exemplars*, "the concrete problem-solutions that students encounter from the start of their scientific education, whether in laboratories, or examinations, or at the ends of chapters in science texts" (Kuhn, 1962: 102). Concerning the structural arrangement of the three cognitive aspects of a paradigm, Eckberg & Hill (1980: 121) suggest that they "are embedded within one another. That is, the greater structure (the metaphysical paradigm) acts an encapsulating unit, or framework, within which the more restricted, or higher-order, structures develop. A specific disciplinary matrix will not develop within just any arbitrary Weltanschauung. An exemplar will be even further restricted." In the end, as the same authors explain, "a paradigm locks its practitioners together within a fairly rigid, highly elaborated framework of beliefs. This is not a serendipitous overlapping of elements from various perspectives. It is made of the consensual beliefs of a self-contained community. No analysis which neglects the *communal* nature of a paradigm can capture the essence of the concept" (Eckberg & Hill, 1980: 122).

As far as the second central aspect is concerned, namely the structural aspect, what Kuhn has in mind is the "community structure," i.e., the community of scholars who practice the cognitive dimension of the paradigm. Shedding light on the importance of a scientific community, Eckbert & Hill (1980: 121-2) tell us how "a paradigm presupposes an integrated community of practitioners. Ongoing puzzle solving, in fact occurs only when a group exists which shares a consistent body of beliefs such that a consensus emerges with regard to the phenomena one/ investigates, the methods one uses, and so forth."

However, while Kuhn's treatment of a paradigm may appear to be rather comprehensive from a Eurocentric standpoint, it is lacking an important dimension, as far as Afrocentricity is concerned. Indeed, we must add a third and critical aspect to the cognitive and structural aspects, namely, a *functional aspect*. From an Afrocentric perspective, where knowledge can never be produced for the sake of it, but always for the sake of our liberation, *a paradigm must activate our consciousness* to be of any use to us. This requirement is reminiscent of the tradition that existed in Ancient Kemet when the priests opened the mouth of the statues of the gods, in order to insufflate life and consciousness in them, thus allowing them to serve the people who served them. Just like without that spiritual act the statues would have remained pieces of rock, without the right type of energy, any set of ideas and practices is unable to move us, and in any case, remains largely irrelevant to our lives. The ultimate test will be our praxis.

Furthermore, given some of the most fundamental assumptions that African culture makes about the nature life, it is necessary to add to the cognitive category identified by Khun as central, two additional categories, namely the affective and conative ones.

Maulana Karenga, in his article devoted to the critical issue of paradigmatic development for Black Studies, does not recognize paradigmatic status to Afrocentricity. While, with his usual insight and articulateness, Karenga correctly and cogently defined Afrocentricity as *"essentially a quality of perspective or approach rooted in the cultural image and human interest of African people"* (1988:404), and described it as a "fundamental building bloc in the conceptual edifice of the Black Studies Paradigm," Karenga did not seem to believe that Afrocentricity was *the* "Black Studies Paradigm" he and others yearned for at the time of his writing. This may be attributed to Karenga's loose definition of a paradigm, a not so uncommon occurrence, as noted above.

Instead, Karenga talks about Afrocentricity as a 'category', although he does not specify what, in his view, a category is to a paradigm.

It is our contention, however, as we shall illustrate below, that Afrocentricity meets the definition of a paradigm, as outlined above. As Karenga himself rightly remarked, the rise of Afrocentricity is intimately linked to African Studies: "Any serious discussion of Afrocentricity must begin by placing it in the context of Africana or Black Studies" (Karenga, this volume). We would like to go even further by asserting that such discussion must also include the development of the Department of African American Studies at Temple University, under the leadership of Professor Asante, for it is within that particular structure that Afrocentricity has been able to evolve into a paradigm. (This also sheds light on the true nature and scope of the attacks launched against the philosophical orientation of that department.)

I. The affective, cognitive, and conative aspects of the Afrocentric paradigm:

A. Metaphysical: the organizing principle that determines the perception of all reality is the centrality of the African experience for African people. This is the one principle that can never be questioned by any person claiming to be Afrocentric: "The Afrocentrist will not question the idea of the centrality of African ideals and values but will argue over what constitutes those ideals and values" (Asante, 1990: 6). The epistemological implications of Afrocentricity are far-reaching; its applications endless: "Afrocentricity questions your approach to every conceivable human enterprise. It questions the approach you make to reading, writing, jogging, running, eating, keeping healthy, seeing, studying, loving, struggling, and working" (Asante, 1988: 45). In the end, it is, as Molefi Asante beautifully states, "the measure of our life."

Inasmuch as it places "African values and ideas" at the center of African life, Afrocentricity espouses the cosmology, aesthetics, axiology and epistemology that characterize African culture. Karenga (this volume) identifies as the core cultural African characteristics the following "shared orientations": 1) the centrality of the community; 2) respect for tradition; 3) a high level spirituality and ethical concern; 4) harmony with nature; 5) the sociality of selfhood; 6) veneration of ancestors; and 7) the unity of being.

Thus, what defines Afrocentricity is the crucial role attributed to the African social and cultural experience as our ultimate reference. This is also what distinguishes it from any previous body of thought. It is not uncommon to hear or read that Afrocentricity pre-dated the publication of Molefi Asante's first book on the topic. Everybody under the sun who had something constructive to say about African people is then casually labeled Afrocentric, from David Walker to Kwame Nkrumah. It is nonetheless fairly easy to understand why such a position (usually the result of professional jealousy) is mistaken once one has correctly identified the fundamental Afrocentric organizing principle. It is simply untrue that any thinker, prior to Molefi Asante, had elaborated and systematized an intellectual approach based on the centrality of the African experience, i. e, Afrocentricity. Certainly, we find in previous scholars the assertion that the African experience is different from the European experience, and must be seen as such –from Blyden's insistence on the infusion of the curriculum with information about African history and culture to Marcus Garvey's emphasis on the necessity to look at the world through "our own spectacles." Also, DuBois's call for a "Negro university" to interpret African and African American phenomena was along the same line. However, it is to Molefi Asante that we owe the making of African epistemological relevance into an operational scientific principle, much like we owe Cheikh Anta Diop the making of the blackness of the Ancient Egyptians into an operational scientific principle (Diop, 1991).

It would be incorrect, on the other hand, to believe that Afrocentricity emerged in a vacuum. As Africans, we are fully aware that nothing is created ab novo but is very much a manifestation of the continuity of life. As such, Afrocentricity has integrated the major principles of several previous philosophical systems. Those principles, which are primary both chronologically and logically, are the foundation upon which Afrocentricity built itself, and function very much as its premises. Asante himself (1980: vi; 104) identifies four major foundational blocks to Afrocentricity, namely Garvey's philosophy, the Negritude movement, Kawaida and Diop's historiography. To these, I have taken the liberty, upon closer examination of Afrocentricity, to add Fanonism.

Marcus Garvey is credited with having developed fully Black Nationalism as an ideology, i.e., as a set of ideas, attitudes, and values about society and the place and role of Black people in it. The main category of thought of Black Nationalism is race, "the essence of man," as far as Garvey is concerned (Wilson, 1982:33). Race is defined primarily as a biological reality, but functions as a political force in society. It provides the key to understanding how particular alliances are forged, or should be forged, among people who look alike. Racial commitment on the part of Black people is a must for Garvey, for upon it is predicated the survival of African people.

In addition, the racial community defined by Garvey is decisively Pan-African:

> "Everybody knows, Garvey declares, that there is absolutely no difference between the native African and the American and West Indian Negroes, in that we are descendants from one common family stock. It is only a matter of accident that we have been divided and kept apart for over three hundred years, but it is felt that when the time has come for us to get back together, we shall do so in the spirit of brotherly love …" (Garvey, 1992:70-1).

Moreover, the commitment to the race is inseparable from a commitment to Africa, the only true home to Black people. In fact, Garvey assigned a special mission, redemption, to those Africans born in the Americas visa vis Africa. His espousal of 'African Zionism' certainly made Garvey the true heir of previous African thinkers such as Delany, Blyden, Bishop Turner and Crummell.

The organizing principle of Black Nationalism as developed by Marcus Garvey is African agency. African agency subsumes a consciousness of victory. Or else, why should anyone want to assume agency if not to achieve victory? How could anyone talk about agency if they did not believe in the possibility of victory? Why should anyone talk about victory if they were satisfied with defeat? The indomitable consciousness of victory that informs all of Garvey's philosophy makes it a truly powerful drive towards self-determination, one that has moved millions of Black people the world over.

Marcus Garvey's conceptualization of African agency is predictated upon two very important ideas: a conception of power as a divine attribute, and a deep commitment to the Ancestors.

A profoundly spiritual man, Marcus Garvey, as several scholars have convincingly argued (Burkett, 1978; McLean, 1982), was consciously building a Black civil religion whose God was Black, Great and Almighty (Martin, 1974: 429). Garvey's emphasis on agency was largely predicated upon his conception of God as one who had made all people equal and masters of their destiny; a God who would be content only if his children lived up to their divine origin and exercised fully their will in determining their life conditions: Garvey, McLean (1982:111) writes in his excellent study, "calls upon the Black race to acknowledge power as a divine right and a functional tool for human upliftment". It was crucial to Garvey that Black people realized and acted upon our godly nature, for victims of white people's bluff, we had accepted the idea of our inferiority, and fallen into a dependent, second-class people category, a most despicable situation, in Garvey's eyes:

> Created in the image of the same God we have the same common rights, and - to see things as they are today I trust that there will be a spiritual and material resurrection among Negroes everywhere; that you will lift yourselves from the doubts of the past; that you will lift yourselves from the slumbers of the past, that you will lift yourselves from the lethargy of the past, and strike out in this new life –in this resurrected life- to see things as they are (Garvey, 1992: 90).

And again,

> I repeat that God created you masters of your own destiny, masters of your own fate, and you can pay no higher tribute to your Divine Master than function as man, as He created you (Garvey, 1992: 91)

Equally important is the fact that Garvey's concept of agency was predicated upon a deep respect and appreciation for the Ancestors, for their accomplishments, struggles and sufferings, from which Garvey derived a profound sense of duty, and victory:

> We are the descendants of the men and women who suffered in this country for two hundred and fifty years under that barbarous, that brutal institution known as slavery. You

who have not lost trace of your history will recall the fact that over three hundred years ago your forebears were taken from the great Continent of Africa and brought here for the purpose of using them as slaves. Without mercy, without any sympathy they worked our forebears. They suffered, they bled, they died. But with their sufferings, with their blood, which they shed in their death, they had a hope that one day their posterity would be free, and we are assembled here tonight as the children of their hope.

I trust each and everyone of you will realize that you have a duty which is incumbent upon you; a duty that you must perform, because our fore-bears who suffered, who bled, who died had hopes that are not yet completely realized. (1992: 79-80)

And again,

What then are you going to do to show your appreciation of this love, what gratitude are you going to manifest in return for what they have done for you? As for me, knowing the sufferings of my fore-fathers I shall give back to Africa that liberty that she once enjoyed hundreds of years ago, before her own sons and daughters were taken from her shores and brought in chains to this Western World. (1992:81)

In the main, "In the theology of Garvey, stress is placed on the Black man as *subject* and *hero* of his history, and is situated within a transnational geographic boundary" (McLean, 1982: 105; my emphasis). While some scholars have chosen to stress the European influence on Garvey's thought (Hill, 1987; Reed, 1986), such focus, in our view, often fails to address and appreciate fully Garvey's unique, outstanding, and lasting contribution to many African people, i.e., a powerful and victorious sense of self as Africans.

The importance of Garvey's philosophy to Afrocentric thought cannot be underestimated: African agency and its attendant consciousness of victory predicated upon ancestor veneration, a Pan-African perspective, a deep commitment to African people and Africa (even though the 'salvation theme' is not as pronounced in Afrocentricity) are all intricate parts of the Afrocentric paradigm, as far as the metaphysical aspect is concerned.

There are also, of course, points of divergence between Garveyism and Afrocentrism. The main one concerns the purely biological definition of race. Indeed, because of its assumption that our main predicament today as African people is our living on imposed European cultural terms, instead of our own, Afrocentricity considers a person's intellectual/cultural point of anchor to be of the greatest relevance, along with their physical outlook and place of ancestry. Although Garvey used 'blackness' and 'Africanness' interchangeably, the two are not synonymous by Afrocentric standards. There is no denying that Garvey could be quite critical of Western civilization. In one instance, he referred to it as "a civilization that is competing with itself for its own destruction; a civilization that cannot last, because it has no spiritual foundation; a civilization that is vicious, crafty, dishonest, immoral, irreligious and corrupt" (Garvey, 1992: 31), and he further warned us that "If the Negro is not careful he will drink in all the poison of modern civilization and die from the effects of it" (Garvey, 1992:13). However, very much like Fanon and Cesaire and many other great African thinkers, Garvey did not seem to be in a position to question the claim to universality made by European culture. As a result, he equated giving ourselves the means to emulate Europeans with putting an end to our predicament as a people. It should be clear at this point that Afrocentricity does not take such a position. Focusing instead on the imperative need to retrieve and embrace African values and ideals, Afrocentricity presents itself as the most potent manifestation of African nationalism today, where 'Africa' refers to a cultural space. It has also been referred to as African Cultural Nationalism.

This acute awareness and embrace of the cultural specificity of African people, Afrocentricity owes, at least in part, to the Negritude movement. However, before examining the Negritude philosophy, it is necessary to review another great African philosopher, who also developed a philosophy and praxis of action, namely Frantz Fanon, and whose influence over Afrocentricity was therefore great.

The well-known African-Caribbean psychiatrist was born in 1925 in the French Caribbean colony of Martinique, and therefore lived at a time when European colonization of the world, and of Africa in particular, was in full swing. It is safe to say that the question that preoccupied Fanon during all of his life was precisely the question of colonization, and of what he saw as its imperative attendant, that is, decolonization. How to end colonialism is a question that haunted Fanon, and informs all of his seminal writings. Effective decolonization, which he understood as a process, and not as some magical transformation happening overnight, first and foremost demanded a correct understanding of the colonization process.

The fundamental characteristic of colonization, Fanon argued, is that it rests on violence. Physical violence, including torturing, violating, massacring (1988: 66), but also, and even more importantly, psychological violence, for Fanon considers that the most horrible crime committed by colonialism "was committed in the heart of man, and consisted of the pathological tearing apart of his functions and the crumbling away of his unity" (1991: 315), which he described in his famous *Black Skin, White Masks*, as resulting in a deep sense of cultural and psychological alienation, based on self-rejection, self-hatred, and a futile and tragic attempt on the part of the colonized to regain their humanity through the apish imitation of white people: "Having judged, condemned, abandoned his cultural forms, his language, his food habits, his sexual behavior, his way of sitting down, of resting, of laughing, of enjoying himself, the oppressed *flings himself* upon the imposed culture with the desperation of a drowning man" (1991: 39). This is because colonization, as a project of "dehumanization rationally pursued" (1991: 64), constructs new ontological categories which confer humanity and superiority to the colonizers, while squarely denying the humanity and equality of the colonized. In that respect,

13

Fanon considers both whiteness and blackness to be colonial inventions, with no referents in reality, but only infused with meanings that will conveniently support the colonial status quo. For example, in his view, the white emphasis on the black man's remarkable sexuality ("In relation to the Negro, everything takes place on the genital level," (1967: 157)), reinforces the racist classification of black people among other mammals, while revealing European feelings of sexual inadequacy (1967: 159), and Fanon thus concludes that "the man who adores the Negro is as "sick" as the man who abominates him" (1967: 8). The problem is that many colonized people, while attempting to free themselves from colonial subjugation, remain stuck in those racist colonial categories, and thus, proclaim their blackness to themselves and the world, while as Fanon sees it, the real issue is the liberation and building of "man" in each of us. Indeed, the major crime of European colonization is the murder of "man": "The disaster and the inhumanity of the white man lie in the fact that somewhere he has killed man" (1967: 231), and again, "Leave this Europe where they are never done talking of Man, yet murder men everywhere they find them, at the corner of everyone of their own streets, in all the corners of the globe" (1991: 311). Thus, in this context, it appears obvious to Fanon, whose reasoning was clearly dialectical, that true decolonization entails, in turn, the destruction of the white oppressors (thus destroying whiteness), not just symbolically, but literally, as he states himself quite clearly: "What the colonial countries want is not a "kind gesture" on the part of the master, but quite literally the death of this master" (1988: 116). Fanon's advocacy of physical violence is well-known, and can only be correctly understood as a necessary component of the decolonization process. It has a therapeutic value, which must liberate the colonized from their fear and inferiority complex vis a vis the colonizer. By making that choice, of fighting back, and killing their oppressors, it is also extremely important to understand that the colonized is asserting his own humanity. Indeed, for Fanon, who was heavily influenced by Existentialist philosophers (such as Jean-Paul Sartre), the destiny of man is to be free. In this context, the removal of any obstacle to one's freedom, including colonization, is definitely a most human act. Only through the physical annihilation of the colonizers can decolonization actually take place, and the colonized regain their freedom. As mentioned above, the true purpose of decolonization is the restoration of their humanity to the formerly colonized people, and ultimately, the development and nurturing of a true, universal, humanism whereas each and everyone will "enrich the world of men" (1991: 115), the final and much-needed synthesis: "For Europe, for ourselves, and for humanity, we must turn over a new leaf, we must work out new concepts, and try to set afoot a new man" (1991: 316), the purpose of all this being, eventually, to "advance" humanity "a step further" (1991: 315).

We have already discussed the dismissal by Fanon of blackness as a racist ontological category, whose main purpose, is to objectify African people in an attempt to better justify our inferior status in the colonial order while rationalizing white supremacy. What, then, of the role of African culture in this process of re-humanization, or relocation, in Afrocentric terminology? It is clear, from reading Fanon, that he believed that role to be minimal. For him, the assertion of the existence of a beautiful and worthy African culture can only be reactionary: "Discovering the futility of his alienation, his progressive deprivation, the inferiorized individual, after this phase of deculturation, of extraneousness, comes back to his original positions. This culture, abandoned, sloughed off, rejected, despised, becomes for the inferiorized an object of passionate attachment." (1991: 41). "The sense of the past is rediscovered, the worship of ancestors resumed ..." (1991: 43). The culture thus embraced, though, is only at best a caricature, for culture is not something to be exhibited, but lived. However, because of the disruption brought upon by European colonization in the lives of African people, African culture "has vegetated since the foreign domination," and not been "reconceived, grasped anew, dynamized from within" (1991: 42). This "rediscovery," which is best understood as a psychological device, a "defense mechanism," is nonetheless "objectively indefensible" (1991: 43) for it is "archaic," "having no relation to technical development" (1991: 42), in other words, backward. In *Black Skin, White Masks*, Fanon asserts in the clearest terms what he sees as an incompatibility between the "past" and the "demands" of the present and the future: "In no way should I dedicate myself to the revival of an unjustly recognized Negro civilization. I will not make myself the man of any past. I do not want to exalt the past at the expense of my present and of my future" (1967: 226). In fact, in Fanon's view, the past can only "encase" us, while our destiny is to be "free." It is painfully obvious, at this point, that Fanon was under the heavy influence of Western rationalist, individualistic and materialistic philosophers. His own dislocation became most apparent when he went so far as to claim to be his "own foundation," (1967: 231), and as not having "the duty to claim reparations for the domestication of my ancestors. There is no Negro mission," he continued (1967: 228). Very much like Marcus Garvey, Fanon took for granted a universal and linear path for "mankind," a most European concept. It may well be his espousal of Marxism that caused him to underestimate the devastating effect of "conceptual incarceration" and, overall, belittle the role of culture in the struggle for freedom, while emphasizing that "we ought to uplift the people; we must develop their brains, fill them with ideas, change them and make them into human beings" (1991: 197) and not hasten "to send the people back to their caves" (1991: 183).

It would be unfair to Fanon, however, not to recognize his own struggle with his intellectual dislocation. He certainly emphasized the need to "stretch" Marxism to accommodate the colonial experience (1991: 41), and the conclusion of his last essay, the *Wretched of the Earth* is a moving plea to "abandon" Europe, for the latter has unmistakably failed, only creating misery and a "monster," the United States. He pleaded that "We today can do everything, so long as we do not imitate Europe, so long as we are not obsessed by the desire to catch up with Europe. Europe now lives at such a mad, reckless pace that she has shaken off all guidance and all reason, and she is running headlong into the abyss; we would do well to avoid it with all possible speed" (1991: 312). These words of caution are certainly reminiscent of the Afrocentric position that the solutions to African problems lie in Africa, not in Europe, or elsewhere. Thus, while we certainly would not embrace Fanon's problematic espousal of European materialistic and individualistic philosophy, we certainly appreciate his understanding of the imperative need to destroy the colonizer *within* ourselves, as well as his conception of African people as agents, not content to be reifed and victimized by European colonizers, but adamant about defining the parameters of our own existence. Fanon died at the early age of thirty-six, and one can only conjecture about how he would have evolved on the issue of the role of culture in the struggle for African liberation. He was at times quite critical of Negritude; yet, in an era of still unabashed and shameless cultural dislocation, forty years after we supposedly regained our freedom on the Continent, the ideas developed by the Negritude movement deserve our full attention.

Negritude is a literary movement that emerged in Paris in the 1930s. Its main proponents were Aime Cesaire, who coined the word 'negritude', Leopold Sedar Senghor, who defined it as the sum-total of the cultural values and expressions of the Black World; and Leon Gontran Damas. Those three men who were then students in France, were quite cognizant of the tenets of the Haitian Indigenist Movement led by Jean-Price Mars a few decades earlier, as Haitians resisted the American military occupation of their country, as well as they were in close contact with the poets of the Harlem Renaissance. Negritude is also, of course, reminiscent of Blyden's efforts to identify the 'African Personality'.

In an interview to the renowned Haitian Poet, Rene Depestre (1982: 74-6), Aime Cesaire explains that Negritude "was really resistance to cultural assimilation (...). Our struggle, he continues, was against alienation. This is how Negritude was born."

One must remember that the French official policy towards its colonial subjects world-wide was openly and unapologetically assimilationist. While an assimilationist policy seems to imply that the colonized can acquire the colonial culture, it is nonetheless predicated upon an even deeper, and more fundamental belief, that is, the inferiority of the colonized. Indeed, if one is not inferior, why should one renounce one's own cultural ways and adopt another culture? Thus, defined as culturally deficient, the Africans were forced to submit to the French culture, supposedly for our own good. The French language was, and continues to be, a crucial component of that precious French cultural package.

Thus, it is in order to counter the 'African cultural deficiency syndrome' fabricated by the French, as well as other Europeans in their attempt to rationalize their white supremacist plans, that Cesaire, Senghor and Damas elaborated the concept of Negritude, i.e., "a certain way of being a man, especially of living as a man. It is sensitivity, and as such, soul rather than thought. African expressions such as "I want you to feel me" as opposed to "I want you to understand me" are significant in that regard" (Senghor, 1988: 139, my translation). The values and attitudes that characterize and define African people, Senghor tells us, constitute a specific Black ontology, the African essence. All the Black people in the world, Senghor asserts, have in common a particular physio-psychology which is unique to us, and which manifests itself independently of where we find ourselves in the world (Ba, 1973). The main characteristic of Negritude, as understood by Senghor (1973), is an intimate, unmediated contact with the cosmos and the life forces, resulting in an extreme sensitivity to rhythm, the pulse of life. Through this positive definition of African culture, Senghor and his friends were attempting not only to deflate all claims of African cultural inferiority, but also to encourage African people to re-embrace what is ours. In one of his poems, Damas demanded that his "black dolls" be given back to him, while Senghor advocated "African socialism" as the ideal political and economic form of organization for African people. In fact, Senghor insisted that "independence of the mind, cultural independence, is the necessary condition for any other independence: political, economic, social" (cited in Ba, 1973:176). Cesaire also made the case for the critical importance of a conscious return on the part of Diasporic Africans to African culture: "It is from Africa, the source of our culture and of our Caribbean identity that I expect our regeneration; certainly not from Europe which can only add to our alienation. Only Africa can revitalize us, repersonalise us in the Caribbean" (Cesaire, cited in Hausser, 1988: 95).

Negritude and Western culture are presented as being in dialectical opposition to each other. Indeed, the Negritude proponents made a critical assessment of Western culture and its many shortcomings: it is materialistic, individualistic, hypocritical and violent, and has only succeeded in creating a world devoid of real life, joy, and imagination. In contrast, the African universe is dominated by life and rhythm, spirituality and mystery, innocence. Unfortunately, the integrity of the African world has been greatly jeopardized by Europe's savage assaults upon Africa. Hence, the necessity to retrieve a pre-colonial consciousness, our true Negritude.

Quite ironically, however, the apostles of Negritude, in particular Senghor and Cesaire, never fully succeeded in removing themselves from the French cultural/intellectual matrix, despite their repeated assertions about the beauty and worth of African culture. For example, Cesaire, in his famous *Return to my native land*, did not hesitate to refer to the Black man as "one who has never invented anything," while Senghor did not have any qualms identifying rational thinking as fundamentally European. There are at least two reasons for this. First, there is the great influence of anthropology, borne out of a fundamentally racist enterprise, over the definition of Negritude. The German anthropologist, Leo Frobenius, played a significant role in that regard: "It is Frobenius who first turned the African into a complete, real, and happy being, while Western man was cut off from the life forces that permeate the cosmos; it is Frobenius who first saw in the African the preservation of true human values, the only hope for tomorrow's humanity; it is Frobenius, the German mystique irritated by European positivism, in particular French positivism, who suggested to the young Black intellectuals an image of themselves which they took upon themselves to rehabilitate" (Corzani, 1973: 119; my translation). Secondly, there is Cesaire and Senghor's deep love and admiration for the French culture and French language. This is particularly clear with Senghor, who went so far as to distinguish a 'true' France from a 'false' one to rationalize his otherwise incomprehensible and paradoxical attachment to France (Towa, 1971:70). The 'false' one, the colonialist France, he condemned. The 'true' one, the 'civilized' one, he venerated. In the end, Senghor in particular argued that there was no contradiction between chanting the merits of Negritude and embracing French culture! Indeed, in the name of humanism, Senghor developed his concept of "Civilization of the Universal," based on the idea that since all cultures have only cultivated fragments of humanity's potentiality, the best of each culture should therefore be gathered and offered to tomorrow's humanity. The main problem with the "Civilization of the Universal" construct is that it negates the self-sufficiency and autonomy of African culture vis-à-vis European culture, while locking African culture in a relationship of dependence and necessity with European culture, a reflection of Senghor' own ambiguity:

> "...we must aim at cultural achievement, in that cultural achievement we must welcome contributions from outside. First among them are the traditional historical contributions of Europe, reaching us through the channel of force; but we must also equally welcome contributions from Asia, from India, or from China. With all these contributions, we have had to build up in Senegal an authentic culture which is rooted in Negro-African values and which, at the same time, expresses itself in French- and that is why we have naturally tried to produce poets" (Senghor, cited in Ba, 1973: 175-6)

It will come as no surprise that Afrocentricity does not embrace the idea of African cultural incompleteness, nor does it cultivate any veneration for European culture and people. On the other hand, it shares with Negritude the idea of an African cultural matrix common to all African people. Its surface manifestations may vary, may be more or less pronounced depending upon the circumstances in which a particular group finds itself. Obviously, Afrocentricity also shares with Negritude the view that African people must consciously reconnect with our cultural matrix in order to truly free ourselves from European hegemony. Finally, Afrocentricity also tends towards humanism to the extent that it assigns Afrocentricity a "humanizing mission on the earth" (Asante, 1988: 106). It should be noted, however, that humanism has been a common tendency among Black nationalists from the beginning (Stuckey, 1972: 27), and a general feature of African culture.

Kawaida, the fourth conceptual building block upon which Molefi Asante erected Afrocentricity emerged in the late sixties, in the wake of the Civil Rights Movement. It was a significant part of the Black Power movement, and played a critical role in the cultural renaissance that prevailed in the sixties in the African American community.

The Black Power movement came in response to, and in opposition to the assimilationist philosophy that characterized the Civil Rights Movement. Indeed, and as aptly noted by Runcie, "One of the weaknesses of the Civil Rights movement was that it offered no cultural programme other than the integration of Blacks into the dominant white culture, and the implications of this type of 'integration' were greater than a growing number of those Blacks were prepared to accept" (Runcie, 1975: 186). Runcie further continues that while "the achievements of the Civil Rights movement encouraged a certain amount of self-esteem and group pride among Afro-Americans, (...) these trends were inconsistent with the basic assumptions of the integrationist philosophy" (Runcie, 1975: 186). The problem that confronted African Americans was thus not different from the one encountered by the Negritude poets discussed earlier, one of defining ourselves positively while rejecting assimilation and its inherent racist assumptions.

The most outspoken and articulate critic of integrationism and Western civilization at that time was certainly Malcom X, who urged us to see ourselves as Africans in America. A Black Nationalist, Malcom revived many of the ideas developed by Marcus Garvey and others. "His aim, explains Moses, was the spiritual regeneration of black Americans, a heightening of their consciousness of themselves as African people. (...) Afro-Americans were urged to go "back to Africa culturally, philosophically, and psychologically, while remaining here physically"" (Moses, 1985: 211). While Malcom X met an early death in 1965, which did not allow him to implement his ideas, his message did not go unheard. In the years that followed, Black cultural nationalism flourished, with a renewed interest in African cultural symbols, African languages (such as Kiswahili), the demand for Black Studies departments, the recognition and validation of a 'Soul'culture, the Black Arts Movement, and Kawaida (Runcie, 1975). The latter, which was formulated by the US organization and its leader, Maulana Karenga, exemplifies best the ideology of Black Cultural Nationalism that Karenga was instrumental in developing: the basis for a Black nation is first and foremost cultural.

According to Maulana Karenga, "Kawaida, at its core, is a theory of cultural and social change. It defines culture in the broadest sense to equate it with all the thought and activity of a given people or society, but places stress on the ideological –i.e., the view which informs social practice" (Karenga, 1981: 16-7). There is a great need for social and cultural change for Karenga contends that the Black community is in a state of "cultural crisis" that Karenga identifies as the "key crisis in Black life" (Karenga, 1981: 17). Our main problem, as Karenga sees it, is that we have a popular culture, as opposed to a national culture: "Popular culture, Kawaida posits, is the unconscious, fluid reaction to everyday life and environment. In other words, it is social thought and practice defined and limited by its unconsciousness, fluidity and reactiveness. By contrast, national culture is the self-conscious, collective thought and practice thru which a people creates itself and introduces itself to history and humanity" (Karenga, 1981: 18). What Karenga is speaking to is the reciprocal relationship that exists between a people and its culture. While it is clearly understood that culture determines one's outlook on life, it is also necessary to understand that people are ultimately the makers of culture. It is possible, and often necessary, as Karenga would argue, to consciously and deliberately affect the course of culture to make it reflect the best that is within us, as well as serve as a source of inspiration and guidance while we thrive to become the best that we can be.

Thus, to reinforce ourselves as a people, as a nation, Africans must fortify ourselves culturally. More specifically, we must rebuild our national culture. Hence, it is correct to say that, quite logically; the main tenet, or organizing principle of Kawaida is African cultural reconstruction. It is in that perspective that one must understand, for example, the creation by Karenga, in 1966, of Kwanzaa, a truly prodigious accomplishment. Kwanzaa is now celebrated all over the world, by millions of Africans who understood and recognized themselves in Karenga's analysis and project.

The influence of Kawaida over Afrocentricity is great and obvious. In fact, Asante explicitly talks of Afrocentricity as a "rebirth," as well as he makes a case for total devotion to "the African cultural project" (1988: 106). As mentioned above, Afrocentricity is the most recent and potent manifestation of Black Cultural Nationalism since the sixties.

Primarily intended as a theoretical and practical guide to action, though, Kawaida could not provide us with an intellectual apparatus sufficiently elaborated to systematically approach the multiple facets of our cultural dislocation. Also, while it stresses the importance of Pan-Africanism, and clearly inscribes African Americans in the African cultural and historical matrix (Karenga, 1977: 12), Kawaida 's focus is on what Karenga labeled "the New African, Afro-Americans" (Karenga, 1981: 17).

Cheikh Anta Diop identified his own major contribution as the making of the blackness of the Ancient Egyptians into an operational concept, as he explained in the introduction to *Civilization or Barbarism* (1991: 2): "Therefore, for us the new, important fact is less to have stated that the Egyptians were Blacks, as one of our principal sources, the ancient writers already did, than to have contributed to making this idea a conscious historical fact for Africans and the world, and especially to making it an operational scientific concept: this is where our predecessors did not succeed.". What Diop is speaking of here is therefore the conscious elaboration of a paradigm whose main principle is the reclaiming of Ancient Egypt, Kemet, for Africa. The implications of such a philosophical posture are profound, and have been responsible for a true revolution in African historiography.

In order to better appreciate the import of Diop's work, it is necessary to place it within the context that was prevailing when Diop first presented his ideas. That context was marked by European racism, as expressed by Hegel's views on African history; and the imposition of European colonial rule on African people.

Seeing all human history as the manifestation and evolution of consciousness or spirit, Hegel stated that Africans had no history. Hegel's philosophy of history posited a universal and linear development of the spirit when it identified three stages through which the latter passes: a) the subjective mind or spirit, where the spirit is still very much a part of the physical world, and as such undifferentiated from nature; b) the objective spirit, where the spirit manifests itself in "objective social phenomena, e.g., legal systems, morality, political philosophy" (Morris, 1991: 199); and finally c) the absolute spirit, the most developed stage, where the spirit is self-conscious, and expresses itself through art, religion, philosophy, etc., as found in Europe. In Africa, however, the spirit has failed to develop, and has fundamentally remained in its first, subjective stage, i.e., African people do not think of themselves as separated from nature. Thus, according to Hegel, who quite ironically never visited Africa,

> The characteristic feature of the Negroes is that their consciousness has not yet reached an awareness of any substantial objectivity –for example, of God or the law- in which the will of man could participate and in which he could become aware of his own being. The African, in his undifferentiated and concentrated unity, has not yet succeeded in making the distinction between himself as an individual and his essential universality, so that he knows nothing of an absolute being which is other and higher than his own self. Thus, man as we find him in Africa has not progressed beyond his immediate existence. (Hegel, 1822-8, cited in Eze, 1997: 127).

In order to reconcile his views with what was otherwise known about African history, in particular the glorious past of Egypt, Hegel further distinguished three Africas, North Africa, Egypt, and 'Black' Africa, the latter being the real Africa. Egypt, Hegel insisted, "does not belong to the African Spirit. What we understand by Africa is the unhistorical, undeveloped spirit, still involved in the conditions of mere nature, and which had to be presented here only as on the threshold of the world's history" (cited in Keita, 1977: 46).

Although it would be naïve to blame solely Hegel for developing a theory of African history that was consistent with the arrogance and the dishonesty of his people, let it be noticed, however, that Hegel's influence has been profound, and that "with the exception of Marx (who was himself influenced by Hegel), no philosopher during the last two centuries has made such an impact on the [European] world" (Morris, 1996: 189). Certainly, his ideas about African history have been widely read and circulated, as attested by statements made only relatively recently by an Africanist, E. A. Ruch (1973), for whom one of the characteristics of African history, is that "its relevance is restricted to a relatively narrow tribal history" (cited in Keita, 1977: 43).

Moreover, colonialism reinforced Hegel's negative ideas about the lack of African history by a) teaching exclusively European history, thus operating a de facto exclusion of the African historical experience and suggesting ipso facto its insignificance in the face of 'real' history (i.e., European history); b) teaching explicitly that Europe had opened Africa up to civilization. History, it was said, started when Africa was placed in the European orbit. In those colonies subjected to French rule, as Senegal was, the Africans even learnt that our ancestors were the Gauls! The situation was worse for Diasporic Africans who were supposed to have been de-Africanized upon contact with the Europeans. The foolish, and unfortunately widespread idea that our history started in the seventeenth century in the Americas was born.

Thus, besides the devastating toll that slavery and colonialism took upon our lives and lands, they induced a major rupture in our historical consciousness, often leaving us without a sense of historical depth and without a sense of cultural unity and continuity, making us, as a result, extremely vulnerable to further attacks.

What Cheikh Anta Diop aims at is precisely our reinscription within our full and common African historical and cultural matrix. The implications of that new historiography, when drawn systematically, are far-reaching. Diop suggests that Africans consciously and deliberately turn to Kemet as the foundation of our cultural selves. Kemet, to use Karenga's concise phrase, must become again a "source of paradigms" for us. It is no longer necessary, nor excusable for us to refer to Greece or Rome as the beginning of our intellectual endeavors. In fact, Diop tells us that Kemet must be to us, Africans, what Greece and Rome are to the Europeans. Furthermore, our common lineage to Kemet allows one to grasp more clearly and consciously the profound cultural unity of Africa, based as Diop explained on linguistic, psychological, as well as historical evidence.

However, Diop himself greatly diluted the impact of the new historiography that he recommended when he declared, quite paradoxically and surprisingly, that given that Africa was the birthplace of humanity, "no thought, no ideology is, in essence, foreign to Africa." "It is therefore, he continued, with total liberty that Africans can draw from the common intellectual heritage of humanity, letting themselves be guided only by the notions of utility and efficiency." (1991: 4) If this is so, it is only legitimate to wonder why we should turn to Kemet at all? Why can't we satisfy ourselves with turning to Europe and its theories, which is what we have been trained to do, anyway? Yet, Diop himself recognized that those ideas which Europeans had received from Africa had not remained intact, but had been "mixed up, reversed, modified, elaborated" (1991: 3). In other words, they had become new ideas, influenced by the European cultural ethos. Interestingly enough, the very notions of utility and efficiency which he recommends to us are European notions, consistent with the fast-speed, quantity-oriented, materialistic European life-style. Similarly, Diop's plan for the redemption of Africa, as expounded in his essay *Black Africa* (1987*)*, seems to take for granted the path followed by the European, in particular with regard to the issue of the industrialization of Africa. However, we do know now that this path has brought the whole word on the brink of ecological disaster. One could also mention Diop's proposed language planning in Africa, an enterprise which is not without serious cultural implications (see Mazama, this volume for a discussion on planning).

Thus, while Afrocentricity inscribes itself firmly within the Diopian project for a new historiography, one which refuses to make African history start with the European so-called "discovery," but one that goes back to the beginning of life and civilization in Africa, and links all Africans back to that first development; it is also obvious that Afrocentricity does not espouse Diop's belief in the 'universality' of concepts and technologies. It is precisely, Afrocentricity will argue, our acceptance of ideas foreign to our cultural reality and ethos, imposed on us by Europeans as 'universal', that has caused the state of great dislocation in which we find ourselves today. There will be no shortcut to liberation and freedom: we will either define the terms of our existence, or continue being incarcerated. This is no small task. Asante warned us in *Afrocentricity* (1988): it is only for the lion-hearted!

B. The sociological dimension of the Afrocentric paradigm

The sociological dimension of a paradigm deals with the establishment of a 'disciplinary matrix', generated by a particular set of metaphysical principles (i.e., unquestioned presuppositions), and characterized by a specific conceptual apparatus, methodology, and set of theories.

Afrocentricity, Karenga correctly reminded us above, cannot be understood outside of the context of African American Studies. What, then, is Afrocentricity to this discipline called African American Studies? I would like to suggest that Afrocentricity functions, or ought to function, as a meta-paradigm to African American Studies.

Indeed, it is most important to remember the purpose and scope of African American Studies from its inception. Karenga again, in his *Introduction to Black Studies*, (1993: 21) defined it as *"the systematic and critical study of the multidimensional aspects of Black thought and practice in their current and historical unfolding"*, stressing how African American Studies is "a discipline dedicated to an inclusive and holistic study of Black life" (1993: 22). As a result, African American Studies covers the social dynamics, the psychological dynamics, the languages, the literary and oratory expressions, the history, the artistic expressions, etc., the whole cultural and historical experience that defines us as a people.

However, while African American Studies is devoted to studying all aspects of our lives, that task is performed for European lives by various departments and disciplines, which taken together form European Studies. What binds those multiple European Studies departments together, despite seemingly disconnected areas of inquiry, is their focus on the European experience *from the European perspective*.

It is therefore simply incorrect to compare, as it is often done, African American Studies with any single European Studies department, like say sociology, or English, or any other white department, and to claim that just as there exists competing theories and paradigms in Sociology for example, there are different perspectives on the Black experience. To do so is to remain blind to the Eurocentric assumptions, the meta-paradigm, shared by European scholars by virtue of being born into European culture, history and biology.

What is true, though, is that much of what that passes for African American Studies is nothing but European studies of Africa. Such confusion and usurpation are made possible by the unquestioned and unproblematized acceptance of the European perspective as universal. It also points to the fact that the perspective, more so that the focus of study, is the most important criterion to locate a particular study.

What ought to bind African American Studies together, what can only make it what it claims to be, and not something else, despite different areas of interest, is our focus on the African experience from an African perspective, i.e., Afrocentricity. Anything else, like Molefi Asante tells us, is not African American Studies.

In order to avoid the clout of conceptual confusion that surrounds African American Studies, as well as stress the crucial metaphysical connection between the study of African lives and African groundedness, orientation, and perspective, i.e., Afrocentricity, Asante used the term *Africology*, which he defined as " the Afrocentric study of phenomena, events, ideas, and personalities related to Africa. The mere study of phenomena of Africa, Asante continues, is not Africology but some other intellectual enterprise. The scholar who generates research questions based on the centrality of Africa is engaged in a very different research inquiry that the one who imposes Western criteria on the phenomena" (1990:14).

In the essay included in this anthology and entitled 'African American Studies: The future of the discipline', Asante discusses in detail the link that unites Afrocentricity and the discipline of African American Studies. While African American Studies Departments and Programs were established in the late sixties, Asante contends that what can be called the discipline of African American Studies itself is intimately linked to the development of Afrocentricity and the establishment of the Temple Doctoral Program, the first Ph.D. program in African American Studies in the United States, in the late eighties. Afrocentricity provided African American Studies with the perspective, the theories and methods that define it as a discipline, Africology, while the Temple Ph.D. program allowed its development. Afrocentricity, Asante explains, is based on the idea of the centrality of the African experience. It focuses on the Africans as subjects, rather than objects, defined from outside by white supremacists. Within Africology, issues pertaining to African cosmology, epistemology, axiology, and aesthetic must be raised. Furthermore, following Karenga, Asante identifies the seven subject Africological fields: communicative, social, historical, cultural, political, economic and psychological, while recognizing three possible approaches: functional, categoral, and etymological. It also goes without saying that Africology concerns itself with the whole African world, i.e., is Pan-African in its scope. A concrete application of these precepts is found within the Temple M.A. and Ph.D. program where Afrocentric faculty have committed 'discipline suicide' (i.e., have renounced the European paradigm and theories upon which the discipline in which they were trained is based), and students are given the choice between two fields of study, the cultural aesthetics field (involved in such studies as the study of ethics, history, motifs, etc.), and the social behavioral field (dealing, for example, with relationships, race, class, gender, etc.). Asante concludes by suggesting that Africology, as a discipline, i.e., fundamentally an intellectual endeavor, is open to all who can share its perspective and methodology.

It is therefore within the context of Africology that the sociological aspect of the Afrocentric paradigm must be apprehended. The metaphysical and sociological dimensions are profoundly embedded, as made explicit in the following statements: "As a discipline, Africology is sustained by a commitment to centering the study of African phenomena and events in the particular cultural voice of the composite African people" (1990: 12); "Centrism, the groundedness of observation and behavior in one's own historical experiences, shapes the concepts, paradigms, theories, and methods of Africology" (1990:12).

    * *Conceptual Apparatus*: The following are the key concepts relied upon by Africologists: Center /Location/Place – Dislocation – Relocation-

    The concept of *'center'* (also *location, place*) occupies, as it could have been expected, a critical place in the Afrocentric conceptual apparatus. It is fundamentally based on the belief that one's history, culture, and biology determine one's identity. That identity, in turn, determines our place in life, both material and spiritual. To practice one's culture *and* to apprehend oneself in a manner that is consistent with one's history, culture, and biology, is to be centered, or to proceed from one's center. On the other hand, *'dislocation'* occurs either when one lives on "borrowed cultural terms" (Asante: this volume), and/or when one apprehends reality through another group's center. Therefore, the concept of 'center' encompasses both our African identity and our disposition towards that identity. The latter is largely determined by our ability (or inability) to assume agency, which itself is predicated upon our reverence (or lack of) for the ancestors (Modupe, this volume). Indeed, the ultimate question about dislocated Africans, is whether or not they are embracing themselves as Africans and defining themselves on their own terms, or whether they are accepting Europeans' definition of their reality, turning their back on the ancestors. For example, can it be said that those Ghanaian politicians who, only recently, banned the public pouring of libations in Ghana, love and respect themselves as Africans, as we would expect *located* Africans to do, or that they believe, consciously or not, African culture to be inferior, thus exhibiting all signs of dislocation? That dislocation, one must admit, is the result of the acceptance of the European definition of the African reality, i.e., in the end, the closing of one's heart to the Ancestors. Thus, one must emphasize, once more, that Afrocentricity cannot be reduced to the practicing of African culture. Indeed, Asante reminds us that central to the Afrocentric idea is self-consciousness, i.e., the deliberate and systematic effort to assume fully one's place in the world.

    Other terms, such as worldview, cosmology, axiology, aesthetics, and epistemology are frequently used by Africologists in our attempt to consciously and precisely delineate the metaphysical contours of the Afrocentric paradigm and the African worldview on which it is based.

* Afrocentric epistemology, methodology and methods

    It is undeniable that methods and methodologies are derived from, and informed by a particular paradigm. Afrocentric methodology and methods are no exception. The essays included in the present volume (Akbar, Myers, Harris, and Asante) reveal the following consensus:

- A people's worldview determines what constitutes a problem for them, and how they solve problems. As a result, Afrocentric scholarship must reflect the ontology, cosmology, axiology, and aesthetics of African people: it must be centered in our experiences.
- The essence of life, and therefore of human beings, is spiritual.

This is not to deny the material aspect of life; however, when all is done and said, what remains is not the appearance of things, but the indivisible essence of life that permeates all that is, the spirit; the ultimate oneness with nature, the fundamental interconnectedness of all things. Therefore, Afrocentric methods, as well as Afrocentrically-generated knowledge must reflect the primacy of the spiritual, the relationship between the physical and the spiritual, as well as the interconnectedness of all things. The integration of spiritual and physical principles may very well constitute a major challenge in an environment dominated by rationalism and positivism. However, Africologists believe that self-knowledge and rhythm play a special role in determining the proper methodology and methods. Indeed, starting with self-knowledge, all Afrocentric inquiry must be conducted through an interaction between the examiner and the subject. Cultural and social immersions are imperative. In addition, all Afrocentric inquiry must be activated by what Asante calls 'soul', which is ultimately linked to rhythm, the inner pulse of the cosmos. Norman Harris in particular reminds us that Afrocentric knowledge is validated through a combination of historical understanding and intuition, i.e., knowing is both rational and supra-rational. In an environment where knowing is narrowly defined as a purely cerebral affair, one must remember always that knowing with one's heart is superior to all and priceless.

- In addition, in keeping with the fact that Afrocentricity's ultimate aim is our liberation, the Afrocentric methodology must generate knowledge which will free us and empower us. Our primary task is to generate knowledge that opens our heart.

To sum up, the Africological methodological principles are the following:

- The African experience must determine all inquiry; the spiritual is important and must be given its due place; immersion in the subject is necessary; wholism is a must; intuition must be relied on; not everything is measurable because not everything that is significant is material; the knowledge generated by the Afrocentric methodology must be liberating.
- The methods used by Africologists vary, depending on their particular topic of study. However, Africological methods devised by particular scholars must be informed by the principles outlined above. In addition, one should not give up one's agency and allow one to be intimidated by the dubious statement that all methods are necessarily Eurocentric, and should therefore be avoided. Such an approach can only lead to intellectual impotence. The fact remains that African people, long before Europeans, observed very carefully and closely the universe that includes and surrounds us. Moreover, although observation, as a method, may be common among researchers working within different paradigms, one should bear in mind that the questions asked about the universe (the research questions) would certainly

be radically different, if they are truly inspired by divergent worldviews. For example, we know that Europeans have been quite puzzled by black skin, and have invested a great deal of energy trying to account for it (usually, of course, needless to say, through derogatory and racist theories). An Afrocentric scholar could certainly not engage in any such problematization of blackness, which is held to be our norm.

* Afrocentric theories

There exists a multiplicity of Afrocentric theories applied to a wide range of topics. This is not surprising since, as discussed earlier, African Studies is devoted to all aspects of our lives. What follows is a review of some of those theories, with a special focus on African women and men relationships, the African aesthetics, language, mental health, social problems, and education.

Clenora Hudson-Weems and Nah Dove have made particularly useful contributions to the Afrocentric discourse on African women and men.

Clenora Hudson-Weems coined the term 'Africana Womanism' in 1987, out of the realization of the total inadequacy of feminism, and like theories, (e.g., Black Feminism, African Womanism, or Womanism), to grasp the reality of African women, let alone give us the means to change that reality. The problems with the adoption of feminism by African women are two-fold. First, feminism is fundamentally a European phenomena. As such, it is loaded with European metaphysical principles, such as the conflictual relationship between the genders whereas men are seen as the primary enemies of women. Secondly, feminism as it developed in the 1880s, was blatantly racist. For these reasons, Hudson-Weems argues, feminism does not and cannot reflect the beliefs or interests of African women. She points out, in particular, how African women do not apprehend African men as our enemies. Nor would it be in our best interest as a people to allow ourselves to be divided along gender lines while living in a highly racialized and racist society. In place of feminism, Hudson-Weems calls for Africana Womanism, which "is grounded in African culture and, therefore, focuses on the unique experiences, struggles, needs, and desires of Africana women" (this volume). Hudson-Weems correctly asserts that the cooperation of African men and women against white supremacy is necessary for the survival and well-being of African people. The term 'Africana womanism' itself is the first step towards defining ourselves, and setting goals that are consistent with our culture and history. In other words, it is the first step towards existing on our own terms.

Nah Dove's concern for, and approach to the lives of African women are very similar to those of Clenora Hudson-Weems. Indeed, in her article entitled 'Defining African Womanist Theory', Nah Dove argues that the fate encountered by African women who live in Western societies, can only be understood within the context of white supremacy and its cultural underpinning. Dove pays particular attention to Cheikh Anta Diop' s Two Craddle analysis, as it relates to the harsh and demeaning treatment of women in Western culturally-dominated societies. Indeed, Dove points out the links between such treatment and the strong patriarchal and xenophobic currents that have characterized

Western culture since the very beginning. Dove rightly reminds us of the great contributions made by African women from antiquity to the present day, either as warriors, or mothers, to the well-being of Africans. In African culture, emphasis is placed on the necessary complementarity, rather than the conflict, that exists between African men and women. What makes a man is a woman; likewise, what makes a woman is a man. Appreciating and understanding this complementarity is at the root of any theory dealing with African women within the Afrocentric paradigm. Indeed, it is not only consistent with African culture, but it is also an act of resistance against the attempts made by white supremacists to further disintegrate and divide the African community.

'Social problems' are also considered within the Afrocentric paradigm, by Jerome Schiele. While it is common for 'people-with-problems', either drugs abusers or young violent crime perpetrators, to be approached by social workers as lacking and deficient, Schiele suggests that in reality, the culprit is the cultural environment in which people are made to live. Of particular concern to Schiele are spiritual alienation, i.e., the fragmentation and desacralization of life, and the subsequent disconnection of people, as well as racism and its attendant oppression. These are the product of Western culture, with its emphasis on materialism, individualism, and its negative view of human beings. Therefore, Schiele stresses the inadequacy of all approaches, even those that claim to be culturally sensitive, that do not deal with the problems inherent in European culture. Afrocentricity, Schiele contends, is the only paradigm that gives African social workers not only the means to analyze correctly the situation, but also proposes an alternative, in the form of a conscious reconnection to one's African core cultural values, especially a profound sense of spirituality and collective existence. The Afrocentric social worker, Schiele further insists, must not attempt to be 'objective', and remain distant from the person who needs assistance. Such a posture would be incompatible with Afrocentricity which stresses the epistemological validity of feelings. Much to the contrary, he or she must work toward establishing a close and reciprocal relationship, based on the recognition of the ultimate interconnectedness of all life forms, in this particular case, of the patient and the social worker. What is labeled 'social problems' may very well, in the end, prove to be 'cultural problems'.

Ama Mazama engages in an Afrocentric critique of the subfield of European Linguistics known as language planning. The latter emerged in the sixties, to deal with the alleged 'language problems' of newly independent states in Africa, Asia, and elsewhere. Language planning, and its attendant language development activities are usually recognized as necessary by the best intended African scholars (e.g., Diop). However, Mazama warns us that one must be careful before engaging in language planning for, much like feminism, it is problematic. First, it is loaded with European cultural assumptions about people and language which are conceived of as tools and puppets that can be manipulated for social control purposes. Secondly, language planning also includes assumptions about the primacy of the written word over the spoken word. As far as the individual is concerned, literacy, it is claimed, allows abstract thinking, and social mobility; as far as the group is concerned, it marks the beginning of true history. Thirdly, language planning is a clear agency of Westernization inasmuch as it has been used to infiltrate the cultural and mental space of people with European ideas, such as Christianity, capitalism, the idealization of whiteness, etc. One must therefore exercise great caution before embarking on 'language planning', realizing that such endeavor is not compatible at all with the African understanding of life, language, the power of the spoken word; as well as it interferes greatly with African cultural relocation.

Afrocentricity was also applied to textual analysis by Molefi Asante. Placing his discourse within a historiography that dismisses Eurocentric and racist claims of African ahistoricalness and inferiority, while focusing on Nile Valley civilizations as the ultimate source for African culture on the Continent and in the Diaspora, Asante insists on the primary importance of the concepts of location and dislocation for textual analysis. The 'cultural address,' location, or place, of a given author must be correctly assessed by any critique. Asante identifies language, attitude, and direction as the main markers of an author's location. Language involves essentially the semantic analysis of the words used; attitude deals with the orientation and response of the writers to situations, ideas, etc. that are presented in the text; while direction manifests itself primarily through the different symbols present in the text. Asante remarks that many African writers, because of their cultural dislocation, have produced texts that he labels 'decapitated', i.e., outside of one's historical and cultural experiences, or 'lynched', i.e., fundamentally European, in terms of themes, images, symbols, etc. On the other hand, writers who proceed from their own center, produce texts that genuinely reflect the African experience. More particularly, Asante analyzes and praises the work of Henry Dumas for telling the authentic story of African people. Asante's application of Afrocentricity to textual analysis has proven quite useful, providing us with a 'Location Theory' that is widely used by Afrocentric scholars.

The identification of aesthetic canons is the task that Kariamu Welsh-Asante set out to accomplish in 'The aesthetic conceptualization of Nzuri'. Indeed, as a result of the Europeans' attempt to place the whole world, including the African world, under European cultural domination, the existence of an African aesthetic has been consistently denied and suppressed. On the other hand, the European aesthetic has been presented as universal, and certainly, as superior. In the artistic domain, this has led African people to some serious distortions, such as the adoption of European cannons, the resort to 'substitution art forms', or simply the production of Eurocentric African art. Kariamu Welsh-Asante's aim is to assert the existence of a Pan-African and Afrocentric aesthetic, which she names Nzuri, and proceeds to describe. Understanding that aesthetic is necessarily based on the historical and cultural experiences of a people, Welsh-Asante identifies spirit, rhythm, and creativity as the key sources of Nzuri, upon which the following seven aspects converge: meaning, ethos, function, mode, motifs, method, and form. Welsh-Asante insists that in order to be Afrocentric, the African aesthetic must be grounded in the multidimensional reality of African people, as well as be informed by a consciousness of victory.

The purpose and form of education is another area that has been explored within the Afrocentric paradigm. Establishing a much useful distinction between *education* and *schooling*, Mwalimu Shujaa argues that "education is a cultural imperative" for African people in the United States. While the main purpose of schooling is social control, and the reproduction of their hegemony on the part of the dominant Euro-American segment of the population over the society, education ensures the transmission to the next generation of values and attitudes that reflect the culture of a given group. Given this state of affairs, it is clear that Africans who attend Euro-American public schools are not becoming 'educated', and should not expect to get educated, while receiving an inordinate amount of negative and debilitating images about ourselves. As a result, many of us behave like 'educated fools', unable to make any contribution to our own community, while adhering to the individualistic, materialistic, and racist European order. School reforms fall short of improving this reality, for what is questioned is not the oppressive system, but its modalities of operation. Shujaa argues that it is ultimately the responsibility of families to take charge of the education of their young, by first assessing the cultural content that needs to be transmitted, and then creating the appropriate venues, if necessary, to pass that knowledge onto the children. It is Shujaa's belief that only Afrocentric independent schools would be in the position to reinforce and nurture the cultural orientation of African children, thus allowing them to know themselves, understand the mechanisms through which oppression is perpetuated, and work to destroy those mechanisms.

Understanding the significance of the African past for our present and future, Asa Hilliard provides a very useful study of education in Ancient Egypt. While his research was hindered by the destruction of texts, as well as the secrecy that surrounded the educational process in Kemet, Hilliard's journey was nonetheless fruitful. Hilliard starts by asserting and establishing the existence of a great and very ancient African historical tradition (that even pre-dates Kemet), responsible for the development of a particular worldview, specific and common to African people, to this very day. Education in Kemet cannot be understood outside of the context of the African/Kemetic worldview. Indeed, the ultimate goal of education is to experience oneness with God, to become one with Maat. This was to be achieved through the unity of the person, the group, and unity with nature, as well as the development of social responsibility, social character, and spiritual power. While initiation was of paramount importance, the teaching and learning process was comprehensive, interactive, and collective and took place in an environment that both reflected and conveyed the total culture of the African people. Hilliard suggests that, as African people seek to educate ourselves properly, we allow the African tradition to be our guide.

C. Exemplars, i.e., "concrete problem-solutions"

The many dissertations produced by our students in the Department of Africology at Temple serve as exemplars for others to use as models. The Afrocentric textbooks that have been published also fall in that category. It may also be said that the present anthology represents an attempt to give the discipline more definite boundaries.

II. The structural aspect of the Afrocentric Paradigm

A paradigm cannot be without "an integrated community of practitioners" (Eckberg et al., 1980:121). The same authors explain that since a paradigm "is made of the consensual beliefs of a self-contained community. No analysis which neglects the *communal* nature of a paradigm can capture the essence of the concept" (1980:122). At the beginning of this introduction, I insisted that the development of the Afrocentric paradigm could not be understood outside of the development of the Graduate Program, in particular, the Ph.D. Program in the Department of African American Studies at Temple University, in 1988. This is where the first and most important community of Africological scholars and scholars-to be emerged. The development of the first Ph.D. Program in Africological Studies was critical to the development of the Afrocentric Paradigm. It was a milestone. Not so much because the Ph.D. validated the African experience, but because for the first time we were systematically and consciously building an army of scholars who were going to challenge white supremacy in ways it had never been before, an army of scholars whose aim it was to finally set us free from mental slavery.

Another important piece in the building of a community of Afrocentric scholars is, of course, the annual *Diop Conference*. This conference, in existence for 13 years too, is a unique opportunity to share with others, especially outsiders our understanding and practice of the Afrocentric paradigm.

The *Journal of Black Studies* is also important, since it provides Africological scholars with an outlet for our research, giving visibility to the Afrocentric paradigm.

Other conferences, such as the *Graduate Students Conference* in the Spring, and other journals, such as *Imhotep*, are also very important for the same reason.

III. The functional aspect of the Afrocentric Paradigm

In order to be considered a paradigm, Afrocentricity, it was stipulated above, must prove able to activate our consciousness, to open our heart in such a way that membership in the Eurocentric plantation is no longer an option. While it is correct and unfortunate that many have attempted to reduce Afrocentricity to an intellectual exercise, confusing it with the creation of a shallow discursive space with no serious and real implications for one's life choices, the lives of many others who have been deeply touched by Afrocentricity, attest that Afrocentricity is indeed a true paradigm for African liberation. In other words, Afrocentricity meets the functional requirement identified as critical.

Afrocentricity's profound impact on African lives can be detected in at least three areas (Asante, in Yaa Asantewaa, 1999): 1) the exhibition of cultural phenomena, such as music, dance, clearly informed by Afrocentric consciousness; 2) the emergence of a new political discourse and praxis in Africa, where leaders such a Mbekhi, for example, have openly acknowledged the need for Afrocentric policies; 3) the building of institutions, such as schools, spiritual centers, in Africa and in the diaspora, whose main purpose is to spread Afrocentric consciousness.

The present volume, in an attempt to contribute to the formalization of the Afrocentric Paradigm, focuses primarily on the first paradigmatic aspect, namely the cognitive, conative and affective one. To that end are included 1) essays that will delineate the metaphysical, epistemological, methodological, as well as the conceptual characteristics of the paradigm; 2) essays that will provide theoretical constructs and analyses generated by those characteristics. The list is long of essays devoted to the Afrocentric analysis of diverse phenomena. The decision not to include some of those essays should certainly not be construed as a negative statement about them, but was rather dictated by space constraints, as well as this editor's personal preferences for some topics.

References

Abraham, Kinfe. 1991. *Politics of Black Nationalism*. Trenton, N.J.: Africa World Press.

Adams, Russel. 1993. African-American Studies and the State of the Art. *Africana Studies: A Survey of Africa and the African Diaspora*. Mario Azeveto (ed.). Durham, NC: Carolina Academic Press. 25-45.

Asante, Molefi. 1980 (1988). *Afrocentricity*. Trenton, N.J.: Africa World Press.

Asante, Molefi. 1987 (1998). *The Afrocentric Idea*. Philadelphia, PA: Temple University Press.

Asante, Molefi. 1990. *Kemet, Afrocentricity and Knowledge*. Trenton, N.J.: Africa World Press.

Asante, Molefi. 1991. The Afrocentric Idea in Education. *Journal of Negro Education*. 60: 170-179.

Ba, Sylvia. 1973. *The concept of Negritude in the Poetry of Leopold Sedar Senghor*. Princeton, N.J.: Princeton University Press.

Burkett, Randall. 1978. *Garveyism as a Religious Movement. The Institutionalization of a Black Civil Religion*. Metuchen, N.J.: The Sacrecrow Press, Inc. & The American Theological Library Association.

Cesaire, Aime. 1989. *Discours sur le colonialisme*. Paris: Presence Africaine.

Corzani, Jean. 1973. *Les Literatures d'Expression Francaise. Negritude Africaine, Negritude Caraibe*. Paris-Nord (Paris XIII): Centre D'Etudes Francophones.

Depestre, Rene. 1982. *Bonjour et Adieu la Negritude*. Paris: Laffont.

Diop, Cheikh Anta. 1987. *Black Africa. The Economic and Cultural Basis for a Federated State*. Lawrence Hill Books. Trenton, N. J.: Africa World Press.

Diop, Cheikh Anta. 1991. *Civilization or Barbarism?* Brooklyn, N.Y.: Lawrence Hill.

Eckberg, Douglas Lee & Hill, Lester. 1980. The Paradigm Concept and Sociology: A Critical Review. *Paradigms and Revolutions. Applications and Appraisals of Thomas Kuhn's Philosophy of Science*. Gary Gutting (ed.). Notre Dame, IN.: University of Notre Dame. 117-136.

Eze, Emmanuel Chukwudi (ed.). 1997. *Race and the Enlightenment. A Reader*. Oxford: Blackwell Publishers.

Fanon, Frantz. 1952. *Peau Noire, Masques Blancs*. Paris: Maspero.

Fanon, Frantz. 1967. *Black Skin, White Masks*. New York, N.Y.: Grove Press.

Fanon, Frantz. 1988. *Toward the African Revolution*. New York, N.Y.: Grove Press.

Fanon, Frantz. 1991. *The Wretched of the Earth*. New York, N.Y.: Grove Press.

Garvey, Marcus. 1986. *Message to the People. The course of African Philosophy*, Tony Martin (ed.). Dover, MA: The Majority Press.

Garvey, Marcus. 1992. *Philosophy and Opinions of Marcus Garvey*, Amy Jacques-Garvey (ed.). Athenum, N.Y.: Maxwell MacMillan.

Hamlet, Janice. 19989. *Afrocentric Visions*. New York, N.Y.: Sage.

Hausser, Michel. 1988. *Pour une Poetique de la Negritude*. Paris: Editions Silex.

Hill, Robert . 1992. Introduction to *Philosophy and Opinions of Marcus Garvey*, Amy Jacques-Garvey (ed.). Athenum, N.Y.: Maxwell MacMillan.

Hill Collins, Patricia. *Black Feminist Thought*. New York, N.Y. & London: Routledge.

Karenga, Maulana. 1977. *Kwanzaa: Origin, Concept, Practice*. Los Angeles, CA.: Kawaida Groundwork Committee.

Karenga, Maulana. 1981. *Kawaida Theory: An Introductory Outline*. Inglewood, CA.: Kawaida Publications.

Karenga, Maulana. 1986. Black Studies and the Problematic of a Paradigm: The Philosophical Dimension. *Journal of Black Studies*. 18 (4): 395-414.

Karenga, Maulana. 1993. *Introduction to Black Studies*. Los Angeles, CA.: The University of Sankore Press.

Keita, L. 1977. Two Philosophies of African History: Hegel and Diop. *Presence Africaine*. 91: 41-49.

Kuhn, Thomas. 1962. *The Structure of Scientific Revolutions*. Chicago, IL: Chicago University Press.

Kuhn, Thomas. 1970. Reflections On My Critics. *Criticism and the Growth of Knowledge*. Imre Lakatos & Alan Musgrave (eds). Cambridge: Cambridge University Press. 231-278.

Martin, Tony. 1976 (1986). *Race First*. Dover, MA.: The Majority Press.

Masterman, Margaret. 1970. The Nature of a Paradigm. *Criticism and the Growth of Knowledge*. Imre Lakatos & Musgrave, Alan (eds). Cambridge: Cambridge University Press. 59-90.

Mazama, Ama. 1999. *The Afrocentric Paradigm*. Keynote Address, Cheikh Anta Diop Conference, Philadelphia, October 16, 1999.

McLean, Roderick. 1982. *The Theology of Marcus Garvey*. Washington, D.C.: University Press of America.

Memmi, Albert. 1991. *The Colonizer and the Colonized*. Boston, MA: Beacon Press.

Morris, Brian. 1991. *Western Conceptions of the Individual*. Oxford & Washington, D.C.: Berg.

Moses, Wilson. 1978. *The Golden Age of Black Nationalism*. 1850-1925. Hamden, CO: Archon Books.

Mudimbe, Valentin. 1988. *The Invention of Africa*. Bloomington, IN: Indiana University Press.

Nantambu, Kwame. 1996. *Egypt and Afrocentric Politics: Essays on European Supremacy*. Kent, OH: Imhotep Publishing Company..

Reed, Adolf. 1986. Pan-Africanism as Liberalism: DuBois and Garvey. *Pan-Africanism: New Directions in Strategy*. W. Ofuatey-Kodjoe (ed.). Lanham, New York, N.Y. & London: University Press of America. 25-60.

Runcie, John. 1975. The Black Culture Movement and the Black Community. *American Studies*. 10 (2): 185-214.

Senghor, Leopold Sedar. 1988. *Ce que Je Crois*. Paris: Grasset.

Stuckey, Sterling. 1972. *The Ideological Origins of Black Nationalism*. Boston: MA: Beacon Press.

Towa, Marcien. 1971. *Leopold Sedar Senghor: Negritude ou Servitude?* Yaounde: Editions Cle.

Weisborg, Robert. 1973. *Ebony Kinship. Africa, Africans, and the Afro-American*. Wesport, VA: Greenwood Press, Inc.

II. THE AFFECTIVE, COGNITIVE, AND CONATIVE ASPECTS

A. METAPHYSICAL FOUNDATIONS

The Afrocentric Idea

Molefi Kete Asante

African cultural interests have been consistently undermined by a determined Eurocentric intellectual conspiracy that began in the 15th century. Our cultural, social, political, economic, and spiritual interests have been systematically assaulted by an array of scholars over the past five hundred years. Their intent was to establish white racial dominance and to maintain a system of hierarchy over Africans and other peoples of the world. We have been the pawns in the game to conquer not just the world, but information about the world, including the African world. Hence, Africans have become marginalized in our own story, held victim by the most ambitious social theorists the West has produced. Many of the major Western scholars have undermined the rights of Africans. Such scholars have pushed their agenda with the idea that they are objective while others who speak against conquest are subjective. They have often assumed that their "objectivity," a kind of collective subjectivity of European culture, should be the measure by which the world marches. A revolutionary intelligentsia can never fall in step with the decimation of a people's culture. Thus, I have seldom fallen in step, insisting that there are other ways in which to experience phenomena rather than viewing them from a Eurocentric vantage point. If African interests are to be protected in the long run they must be protected by a group of committed scholars who understand the Afrocentric perspective.

Any real Afrocentric work must constitute a radical critique of the Eurocentric ideology that masquerades as a universal view in the social sciences and humanities. I mean that it is radical in the sense that it suggests a transformative turnabout, an alternative perspective on phenomena. It is about taking the globe and turning it over so that we see all the possibilities of a world where Africa, for example, subject and not object. Such a posture is necessary and rewarding for both Africans and Europeans. But it is absolutely necessary for the survival of the African world. The inability to "see" from several angles is perhaps the one common weakness in provincial scholarship. Those who have delighted us most thoroughly and advanced thought most significantly have been those thinkers who explored different views and brought new perspectives for analysis.

My principal objective has always been to introduce a critique that propounds a cultural theory of society by the very act of criticism. In other words, I believe that to provide a radical assessment of a given reality is to create, among other things, another, more liberating, reality. Furthermore, any criticism of society is, definitionally, a criticism of the ruling ideology of that society. I have the insight that comes from having been born black in the United States. That fact puts me in a critical mood within the intellectual and social milieu I share with Eurocentricists. As the critic, I am always seeking to create a new world, to find an escape, to liberate those who see only a part of reality.[1]

The most valuable critique a person can make of the dominant ideology of society is one that proposes in its critique an advancement of science. As a writer involved in the movement for human liberation and aligned with the basic human values of harmony, justice, righteousness, order, balance, harmony, and reciprocity, I am by definition in defiance of an oppressive situation.

The crystallization of this critical perspective I have named Afrocentricity, which means, literally, placing African ideals at the center of any analysis that involves African culture and behavior.[2] For example, the communicationist who defines a speech as an uninterrupted spoken discourse demonstrates either a disregard or ignorance of the African tradition of speech, much as Leslie Fiedler was using a purely European conception of fiction when he contended that romance was a central theme in literature. Fiedler's reaction to literature was essentially a Eurocentric contextual affair.[3] Familiar with the classics of American and British literature, he apparently accepted Western literature as world-defining. Although an able critic of Eurocentric culture, he failed to analyze his genre from a worldwide perspective—or, at least, to acknowledge the possibility of such an analysis. Traditionally, African writers are not concerned with the romance variety of literature, but Fiedler, like many Eurocentric writers, gives us no awareness of this fact. We are thus left with his word for literature—a truncated word, parading as universal. Charles Larson wrote a perceptive essay, "Heroic Ethnocentrism: The Idea of Universality in Literature," in which he examined the European notion of universality.[4] Larson had first come face to face with the problem of universality while teaching an English literature course in Nigeria—a good place, I might add, to come to grips with ethnocentric ideas of all kinds. His students did not understand the idea of kissing in the Victorian novel, and how Larson handled the situation is revealing. He groped for words to explain the work of such a celebrated writer as Thomas Hardy to his African audience. He learned, of course, how culture shapes the interpretation of literature. But since culture itself is shaped by the constant demands of society and the environment, Larson concluded that kissing and description have not found counterparts in the African novel—not yet, at least. He writes, "Usually, when we try to force the concept of universality on someone who is not western, I think we are implying that our own culture should be the standard of measurement."[5] Larson is correct to see Fiedler's assertion that the romance is universal as another Western analysis imposed on world literature. Since there are entire cultural areas where the romance is nonexistent, its universality is doubtful. There are no major African novels where the plot progresses because of a hero's attempt to attract a mate. An Afrocentric discussion of literature thus would guard against this ethnocentric promotion of a group's claim of universality. The central problem with Fiedler and others who write in this vein is that, just as fifteenth-century Europeans could not cease believing that the earth was the center of the universe, many today find it difficult to stop viewing European/American culture as the center of the social universe. Thus, the work they produce seldom considers the possibilities of other realities or, indeed, shared realities. A number of scholars have challenged such a narrow view of the arts and the social sciences. Their works speak to the abiding problem of Western formulations based on parochial observations.[6]

But Robert Armstrong declares, in a more direct way, that Europeans tend to speak as Fiedler had, tying themselves to all that is supposedly universal, because they have "an ethnocentric crypto-aesthetics" that links them to what they perceive as a "universal cultural phenomena."[7] What is particularly troubling in these formulations by European and some African and Asian writers, who have been thoroughly trained in Eurocentrism, is that they assume that everyone else should simply acquiesce in their expansive provincialism. They not only make their arguments with a bewildering array of tropes, figures, and oxymorons, but they assert them as if there were no other reality, no other perspective. It is striking that some feminist critics have addressed the same conceptual issue, though from a different point of view. For example, Karen Sacks has attacked Social Darwinist anthropology for its industrial-capitalist bias. In her study of six African societies, she argues that anthropology's inherent hierarchical and competitive dimensions create, as well as rein force, beliefs in the natural superiority of men over women. According to Sacks, "the center of the struggle lies in changing institutionalized patterns of behaviors and allocations of social roles."[8] Since Marxism does not presume such inequality, Sacks extols its analytic advantages in the feminist movement: Social Darwinist and Marxist theories "are diametrically opposed ways of seeing the same social order(s), and they represent opposed class views and needs."[9] However, her argument, like those of other Marxist theorists, rests on a reaction to the industrial-capitalist order and must use its language to demonstrate the opposition. Thus, though the opposition is real, the balance is weighted toward Social Darwinism.

While Afrocentric thinkers must also confront presumptions of inequality, Marxism is likewise not helpful in developing Afrocentric concepts and methods because it, too, is a product of a Eurocentric consciousness that excludes the historical and cultural perspectives of Africa. I am sympathetic to Sack's view to the extent that she criticizes the Social Darwinist perspective and attempts to find, as I have done, a way of seeing based on people's needs and experiences. But because Marxism emerged from the Western consciousness, it is mechanistic in its approach to social understanding and development, and it has often adopted forms of Social Darwinism when explaining cultural and social phenomena.

I have challenged the African American Marxists, who have claimed to be radical democrats under the new philosophical regime in which Marxism appears weakened by the demise of the Soviet formula, to understand that the structural problems they identify in the American system are not primary causes of the economic dislocation of African people. While it is true that the American system, with its new technological thrust away from the old industrial order, is structurally organized by the energy it gathers to dislocate and disorient African people, it is dependent on the cooperation of systemic racism. In other words, the system exists because of the racism, not the other way round. One cannot claim that the industrial age was any better for Africans than the new structural situation. Furthermore, what appears to Cornel West and others as evidence of nihilism in the African American community is simply the failure of the American economic system to deliver its goods equitably, not some imperfection in African people.[10] Actually the system, as designed, has worked quite well in marginalizing the African American and other ethnic populations. Interestingly, in trying to pinpoint the nature of this nihilism in the African American community, of West, Angela Davis, and Manning Marable,[11] radical democrats all, none has been able to offer a way to eliminate the nihilism, except to argue that there must be some sort of structural change in the American economy. To be sure, Marable is more specific in calling for a socialism committed to human equality in which liberty is not simply a function of the power and privilege of the wealthy.

What I, as an Afrocentrist, am concerned about is not nihilism per se but the underlying problem of a strictly class analysis of the African American situation. I do not accept the thesis that the material condition creates ideas in an absolute sense. One sees this precisely in the manner race operates differently for the white worker and the black worker. There is no consistent, provocative revolutionary sentiment, as Harold Cruse would say, evident in the white proletariat.[12] On the other hand, African Americans want fundamental change in the way we are perceived. It is clear to me that Afrocentricity assists us in understanding how people come to create material realities, whether those realities are based in class or race conditions. Furthermore, it is not true now, nor has it ever been true, that the white poor see themselves as united with the black poor against the white elite in the struggle to bring about a more equitable society. In fact, the white poor and working classes believe (witness the various white separatist and paramilitary groups) that the black poor and the white establishment work in tandem. While radical democrats argue that the failure of the Soviet Union was not the failure of communism, Soviet communism is the only grand communism that we have known. Such is the limit of class thinking in racist societies.

While inquiring into the nature of the African condition in the Americas, Cornel West concluded that the fundamental problem was the loss of values, a sort of nihilism that has derailed the best intentions of the African American genius. Although West has expressed this belief in many places, it is especially pronounced in *Prophetic Thought in Postmodern Times*, where he contends that the period between 1965 and 1992 produced "the highest level of forms of self-destruction known in black history." With the passion that only West can bring to an issue, he reiterates in his unique manner that "these demons which are at work, the demons of meaninglessness, of hopelessness, a sense of nothingness conjoined with the institutional and structural marginalization of large numbers of black people ... But, for the most part, it has produced the highest level of self-destruction known to black people since we arrived."[13]

My response to what West sees as nihilism has been to present an Afrocentric vision wrapped in the optimism that remains the attitude of the African multitudes in the United States. By raising some important issues in regard to the loss of values, West has struck the same chord as the African American conservatives from whom he distances himself They argue that the loss of values means that African Americans need to acquire the habits and values of the white population in order to become fully functioning citizens of the United States. To his credit West does not go this far and indeed has taken issue with the conservatives Glenn Loury and Thomas Sowell, who have made a rather straightforward critique of the conservative position by framing this question of values in terms of individual choices rather than in terms of what the structural dimensions of society have created as choices.

But the concentration on the loss of values by the conservatives, West, and, to a lesser extent, Marable and other radical democrats is misplaced. I have tried to demonstrate that there is no loss of values in the African American community, and that the values that we honor and respect are as strong today as they have ever been. Of course, changing economic and political realities do highlight certain antihuman behaviors by some individuals, but these actions are neither acceptable to African Americans nor unprecedented in our nation's past. Although our traditional values such as harmony, justice, equality, patience, diligence, and good-naturedness are not foreign to us today, they are rarely represented in the media, which instead produces a flood of images and ideas about how nihilistic we have become. Although I do not dismiss the realities of violence and other destructive behaviors, I believe that the media make them seem more pervasive than ever.

If we have lost anything, it is our cultural centeredness; that is, we have been moved off our own platforms. This means that we cannot truly be ourselves or know our potential since we exist in a borrowed space. But all space is a matter of point of view or interpretation. Our existential relationship to the culture that we have borrowed defines what and who we are at any given moment. By regaining our own platforms, standing in our own cultural spaces, and believing that our way of viewing the universe is just as valid as any, we will achieve the kind of transformation that we need to participate fully in a multicultural society. However, without this kind of centeredness, we bring almost nothing to the multicultural table but a darker version of whiteness.

There is therefore nothing strange about the Afrocentric idea. All distorted or otherwise negative understandings of it are rooted in the society's manner of viewing Africans. This is not to say that all who reject the Afrocentric idea are racists, but rather that their failure to appreciate its context and objectives suggests their seduction by the structural elements of a hierarchical society that fails to recognize African agency. We have, however, arrived at a point at which the entire process of human knowledge is being assessed and reassessed in order to help us discover what we know about each other. As we open the doors to return to our own platforms, we greatly enrich the world.

What makes Afrocentric concepts more inclusive is that they seek to reorient our world-view in ways that challenge Social Darwinism, capitalism, and most forms of Marxism— all of which are grounded in their own particularity. The invalidity of an idea arises not from its exponents but from its own fundamental flaws. This is the point at which the feminist critique converges with the Afrocentric line of reasoning. What I seek to do here is to move closer to a post-Eurocentric idea that makes true transcultural analyses possible; this can be accomplished alongside a post-paternalist ideology as we unlock creative human potential.

It should be clear that while numerous issues remain unresolved in the discourse of Afrocentricity, I am not opposed to any conception of the human being that is rewarding and liberating. Indeed, we can only advance communally in the context of freedom, personal liberty, and collective liberation as conceived by many scholars.

While I, as an Afrocentrist, argue the primacy of the cultural crisis in the context of a heterogeneous racist society, I am aware of the varieties of oppressions in our contemporary situation, and, like other Afrocentrists, I believe that it is necessary to confront all forms of discrimination, persecution and oppression simultaneously.

But what of the poststructuralist and, by extension, post modernist concern about the perceived restructuralism inherent in Afrocentricity? This question is meant to sharpen the conflict that frequently exists between the postmodernist and the Afrocentrist on the cultural issue. Afrocentricity cannot abandon the structuralism of modernism without betraying the achievements of culture. African Americans are a preeminently cultured people within American society, and our contributions to what is called "popular American culture" are immense. To seek to transcend the African cultural presence in contemporary society is to quest for anonymity at the very time that African Americans and Africans are most capable of asserting their culture. Robert Farris Thompson has argued that the modern world is fundamentally a world created by the presence of Africans in the Americas.[14] Thus, African presence in art, science, Egyptology, literature, politics, and democracy is a decisive force in the modern world as it either affirms or rejects that presence. That we Africans have been involved in making the modern world is precisely why Afrocentrists question the abandonment of modernism. We are not, however, running away from ourselves, and while we are in the midst of projecting ourselves to the world, we do not lose sight of the structural ideas of *location, place, community,* and *stance.* These may be anathema to the poststructuralist but they are precisely the keys to centeredness in the African context.

Nevertheless, the quest for transcendence, in the sense of going beyond the simple affirmation or rejection of African presence, does not have to be detrimental to good society; it can be affirming and fulfilling so long as an Afrocentric agency is constituted in the creation of a new world. We must conclude that modernism's problem is with the use of Africans rather than with the agency of Africans. If this unsettles some to the point that they question the restructuring of the world, it serves to demonstrate that the deconstruction process was never completed in the first place. If it had been completed, it would have had to serve up the abandoned concepts of white racism on the altar of progressive sacrifice so that we could have a more fully creative world. What needs to be deconstructed are the means by which human beings in the Western world have defined a triumphal vision that diminishes other people. I know that this is a difficult road for those who are committed to the detours of literary analysis and historical speculation, because once again we are in the area of the forbidden when we question the Eurocentric ideas about culture.

Unless they are subjected to severe criticism, the preponderant Eurocentric myths of universalism, objectivity, and classical traditions retain a provincial European cast. Scholarship rooted in such myths obviously lacks either historical or conceptual authenticity. The aggressive seizure of intellectual space, like the seizure of land, amounts to occupying someone else's territory and claiming it as one's own. When this occurs, cultural analysis takes a back seat to galloping ethnocentric interpretations of phenomena.

Applied to the African world, such conceptions become limiting, restricting, and parochial. For example, a discussion of African cultural history rarely calls forth African culture in the American context. There is a clear separation of African peoples. Those who remain on the continent and may have been exploited on their own lands and those of us who were brought across the ocean are seen as fundamentally different. In fact, the similarities are overwhelming when it comes to the attempt to destroy our cultures, minimize our histories, and to eliminate the contributions made by Africans. Like the literary critics, the historians often dismiss the African elements that survived and developed on the American continents as purely temporal. They usually refer to them as "Negro culture," or speak of "the African slave in the New World" or "Negro emancipation." The fact that the spatial referent is Africa is ignored, and Negro becomes a crypto-term that is used to designate our degradation. In this way the Eurocentric writer ties the African to the Negro, a false concept and a false history, separate from any particular spatial reality. The word Negro did not exist prior to slavery; both the term and its application were products of the social and economic context of the slave trade. Consequently, the attachment of the term Negro to African means a negation of history and culture.

Furthermore, the Eurocentric formulations recognize neither African classical thought nor the African classical past. We are essentially left with a discontinuous history and an uncertain future. By contrast, the Afrocentric analysis reestablishes the centrality of the ancient Kemetic (Egyptian) civilization and the Nile Valley cultural complex as points of reference for an African perspective in much the same way that Greece and Rome serve as reference points for the European world. Thus, the Afrocentrist expands human history by creating a new path for interpretation, making words like Negro and colored obsolete and anachronistic. African is identified with time, place, and perspective. Without the Afrocentric perspective, the imposition of the European line as universal hinders cultural understanding and demeans humanity.

Such deliberately separatist views carry the false assertion that Africans in the Americas are not Africans connected to their spatial origin. While differences exist between Barbados and Zimbabwe, these differences are much like the differences between Florence and Brisbane. African American culture and history represent developments in African culture and history, inseparable from place and time. An analysis of African American culture that is not based on Afrocentric premises is bound to lead to incorrect conclusions. In a similar manner, the interpretation of historical data from a strictly Eurocentric perspective can cause serious intercultural conflict, based on wrong premises.

Let me give an example of how cultural misunderstandings can be propagated by different views. In the nineteenth century, Cecil John Rhodes sought to gain control of a large territory of southern Africa that was ruled by the Ndebele King Lobengula, and he sent emissaries to the powerful king in an effort to secure his consent. After many days of discussion with Lobengula, the white emissaries returned to Rhodes with the king's signature on a piece of paper. They told Rhodes that Lobengula had given him all of his territory, and Rhodes sent a column of soldiers into the area with the instruction to shoot any black on sight. Thus began the country of Rhodesia.

Rhodes may have believed that King Lobengula had given him title to the land, but Lobengula never believed that he had. Thus, their two cultural views of the world clashed, and the Europeans automatically assumed the correctness of their view. An Afrocentric analysis points out that Lobengula could never have sold or given the land away, since it did not belong to him but to the ancestors and the community. He could grant Rhodes permission to hunt, to farm, and even to build a house, but not to own land. Only in this manner could the king follow the discourse of his ancestors. It took nearly one hundred years, two revolts, and a seven-year war to correct the situation. A rigid Eurocentrism made Rhodes believe that Lobengula had signed his country over to him.

Similarly, I am certain that the American Indians did not believe they had sold Manhattan Island for twenty-three dollars worth of trinkets, no matter what the Dutch thought. Native Americans revere the land in much the same way that Africans do. No king or clan leader could sell what did not belong to him. On the basis of European contractual custom, the Dutch may have thought they were purchasing the island from the Indians, but this was obviously a view based on their own commercial traditions.

One has to ascertain other points of view to understand human phenomena. African responses and actions, however, have too often been examined from

Eurocentric perspectives.[15] The misunderstandings between Europeans and others have provoked in me an interest in alternative perspectives.

A Place to Stand

I turn now to a related area of concern. I have been criticized as an essentialist, a bad thing to be, according to deconstructionists. They believe that when one argues for certain characteristics of culture that constitute a given community, one is taking an essentialist position. The problem with such a position, according to these critics, is that it denies the fluidity of cultures and the possibility that cultures can change. As developed by Cornel West, the idea is that "Molefi Asante believes that one has to be centered, rooted, but I believe that one must go with the flow, move and groove, and be dynamic." My reply is that I, too, believe that one must be "open to the possibilities of dynamism, moving and flowing, but you have to be moving and flowing from some base. Those who do not move from a base are just floating in the air."[16] It is clear to me from my own study of history that cultures do exist and in fact persist for centuries with many basic characteristics hardly changed. This is the nature of human societies operating on the foundations of myths, history and memories. The African American community is no different from others in this regard. There are certain essential characteristics that identify the contours of our African American community. These are not immutable characteristics in the sense of being inborn, but rather the fundamental outlines of what we regard and preserve as characteristic of our society.

Thus, while I may answer to being an essentialist, I am not an *immutabilist*. It is unreasonable to expect African Americans to divest themselves of culture when such unilateral divestiture is neither required nor expected of other cultural groups. Imbedded in the suggestion is a notion of power and hierarchy according to which only communities considered of low status are required to abandon their essential characteristics, while others seek to preserve their characteristics for generations yet unborn. Look at the degree to which the French are fighting to preserve their cultural essentials. Look at the concern among Japanese Americans and Jewish Americans that high rates of intermarriage will erase their cultural heritage. To claim an African identity and an Afrocentric place to stand is no more essentialist than the positions taken by critics in feminist, gay/lesbian, or cultural studies, who challenge established hierarchy.

The Afrocentric critic's chief problem is finding a place to stand—so to speak—in relation to the Western standards that are imposed as interpretative measures on other cultures. I have familiarized myself with the leading proponents of the logic of scientific discovery, only to find their reductionist views of the world incapable of adequately dealing with African cultural data. In fact, I question whether they are able to examine any data that are dynamic and transformational. Since the time-space domain is not stationary and has not been considered to be so since the Newtonian view was shattered by the quantum theory's evidence of particle-wave behavior, there needs to be an accommodating, flexible frame of reference that permits the dynamic.

A promising attempt to account for the harmony of opposites and break down the false dichotomies that occur in much social science and physical science research is found in the work of Thomas Kuhn. It is promising as a heuristic, not an accomplished, end, because Kuhn does not question the ground upon which he stands. The procedure for scientific discovery, in Kuhn's view, has two components: verifiability and falsifiability.[17] However, the Kuhnian paradigm has been considered a copy of Karl Popper's logic of discovery. Kuhn pointed out the similarities and differences between his views and Popper's in a rather lengthy paper that contrasts the logic of discovery and the psychology of research.[18] Although he admits that he and Popper selected the same scientific aspects to investigate, he says they differ in how they perceive these aspects and in how they evaluate their significance. The two agree on the following: (1) scientific development is a dynamic process; (2) science is not the accretion of concepts but rather a transformation of conceptual frames; (3) history of science provides facts; and (4) outstanding science should be viewed as revolution. However, Kuhn argues, he and Popper arrive at these conclusions by different analytical modes.

Both Kuhn and Popper are primarily concerned with falsification and verification. While Popper believes that scientific revolutions occur when there is falsification of a theory Kuhn argues for the joint approach of verification and falsification. The progress of science is supposed to occur when the crises of revolution are resolved. In my view, both the Kuhnian and the Popperian arguments, while certainly powerful within the context of European science, fail to raise the first-order question, which asks for a justification of the scientific endeavor itself. Rather than discuss the relative differences between revolutionary and normal science, one might question the scientific perspective itself or, as Stephen Toulmin did, the notion of the revolutionary when used in connection with science. Yet it is clear that Kuhn has introduced a controversial and creative idea, although he must, as he says of scientists, defend his own commitments while assuming a universal role. He cannot question the ground he stands on. It is essentially a materialist view.

The materialistic view of reality seems to have its roots in Greek philosophy. Aristotle (384-322 BC.), who is sometimes described by Westerners as "the master of all who know,"[19] defines the soul as the function of the body and argues that body functions are the individual's behaviors that are observable and therefore should be measurable. This is a stance that articulates the empirical trend in Greek philosophy. The inductive approach for collecting data and, later, for verifying it by the logical, deductive approach, is a major contribution of Aristotle. His view of humans is, in the final analysis, a reductionist, deterministic, operationist, positivistic view that has motivated the modern behavioristic school to call for real science free from mentalistic concepts and subjective methods.

I consider Aristotle a reductionist because he views behavior as a function of the body and assumes that nothing goes beyond what the organism does. He views the psychological functions in relation to physiological mechanisms. He is deterministic because he assumes that everything that happens in the universe can be accounted for by definite laws of causation. His view assumes that human behavior is subject to natural laws and must, therefore, be explained in terms of causative factors within the individual's heredity and environment. Aristotle is an operationist since he instructs the scientist to check the validity of his or her findings by examining the validity of the operations used in reaching them. He is a positivist since he assumes that the goal of the scientist is to verify a hypothesis by searching for a natural principle.

Fundamental to the materialist idea is the separation of mind and body. From the seventeenth to the nineteenth century, philosophers assimilated new information of scientific discovery in physics, chemistry, and biology, and, accordingly, sharpened their philosophical views to articulate new opinions on human nature. The mind-body dichotomy persists in the literature of Western philosophy to the present day. The psychologist William Quill points out:

> In considering the body-mind problem, one embarks upon a tradition of inquiry which many have undertaken during the long history of philosophical thought—how ever, the whole issue of mind and body has been periodically discredited as a pseudo-problem and hence repressed. This latter attitude has been predominant during the last forty years, particularly in positivistically oriented "philosophies" and "psychologies." One of the increasing number of current testimonies to the fact that [the] mind-body problem is still highly problematic is that the Minnesota Center for Philosophy of Science devoted an entire volume, entitled Concepts, Theories, and the Mind-Body Problem, to studying the issue.... Obviously men of great ability—men who formerly regarded the mind-body problem as a pseudo-issue—in response to valid criticism, now find the problem to be a genuinely substantive one.[20]

Who makes this a genuine problem? The Afrocentric writer knows that oppositional dichotomies in real, everyday experiences do not exist. The speaker or the writer is fully engaged in every way, not merely in ways that seem measurable. You may use the computer, but you cannot understand all that is involved in my writing by simply observing my fingers. I may experience hunger, joy, pain, or pleasure while I write. I might even get an electric shock or two, but you would not know that from observing my hands, unless I shrieked. I might experience the most delightful romantic thoughts while I strike the keyboard to produce unromantic prose. This flow of energy cannot be accounted for by the mere observation of my physical movements as I write, nor by my report of what I describe in my writings, nor even by what I say has crossed my mind while I was writing. The interaction of my physical and metaphysical world leads to my behavior at the moment, and this interaction cannot be reduced to separate units of an either/or nature of body-mind. It cannot be assumed that the body causes the mental activities or that mental activities cause the body to function. Accounting for different perspectives or allowing them to emerge becomes the principal aim of a truly liberating perspective. While the contributions of the Eurocentric philosophers and scientists have been important and valuable, they have not been fully expressive of the extent or power of human ways of knowing. The arguments that have been advanced for the Western formulation of science are not convincing. Marvin Harris, for example, writes as good an apologia as anyone for the values of science:

> Science is a unique and precious contribution of western civilization.... No other way of knowing is based on a set of rules explicitly designed to transcend the prior belief systems of mutually antagonistic tribes, nations, classes, and ethnic and religious communities in order to arrive at knowledge that is equally probable for any rational human mind.... The real alternative to science is not anarchy, but ideology: not peaceful artists, philosophers, and anthropologists, but aggressive fanatics and messiahs, eager to annihilate each other and the world if need be in order to prove their point.[21]

Harris characterizes the scientific approach as superior to others and claims that it is uniquely rational among systems. He is perhaps at his Eurocentric best as an interpreter of the nonscientists of other cultures. He readily admits that there are "domains of experience the knowledge of which cannot be achieved by adherence to the rules of scientific method."[22] But he sees this "nonscientific" knowledge, particularly the ecstatic knowledge of mystics and saints; the visions and hallucinations of drug users and of schizophrenics; and the aesthetic and moral insights of artists, poets, and musicians," as being beyond his understanding.[23] This is almost fantastic: an admission that he cannot distinguish between the euphoria of drug users and saints or schizophrenics and the insights of artists and poets!

Harris's characterization of the Western scientific method is by no means unique. Yet his ability to denigrate other ways of knowing creates a false impression of science itself. Science does not exclude moral or aesthetic insight. The special disciplines and rigors of the arts and the regularized, methodical procedures of the so-called mystics cannot be easily discounted, for they have added knowledge and richness to the human experience.

What Harris and other apologists of this peculiarly narrow version of the scientific adventure argue against is what they perceive as the random, mystical type of discovery. They see it as valuable only when it is transformed into precise, logical verification. Thus discovery is separate from verification. In effect, Harris's view would dismiss the creative process, divest itself of discovery, and concentrate on the verification process. My desire is to see a paradigm of complementarity that integrates discovery with verification where necessary. In this manner, Afrocentricity expands the repertoire of human perspectives on knowledge.

The Afrocentric View

Because the Afrocentric idea is unthinkable without African agency, I feel compelled to resolve the confusion surrounding the terms Afrocentricity and Africanity. How one approaches these concepts in large measure determines the efficacy of a challenge to hierarchy. The substance of one term is not that of the other, and the consequences of one can create problems for the other. In other words, one—Afrocentricity—seeks agency and action, and the other—Africanity—broadcasts identity and being. Actually, Africanity refers in its generality to all of the customs, traditions, and traits of people of Africa and the diaspora. On the other hand, Afrocentricity is very specific in its reliance on self-conscious action. To say, for example, that Afrocentricity has no role in Africa because the people there already have an African perspective is to misunderstand the practical dimension of Afrocentricity. To be African is not necessarily to be Afrocentric. It is possible, however, to develop a nexus between Africanity and Afrocentricity in order to generate a more productive architectonic African culture of balance and harmony.

The term Afrology, which I coined in *Afrocentricity: The Theory of Social Change* denotes the Afrocentric study of African concepts, issues, and behaviors.[24] In recent years Winston Van Horne of the University of Wisconsin at Milwaukee has promoted Africology as a more fluent term to describe the discipline, and his department is now known by that name. I have adopted his word since the publication of the first edition of *The Afrocentric Idea* and believe that in time it will replace such names as African American Studies, Africana Studies, and Black Studies. As used by Van Horne, Africology is the trans-generational and transcontinental Afrocentric study of African phenomena.

Studies of Caribbean culture, the African presence in South America, and the African trade with India as well as African American experiences in the United States are all within the purview of the discipline of Africology. Most of the relevant research involves the systematic exploration of relationships, social codes, cultural and commercial customs, and oral traditions and proverbs, although the interpretation of communicative behaviors, as expressed in spoken or written discourse, and techniques found in jazz and urban street-vernacular signifying, is also included. There are three fundamental existential postures that one can take with respect to the human condition: feeling, knowing, and acting, which are sometimes known as the affective, cognitive, and conative positions. Africology recognizes these three stances as being interrelated, not separate.

The affective component deals with a person's feelings of like or dislike about an object or idea. The cognitive refers to how an object is perceived, or its conceptual connotation. The conative stance is the person's behavioral tendencies regarding an object. In Africology, an object or idea is best studied when all three components are interrelated. This present book, therefore, is an Africological undertaking.

Perhaps the most important theoretical impetus to this line of study came from the theorizing of Wade Nobles and Maulana Karenga.[23] Nobles is primarily concerned with the psychological states and conditions of an oppressed people, whereas Karenga is interested mainly in developing theories of cultural reconstruction. Both argue that because diasporic Africans are often disconnected from positive African values, cultural reconstruction is necessary. Their work has thus contributed to my Africological enterprise and to my understanding of the enormity of the task Afrocentrists confront in challenging the intellectual taboos of the academy.

My aim in writing *The Afrocentric Idea* was to inject the agency of Africans into the equation of social and political transformation.

Heretofore the discussion of African Americans has always taken place within the framework of Europe and then most frequently in the margins of Europe. Since Europe was the center of the world and European people the centers of history in these constructions, Africans did not have any agency except as it was granted by Europe or by contact with Europeans. Thus, Robert Speke's search for the source of the Nile is historically significant because the river's origin had not yet been discovered by Europeans, even though it was not unknown to Africans. African American communities became important because whites developed an interest in them and decided they must be studied, modified, or eliminated. African scholars were declared honorary whites when they expressed anti-African sentiments. Whatever whites decided about blacks became the ultimate determinant of the fate of blacks. In almost every field of human endeavor, the situation was the same. If whites considered a black person important to the advancement of the ideological framework of Western triumphalism, then that person took on significance to whites even if he or she were anti-African. Some Africans may have been given positions, promoted in jobs, and paraded by whites as significant (although they had no social or political legitimacy in the African community) simply because they were useful smoke screens for the continued attacks on the African community. Certainly, some of these blacks so used by whites have turned the tables and become outstanding antiracist campaigners. However, it is their anti-Africanness that defines them as important within the context of the ideology of white supremacy. When they no longer express their dislike of their own cultural traditions, or when they no longer condemn their own ancestors, they are without worth to the racists.

Afrocentricity liberates the African by establishing agency as the key concept for freedom. I am most free when I am most active on the basis of my own volition. Even if I am active and believe myself to be free under the will of another, I am not truly liberated. In the early years of African American Studies, I was the director of the Center for Afro American Studies at UCLA and wrote an essay calling for the development of courses from a black perspective. I had not called that perspective "Afrocentricity" in the 1970s, but the incipient idea existed in the notion of self-defining characteristics and self-determining actions. Furthermore, the opening of the cultural discourse to the topic of African agency pushed through the conception of African people as subject rather than object in the European experience. For the non-African, the

Afrocentric idea positions intellectual discourse in the African agency that is often denied by Eurocentric conceptualizations of our roles.

What I have done is to bring the consciousness of rhetorical structure to the study of African communication, particularly discourse by explaining the rhetorical condition as a phenomena with an implicit structure. Thus, African American oratory becomes the totalization of the Afrocentric perspective, emphasizing the presence of nommo, the generative and productive power of the spoken word, in African discourse with respect to resistance to the dominant racist ideology. In the oratorical experience, much as in the jazz experience, the African person finds the ability to construct a discourse reality capable of calling forth nommo in every instance of human communication.

The idea that the political and social protocols of a society are based on the very nature of the laws and customs of that society leads to the formation of a structure that dictates the relationships between people. Just as it is possible to speak of a culture that seeks to predict and control and another that seeks to understand and interpret, one can also see that different human objectives are derived from different historical and cultural experiences. Actually this is what Ama Mazama means when she describes Afrocentricity as a paradigm.[24] What occurs in any science or art is a debate over mode, structure, and condition; that is, the guidelines for the valid discussion of discourse are at the center of any polemic. On a larger scale, a topic is an ongoing conversation about the plurality of visions in the context of reality.

We all possess the cultural capacity to see, explain, and interpret from the vantage point of our existential location. In the West and elsewhere, the European, in the midst of other peoples, has often propounded an exclusive view of reality; the exclusivity of this view creates a fundamental human crisis. In some cases, it has created cultures arrayed against each other or even against themselves. Afrocentricity's response certainly is not to impose its own particularity as a universal, as Eurocentricity has often done. But hearing the voice of African culture with all of its attendant parts is one way of creating a more sane society and one model for a more humane world.

Endnotes and References

1. Asante, Molefi. 1980. *Afrocentricity: The Theory of Social Change.* Buffalo, N.Y.: Amulefi. The argument of this volume is essentially a sort of congruence position. I maintain that African Americans can never achieve their full psychological potential until they find congruence between who they are and what their environment says they ought to be. To be Afrocentric is to place Africans and the interests of Africa at the center of our approach to problem-solving.

2. Fiedler, Leslie. 1966. *Love and Death in the American Novel.* New York, N.Y.: Stein & Day.

3. Larson, Charles. Heroic Ethnocentrism: The Idea of Universality in Literature. *American Scholar.* 42 (3): 463-467.

4. Larson, Charles. Heroic Ethnocentrism: The Idea of Universality in Literature. *American Scholar.* 42 (3): 463-467. 465.

5. Cedrix X; McGee, D. Phillip; Nobles, Wade & Luther X. 1975. *Voodoo or IQ: An Introduction to African Psychology*. *Journal of Black Psychology*. 1(2): 10. Another brilliant scholar in African psychology is Joseph Baldwin of Florida A & M University. Baldwin has contended that to speak as if "Black people and Black experience outside of the context of African culture and African experience is utterly meaningless." See Joseph A. Baldwin. 1986. African (Black) Psychology. *Journal of Black Studies*. 16 (3): 241. Baldwin believes that African psychology is an affirmation of centrality in the natural order.

6. Armstrong, Robert Plant. 1975. *Wellspring: On the Myth and Source of Culture*. Berkeley, CA: University of California Press. 14.

7. Sacks, Karen. 1979. *Sisters and Wives*. Westport, CT: Greenwood Press. 3.

8. Sacks, Karen. 1979. *Sisters and Wives*. Westport, CT: Greenwood Press. 4.

9. West, Cornel. 1988. *Prophetic Fragments*. Grand Rapids, MI: Eerdmans.

10. Marable, Manning. 1996. *Speaking Truth to Power*. Boulder, CO: Westview Press.

11. Cruse, Harold. 1969. *Rebellion or Revolution*. New York, N.Y.: William Morrow. 11-32. He addresses similar themes in *The Crisis of the Negro Intellectual*. New York, N.Y.: William Morrow (1967).

13. West, Cornel. 1993. *Prophetic Thoughts for Postmodern Times*. Monroe, MN: Common Courage Press. 150-1.

14. Thompson, Robert Farris. 1984. *The Flash of the Spirit: African and Afro-American Art and Philosophy*. New York, N.Y.: Random House. In this work Thompson is interested in the way Africans made the Americas; the essence of modernity is bound in the rhythms and rituals of Africa turned to America.

15. Asante, Molefi & Vandi, Abdulai (eds). 1981. *Contemporary Black Thought*. Beverly Hills, CA: Sage Publications. See particularly the introduction.

16. These comments were exchanged in a debate at the United Theological Seminary in Dayton, Ohio, on April 12, 1995.

17. Kuhn, Thomas. 1970. *The Structure of Scientific Revolution*. Berkeley, CA: University of California Press.

18. In Lakatos, Imre & Musgrave, Alan (eds). 1970. *Criticism and the Growth of Knowledge*. Cambridge: Cambridge University Press.

19. Munro, P. 1912. *A Brief Course in the History of Education*. London: McMillan. 8.

20. Quill, W. 1972. *Subjective Knowledge*. New York, N.Y.: Spartan Books. 4.

21. Harris, Marvin. 1979. *Cultural Materialism: The Struggle for a Science of Culture*. New York, N.Y.: Random House.

21. Harris, Marvin. 1979. *Cultural Materialism: The Struggle for a Science of Culture*. New York, N.Y.: Random House. 28.

22. Harris, Marvin. 1979. *Cultural Materialism: The Struggle for a Science of Culture*. New York, N.Y.: Random House. 28.

23. Asante, Molefi. 1980. *Afrocentricity: The Theory of Social Change*. Buffalo, N.Y.: Amulefi. 67.

24. Mazama, Ama. 2001. *The Afrocentric Paradigm: Contours and Definitions. Journal of Black Studies*. 31: 387-405.

The Afrocentric Philosophical Perspective: A Narrative Outline

Danjuma Sinue Modupe

To facilitate understanding of the Afrocentric philosophical perspective, a term utilized here as emblematic of the major and defining structure of Afrocentric theory, the Afrocentric academic framework, Afrocentric theory must be understood in its entirety and as a number of interrelated and interconnected component parts. A narrative outline of the theory is assumed the best method for providing both the whole and its components parts within the spatial constraints of a single essay. On the one hand, therefore, this essay is an attempt to provide the minimal amount of concepts necessary for understanding Afrocentricity as a whole; on the other, it is an attempt nevertheless to present a complete picture. At this point in the development of Afrocentric theory, such a picture necessitates the presentation of both established and newly created categories. Such an endeavor reveals Afrocentric theory capable of being divided into seven basic components, each of which is defined and given function in relationship to the whole. The components are 1) the Afrocentric objective, 2) the consciousness matrix for definition, 3) the formal academic framework, 4) the condition complex, 5) theoretical constructs, 6) the structural gluon, and 7) victorious consciousness. Afrocentricity's source and the term Afrocentric philosophical perspective, which has become emblematic of the theory as a whole, complete the picture.

In an attempt to present Afrocentricity in an even more structured and developmental fashion, this narrative essay provides conceptualizations inclusive of, first, Afrocentricity's source, definition and ultimate objective.

Second, it makes explicit the implicit Afrocentric framework and its dynamic component parts. Third, it explores Afrocentric framework engagement with the problematics of the condition complex, an engagement which results in what has become known as the hallmark of Afrocentric theory, theoretical constructs, concepts such as agency, centeredness, situatedness, etc. Fourth, the narrative presents the structural gluon of Afrocentric theory, or the language and language devices which hold the theory together. Finally, the narrative presents Afrocentricity's culminating achievement, victorious consciousness.

In general, through my analysis and interpretation of Afrocentric texts, the essay attempts to advance Afrocentric theory not only by delineating new categories and adding nomenclature but also by reaffirming and extending established categories and their functions, with the specific intent of further formalizing Afrocentric theory. Due to the relative newness of Afrocentric nomenclature, I have taken the liberty of using bold italics to emphasize component parts and their basic elements. For all of my formulations, I utilize the theoretical work developed by Molefi Kete Asante, although I include that of other theorists.

THE COMMUNAL COGNITIVE WILL

Usually, theorists provide a compelling understanding or insight for their theory's source. For Molefi Kete Asante, this source is the African's collective cognitive will, the continuous spiritual and intellectual thrusts towards psychic and cultural liberation. Thus Afrocentric theory makes claim to being in tune with, to serving as a link to, and to advancing the African's collective cognitive will. In *Afrocentricity*, fidelity to this "will to liberation" is interpreted as being "imperative." As both the product and creative maintenance of that will, Afrocentric theory is viewed as the fulfillment of that imperative; and thus fidelity to Afrocentricity is viewed as fidelity to that will. (Being that "collective" implies a group of individuals coming together for a common end, whereas communal implies a spiritual connectedness, an inherent wholeness independent of individual decision, for theory consistency I employ the term "communal.") Molefi Kete Asante writes;

> [The communal cognitive will] is the overwhelming power of a group of people thinking in the same direction. It is not unity in the traditional sense of a group of people coming together to achieve a single purpose, it is a full spiritual and intellectual commitment to a vision which constitutes the [communal] cognitive imperative. (53)

Here, the communal cognitive will is characterized as a spiritual and intellectual vision by which Africans are linked to other Africans, a vision of psychic and cultural liberation which derives its power from a communal "direction of thought."

AFRICAN DEVELOPMENT

First and foremost, Afrocentricity is a theory about *African development*, psychic and cultural, of the person and of the people, as African. Therefore, African development is Afrocentricity's ultimate *objective*. Although Molefi Kete Asante makes this clear in the first page of *Afrocentricity* when he defines Afrocentricity as "human regeneration" and implicitly as "personal and collective growth and development," it is much later in the text, when Asante compares African development to European progress, that the definition takes on its important distinctions and implications:

> Marxism's Eurocentric foundation makes it antagonistic to our world view; its confrontational nature does not provide the spiritual satisfaction we have found in our history of harmony. This history of harmony, stemming from a strong sense of God-consciousness in nature and each other, is denied by European materialism which views harmony as a lack of progress. Progress, in a Eurocentric manner, grows out of conflict, a sort of dialectic of forces. For us, life is culture, spirit and harmony. (1988: 80)

Later in the text, Asante writes,

> Progress, in an Afrocentric manner, is related to the development of human personality because we are the source of life for the material and the spiritual; when we become more conscious of ourselves we shall be advanced and will make progress. (1988: 81)

African development, Asante makes clear, takes place within the context of "an ideal ideological commitment to harmony," (1988:22) what Afrocentrics and other scholars have concluded to be the original and continuing African context for fulfilling the African cultural objective.

CONSCIOUSNESS MATRIX

To achieve the objective of African psychic and cultural development, within the context of an African communal consciousness, Afrocentric theory postulates what can be perceived as a *consciousness matrix* [as the seat where and the apparatus for attaining that objective.] As described in *The American Heritage Dictionary of the English Language*, by matrix is meant "A situation or surrounding substance within which something else originates, develops, or is contained," ... "a binding substance." This Afrocentric consciousness matrix is the "binding substance" out of which "originates, develops," and is "contained" a conceptualization of *consciousness for psychic liberation* and a conceptualization of *consciousness for cultural reclamation*. Perceived as different from the previous African American postulation of "unity in struggle" as matrix or binding substance for liberation, Molefi Asante describes Afrocentric consciousness as "the next act in our drama." Asante writes, "It is not unity that we must seek, but [communal] consciousness... a remarkable surge of consciousness that transcends the current emphasis on unity ..." (1988: 24). Consciousness precedes unity! It is a personal and communal consciousness which moves toward "victory," allowing for the expression of a "victorious consciousness" (1988: 50-1). Moreover, Asante stipulates that "The type of relationship between our consciousness and our history [and culture] is *the true character of Afrocentricity*" (1988:51) [Emphasis mine].

It can thus be said that the Afrocentric consciousness matrix "moves toward" or *operates* in two directions in the "surge" of consciousness, toward African psychic liberation and African cultural reclamation. In turn, African psychic liberation and African cultural reclamation are concomitant, and increasing levels of each contribute to the expansion of the base consciousness matrix. The consciousness matrix, in its attempt to attain communal self-fulfillment, acts upon or *motivates* the person of African descent by making clear the need for psychic liberation and African cultural reclamation. Therefore, African psychic liberation and cultural reclamation presuppose an understanding and acceptance of *the need* for each, a conceptualization and understanding which in themselves in turn make a vital contribution to the consciousness matrix. It is also, therefore, the consciousness matrix which allows for the ultimate expression of a victorious consciousness –*knowing that* and *understanding how* the person has achieved African psychic and cultural development, as African, or know how the person has *won*.

PSYCHIC LIBERATION

As a theory of development, as opposed to a theory of unity or a theory of resistance to oppression, Afrocentricity postulates a two-pronged conceptualization of liberation; and the conceptualization of liberation itself is grounded by the African American conceptualization of *freedom*. In such a development as opposed to resistance theory, psychic liberation would necessarily comprise, first and foremost, the *freedom* to develop. However, because the reality in which the "freedom to" is situated, the *freedom from* the oppression which impedes that development comprises the second part of this two pronged conceptualization. For a definition of freedom, I utilize Norman Harris' essay, "A Philosophical Basis for an Afrocentric Orientation," in which Harris indicates that one of the "philosophical assumptions which seem(s) to structure the application of all Afrocentric approaches" is that "the central motivation in African American life is the desire to achieve freedom ..." (this volume). "Freedom," he writes, "is the ability to conceptualize the world in ways continuous with one's history" (this volume). Thus, both the freedom to develop and the freedom from oppression are conceptualized in a fashion which indicates the African person's ability to conceptualize the world in ways continuous with the African's history.

What this formulation presupposes is that, though related, the freedom to develop can be distinguished from the freedom to resist oppression. The freedom to develop presupposes an Afrocentric relationship to, and a desire for, African psychic and cultural development, as African; whereas, freedom to resist oppression, the dominant mode of African American theory to date, has not necessarily comprised either the necessity for the Afrocentric relationship to Africa nor the same desires for development as African. However, for the Afrocentric, both these concepts are expressed with the implicit assumption that *African* freedom to develop and *African* freedom from oppression have a specificity of time, place and condition, derived out of African history and culture and thus different from any "universal" or European conceptualizations of freedom, development, and oppression, as described either by Europeans for themselves or as described by Europeans for the African (Asante, 1988: 24-30).

CULTURAL RECLAMATION

African development presupposes more than the mere traditional African American investigation and absorption of extant African cultural material and immaterial reality; the nature of the need for African development, in the context of cultural development as Molefi Asante has described it, as "under duress," along with the type of oppression undergone – the type of duress, mandates the African person's conscious effort to understand *what is African*, then the pursuit and utilization of and the participation in African culture – as rendered theoretically. In effect, this formulation for relating to African culture is termed African *cultural reclamation*: the resurrection, reconstruction, and revitalization of African culture. (As Molefi Asante has so made emphatic, "Europeans have gone on their cultural project but we [people of African descent] have not gone on with ours.")

It is thus this consciousness matrix, which is contextualized by the African communal consciousness and which allows for victorious consciousness, psychically liberating and cultural reclaiming, which in turn is definitive of Afrocentricity. One can thus, as definition, envision Afrocentricity as *a consciousness matrix utilized in the pursuit of the objective of African psychic and cultural development, as African.*

AFRICAN DEVELOPMENT, AS AFRICAN

The definitive characteristic of an Afrocentric theory of African development, of the person and of the people, is *as African*. That is, Afrocentricity theorizes about the development of people of African descent, as African people. This is in contradistinction to all theories which posit Africans in the diaspora as culturally "Western" and thus which necessarily posit diasporan Africans in the pursuit of the development of culture extending out of European origins. Implicit in the concept of African development, as African, is a particular conceptualization of African origins, history, culture and African cultural "retentions" in the diaspora. This understanding draws heavily upon the "ancient" as opposed to the "Aryan" model of history, consisting of African Nile Valley Civilization origins, the subsequent spread of this culture throughout the African continent, and the forced out-migration of Africans who carried their culture with them to what is now the African diaspora, where African culture proceeded "under duress." In *Afrocentricity* Asante (1988: XI) writes, "Afrocentricity [is] a reconnection, in our minds, of Egypt to Africa ... the assertive challenge Afrocentricity makes to non-African and anti-African perspectives ... a historiography that re-writes Africans to the classical periods." This theoretical position on African culture exists in contradistinction not only to the "Aryan" model of history but also to African development as theorized in any number of contexts other than *as African*. The position is particularly relevant to the theories which relegate African American culture and history to the beginning of European enslavement of the African, which has been said to create a "slave history and culture." Different conceptualizations of the African American, historically and culturally, demand different theoretical objectives, each objective demanding a different theoretical praxis and producing different ends.

AFRICAN PERSONALISM

The philosophical understanding which undergirds Afrocentric consciousness as it relates specifically to the person, and which thus situates the person in the context of the conceptualization of the consciousness matrix, Molefi Kete Asante has termed African *personalism*, a West African philosophical position originating out of the *sudic* ideal, the *quest for and commitment to harmony*. In essence, personalism describes the *activating energy* contained in the person in pursuit of harmony, an activating energy which, in turn, determines the *nature of reality*. Thus it can be said that in the context of the consciousness matrix the activating energy in the pursuit of and the commitment to harmony of the person determines the nature of Afrocentric consciousness. In effect, personalism is what activates and gives form to the consciousness matrix: psychic liberation and cultural reclamation. Thus personalism is also what allows for the possibility of victorious consciousness. In the context of the Afrocentric objective of African psychic and cultural development, as African, an Afrocentric personalism determines the manner in which that activating energy is utilized by the person in the attainment of the Afrocentric objective. Ultimately, of course, a philosophical belief which defines the nature of reality and the manner of personal consciousness activity for achieving that reality, determines for the African person the *meaning* of reality, which in turn can be said to originate out of a particular world view described as African, as distinguished from the world views of other cultural groups.

Dividing world cultures into three distinct culturally evolving groups, the European, the Asian, and the African, scholars have arrived at three distinct world views. The cultures of the East are postulated as favoring the world as spiritual and the cultures of the West as favoring the world as basically material. African culture is said to favor neither, but instead to see the world as spirit manifesting, or the material world as manifestation of an animating spiritual world. In *The Afrocentric Idea*, Molefi Kete Asante (1987: 22) writes, "This view is similar to the position I advanced in intercultural communication theory regarding the Afrocentric personalism, Asiocentric-spiritualism, [and] Eurocentric-materialism categories of reality." Asante writes further, "... the *sudic ideal, personalism* ... is itself an ideal ideological *commitment to harmony*, and the fundamental Afrocentric response to phenomena." He adds,

"There is nothing to the spiritual, nor to the material, that is not activated by the person. So I can say that personalism, in the African and African American sense, is neither spiritual nor material, but the activating energy contained in the person" (1988: 202). This of course, brings a particular kind of reality into existence.

This conceptualization is extremely important in the context of the person in the African and African American community, where the person, in order to contribute to and maintain the proper functioning of order or harmony, is obligated to pursue happiness. Unhappiness brings disruption of order or disharmony. Such a postulation posits a different conceptualization of the "nature" of the person as human being and thus brings the "possibility" of harmony or happiness for the person in community than that described by Western culture, which posits in drama, literature, art, history, and theology the tragic and alienated individual in community. In further contrast, the Eastern conceptualization of the individual in community, which is defined by the height of spiritual existence, allows for the existence of such an individual apart from community. However, the African receives his/her understanding of the "nature of life" and its "possibility for happiness" as defined by the African world view in the context of "life in community." Alienation and tragedy are thus modes of "disharmony," not modes of life. Personalism thus defines the African person's existence in relation to the material and immaterial worlds as the quest for and commitment to achieving harmony in community. The activating energy of the person can thus be viewed as the fuel for personal Afrocentric consciousness, while at the same time being defined by the parameters set forth by African reality or by the African world view. It is the African world view which, as we will see, is considered foundational to the explicit, formal Afrocentric framework in the rise to an Afrocentric consciousness.

AFROCENTRIC PRAXIS

Afrocentric praxis, on the level of theory, can be defined as Afrocentric *engagement* with phenomena. Afrocentric praxis includes all of the conceptualizations which make that engagement possible: an academic discipline, a paradigm, a philosophical undergirding, a theoretical framework, framework dynamics, and methodologies of *engagement* in the utilization of the Afrocentric framework. In addition, one can distinguish Afrocentric theory praxis in the literature as the utilization of particular, categorized results of the Afrocentric framework engagement with phenomena, called *theoretical constructs*. Theoretical construct engagement with phenomena demands a different methodology. A model of praxis for a particular discipline is called a paradigm, or one of the logical procedures utilized to effect the objectives of the discipline of Africology. In the Afrocentric Idea, Asante (1987: 175) writes:

> Afrocentric scholarship is itself praxis. Afrocentricity as paradigm has propaedeutic value because a myriad of assumptions and basic propositions employed by African American Studies can be examined. Such scholarship as praxis reduces the tendency for individuals to make random, non-

connected comments, even though those comments might be informative. The logic of procedure provides groundwork for others to follow; this is the value of Afrocentric scholarship as work.

The logic of procedure in Afrocentric praxis, "Scholarship as work," can be described, formally, as, first, the explicit Afrocentric framework's engagement with problematic phenomena, or with a *condition complex*; and second, as the explicit utilization of Afrocentric theoretical constructs.

Asante (1987: 175) adds to his perspective on praxis, "This position is in keeping with my contention that African American Studies must be defined not by subjects or themes, but by an *Afrocentric [philosophical] perspective* that is central to the paradigm." The Afrocentric philosophical perspective is both inclusive and a product of the implicit framework. The discipline is called Africology; the paradigm is Afrocentricity; and the framework I have described as a pyramid, reflecting the dynamic and interactive Afrocentric pyramidal rise to consciousness.

THE AFROCENTRIC FRAMEWORK

Thus far in the literature the Afrocentric framework is recorded implicitly, through praxis, although all of its component parts have received ample and serious critical attention. However, my attempt here is to present the framework as a conceptual whole. Generated and informed by the knowledge, experience, history and culture of people of African descent, the Afrocentric framework is designed to achieve the Afrocentric theory objective of African development, as African, though its interactive and interrelated, dynamic process of the rise to consciousness. *Emblematic* of this process is the Afrocentric philosophical perspective. What is meant here by emblematic is that although the Afrocentric framework consists of a dynamic process of the pyramidal elements in the rise to consciousness, the Afrocentric philosophical perspective is inclusive in that process, it is representative, symbolic of both the process itself and the results of that rise. We can now state that the Afrocentric objective is African development, *as the African, as achieved though the specificity of the Afrocentric framework engagement with phenomena, emblematic of the philosophical perspective.*

In *Afrocentricity*, Molefi Kete Asante has established three basic conceptualizations of elements of what can be termed the implicitly Afrocentric framework: grounding, orientation, and perspective, which I will present here into a structure for a formal, explicit framework, accompanied by a diagrammatic functioning. (See below) Following the ancient practice of dedication to the ancestors, I have described these elements as building blocks of a pyramid. I thus refer to them as the *pyramidal elements* of the Afrocentric rise to consciousness. Simply defined, they are as follows:

- Grounding is the acquisition of knowledge and experience centered in the history and culture of people of African descent, continental and diasporan.

- Orientation is having and pursuing intellectual interest in the African and the formation of a psychological identity direction, based upon that interest, in the direction toward Africa.
- Perspective is a self-conscious "way of seeing" and "shaping" the world which reflects African best interest and which is indicative of the quality, kind and amount of grounding and orientation.

Descriptive modifiers, reflecting the area of study and purpose of the pyramidal elements, distinguish pyramidal element categories from that of other frameworks. Thus, grounding has been theorized as *African-centered*; orientation, as *psycho-intellectual*; and perspective, as *philosophical*. In addition, each pyramidal element has been demonstrated to correspond best to a particular philosophical principle. African-centered grounding corresponds to the philosophical principle of epistemology; psycho-intellectual orientation to axiology; and the philosophical perspective to ontology and cosmology.

FRAMEWORK INTEGRITY

Though the Afrocentric framework is conceived and diagrammed as a pyramid, with an African-centered grounding base and a psycho-intellectual orientation rise in consciousness to the pinnacle of a philosophical perspective, Afrocentric consciousness takes place over time as a dynamic process. Contoured and controlled by the Afrocentric objective of African psychic and cultural development, as the African, the pyramidal elements work in an interactive, interconnected process which, though resulting in a definite increase in the level of consciousness, is not necessarily a linear climb. In addition, without the struggle to achieve the concrete objective to which the framework aspires, which again is defined as consciousness matrix which fosters psychic liberation and cultural reclamation, pyramidal elements loose their functional direction, shape, and scope. What this means is that no one pyramidal element is independent of the others; no one pyramidal element is and of itself is capable of fulfilling the Afrocentric objective; and thus no one pyramidal element is definitive of the Afrocentric framework or of Afrocentricity as a theory.

Moreover, the process of the rise to consciousness provided by the pyramidal element dynamic requires, necessarily, self-conscious activity. Such activity is necessitated by the nature of the African's particular requirements for development, which take the form of psychic liberation and cultural reclamation under the tremendous pressure and weight of a particular kind of European oppression perpetrated against the African for nearly five hundred years. That is, to obtain a liberation which houses the psychic freedom to develop and the freedom from oppression concomitant with African cultural pursuit, it takes self-conscious effort. This effort takes the form of belief in the dynamic process of the Afrocentric framework, which means its study, understanding, and praxis, which adds up, of course, to *commitment*. In other words, in order to counter what has become centuries of a normalized psychic oppression and cultural obstruction, which have impeded not only the means to African development but also actually impeded the African's desire for it, as the African, it is imperative that the African commit to the understanding and practice of the dynamics of the Afrocentric framework.

At this point, one can see that the Afrocentric framework consists of particular parts designed to perform particular functions in the effort to achieve a specific objective. To make such a statement is not to deny or exclude other theories or theorists with different functions and objectives claiming to be Afrocentric but to maintain Afrocentric theory integrity – which actually makes Afrocentricity viable and effective as a theory. It is the Afrocentric framework dynamic in meeting its challenge to a rise in Afrocentric consciousness in order to fulfill its ultimate objective of African development, as African, and thus the framework's implications and permutations, which makes all Afrocentric nomenclature and taxonomy particular and different.

CONDITION (CEA) COMPLEX (Cause/Effect/Alleviation)

An Afrocentric methodology of *engagement* has already begun to establish as representative of the discipline of Africology, one which I have termed *internal* engagement, due to its utilization of the elements internal to the framework. An engagement reflective of the perceived effectiveness of addressing the whole of an African problematic condition, it promotes an African *holism*. I have termed this pattern of engagement the "condition" or "CEA" complex, meaning that *cause, effect*, and *alleviation* of any problematic condition are viewed and treated holistically or as a complex. In effect, the Afrocentric framework engages not merely the cause of condition or its effects upon the African or the theorized alleviation of those effects but views the condition as forming a complex deserving of an understanding as an interrelated and interconnected conceptual whole. In "Afrocentricity, Race, and Reason," Molefi Kete Asante suggests such a mode of engagement when, taking the form of *analysis, critique*, and *corrective*, an Afrocentric critical theory is proposed. In that such a methodology privileges corrective as opposed to critique or to the problematizing of things African, it is considered to serve best the objective of a theory of *development*. This is not to say that cause, effect, alleviation are absolutely necessary in Afrocentric engagement but that Afrocentric theory is highly suggestive of such a methodology and it is thus *preferred*.

THEORETICAL CONSTRUCTS

Theoretical constructs are defined as accumulations of knowledge and understanding resulting from the effective engagement of the Afrocentric framework with a problematic African condition. Once developed, or described and categorized, each theoretical construct can be utilized in a methodology different from that of Afrocentric framework with condition complex. Because theoretical constructs are outside the Afrocentric framework, the methodology is termed external engagement. Thus far, I have formulated seven theoretical constructs, and these distinct but related conceptualization can be said to consist of Afrocentric accumulated wisdom, or the philosophical "should" of thought and behavior deemed necessary for African psyche and cultural development, as African. Thus, as tools in the fulfillment of the Afrocentric objective, it is assumed that the first and primary argument or the philosophical "should" implicit in and undergirding all theoretical constructs – those listed and others to be discovered- is *African development, as African*. In addition, as Molefi Kete Asante states in *The Afrocentric Idea* (1987: xvii), there is the implicit assumption that theoretical constructs can and do serve as "a perfectly valid and scientific basis for the exploration of African historical experiences." In *Race and Class*, in his formulations toward an Afrocentric critical theory, Asante employs a logic of procedure different from that employed with the condition complex ("cause," effect," "alleviation), that of "analysis," "critique" and "corrective." A close reading of Afrocentric literature reveals in general, however, not only the need for further categorization but also the necessity of "unpacking" already extant categories.

• *Agency* is a conceptualization which argues for and employs the philosophical "should" of Africans being subjects of history and culture, an efficacious habit of being in which the African acquires the "desire" and "capability" of recognizing and effecting African subjectivity. The African perceives self as "cultured" and forms self-developmental cultural objectives, or African instrumentality. The problematic is the African normalized as object of European history and culture, which induces the lost desire for creating African cultural objectives, often producing "anti-agency" or dysfunctional behavior, which negates recognition of the African as actor and of positive projections of the African self in the future.

• *Centeredness* is a conceptualization which argues for and employs the philosophical "should" of Africans having knowledge and understanding of their historical origins and cultural development which provides *connectedness* to and the necessary reverence for the ancestors, and thus an *efficacious perception* of "self in culture." The problematic is decenteredness, having a false connection to European history and culture and thus a *(mis) perception* of reality which often causes a psychopathological *disconnectedness* from the ancestors, from African culture, and at times even from people of African descent. A form of *self-alienation*, this impedes a common cultural knowledge source for understanding in community and thus preventing effective communication, particularly inter-generational.

• *Situatedness* is a conceptualization which argues for and employs the philosophical "should" of Africans acquiring and/or creating an efficacious intellectual and psychic space, a "place to stand," for an *anchored* and *proactive stance* from which to form the "proper attitude" toward African phenomena in general and data in particular. The problematic is one of current *location* due to *dislocation* and the absence of the means to *relocation*. With dislocation, the African is forced to exist outside of proper place, *unanchored* and *reactive*, exhibiting the "improper attitude" toward African phenomena, particularly data, the *"process of disbelief,"* thus residing at the "borders" of European history and culture – *marginality*.

- *Psychic integrity* is a conceptualization which argues for and employs the philosophical "should" of Africans being capable of making distinctions which allow for the achievement of thought and behavior conducive to African psychic health, or sanity, which demands 1) ethical clarity, 2) privileging one's own knowledge and experience, and 3) an efficacious amount of cultural knowledge. The problematic is the normalized ill health of the African psychic serving the needs of European psychic health, or insanity, which reflects 1) a misconstrued ethics, 2) mistaking white intentions, 3) privileging white experience, and 4) cultural transubstantiation. Currently, *mis-orientation* and/or *disorientation* are the formal psychological terms utilized.

- *Discursive acumen* is a conceptualization which argues for and employs the philosophical "should" of Africans creating and evolving *language* which depicts and constructs and African reality reflective of 1) an African *knowledge and experience*, 2) the *wisdom (Philosophy)* of African people, 3) a *culturally positive discourse*, and 4) an *accurate categorization* of the nature of white, Western, European oppression. The problematic is Africans being normalized into a European reality which depicts and is constructed by language reflective of European best interest, knowledge and experience, Philosophy, and an *anti-African discourse*, formed by categorizations which deny and obscure the nature of European oppression of the African.

- *Cultural fidelity* is a conceptualization which argues for and employs the philosophical "should" of African cultural reclamation, building upon the continental African philosophical concept of Sankofa, the responsibility and maturity of "reaching back and fetching it," or the acceptance and self-conscious pursuit of African historical and cultural knowledge. The problematic is mistaken or forced participation in African cultural obliteration, a normalized hegemony governed by the absence or distortion of knowledge and the creation of an illusion for (mis) recognition, comprising the irresponsibility and immaturity of cultural infidelity.

- *Ownership* is a conceptualization which argues for and employs the philosophical "should" of the African's recognition of and the responsibility for ownership of all that is psychically and culturally African, in order to establish Afrocentric psychic and cultural literacy, literacy as the extension of Harris' definition of freedom, as "the application of historical [and cultural] knowledge as the confluence between personality and situation dictates (this volume)." The problematic of *dis-ownership*, the "ideological" imposition placed upon African people's psyche and culture over the last three-hundred years, created by enslavement, colonization, imperialism, and white supremacist domination and control.

Combined, theoretical constructs not only demonstrate the results of framework engagement with African problematic conditions, they represent the major philosophical concerns of an *Afrocentric philosophy*, the conclusion reached about how Africans should live their lives, while the African continental philosophical praxis can be described as *Afrocentricity as philosophy*.

Afrocentric philosophical praxis, or "doing philosophy," fulfills the Afrocentric objective by arguing for and demonstrating the value of Afrocentric accumulated wisdom, or theoretical constructs.

CRITICAL THEORETICAL DISTINCTIONS

At this point, it is necessary to make the critical distinction between two different schools of thought, one which utilizes an *African world view* as framework, and one which utilizes an *Afrocentric philosophical perspective* as framework. The latter, I have termed the *Asantean* school of thought. The former is composed predominantly of scholars who self-identify as Africentric, Africanity, and African-centered theorists and who are mostly in the areas of Black Psychology and African Personality Theory. As a phenomena achieved by a people over time, in response to nature and their physical environment, world view is for a people a way of making sense of the world based upon a people' s particular historical and cultural development. However, world view allows for different philosophical perspectives, and different world views (such as European, Asian and African world views) allow for different sets of perspectives. Thus, world view cannot be considered the same as philosophical perspective, and it is important to note that Afrocentricy claims to be neither a world view nor does it claim an African world view as framework.

Along with the perspective/world view distinction, the Asantean Afrocentric theory needs to be distinguished from other theories of similar and dissimilar nomenclature. For example, the late Black Psychology professor Amon Wilson, though utilizing traditional Western psychoanalytical tools, worked out of an Afrocentric philosophical perspective. In a text entitled *Understanding an Afrocentric World View*, Linda James Myers nevertheless frames her "Optimal Psychology" from an African world view, while Kwame Agyei Akoto's *Nationbuilding: Theory and Practice in Afrikan Centered Education* utilizes an Afrocentric perspective (1992: 25). Similarly, Marimba Ani, who in the introduction to her text, *Yurugu* (1994) cites herself as an Afrocentric theorist and works out of an African-centered culture paradigm. For clarity's sake, these four theorists need to be distinguished from an Asantean Afrocentricity for a number of reasons: 1) an Asantean Afrocentricity does not proceed from traditional Western analytical tools, 2) does not claim an Afrocentric world view, 3) does not claim to be centered in any traditional Continental African culture, and 4) does not claim to operate out of an African-centered cultural paradigm. (I feel it would be of great help to current and potential students in Africana Studies if theorists working out of an African-centered paradigm would define exactly what this concept means, particularly if it is to be distinguished from an Afrocentric paradigm. Or is an African-centered paradigm merely a way of utilizing Afrocentric theory under a different nomenclature?)

At the same time that it is important to disclaim Afrocentricity as a world view, Asantean Afrocentric scholars make extensive use of the excellent African world view delineations made available by a number of the above and other African culture theorists. For example, James A. Anderson in "Cognitive Styles and Multicultural Population" (1988: 6-7) and Linda Myers in an addendum to her text have provided invaluable delineations of the cognitive dimensions and philosophical principles of an African world view. Clovis Semmes, while carving out an Afrocentric sociology, provides helpful distinctions between world view theorists and other theories in *Cultural Hegemony and African American Development* (1992: 20-3). However, in contradistinction to world view, Afrocentricity as a philosophical perspective is the result of the dynamic rise to consciousness afforded the self-conscious pursuit of the Afrocentric objective, African psychic liberation and cultural reclamation. As a function of its *cultural reclamation*, Afrocentricity advocates African cultural resurrection, reconstruction and revitalization. This implies an understanding and conscious utilization of the African world view as one of the major constituents of African-centered grounding, which forms the pyramidal element base of the Afrocentric academic framework. Thus, African-centered grounding is not utilized as framework, but as a particular *element* of a particular *component* (the Afrocentric framework) of Afrocentric theory.

Thus, when applied to phenomena with respect to analysis, interpretation or critique, an African world view does not yield the same types of results as does an Afrocentric philosophical perspective. For example, an African born and raised in a traditional, African continental culture – let us say, for example, an Ibo – has an African world view, not an Afrocentric philosophical perspective; and this world view is indicative of neither the thought nor the dictates of behavior implicit in an Afrocentric philosophical perspective. The application of this person's world view to phenomena – let us say, to the condition complex of African American internalized inferiority – does not yield the same results as the application of an Afrocentric philosophical perspective.

In addition, critical to note also is that an *Asantean* Afrocentricity does not privilege any one aspect of Afrocentric theory as equal to or definitive of the whole of Afrocentric theory. Parts of the whole are viewed as components or elements of components or constituents of elements. Partial definitions of Afrocentricity, when conceptualized as the whole, appear to serve best the needs of a particular scholar's discipline, while an *Asantean* Afrocentricity serves best the Afrocentric objective and thus purports the Afrocentric framework as paradigm for the discipline of *Africology*.

STRUCTURAL GLUON

The structural gluon of Afrocentric theory, that which holds it together, is defined as the material and nonmaterial reality in which Afrocentric theory exists, bound by the framing philosophical principles which govern that existence, and the philosophical concerns which provide its particularity. Afrocentricity exists in culture, on the level of language, and is governed by particular African/African American philosophical principles and concerns. As stated by Molefi Kete Asante in *Afrocentricity, Kemet and Knowledge* (1990), the principles of Afrocentricity are epistemological, axiological, and ontological/cosmological; and the philosophical concerns favored by African culture are ethics and aesthetics: Ma'at. To the theoretical component which defines the structural gluon, I have given the name the *language environment*. The component of Afrocentric theory which interprets the nature of language and prescribes its use, I have termed, simply, the Afrocentric language environment. Language, as psychological, social and cultural reality, is where Afrocentric theory exists; that is, language comprises the *environment* in which all Afrocentric theory has been created and in which all Afrocentric theoretical praxis takes place. Thus the term "environment," in the context of Afrocentricity's relationship to language, takes on a unique meaning; for language environment establishes the relationship between Afrocentric theory and *itself*. In Webster's Collegiate, there are two related definitions for environment:

> 1. The circumstances, objects, or conditions by which one is surrounded ; 2a. A complex of physical, chemical, and biotic factors (as climate, soil, and living things) that act upon an organism or an ecological community and ultimately determine its form and survival; 2b. The aggregate of social and cultural conditions that influence the life of an individual or community.

"Environment" is thus suggestive of a complex of factors, circumstances and/or conditions which influence the life, the form and the survival of a particular kind of organism or community. In this particular formulation, therefore, language environment is viewed as factors, circumstances or conditions (psychological, social and cultural); and Afrocentricity is viewed as an organism. Afrocentric theory receives its life, its form and its means of survival from its language environment. It would follow then, that within the language environment, the more *conducive* are the complex of factors, circumstances and/or conditions (psychological, social and cultural) to the particular organism (Afrocentric theory), the better the quality of the life, the survival and development of that organism.

Thus, Afrocentricity as theory is "language bound" and ultimately as effective as its language environment. Thus, the Afrocentric concern with language exists necessarily on two different but related planes; one, the *efficacious use of language* in the effort of Africans, as African, and second, the *nature of the language environment* in which that effort is being made. The concrete, structured entities utilized to achieve the Afrocentric objective of psychic and cultural development, as African, within the language environment is described as *language/discourse*. Thus we have language on the level of environment and as concrete reality within that environment. For the African American, the language environment exists as 1) Ebonics, 2) African American Standard Ebonics (AASE), and 3) Afrocentric Standard Ebonics (ASE). (These elements of this theory were developed in a paper entitled "The Afrocentric Writing Project"). The language/discourse is defined by Afrocentric Ebonics utilized to achieve an Afrocentric objective in language. This is reflective of the understanding that language contains the wisdom of a people.

With respect to methodology, my concern here is limited to describing one particular technique within an Afrocentric discourse. Though not yet made explicit, this technique is essential to all Afrocentric methodological engagement. Reflecting its function, I have named it *(Re) Framing*. (Re) Framing involves positioning any material engaged by the Afrocentric framework or theoretical constructs within an *Afrocentric discursive field*, a field which has implicit in it language reflective of the wisdom, and thus the best interest, of African people. This field restructures questions, concepts and problematics so that they are reflective of the African objective, and thus allows the best application of Afrocentric and global methodology.

VICTORIOUS CONSCIOUSNESS

Victorious consciousness begins at a level of Afrocentric consciousness appropriate to having achieved the knowledge and understanding that the African has *won*. When the dynamic rise to consciousness reaches a particular level – meaning the achievement of an amount and quality of African-centered grounding, psycho-intellectual orientation, and philosophical perspective – victorious consciousness is capable of being actualized. In effect, *Afrocentricity achieved* creates a desire and need, and thus a *propensity*, for a vision of the African as victorious. Despite the white supremacist construction of African denigration normalized throughout the world culture, Afrocentrics, now, are capable of conceptualizing African history and culture, and thus the African, as victorious. Victorious consciousness, in fact, becomes *normalized*. Concomitantly, white supremacy and "whiteness" are demystified. The dominant manifestation of victorious consciousness is the Afrocentric person' s *attitude*, which is manifested in the manner which the Afrocentric applies this knowledge and understanding to African phenomena. Thus, Afrocentricity achieved, the person of African descent has acquired the propensity for perceiving him/herself, personally, as having *won*. In *Afrocentricity*, Molefi Kete Asante writes, "Victory means that you have won, not that you are expecting to win ... Being Afrocentric is being victorious" (1988: 55). The Afrocentric, through his/her orientation, thus maintains an attitude which demonstrates the knowledge and understanding of that victory.

Aspects of Consciousness: "There are two aspects of consciousness: (1) *toward* oppression and (2) *toward* victory," Asante writes in Afrocentricity (1988: 50) [Emphasis mine]. In addition, "towards victory" can be divided into four different levels of reality. Consciousness of victory exists, first, in the concrete reality of the victorious nature of African history and culture itself, and second, in the possibility of the existence of that victorious reality, and third, the ability to arrive at this particular level of consciousness, and fourth, in the knowledge that it is achievable by all Africans. Victorious reality itself, in the concrete, is constituted by the knowledge and understanding of African history and culture, which says that there is concrete data and experience to demonstrate this victory. And about the possibility of that victorious reality Asante writes, "Consciousness of victory is the awareness that all attitudes and behaviors are achievable" (1988: 52). In turn, these two levels of reality are constituted by the

Afrocentric's ability to understand "objective" and "subjective" conceptualizations of African history and culture. Asante writes (1988: 51-2):

> If we are Afrocentric, then we know that objective and subjective, while not arbitrary designations, are not ironclad. We determine what constitutes objectivity and subjectivity by deciding what is necessary in order for the relationship between history and consciousness to work ... the true character of a people resides in how they relate their history to the present and future. No Afrocentric person can ever have merely a consciousness of oppression, pain, and suffering. The present and future must be projected as victory, indeed the present must be lived victoriously.

Victorious consciousness is therefore an attitude based upon the understanding of the *relationship* between African history, derived of African culture, and African consciousness, which is in turn governed by the Afrocentric's understanding of the subjective and objective nature of reality. In turn, this is definitive of the particular character which the attitude takes on in its manifestation of Afrocentricity. As we have already noted, "The type of relationship between our consciousness and our history is the true character of Afrocentricty" (1988: 51).

THE AFROCENTRIC PHILOSOPHICAL PERSPECTIVE

Concluding, we can now arrive at an understanding of the Afrocentric philosophical perspective as emblematic of Afrocentricity as a whole. Originating out of the consciousness matrix of Afrocentric definition, which consists of psychic and cultural development, as African, and necessitating therefore the fulfillment of the Afrocentric objective of psychic liberation and cultural reclamation, the Afrocentric philosophical perspective is structured within the formal Afrocentric framework, where it is distinguished as a pyramidal element, contributing to and operating out of the dynamics of the Afrocentric rise to consciousness. Here, interacting dynamically with African-centered grounding and psycho-intellectual orientation, it is defined as "a way of seeing" and "a way of shaping" the world; it is designated philosophical and corresponds to the philosophical principles of ontology and cosmology. In this capacity, it serves as the culminating force of the Afrocentric framework. Employed in methodological engagement with phenomena or problematics, which consist of a CEA complex, the Afrocentric philosophical perspective is instrumental in the formulation of the theoretical constructs resulting from that engagement. Apart from being viewed as the centerpiece of the Afrocentric framework, the Afrocentric philosophical perspective is instrumental in providing the necessary "way of seeing" and "shaping" the world which allows for Afrocentricity's crowning achievement, its victorious consciousness.

References

Akoto, Kwame Agyei. 1992. *Nationbuilding: Theory and Practice in Afrikan Centered Education*. Washington, D.C.: Pan African World Institute.

Ani, Marimba. 1994. Introduction. *Yurugu*. Trenton, NJ: Africa World Press.

Anderson, James A. 1988. Cognitive Styles and Multicultural Populations. *Journal of Teacher Education*.

Asante, Molefi Kete. 1988. *Afrocentricity*. Trenton, NJ: Africa World Press.

Asante, Molefi Kete. 1987. *The Afrocentric Idea*. Philadelphia, PA: Temple University Press.

Asante, Molefi Kete. 1990. *Kemet, Afrocentricity and Knowledge*. Trenton, NJ: Africa World Press.

Asante, Molefi Kete. 1993. *Malcom X as Cultural Hero and Other Afrocentric Essays*. Trenton, NJ: Africa World Press.

Asante, Molefi Kete. 1993. Afrocentricity and the Question of Youth Violence. *Malcom X as Cultural Hero and Other Afrocentric Essays*. Trenton, NJ: Africa World Press

Asante, Molefi Kete. 1994. Afrocentricity, Race, And Reason. *Race & Reason*. Columbia University.

Evans, Henry. 1996. The Afrocentric Writing Project. *Writing in Multicultural Situations*. New York, NY: Modern Language Association.

Harris, Norman. 1992. A Philosophical Basis for an Afrocentric Orientation. *Western Journal of Black Studies*. (3).

Karenga, Maulana. 1993. Introduction. *Introduction to Black Studies*. Los Angeles, CA: University of Sankore Press.

Myers, Linda James. 1988. *Understanding an Afrocentric World View*. Dubuque, IO: Kendall/Hunt.

Seemes, Clovis. 1992. *Cultural Hegemony and African American Development*. Westport, CN: Praeger.

Afrocentricity and Multicultural Education: Concept, Challenge and Contribution

Maulana Karenga

I. Introduction

I.1 Generative Assumptions

The current debate on the character and content of quality education in a multicultural context offers new possibilities not only for the reconception and reconstruction of public and higher education but also for the reconception and reconstruction of society itself. For the debate is in essence about power and place, standards of relevance and the quality of relations among the various cultural groups which compose U.S. society and indeed the world. This paper is offered as a contribution to this discourse and is based on and informed by several interrelated assumptions: 1) that both our society and the larger human community is fundamentally characterized by diversity and that human diversity is human richness; 2) that to benefit from this rich diversity, we must not simply tolerate it but embrace and build on it; 3) that each people has the right and responsibility to speak its own special cultural truth and make its own unique contribution to the forward flow of societal and human history; 4) that the search for truth in the service of a fuller and freer humanity must of necessity include travel on paths opened and paved in history by humanity in all its rich, complex and instructive diversity; 5) that given these realities, multicultural education is at the heart of any meaningful concept of quality education; 6) that the imperative of a truly multicultural education rests on substantive moral, intellectual and social grounds, and finally; 7) that the Afrocentric vision of quality education located within the Africana Studies project offers in content, perspective and methodology an important contribution to this urgent quest for both quality education and the multicultural context for it and its correlative project a just and good society.

I.2 Grounding of Multicultural Education

It is important to stress, as cited above that the thrust for a multicultural education rests on solid moral, intellectual and social grounds. The moral grounds rests in a real respect for the concrete human person in all her/his diversity. Here the student and teacher are not abstracted from concrete conditions for critical understanding but are engaged from the vantage point of their own experience. They speak from their own experience and location in history and culture and thus enrich educational discourse and prefigure and express a democratic public life rooted in cooperative forms of participation and exchange.

The intellectual grounding of multicultural education is revealed, as I (Report, 1991:3) have argued elsewhere, in its use and value as 1) "a necessary corrective for the conceptual and content inadequacy of the exclusive curriculum which omits and diminishes the rich and instructive" variety of human cultures; 2) an equally important corrective for racist, sexist, classist and chauvinistic approaches to knowledge and education which deny, demean or diminish the meaning, experience and voice of the other; 3) a necessary reflection of the diverse multicultural society in which we live, "thus, providing an intellectual competence otherwise diminished or denied" and 4) a creative challenge to the established order of things, in which the university is reduced to a warehouse of Eurocentric goods to be authoritatively transmitted and imposed as a sacrosanct canon or unproblematic body of deference-deserving knowledge. For multicultural education, especially in its Afrocentric form, comes into being and establishes its raison d'etre as uncompromising and relentless critique of the established order and then joins this with correctives pointed toward creating not only a richer and more varied educational experience but also a just and good society.

The social grounds of multicultural education rise from its function as: 1) a just response to the demand of marginalized and excluded peoples and groups for an education reflective of and relevant to their own life experience ; 2) an indispensable preparation of students and teachers for the world in which they live, work, study and exchange; 3) preparation of youth for the "burden of support" of an older and different populations based on principles of appreciation for diversity, mutuality and interdependence, and 4) "part and parcel of the thrust to create a just and good society, to avoid civil strife, and to enhance the quality of social life through cultivation of democratic values of and for civility, cooperativeness, mutuality, mutual respect, equality, justice and interdependence" (Report, 1991:4).

If quality education is at the same time and of necessity multicultural education, then, the challenge here is not to provide an Afrocentric paradigm for the entire curriculum in schools and universities, but rather to propose an Afrocentric contribution which will and should become a constitutive part of the overall multicultural project. Thus, in a multicultural context, the curriculum cannot be totally Afrocentric or it will become hegemonic as is the current Eurocentric model. On the contrary, the curriculum will and should be multicultural with various cultural visions, including the Afrocentric vision, as fundamental constitutive parts of the educational process. This position in no way suggests that Africana Studies departments and programs should not be Afrocentric. On the contrary, they must be Afrocentric; otherwise the distinctiveness of their contribution to multicultural discourse is called into question and ultimately undermined.

I.3 Delineating the Afrocentric Vision

A successful delineation of the Afrocentric vision of quality education and its contribution to multicultural education requires the accomplishment of several interrelated tasks. First, Afrocentricity, the central concept in the Afrocentric vision, must be explained in its own terms (Asante, 1990; Karenga, 1986). In this way it is freed from the imprecise and varied descriptions posed as workable definitions by some of its adherents. And it is also saved from the hype and hysteria of media and academia which are often simply interested in preserving privileged position and canon rather than facilitating and clarifying discourse (Schlessinger, 1991; Ravitch, 1990).

Secondly, the successful delineation of an Afrocentric vision of quality education requires that it be distinguished from the established-order Eurocentric educational process in its most negative form. And, thirdly, such a delineation must present and explain the value of the areas of fundamental focus and practice of such an educational project. This would include simultaneous discussion of the pedagogy which informs and implements the basic demands of the paradigm.

II. Afrocentricity and Africana Studies
II.1 The Africana Studies Project

Any serious discussion of Afrocentricity must begin by placing it in the context of Africana or Black Studies. For it is within this context that one discovers both its genealogy and grounding. It is in the latter half of the 60's that Africana Studies emerges as both a social and academic project to challenge and change the Eurocentric educational paradigm and simultaneously contribute to a process and movement of social change (Brisbane, 1974; Karenga, 1989, Chapter 1). In the process of both social and academic struggles, Africana Studies develops as an emancipatory project which suggests a reconception and reconstruction of both academia and society as multicultural realities. It is Africana Studies' stress at its inception on relevance in education and on the inseparability of the social and the academic, as well as on the interrelatedness of the campus and community and of intellectual and social emancipation that aided in creating both the context and dynamic for discourse on the need for the university and its curriculum to reflect and speak to the cultural communities which it serves (Hare, 1969; Robinson, 1969; Blassingame, 1973). Moreover, as critique and corrective of established-order discourse and practice, Africana

Studies continues to contribute to the definition, clearing and maintenance of space for the multicultural project.

In its dedication to academic excellence and social responsibility, Africana Studies discourse and practice are informed by four basic concerns: (1) the critical and persistent search for meaning and truth in history and social reality; (2) a rigorous intellectual challenge to established ways of viewing social and human reality; (3) a moral critique of the social constraints on human freedom, especially those rooted in race, class and gender considerations; and (4) cultivation of commitment to the historical project of creating a truly multicultural, democratic and just society based on mutual respect of persons and peoples and mutual cooperation for mutual benefit.

Africana Studies as a discipline, however, is not simply a body of data but also a way of approaching and interpreting data as Molefi Asante (1990:7) has observed. It thus, seeks not simply to offer information, but also to teach critical thinking and knowledge from an African-centered standpoint. It is at this point that Afrocentricity becomes an indispensable aspect of the Africana Studies project and contributes to the enrichment and expansion of educational discourse and practice.

II.2 The Category Afrocentricity

Afrocentricity as an intellectual category is relatively new in the discourse of Africana Studies, beginning with its introduction in the late 70's by Molefi Asante (1980). It is Asante who attempted to conceptually unify the varied African centered approaches to Africana Studies by designating them as Afrocentric. This is not to suggest that Afrocentric study and teaching are, themselves, new, for there are important works in African intellectual history which represent a long-term stress on the need for African-centered thought and practice. For example, one can cite among others works by W.E.B. DuBois (1975), Anna Julia Cooper (1988) and Carter G. Woodson (1969) on education.

Asante's (1980, 1987, 1990) essential contribution to this orientation in Africana Studies is the provision of the category Afrocentricity itself and an accompanying literature which contributes definitively to the delineation of a conceptual framework for a self-conscious, unified and effective way of understanding, appreciating and utilizing the rich and varied complexity of African life and culture. Since the introduction of the category, the discourse around it and within its conceptual framework has been extensive and varied. And therefore when one speaks of the Afrocentric project, one should always keep in mind that one is not talking about a monolithic position but rather a general conceptual orientation among Africana Studies scholars whose fundamental point of departure and intellectual concerns and views are centered in the African experience.

Within Afrocentric discourse two nominal categories are given from which the adjectival category, Afrocentric, is derived: Afrocentricity and Afrocentrism. In my contribution to discipline discourse, I prefer and use Afrocentricity for several reasons: 1) to stress its intellectual value as distinct from its ideological use; 2) to clearly distinguish it from Eurocentricism which is an ideology of domination and exclusion; and 3) to establish it as a quality of thought and practice rather than thought and practice itself. The need to stress its intellectual value as opposed to or distinct from its ideological use appears obvious. For if it is to fulfill its educational potential and promise, it must prove itself essentially an intellectual category regardless of the use and misuse people make of it. Secondly, Afrocentricity rather than Afrocentrism is used here because of the equally obvious need to distinguish the category from uninformed or manipulative associations of it with Eurocentrism. In this respect, it is important that the specific cultural and general human character of Afrocentricity be stressed. For Afrocentricity must never be conceived of or employed as a reaction to or an African version of Eurocentrism with its racist and structured denial and deformation of the history and humanity of peoples of color. As I (1986) have stated, "Afrocentricity, at its best, is a quest for and an expression of historical and cultural anchor, a critical reconstruction that dares to restore missing and hidden parts of our historical self-formation and pose the African experience as a significant paradigm for human liberation and a higher level of human life." Moreover, "To be no more than an 'obscene caricature of Europe' - to use Fanon's phrase - is to violate historical memory and vitiate historical possibilities inherent in the special truth Africans can and must speak to the world, given their ancient, rich and varied experience."

The Afrocentric vision, critically defined and developed, then, demands that Africana Studies root itself in the African experience and in the worldview which evolves from and informs that experience. For inherent in the assumption of the legitimacy and relevance of the discipline is its correlative assumption of the validity and value of studying Africans as a paradigm and field of focus in understanding humanity in both its particularity and commonality. However, having rooted itself in the African experience, which is the source and substance of its raison d'etre, Africana Studies as a mode of grasping reality, expands outward, to the acquisition of other relevant human knowledge and the knowledge of other humans. For even as there are lessons for humanity in African particularity, there are lessons for Africans in human commonality. And African humanity is enriched and expanded by mutually beneficial exchanges with others. Moreover, in understanding human history as a whole, Africans can even more critically appreciate their fundamental role in the origins of human civilization and in the forward flow of human history.

Thirdly, the category Afrocentricity is preferred to focus on the cultural and human quality of the thought and practice rather than on the thought and practice as ideological conception and conduct. As a quality of thought and practice defined by its particular African and shared human character, it allows for greater intellectual use and value and again avoids reductive translation as just another ideological posture. It is, in a word, a category of African culture and shared human interests and thus fits within the particular and universal demands of multicultural education and exchange.

Afrocentricity can be defined, then, as a quality of thought and practice rooted in the cultural image and human interests of African people. To be rooted in the cultural image of African people is to be anchored in the views and values of African people as well as in the practice which, in a generative dialectic, emanates from and gives rise to these views and values. To be rooted in the human interests of African people is to be informed and attentive to the just claims on life and society Africans share with other peoples, i.e., respect and concern for truth, justice, freedom, the dignity of the human person, etc.

Afrocentricity as a culturally rooted approach to thought and practice brings, then, both a particular and universal dimension. It contributes a particular cultural insight and discourse to the multicultural project and in the process finds common ground with other cultures which can be cultivated and developed for mutual benefit. In fact, Afrocentric thought shelters the assumption that the rich, varied and complex character of African culture is a critical resource in understanding and engaging the human community. Moreover, in an educational context, Afrocentric contributions to research and teaching not only challenge established-order discourse but contribute to the broadening and deepening of the educational project.

It is important to state here that my use of the terms African-centeredness and Afrocentric does not intend to suggest any more for the conceptual category "African" than is indicated by the terms "European" (Western), "Asian" (Oriental) or "Latin American." The categories African philosophy, worldview, values, etc., simply suggest shared orientations born of similar cultural experiences. As Gyekye (1987:x) notes, "(i)t is the underlying cultural unity or identity of the various individual thinkers that justifies references to varieties of thought as wholes, such as Western, European or Oriental philosophy." In other words, he continues, " . . .even though the individual thinkers who produced what is known as Western philosophy are from different European or Western nations, we nonetheless such body of philosophical ideas as western philosophy (in addition to, say, French, German or British philosophy)." One can justifiably conclude that "the real reason for this is surely the common cultural experience and orientation of those individual thinkers."

Likewise, in spite of the obvious differences between Indian, Chinese and ancient Persian philosophy, as well as the difference between Hindu, Buddhist, Confucian and Taoist thought, they are generally called Asian philosophy. And as Tu Wei Ming (1985:7) states, it is based on the notion of "shared orientations." Therefore, to say African philosophy, worldview or values is to assume certain shared orientations based on similar cultural experiences. Among these shared orientations are: 1) the centrality of community; 2) respect for tradition; 3) a high level spirituality and ethical concern; 4) harmony with nature; 5) the sociality of selfhood; 6) veneration of ancestors; and 7) the unity of being. This is also not to say that there are not other African core values which one could focus on as central to the Afrocentric vision. However, I do maintain that these are a conceptual and indispensable minimum regardless of other additions. Having identified these basic components of the African worldview, the task now is to demonstrate how these inform the conceptual contributions of Africana Studies to the multicultural educational enterprise.

III. Afrocentric Conceptual Contributions

Within the context of an Afrocentric cultural paradigm, then, several conceptual contributions can be offered as an enrichment of multicultural discourse and education Among these are: 1) centeredness or groundedness and insight from one's own culture; (this is also called location or orientation); 2) the multidisciplinary requirements of knowledge; 3) critique and corrective as a joint project in the educational enterprise; 4) the essentiality of an historical perspective; and 5) the indispensability of an ethical dimension to the educational project both in terms of reaffirmation of the worth and dignity of the human person and knowledge in the service of humankind and the just and good society. All of these contributions are interrelated and mutually reinforcing and offer a paradigm of difference as possibility in a multicultural contest.

III.1 The Concept of Centeredness

Certainly, the first and most fundamental contribution an Afrocentric project brings to the broadening of its knowledge base and expanding and enriching approaches to knowledge is its stress on centeredness which is also called place, location and orientation. This is a particularly challenging and, at times, even problematic concept, given the current stress in academia on decentering and deconstructionism as both an aid to more critical learning and greater social exchange (hooks, 1990; Hassan, 1987). However, Afrocentric scholars as well as many feminists and Marxists also recognize the problems of unlimited deconstruction which subverts the emancipatory possibilities in ethnic, national, gender and class theory and practice, and undermines human agency by decentering the subject and denying difference its oppositional, enriching and essential role in both education and social practice (Ferguson, et al, 1990; Hooks, 1992; Giroux, 1992; Karenga, 1986). History and culture, then, are essential points of rootedness and departure for Afrocentric studies. And thus, in an Afrocentric vision of learning, one does not step out of one's history to learn or practice but rather engages in it to ground oneself and grasp both the particular and the universal. As Asante (1990:5) argues, "One steps outside one's history (only) with great difficulty." "In fact, the act itself is highly improbable from true historical consciousness." Moreover, he continues, "There is no anti-place, since we are all consumers of space and time." Given this, he states, "the Afrocentrist seeks knowledge of this 'place' perspective as a fundamental rule of intellectual inquiry. . .." Moreover, Asante maintains that "All knowledge results from an occasion of encounter in place," and that such a "shaped perspective (then) allows the Afrocentrist to put African ideals and values at the center of inquiry."

However, recognizing the problematic of centeredness, as an educational positive in the midst of a thrust toward decentering and deconstruction, Asante (1990:12) notes that centeredness "the groundedness of observation and behavior in one's own historical experiences," shapes the Africana Studies project but allows for a similar posture and process for all other cultures. Thus, he states, Africana Studies "secures its place alongside other centric pluralisms without hierarchy and without seeking hegemony." Here Asante answers critics who incorrectly contend that Afrocentricity claims a privileged and hegemonic racial position for Africans in human history and culture. He does this by posing centeredness as an essential and effective orientation and point of departure for all cultures. In this stress on the value of location, place or orientation, Asante reaffirms the contentions of earlier African scholars like W.E.B. DuBois (1975) who argued against simply teaching of what he called general and disembodied knowledge of science and human culture and instead argued for beginning with the particular experience of a people and expanding to understand the whole of humankind.

DuBois (1975:98) in his seminal essay, "The Field and Function of the Negro College" had early argued for an education located in and oriented toward the concrete experience of the students being taught. No teacher, Black or White, who comes to a university like Fisk, filled simply with general ideas of human culture or general knowledge of disembodied science, is going to make a university of this school," he stated. For "a university is made of human beings, learning of things they do not know from things they do know in their own lives." What DuBois argues against then is the assumption of the effectiveness of transmission of simply "general ideas of human culture or general knowledge of disembodied science." His position which informs the Afrocentric vision of quality education is that there is no real substitute for an embodied knowledge, a knowledge rooted in and reflective of the concrete situation of the student starting, as DuBois says, from what they know to teach them and assist their learning what they do not know. It is both to use the familiar as instrument to discover the unknown and unfamiliar and as a particular and rich resource for understanding the universal, i.e., humanity as a whole.

Moreover, the Afrocentric vision is one of generating problematics from one's own life experience, and then relating and comparing it to the experience of others. Here again DuBois is instructive. He (1975:95) argues that an effective education, in this case of African Americans, starts with present facts and conditions about Africans and then "expands toward conquest of...knowledge" of the world. Likewise, such a centered study, he continues, begins with African history and through this lays a foundation "to interpret all history," and in the same way begins with the study of the current and historical social development of African peoples and on this foundation strives "to interpret and understand the social development of all mankind in all ages." This centered approach then invites and lays the foundation for comparative analysis which stands at the heart of the Afrocentric education thrust with its stress on the particular and the universal, similarity and difference.

The point which DuBois (1975:96) makes here, is that a quality education is especially attentive to the process of "beginning with the particular and going out to universal comprehension and unhampered expression. . ." (emphasis mine). Thus, he criticizes much of the literature of the Harlem Renaissance which was, he contends, "written to the benefit of white readers, and starting out primarily from the white point of view." Therefore, the movement eventually declined for "it never had a real (Black) constituency and it did not grow out of the inmost heart and frank experience of (Blacks); (and) on such an artificial basis no real literature can grow." Again, the point is that a disembodied knowledge, an abstract discourse on humans cannot and does not produce a quality education. The need, then, is to begin with each culture's experience and then translate it into a process of understanding others' experience as well as the varied and collective experience of society and humankind.

In summary, then, the concept of cultural orientation in education suggests several basic advantages in the multicultural educational project in particular and the educational project in general. First, it recognizes peoples' experience as a rich resource for study and therefore broadens the base of knowledge without hegemonic distortions and demeaning. Secondly, it is the value of the concrete and the known as the essential point of departure for learning the abstract and unknown. Thirdly, it values particular cultural and historical experiences as fruitful grounds from which to generate reflective problematics and to critically understand self, society and the world. And finally, orientation as a category of intellectual thought and practice gives one the grounds and context for a comparative and contrastive study of self, society and the world and thus enriches and deepens our understanding of each.

III.2 The Multidisciplinary Requirements of Knowledge

A second contribution the Afrocentric project brings to the enterprise of quality education in a multicultural context is the stress on the multidisciplinary requirements of knowledge. As James Stewart (1984:296-297) remarked, this focus is both an intellectual challenge and a mark of uniqueness of the Africana Studies enterprise. At its inception Africana Studies conceived of itself as an interdisciplinary and multidisciplinary project. As I (1982:33) have stated, "The scope of Africana Studies was established by its self-definition and by the parameters it posed for itself as a multidisciplinary discipline." By definition Africana Studies is a systematic and critical study of the totality of Black thought and practice in their current and historical unfolding. The use of the category totality is intended to suggest a holistic approach to the study of Black life. This means, first of all, an intellectual engagement which stresses totality as an inclusive social dimension, i.e., the various interrelated fields such as history, religion, sociology, politics, economics, creative production and psychology, etc. But it also is designed to stress the importance of totality in time, i.e., historical and current analysis joined to potential projections of tendencies and possibilities inherent in the historical and social process. This is what is meant by the phrase, the study of Black life in its current and historical unfolding.

Thus the inclusive approach of Black Studies commits it to a multidisciplinary educational process. It therefore integrates various subject areas into a coherent discipline reaching across what James Turner (1984:xi) calls "the voids that have inevitably occurred as a result of artificial disciplinary demarcations."

In addition to this motivation for a multidisciplinary approach by the very definition and nature of a discipline itself, Africana's stress on this requirement of knowledge is also informed by an African ontology that argues the unity of being and an epistemology that sees both being and truth about it as whole.

Speaking of classical African ontology as expressed in ancient Egypt, Finnestad (1987:31ff) notes its stress on "the affinities and connections" rather than differences in its conception of reality and being. In such a conception human life "merges with that of the entire world and being is conceived as an 'integrated whole.'" The logic of such a position, of necessity, leads to the epistemological assumption that the truth of being is also whole and any partial approach to it must yield only understanding of it. It is important to note, however, that such holism does not deny the value of the temporary analytical decomposition of subjects of study for a more intimate or detailed study. But it stresses the need to guard against losing sight or understanding of affinities, connections or the interrelatedness of each part to the other and all to the whole. The implications of such a view for both social study and practice are numerous and important as are they for a correct study and ethical practice toward the environment. Such a holistic position which moves away from Cartesian dualism and rigid lines of demarcation in both conception of the world and approaches to it is becoming increasingly important in social and intellectual discourse. In addition to its stress in Africana Studies, other ethnic studies, women studies and some socialist studies also assume such a holistic position. This offers an excellent opportunity for creative dialog and challenge to the established-order dualistic conception and promises a useful and ongoing discourse.

III.3 The Joint Project of Critique and Corrective

A third conceptual contribution Afrocentric studies offers to the enrichment and expansion of multicultural education is its stress on critique and corrective as a joint project in the educational enterprise. This stress on critique and corrective is rooted in the very conception and earliest practice of Black Studies as a discipline. From its inception Africana or Black Studies has had both an academic and social thrust and mission which involved critique and corrective as essential to the meaning and mission of the discipline (Karenga, 1989:Chapter 1). Black Studies evolved in the midst of the emancipatory struggles of the 60's which linked intellectual emancipation with political emancipation, campus with community, intellectuals and students with the masses and knowledge in the academy with power in society (Hare, 1969). What emerged in the process of both struggles on campus and in society was a paradigm of critique and corrective designed to critique and end domination, to expand the realm of freedom and just and good society.

The Critical Dimension

The Afrocentric stress on critique as essential to the educational enterprise emerges, then, from the actual conditions in and under which Africana Studies comes into being. As a component part and an intellectual arm of the overall Black Freedom Movement in this country, Black Studies becomes an essential critique of domination in its various forms. It is concerned about the distortion and deficiency of what is present in the curriculum and larger social discourse and about the abundance and emancipatory possibilities of that which is absent.

It seeks to rescue and reconstruct Black history and culture in order to define more correctly Black humanity. Thus, its critique can be defined as "a systematic unrelenting battle against both ignorance and illusion, the struggle against the poverty of knowledge as well as the perversion of truth" (Karenga, 1986:410). Moreover, it involves realizing that the greatest part of truth both rests and is continuously hidden beneath the surface, and that therefore, there is a constant need to reach beyond and below the surface manifestations of society and the world to penetrate and grasp the warp and woof of the relations which give them their motion, meaning and character. Moreover, the Afrocentric critique requires focus on contradictions in society, especially ones of race, class and gender, looking again not only for what is present and distorted in the discourse but also for what is absent and undiscussed, not only for codified ignorance but also for canonized illusion.

Such an approach not only contributes to the encouragement of critical thinking about the present and absent, the given and the possible, but it also calls for a redefinition in practice of the university itself. In such a context the university became in the struggles of the 60's not simply a place to transmit authoritative views and values but a ground of contestation; contestation over intellectual issues, but also over the structure and meaning of the university itself and the society for which it served as brain and apologists. Contestation, then, became and continues to be posed in Africana Studies as a fundamental mode of understanding self, society and the world. In such a process Africana Studies sought and seeks to create a space and a process for students to recover, discover and speak the truth and meaning of their own experience, to locate themselves in social and human history and having oriented themselves, bring their unique contribution to multicultural exchange in the academy and society. Ideally what results from this critique of established-order discourse and contestation over issues of intellect and life is the multicultural cooperative production of knowledge rather than its Eurocentric authoritative allocation.

In the process of bringing one's own experience and unique cultural contribution to the educational process several paths are pursued. First, one is compelled to create both a different language and logic. For the established-order language and logic are not conducive to the emancipatory project which Africana Studies represents and nurtures. As Malcolm X (1968:133) argued in a lecture at Harvard, "the language and logic of the oppressed cannot be the language and logic of the oppressor" if an emancipatory project is to be conceived and pursued. Thus, Africana Studies began to develop and use new categories and modes of analysis and give new definition to old terms and concepts. For example, within Africana Studies "classics" is no longer an exclusive category of European achievement, but rather a category of achievement for humans in general. Stripped of all its Eurocentric pretensions, the category "classics" can be defined as works whose level of creativity and achievement deserve and demand both preservation and emulation. Thus, classical music, art, literature, civilizations, etc., are present in African, Native Americans, Latino and Asian cultures as well as in Europe.

Secondly, given this and the multicultural demands of education, one moves beyond the Eurocentric self-congratulatory narratives in various disciplines and engages in a multicultural discourse which reveals the rich variousness of human culture and poses a necessary creative challenge to European hegemonic discourse and practice. Using political science as an example, the thrust becomes one of moving beyond and before Plato to include the study of classical African texts from ancient Egypt such as *The Book of Ptahhotep* which offers a discourse on leadership as a moral vocation (Lichtheim, 1975:61ff; Simpson, 1973:159ff) and *The Book of Khun-Anup*, the oldest treatise on social justice (Lichtheim, 1975:97ff; Simpson, 1973:31ff). Likewise, the study of literature would include in a multicultural curriculum both ancient and modern African classics, i.e., classical praise poetry of the Zulu, Izibonao, (Cope, 1968), of the Tswana, Maboko (Schapera, 1965) as well as selected literature of the Harlem Renaissance and the 60's. Finally, as another example, discourse on ethics need not begin or end in Judaism and Christianity but extend back before such frameworks to Maatian ethical texts of ancient Egypt which offers both parallels and sources of Jewish and Christian concepts and practices (Breasted, 1924: Morenz, 1973:Chapter 6; Karenga, 1988). It is important to note here that the use of African classics and other achievements to enrich multicultural education and discourse must and does assume and require a similar and equal contribution of other cultures.

Thirdly, within the framework of developing a new language and logic one can pose different points of departure for understanding social and human reality. From an Afrocentric view, one can and does study society from a communitarian rather than individualistic view (Mbiti, 1970; Menkiti, 1984). Also, one poses the study of politics not simply as a struggle for power, but also, as in Maatian ethical texts, i.e., the Sebait, as a collective vocation to create a just and good society (Karenga, 1988). Likewise, one can and does pose communal and substantive democracy against "herrenvolk" and procedural democracy, and engages Malcolm X's (1965:26) concept of being a "victim of democracy" for all its "fruitful ambiguity." For in an age of praise and pursuit of democracy as a central human good, one is challenged to understand and explain why Malcolm claims, in this particular case, such a negative role for it.

Finally, there is a thrust in Africana Studies to redefine the parameters, focus and central categories of intellectual discourse in the social science and humanities. Therefore, for example, one talks of the holocaust of enslavement rather than "slave trade" as the most instructive and correct way of discussing the genocidal tragedy which marked the loss of millions of African lives. Here, one poses enslavement as an ethical issue rather than a commercial one and defines holocaust as an act of genocide so morally monstrous that it is not only against the people themselves but also against humanity. Such a redefinition of the experience of enslavement as a holocaust invites a rich comparative and contrastive discourse on other holocausts - Native American, Native Australian, Jewish, Roman, Palestinian, Armenian, Kurdish, et al. In conclusion, then, the practice of critique and corrective means that suppressed and marginalized voices of various cultures will bring an enriched and enlarged agenda to the educational table.

Various ways of viewing and approaching human reality will challenge and change Eurocentric hegemony and pose in its place a democratic and multicultural education which prefigures and points to the possibility of a truly democratic and multicultural society.

The Corrective Dimension

It is at this point that critique is joined by correctives in the Afrocentric project, not only in the intellectual ways discussed above but also in a concrete way which suggests and encourages social practice. Such a stress, as noted above, emanates from both the emancipatory role assigned to education and the educated by earlier African scholars and leaders and from the emancipatory struggles of the Sixties which assigned Africana Studies both an academic and social mission. Moreover, such an Afrocentric concept of education grows out of the African communitarian worldview with its interrelated concepts of the centrality of the community and the sociality of selfhood. This communitarian African worldview, as Gyekye (1987:157) states, contains within it "such social and ethical values as social well being, solidarity, interdependence, cooperation and reciprocal obligations - all of which conduce to equitable distribution of resources and benefits of society." In such a context, "inherent in the communal enterprise is the problem of contribution and distribution" then. This translates in an educational context as recognition of the fact that instead of conceiving of education as "knowledge for knowledge sake," one approaches education within a concept of "knowledge for humans' sake." This means that knowledge as a key social value is conceived as belonging not simply to the student and intellectuals but also to the community and that both the mission of students and the university must relate to and contribute to the historical vocation of human flourishing in the context of a just and good society.

Inherent in this communitarian concept of education is the concept of mission which has long been a central theoretical pillar in Africana Studies' conception of itself. W.E.B. DuBois' conception of the Talented Tenth stands as a classic example of mission as an inherent aspect of the educational project. Education, he argued, is "a difficult and intricate task" whose "technique is a matter for educational experts, but its object is for the vision of seers" (Paschal, 1974:31ff). The fundamental challenge of education was for him at that time to "develop the best" to guide the community, and to avoid focus simply on career preparation. The task is not to develop moneymakers or even artisans but men and women of intelligence and character, with "knowledge of the world that was and is," and commitment to community. Although he later modified stress on the Talented Tenth to deal with its class problematic, he still maintained that service to the people was key to any viable and valuable concept of education (Stewart, 1984: 306ff).

Also, one finds the concept of mission in Mary McLeod Bethune's (1939:9) concept of education as a process of searching for truth, critically interpreting it and then spreading it. In a word, she (1938:10) says it is "to discover the dawn and to bring this material within the understanding of the child and the masses of our people." For, she continues, although "we are living in a great age of science and invention...we still have the human problem of distribution of natural resources and of seeing that the fruits of science and invention are within the reach of the masses who need it most." The need she concludes is an ethically focused education which teaches one obligations not simply to self but to community, society and humanity and to look forward at the end of one's life to stand tall "on the platform of service" (Bethune, 1975:46).

The stress on the academic and social nature of the educational project was also expressed in the relationship of the university to the community. Again, early in Black Studies history, Nathan Hare, one of the founders of the discipline, defined such a relationship as important even indispensable. Hare (1969, 1972, 1975), who established the first Black Studies programs, made essential to his conception of the discipline the joining of the university and the community in a mutually beneficial ongoing relationship. His conception was summarized in the statement, "bring the community to the campus and take the campus to the community."

Such an exchange would involve at a minimum several aspects. First, it would mean the university's recognition and reaffirming in practice its obligation to serve the community or communities in which it is located and those from which its students come. This implies not only the teaching of students but also joining with the community in cooperative projects to address critical issues and challenges. Secondly, such a relationship would necessitate the community's active involvement in the determination of what constitutes quality education and in ongoing campus-sponsored educational projects on campus and in the community or any other projects of mutual benefit. And thirdly, such an exchange would mean that students again, as DuBois argued, would use their own experience to understand social and human reality and also enrich the educational process with it.

In such a process of reciprocal engagement on and off campus, students are challenged to frame questions and projects from their own experience and for their own future. They raise and seek to answer questions about the meaning, quality and direction of their lives, not as abstracted individuals but as persons-in-community. Therefore, their thrust becomes not simply to understand self, society and the world but to change it. And education and the corrective social practice it encourages and sustains becomes a practice of freedom.

Such a joining of critique and corrective, in both the intellectual and practical sense, poses an important model, then, for discourse and practice in a multicultural educational process. First, the stress on critique and corrective focuses on critical thinking, challenging the given, and posing plausible alternatives to the established order of things. Secondly, this means that the university can no longer be seen and posed as simply a place for the authoritative transmission of sacrosanct knowledge of the Eurocentric world, but also as a context for contestation and the cooperative discovery and production of knowledge of the real multicultural world. Thirdly, such a conception and practice encourage the creation of space and process for students to discover and speak the truth and meaning of their own cultural experience, to locate themselves in social and human history and having oriented themselves, project possibilities of where they wish to and will go. Fourthly, the concept of mission and social obligation removes education from the role of simple transmission of canon and job preparation to a context of contestation and cooperative engagement over vital issues concerning self, community, society and world which in turn reaffirms the imperative of critical thinking, below-the-surface searching for new and more ethically and culturally sensitive conceptions of society and human life. Finally, the university defined as a partner with the communities it serves creates the concept of joining the intellectual and practical in a project of a relevant education and social practice to create and sustain the good and just society.

III.4 The Essentiality of the Historical Perspective

Another contribution which the Afrocentric vision of a quality education offers is its emphasis on the indispensability of the historical perspective in understanding social and human reality (Keto, 1991). Africana Studies is not to be equated with history, but it is considered within this framework the key social science, given each discipline's dependence on it for grounding (Karenga, 1982:43). As Malcolm X (1965:8) noted, "of all our studies history is best qualified to reward our research." For history is the central discipline of contextualization and orientation, and the Afrocentric stress on centeredness is both a historical and cultural concept. Thus, the first value and use of such historical stress is its function as a mode and means of centering.

Secondly, history for Africana Studies has been the key means in the central and ongoing project of rescue and recovery. In a multicultural context, this means that African and other cultures are prized as treasure troves of rich and varied experiences, narratives, knowledges and ways of being in the world. Thus, one rescues and reconstructs one's history as a part of the process of rescuing and reconstructing one's humanity. The study, writing and discussion of history, then, become ways of giving freedom to suppressed voices. It is, as the ancient Egyptian texts teach, a process of "restoring that which is found in ruins, repairing what is found damaged and replenishing what is found lacking" (Lichtheim, 1988:43).

Central to Africana Studies and the Afrocentric concept of education in this respect is the concept of Sankofa, an Akan concept of historical recovery. As Niangoran-Bouah (1984:210) states, Sankofa "is made of the words san (to return), ko (to go) and fa (to take). The literal translation is: come back, seek and take or recover." The Sankofa ideogram is a bird reaching back with its beak into its feathers and "is a symbol representing the quest for knowledge and the return to the source." Niangoran-Bouah further states that the ideogram implies that the resulting knowledge "is the outcome of research, of an intelligent and patient investigation." This concept of Sankofa with its dual emphasis on the quest for knowledge and return to the source has become a central concept in Africana Studies in all its fields, i.e., history, religion, sociology, political science, economics, creative production, psychology, etc. But it gets its greatest use in reference to the quest for historical paradigms to place in the service of the present and future.

Such a function of historical knowledge and paradigm is evident in the identification and beginning restoration of ancient Egypt (Kemet) as a paradigmatic classical African civilization. It is Cheikh Anta Diop (1982:12) the Imhotepian or multidisciplined scholar, who posed ancient Egypt as the essential paradigmatic African civilization, arguing that "a look toward ancient Egypt is the best way of conceiving and building our culture future." In fact, he maintains that "...Egypt will play, in a reconceived and renewed African culture the same role that ancient Greco-Latin civilization plays in western culture." In a word, he concludes, for African peoples "the return to Egypt in all fields is the necessary condition to reconcile African civilizations with history, to build a body of modern human sciences and renew African culture." Afrocentric scholars have accepted the validity and urgency of this task and have begun to do work important to its completion (Karenga, 1984; Carruthers, 1984; Karenga and Carruthers, 1986; Karenga, 1990a, 1990b; Asante 1990).

The African rescue and recovery of ancient Egypt as a paradigm, which precedes and parallels in intellectual function as well as contributes to the Greek paradigm for Europe, has created an important source of contestation in the academy (Diop, 1982; Bernal, 1987; Arethusa, 1989). The importance of this contribution lies in several areas. First, it provides an important creative challenge to Africana scholars who, in presenting and defending the paradigm and the work surrounding it, challenge and are challenged by Eurocentric scholars. Secondly, the contestation becomes for Africana Studies another critique of domination, in the form of the Eurocentric desire and efforts to maintain cultural hegemony and an exclusive canon and denial of the historical capacity and achievement of Africans and other peoples of color. In such a struggle, the falsification of African history becomes a metaphor for the falsification of human history. For central to Europe's falsification of human history was its removal of Africa from Egypt, Egypt from Africa and Africa from human history.

Likewise, the emancipatory, intellectual and practical struggles to return African to its own history and to human history becomes a metaphor and model of a similar return of all people to their history as well as to human history. And Diop's concept of reconciling African civilization with human history becomes a metaphor and impetus for reconciling all excluded civilizations and cultures with human history, by returning them to their rightful place, restoring the rich variousness of their voices and learning the complex and often contradictory messages they offer to teach. Also, such a contestation as both paradigm and process reaffirms the value and function of critical thinking in both its demand for intellectual skill and human and ethical sensitivity.

Finally, the Afrocentric conception of history reveals history as a living concreteness. History, as I (1982:43) argued elsewhere is not simply a record but rather a struggle and record of specific peoples and humanity as a whole in the process of shaping their worlds and the world in their own image and interest.

Here one sees the dynamic and dialectic of the particular and the universal, for as each people shapes its own world, it contributes to the shaping of the whole world. And in this process it is important that no people impose their worldview and practice on others or in rationalized delusion and illusion of superiority assume and assert themselves as the single paradigm for human thought and practice. Such is the history of Europe in its drive for political and cultural hegemony. And it is the history of peoples of color which reveal liberational struggles in society and academy to challenge, check and end this hegemony.

At this point one sees how history, for Afrocentric scholars, as their critics charge, is not simply a neutral record. On the contrary, it is neither neutral nor simply a record. It is above all a struggle, a lived concreteness. At the heart of this process called history is the struggle to clear and create space for human freedom and human flourishing. Such is the history of Africans and thus, for them history cannot be an abstract intellectual process. It is their lives unfolding or being checked, their perceptions given wings or restrained, and their struggle to be free and productive through emancipatory thought and practice. Such a conception of history offers multicultural education a mode of critical engagement in discourse and practice essential to the concept and process of quality education. For again students are challenged to discover, recover and speak the truth and meaning of their own experience, locate themselves in the larger realm of social and human history, and pose paradigms of human culture and society which contribute not only to our critical understanding of the world, but also to our thrust to change it in the interest and image of human good. This, in turn, encourages and cultivates critical thinking, below-the-surface searching, and ethical concerns and conceptions of human life and society.

III.5 The Indispensability of the Ethical Dimension

A final contribution of the Afrocentric concept of education to the paradigm of a quality and multicultural education is the centrality of the ethical dimension. Again, since its inception, Africana Studies has stressed the centrality of ethics to a quality education. This stress has its roots in several basic factors. First, it evolves from the emancipatory nature of the Africana Studies project itself which has at its central thrust a critique and corrective of domination and the posing of paradigms of human freedom and human flourishing. As mentioned above, the critique is essentially a moral critique of constraints on human freedom and the correctives are always undergirded by the moral project of creating a just and good society.

Secondly, the focus on the ethical evolves from the definition of the dual mission of Black Studies', i.e., academic excellence and social responsibility, a social responsibility which conceptually and practically is an ethical obligational task. It is an ethical responsibility to create the kind of community which practices and promotes human freedom and human flourishing, in a word, to create the kind of moral community one wishes to live in. In the earliest stage of Black Studies in the U.S., DuBois (1971:64) argued that education was "primarily scientific a careful search for truth conducted as thoroughly, broadly and honestly..." as possible. However, he noted in its more expansive form, the educational process was "not only to make the truth clear but (also) to present it in such shape as will encourage and help social reform."

Thirdly, the very practice of generating reflective problematics and correctives from the African experience, which is defined by oppression, resistance and the creation and maintenance of free space for proactive practices in spite of social oppression raises continuous ethical questions. Both oppression and resistance unavoidably generate ethical questions and thus much of Africana Studies discourse, regardless of the specific field, revolves around specific and general issues of right and wrong, and the grounds and meaning of human freedom and human flourishing.

Fourthly, the stress on the ethical dimension evolves from an ancient tradition of emphasis on civic moral education extending back to ancient Egypt with its concern for moral leadership and a just and good society (Karenga, 1989; Carruthers, 1984). Classical African philosophy in ancient Egypt posed the human ideal as a reflection of the universe which was grounded in and ordered by the principle of Maat. Maat was rightness in the social, nature and divine sphere and translated as truth, justice, propriety, harmony, balance, reciprocity and order.

Also key to this is the African worldview in general with stress on freedom as responsible personhood-in-community. It stresses persons-in-community acting with shared initiative and responsibility to collectively conceive and create a social context for maximum social solidarity and human flourishing (Gyekye, 1987; Wright, 1984).

This communitarian philosophy and emphasis of African culture serves as an essential framework for the conceptualization and pursuit of the just and good society, a society marked and moved by civility, reciprocity and equality in all area of human life and practice.

The contribution of this discourse to a quality multicultural education begins with its encouraging students and faculty to frame questions and generate problematics around the quality, purpose and direction of social and human life. It cultivates an appreciation for framing and discussing issues of life and death in ethical terms rather than vulgarly pragmatic and egoistic ones. Secondly, such an ethical dimension to the educational process also encourages critical thinking because only in matters of faith are such issues of life and death exempt from complexity and most often ambiguity. One, then, is compelled to do below-the-surface searching to confront and be confronted in a mutually benefiting process.

The Afrocentric stress on ethics also becomes a way to begin to integrate the disciplines for it rightly raises questions about the relevance of knowledge and its pursuit to the human person and the human community. This means that ethical questions about the world or ethical questions of life and death are no longer safely assigned to religion, but rather that each discipline raises its own ethical questions as well as participates in discourse on general ethical issues. This would include the hard sciences which often conceive of themselves as exempt from and beyond valuative discourse and ethical judgment. However, it is the hard sciences physical and technical - which have produced products and processes of the greatest threat to humankind and the environment. Thus, neither they nor their practitioners can be exempt from discussion of how they conceive, approach and affect the world.

Finally, the Afrocentric stress on ethics as a fundamental component of a quality education brings to the multicultural process of exchange support for the concept of pursuit of the common good. For pursuit of the common good is at heart an ethical project in the philosophical and practice sense. And it translates as democratic multicultural discourse on and pursuit of social policies aimed at creating a context of maximum human flourishing. Given the historical and current vanguard role African Americans have played in setting and pursuing the moral and socially progressive agenda in this country, it is only logical that they would play a vanguard role in creating space and impetus for a generalized and deepened ethical discourse in the academy. Not only does African culture have the oldest ethical texts in the world, but it is the African American struggle which has been at the heart of fundamental changes in the quality of life in this country and has posed a paradigm of struggle for a just and good society respected and referred to around the world. Thus, among other people of color, women, the disabled, the seniors and other marginalized groups in this country, as well as among peoples in South Africa, South America, the Philippines, China, Eastern Europe and with the Palestinian and Israeli Peace Movement, the African American liberation struggle became a focus. In these struggles, the participants borrowed from and built on the moral vision and moral vocabulary of the African American struggle and embraced it as a paradigm for struggle of human liberation.

Jesse Jackson (1989:14) contends rightly that the "greater good is the common good" which is clearly "a good beyond personal comfort and position." It is a good created out of the common aspirations of many peoples, groups and cultures who share this society and want and are willing to cooperate in building a just and good society. This aspiration finds itself needing a public philosophy beyond liberal myths of melting pots and Eurocentric concepts of universality. It seeks and must be grounded in a public philosophy which teaches above all the reality that U.S. society is not a finished white product but rather an ongoing multicultural project and that each person and people has both the right and responsibility to speak their own special cultural truth and make their own unique contribution to the forward flow of societal and human history. Moreover, such a public philosophy will build on the best ethical traditions of the many cultures that constitute the U.S. social project. These traditions will, of necessity, contain and concede the necessity of civic virtue, voluntarism, reciprocity, cooperativeness and together resolve the tensions between the personal and the collective, community and society, the private and the public difference and commonality.

Finally, these traditions must merge in the public sphere in redefining politics in the classical African sense as an ethical and collective vocation to create a just and good society. Such an ethical vocation will be one of shared responsibility in a shared public life of mutual benefit and cooperation, a democratic political and economic sphere.

All this, of course, requires public debate and discourse and the academy becomes an indispensable context for conception and discourse based on civility, reciprocity and equality. The challenge, then, is to initiate and sustain such a discourse and the companion practical project which gives such discourse its relevance and ultimate reality.

References

Arethusa. Fall 1989. Special Issue.

Asante, Molefi. 1987. *The Afrocentric Idea.* Philadelphia, PA: Temple University Press.

Asante, Molefi. 1980. *Afro-centricity: The Theory of Social Change.* Buffalo, N.Y.: Amulefi.

Asante, Molefi. 1990. *Kemet, Afrocentricity and Knowledge.* Trenton, NJ: Africa World Press.

Bernal, Martin. 1987. *Black Athena: The Afro-Asiatic Roots of Classical Civilization*, Volume I. London: Free Association Books.

Bethune, Mary McLeod. 1939. The Adaptation of the History of the Negro to the Capacity of the Child. *Journal of Negro History.* 24: 9-13.

Blassingame, John. 1973. *New Perspectives on Black Studies.* Chicago, IL: University of Illinois Press.

Brisbane, Robert. 1974. *Black Activism.* Valley Forge, PA: Judson Press.

Carruthers, Jacob H. 1984. *Essays in Ancient Egyptian Studies.* Los Angeles, CA: University of Sankore Press.

Cooper, Anna Julia. 1988. *A Voice From the South.* New York, N.Y.: Oxford University Press.

Cope, Trevor. 1968. *Izibongo: Zulu Praise Poems.* New York, N.Y.: Oxford University Press.

Diop, Cheikh Anta. 1982. *Civilisation ou Barbarie.* Paris: Presence Africaine. English translation, *Civilization or Barbarism*, Brooklyn, NY: Lawrence Hill, 1990.

DuBois, W.E.B. 1975. *The Education of Black People: Ten Critiques. 1906-1960.* New York: Monthly Review Press.

Ferguson, Russell, Martha Gever, Trinh T. Minha and Cornel West. (eds.) 1990. *Out There: Marginalization and Contemporary Cultures*, Cambridge, MA: MIT Press.

Finnestad, Ragnhild B. 1989. Egyptian Thought About Life as a Problem of Translation. *The Religion of the Ancient Egyptians: Cognitive Structures and Poular Expressions*, Gertie Englund, (ed.). Uppsala: Acta Universitatis Upsaliensis.

Giroux, Henry. 1992. *Border Crossings: Cultural Workers and the Politics of Education.* New York, N.Y.: Routledge.

Gyekye, Kwame. 1987. *An Essay on African Philosophical Thought: The Akan Conceptual Scheme.* New York, N.Y.: Cambridge University

Hare, Nathan. 1972. The Battle of Black Studies. *Black Scholar.* 3 (May): 32-37.

Hare, Nathan. 1975. A Black Paper: The Relevance of Black Studies. *Black Collegian*. 6 (September/October): 46-50.

Hare, Nathan. 1969. What Should be the Role of Afro-American Education in the Undergraduate Curriculum? *Liberal Education*. 55 (March:42-50.)

Hassan, Ihab. 1987. *The Post Modern Turn: Essays in Postmodern Theory and Culture*. Columbus, OH: State University Press.

Hicks, Florience (ed.). (Undated). *Mary McLeod Bethune: Her Own Words of Inspiration*. Washington, D.C.: Nuclassics and Science Publishing Company.

Hooks, Bell. 1990. *Yearnings: Race, Gender and Culture Politics*. Boston, MA: South End Press.

Hornung, Erik. 1985. *Conceptions of God in Ancient Egypt*. Ithaca, NY: Cornell University Press.

Karenga, Maulana. 1988. Black Studies and the Problematic of Paradigm: The Philosophical Dimension. *Journal of Black Studies*. 18 (4):395-414.

Karenga, Maulana. 1990. *The Book of Coming Forth By Day: Ethics of the Declarations of Innocence*. Los Angeles, CA: University of Sankore Press.

Karenga, Maulana. 1991. *The Challenge of Diversity and Multicultural Education: Report of the President's Task Force on Multicultural Education and Campus Diversity*. Long Beach, CA: California State University, Long Beach.

Karenga, Maulana. 1987. *Introduction to Black Studies*. Los Angeles, CA: University of Sankore Press.

Karenga, Maulana (ed.). 1990. *Reconstructing Kemetic Culture*. Los Angeles, CA: University of Sankore Press.

Karenga, Maulana. 1984. *Selections From the Husia: Sacred Wisdom of Ancient Egypt*. Los Angeles, CA: University of Sankore Press.

Karenga, Maulana. 1989. Towards a Sociology of Maatian Ethics: Literature and Context. *Journal of African Civilizations*. 10(1): 352-395.

Karenga, Maulana & Carruthers, Jacob (eds.) 1986. *Kemet and the African Worldview*. Los Angeles, CA: University of Sankore Press.

Keto, C. Tsehloane. 1991. *The Africa Centered Perspective of History: An Introduction*. Laurel Springs, NJ: K.A. Publishers.

Lichtheim, Miriam. 1988. *Ancient Egyptian Autobiographies Chiefly from the Middle Kingdom*. Feiburg, Switzerland: Universitatsverlag.

Lichtheim, Miriam. 1975. *Ancient Egyptian Literature*. Volume I, Berkeley, CA: University of California Press.

Locke, Alain. 1968. *The New Negro*. New York, N.Y.: Atheneum.

Malcolm X. 1965. *Malcolm X Speaks*. New York, N.Y.: Merit Publishers.

Malcolm X. 1968. *The Speeches of Malcolm X at Harvard*, Archie Epps (ed.). New York, N.Y.: William Morrow and Co.

Menkiti, Ifeanyi. 1984. Person and Community in African Traditional Thought. *African Philosophy: An Introduction*, Wright, Richard (ed.). Lanham, MD: University Press of America.

Ming, Tu Wei. 1985. *Confucian Thought: Selfhood as Creative Transformation*. Albany, N.Y.: State University of New York Press.

Morenz, Siegfried. 1973. *Egyptian Religion*. Ithaca, N.Y.: Cornell University Press.

Niangoran-Bouah, G. 1984. *The Akan World of Gold Weights: Abstract Design Weights*. Abidjan, I.C.: Les Nouvelles Editions Africaines.

Paschal, Andrew (ed.). 1974. A W.E.B. DuBois Reader. New York, N.Y.: Macmillan Publishing Co., Inc.

Ravitch, Dianne. 1990. Multiculturalism. *American Scholar* (Summer): 347.

Robinson, Armstead, et al.. 1969. *Black Studies in the University*. New York, N.Y.: Bantam Books.

Schapera, I. (ed.). 1965. *Praise Poems of Tswana Chiefs*. New York, N.Y.: Oxford University Press.

Schlessinger, Arthur. 1991. *The Disuniting of America: Reflections on a Multicultural Society*. Knoxville, TN: Whittle Direct Books.

Simpson, William K. (ed.). 1973. *The Literature of Ancient Egypt*. New Haven, CT: Yale University Press.

Woodson, Carter G. 1969. *Mis-Education of the Negro*. Washington, DC: Associated Publishers, Inc.

B. SOCIOLOGICAL DIMENSION

1. AFRICOLOGY AS THE AFROCENTRIC DISCIPLINARY MATRIX

African American Studies:
The Future of the Discipline

Molefi Kete Asante

To the Ancestors in whose path I walk and the Elders whose son I am I give thanks for being invited to participate in this historic conference.

It is my intention to discuss the maintenance and future of African American Studies within the context of contemporary intellectual ideas. I will begin, of course, where I always begin, with a discussion of Afrocentricity as a theoretical instrument for the examination of phenomena. Afrocentricity is a simple idea. The reason that I know it is simple is because I have yet to meet a person on the streets of North Philadelphia who could not understand it. I also know it is simple because I have met a lot of Africans and Europeans in the Academy who deliberately misunderstand it. At its base it is concerned with African people being subjects of historical and social experiences rather than objects in the margins of European experiences. I recall seeing the book by Charles Wesley and Carter Woodson entitled *The Negro In Our History* and feeling that they were truly speaking from and to a Eurocentric perspective if they felt that such a title captured the essence of our experience. These were two of the most successful African American historians and yet they could not totally disengage their critical thinking from the traditional views held by whites. Viewing phenomena from the perspective of Africans as central rather than peripheral means that you secure a better vantage point on the facts. It also means that you have a better handle on your own theoretical and philosophical bases. It is not a biological issue, anybody can see if they have the right vantage point. There are two aspects to Afrocentricity, the theory and the practice. One could master the theory and not be involved in the practice or vice versa. In my case, I have tried to merge the two aspects in my intellectual work and lifestyle. Of course, if one is not culturally African, that is, if one does not possess the historical and social memories that constitute Africanity, and practices Afrocentricity as a life style it would be strange although it is possible, just as weird and possible as Africans who have adopted Eurocentric styles.

Dislocation, location, and relocation are the principal calling cards of the Afrocentric theoretical position. My attempt is always to locate a situation, an event, an author. I have identified through historical and literary analysis two fallacies of position: the locational fallacy and the linguistic fallacy. The first occurs when a person is de-centered, misoriented, or disoriented and cannot possibly be looking from the proper angle. This is the problem Malcolm X recognized when he spoke of some enslaved Africans thinking they had come to America on the Mayflower or when he told us that there were some who took the slave master's perspective when it came to the plantation. Such people are not only dislocated but disoriented. The second fallacy occurs when a person is located in the proper place but does not have the experience or the ability to explain or to describe what is being seen. The second fallacy leads to a sort of naive nationalism because the viewer has only a vantage point but no adequate discipline or skill for analysis. Both types of persons abound in the academy.

The Nature of Criticism

The critics of Afrocentricity fall into two classes, those who are simply opposed to any African self determination and those who favor African self determination within the framework of European experiences. Africans and Europeans occupy places in each category of those who have attacked the theoretical position staked out by a growing number of Afrocentric theorists. There are Marxists, liberals, reactionaries and various apologists for white racism in both groups. Recently Anne Wortham, the "colored" sociologist as she referred to herself at a symposium "Education and Afrocentrism" organized by the Heritage Foundation, went so far as to say that Afrocentricity was much like Nazism because it articulated a cultural viewpoint. I could not tell from listening to her on C-Span whether she actually believed that Afrocentricity was like Nazism or was doing as the late Louis Lomax once said some blacks do, "fooling white people." She could have received nothing from my works, which she attempted to discuss, to lead her to such a silly conclusion. There is nothing in the form or substance of Afrocentricity that is like Nazism.

In an opposing lecture from the left, Harold Cruse, in a major address on Afrocentricity at Temple University said it was like Marxism in its transformative potential. Cruse saw the metatheoretical possibilities of the idea extending to the psychological, cultural, and economic recovery of African people for ourselves. His criticism of the idea was essentially around the abstract nature of the metatheory. He kept asking, where is the practice? This is a legitimate question to ask of any Africological theory. The answer in African American Studies at Temple is the doctoral program itself, a product of

Afrocentric theory and practice. Of course, Diane Ravitch, William Raspberry, Henry Gates, Manning Marable, Michelle Wallace, Orlando Patterson, Arthur Schlessinger, Glen Loury, George Wills, and other less well known lights have had something to say about Afrocentricity. Much of what many of them have had to say is a result, not of reading or quoting my works but of responding to a popular cachet. Let me add that these are not all individuals of the same quality or insight.

I shall attempt to clarify several points with reference to Afrocentricity and the future of African American Studies or Africology. Let me start with a rather broad statement that in a white supremacist environment, You are either for white supremacy or you are against it. There is no middle ground for the intellectual in an oppressive society. White supremacy is not just a sociological or political theory or ideology, it is also a literary project in the sense of the Great Books of the Western World as described by Mortimer J. Adler and William Buckley. One hundred and thirty authors and not one African American is included, not even an African who sees herself or himself on the margins of the European experience. To an Afrocentrist, of course, some things are arrogant imposition of a particular view as if it is a universal view. Such a position is ethnocentric and leads to racism when it is enforced by custom, law, or physical force. It degrades other views and valorizes the European viewpoint.

The African American Studies Idea

My thesis is simply stated. During the past twenty or so years since the establishment of African American Studies, two major changes have occurred in the American Academy in reference to African American Studies which have altered the academic landscape for years to come. The first was the institutionalization of African American Studies, Africology, as a discipline alongside other disciplines within the Academy. The second was the creation and mounting of the first doctoral program in African American Studies in the nation at Temple University. The first transformed the student movement of the 1960s into a concrete reality in academic units as well as in theories and methods. The second transcended the parochial and provincial role which had been assigned to the field by keepers of the Academy. What were the characteristics that manifested themselves in this flowering of a new intellectual reality?

I am a child of the Black Studies Movement having been born to it in the late night and early morning labors of love and emotion that saw young men and women at UCLA, members of the Harambe Club, and later SNCC-UCLA of which I was chair, totally absorbed in the creation of the new, the novel, the radical. The processes by which the curricula documents were produced by African American students in the late 1960s and early 70s were unknown in the history of the creation of academic fields and very few of us at that time had any real idea what the future would bring. We knew that curricula were to universities what oxygen is to the lungs. Curricula were inseparable from the concept of the university, just as lungs and breathing could not be separated from the inhaling and exhaling of oxygen. With the curricula changes there would have to be fundamental changes in the institution. We knew this, it now seems, instinctively because the few African American professors who were on those campuses often had not been there long or could not give us advice. As the first permanent director of the UCLA Center for Afro American Studies I wrote the interdisciplinary M.L.A. program and in 1969 started, along with Robert Singleton, who had been an interim director at the Center, the *Journal of Black Studies*. We knew then, as most of you knew, that Black Studies was not the mere aggregation of courses about our experiences but had to be courses taught from what we called at the time "The Black Perspective." In our rush to establish the perspective, we even demanded that only Black teachers teach in the programs until we discovered that perspective is not a biological issue. Some of the Black professors taught from a white perspective. It is from this reality that I shall attempt to answer the question posed above regarding the nature of disciplinary transformations, their characteristics, and future.

The Context of Discipline Development

African American Studies is a discrete discipline with certain critical perspectives, theories, and methods which are necessary for its role in discovery and understanding. Inherent in this statement is the radical idea that African Americans are largely responsible for producing the only new discipline in the social sciences and humanities in the last fifty years. The attendant propositions suggest creativity, innovation, genius, and authority in disciplines. Assaults on Africology as a discipline, as we shall see, are nothing more than attacks on the idea that African Americans can neither create theories nor disciplines, and is ultimately the same tune played in previous discussions of African intelligence. A number of books, such as George Mosse's *A History of Racism* in Europe, Michael Bradley's *The Ice Man Inheritance*, and Stephen J. Gould's *The Mismeasure of Man*, exist on this subject. When this tune is played by Africans themselves it is often the results of dislocation, that is, the assumption of the place where Africans have been pushed by white racial hegemony in the Academy. In such situations the African feels that he or she must act much more correct in the white sense than even whites themselves. There is a felt pressure to be hard, as it were, on any African who raises the possibility of escape from the mental plantation. What I am saying is that it becomes necessary to suspend judgment or to kill one's traditional sensibilities so to speak in order to understand the language of the new reality, that is, Africans as subjects instead of objects in the European project. This is difficult to discern from the same tired portals of traditions which are rooted in the conquest of Africans by Europeans. Africology becomes a discipline whose mission is, interalia, the critique of domination. Of course, there are implications for institutional and organizational issues in the disciplinary question. That is, whether or not departments are more valuable in the maintenance of the discipline than programs in which faculty members share joint appointments. There is also the issue of the symbolic meaning, as well as the political implication, of joint appointments. At Temple University it was to our advantage to share the same paradigm of power and structure as the other organized academic units. Thus, the department is the basic unit and all of our faculty have full appointments in the department.

To examine these issues I will discuss the principal areas of inquiry, the shape of the discipline, classificatory aspects of the discipline, and heuristics for method.

Issues in Inquiry

I am not sure whether it is necessary any longer to debate the question of perspective in terms of the Africological discipline as had been the case during the past twenty years; at least, in the circle of scholars with whom I am associated it is pretty well agreed that the fundamental basis for Africology as a separate discipline is its unique perspective. Nevertheless, the ground is clearly established in the works of Linda James Myers, C. Tsehloane Keto, Maulana Karenga, Dona Richards, and Wade Nobles. Their arguments are expertly placed within the on-going creative project of African liberation, now more than ever, an intellectual liberation. Therefore, the Afrocentric enterprise is framed by cosmological, epistemological, axiological, and aesthetic issues. In this regard the Afrocentric method pursues a world voice distinctly Africa centered in relationship to external phenomena. I did not say distinctly African, which is another issue, but Africa-centered, a theoretical perspective.

Cosmological Issue

The place of African culture in the philosophy, myths, legends, literatures and oratures of African people constitutes, at the mythological level, the cosmological issue within the Afrocentric enterprise, which is an enterprise entirely consistent with the Africological discipline. What role does the African culture play in the African's interface with the cosmos? The debate over "African cultures or culture" is answered definitionally within the context of the Afrocentric perspective so I will not discuss it at this juncture, no more than to say that it has been dealt with in the writings of Afrocentric scholars. One might see particularly the book *African Culture: The Rhythms of Unity* edited by Asante and Asante for a discussion of this issue.

Among the questions that might be dealt with under the cosmological umbrella is, what dramas of life and death, in the African tradition, are reflected in metaphysical metaphors? How are those dramas translated by lunar, solar, or stellar figures? The fundamental assumptions of Africological inquiry are based on the African orientation to the cosmos. By "African" I clearly mean a "composite African" not a specific discrete African ethnicity, which would rather mean, African American, Yoruba, Ibo, Fulani, Zulu, Mandingo, Kikongo, etc. C. T. Keto has taken this up in his book *Afrocentricity and History* by writing that "African American thinkers were among the first to feel the need to create the concept 'composite' African and, in so doing their reference was the whole of the African continent which included, historically, ancient Kemet." (Keto, 1991:5). He continues that "denied a precise ethnic linkage, they created a holistic African vision that ... influenced Africans on the continent." (Keto, 1991:5)

There are several concerns which might be considered cosmological in that they are fundamental frames for research initiatives in this discipline. I shall only make reference to them here and refer you to my recent book, *Kemet, Afrocentricity and Knowledge*, for greater commentary. The concerns are: Racial Formation, Culture, Gender, and Class. Race as a social factor remains prevalent in heterogeneous but hegemonically Eurocentric societies. In the United States, the most developed example of such a society, the question of race is the most dominant aspect of intersocial relations. Cultural questions are usefully viewed in the context of shared perceptions, attitudes, and predispositions that allow communities of people to organize responses in similar ways. Gender also must be seen as a substantial research area in questions of social, political, economic, and cultural dimensions. Since the liberation of women is not an act of charity but a basic premise of the Afrocentric project, the researcher must be cognizant of sexist language, terminology, and perspectives. Class becomes for the Afrocentrist, aware of our history, much more complicated than capitalists and workers, or bourgeoisie and proletariat. Finding the relevant class positions and places in given situations will assist the Africological scholar with analysis. Indeed, Eurocentrism with all of its potential for asserting its particular self as universal becomes the repository for race, class, and gender conflict. Rather than an isolated or isolatable discussion of race, or class, or gender one begins to view the dominant Eurocentric myths as containing all of these elements.

Epistemological Issue

What constitutes the search for truth in the Afrocentric enterprise? In Africology, language, myth, ancestral memory, dance music-art, and science provide the sources of knowledge, the canons of proof and the structure of truth.

Discussions of language from an Afrocentric perspective or research into African language, diasporan or continental, may lead to understanding about the nature of truth. Ebonics, the African American language, serves as the archetype of African American language in the United States. A variety of languages in Brazil, Ecuador, Colombia, Panama, and Belize serve this functions in other American communities. One of our students, for example, is centering her research on the Garifuna people of Belize. However, while her work will include much that is historical and linguistic, she is principally concerned with an epistemological question rooted in the inquiry on methods of retention as expressed in the declarative, as opposed to cognitive culture, of the people.

The strong, expressive, inescapable myth of the African presence in America, indeed, in the world has value for the discovery of truth in many dimensions of human life. Thus, behind and in front of our banquet of possibilities are the refracting elements of myths which appropriately mediate our relationships. Knowing those myths, making a habit of investigating them in a serious manner, allows the researcher to form new metaphors about our experiences. In dance music-art, performing and representational art forms are central to interpretation of cultural and social reality. Our analysis is informed by the way dance is seen in African culture, even in the way we view the Africanization of the walkman.

Axiological Issue

The question of value is at the core of the Afrocentric quest for truth because ethical issues have always been connected to the advancement of the discipline. One cannot speak of Africology apart from its origin in the drive to humanize education, to democratize the curriculum, to advance the understanding of humanity. This is the birthright of the discipline more than any other discipline in the social sciences or humanities. What constitutes the good is a matter of historical conditions and cultural developments within a particular society. A common expression among us relates to the good and beautiful in this way, "beauty is as beauty does." We are also sure that a person "is beautiful because he or she is good." When a sister says, "that's a beautiful brother," she is usually meaning something more than his physical looks. Doing good is equivalent to being beautiful. The Afrocentric method isolates conduct and action in social or literary analysis. The aim is to see what conduct has been sanctioned, and if sanctioned, carried out.

Aesthetic Issue

Kariamu Welsh Asante has identified seven aspects of the African aesthetic which she calls "senses". Based upon her field research into Zimbabwe dance she isolated polyrhythm, polycentrism, dimensionality, repetition, curvilinearity, epic memory, and wholism as investigative categories for African aesthetics. Each aspect might be examined from the disciplinary perspective by any researcher using the idea of African centrality. Particularly useful in the context of drama, dance, the plastic arts, and literature, the aesthetic senses represent an Afrocentric approach to the subject of African art.

The Shape of the Discipline

The groundedness of observations and behaviors in the historical experiences of Africans becomes the main base for operation in the field of African American Studies. Centrism, the operation of the African as subject or the Latino as subject or the European as subject, and so forth, allows Africology to take its place alongside other disciplines without hierarchy and without hegemony. As a discipline, Africology is sustained by a commitment to centering the study of African phenomena, events, and persons in the particular cultural voice of the composite African people. But it does not promote such a view as universal. Furthermore, it opens the door for interpretations of reality based upon evidence and data secured by reference to that world voice.

The anteriority of the classical African civilizations must be entertained by any Africological inquiry, simply because without that perspective, our work hangs in the air, detached, and isolated or becomes nothing more than a sub-set of the Eurocentric disciplines. As I have often said, without Afrocentricity in this way, research becomes disconnected, without historical continuity, incidental, and nonorganic.

The Eurocentric dogma creates an intellectual structure that locks the African in a conceptual prison. One key to this dogma is that philosophy is the highest discipline and that philosophy is Greek. Thus, Greece becomes the model for the structure of knowledge in the West. According to this dogma, everything starts with the Greeks: philosophy, politics, art, drama, literature, and mathematics. There is no philosophy in Africa, Asia, or the Americas, only the Europeans have philosophy. However, since the first Greek philosophers, Thales and Socrates, studied philosophy in Kemet (Ancient Egypt), philosophy could not have started with the Greeks. Cheikh Anta Diop, perhaps the greatest African intellect of the 20th century, argued that there could be no understanding of things Africans without linkage to ancient Kemet. Thus, Egypt is to the rest of the African world as Greece is to the rest of the European world. Europe constitutes itself around several principles including its connection, however mythical or distant, to ancient Greece, to certain ideas that are traced to the Greeks and to the Romans, and to Christianity as a unifying theme from the 10th century A.D.

Subject Fields

To say that Africology is a discipline does not mean that it is without subject fields or interest areas. There are seven general subject fields which I have identified following the work of Maulana Karenga in *Introduction to Black Studies:* communicative, social, historical, cultural, political, economic, and psychological. Most of the people who are working in the field are approaching their work from one of the above subject fields. A student of Africology chooses a research issue which falls within one or more of these subject fields. In any endeavor to uncover, analyze, criticize, or anticipate an issue, the Africologist works to use the appropriate methods for the subject. To examine cultural nationalism, for example, within the historical or political subject field would require a consonant method for research.

There are three paradigmatic approaches to research in Africology: functional, categoral, and etymological. The first represents needs, policy, and action orientations. Categoral refers to schemes, gender, class, and themes. The etymological paradigm deals with language, literatures, and oratures. Studies of either sort might be conducted in the context of African society, either on the continent or in the Americas. The aim is to provide research results that is ultimately verifiable in human experience.

A student of Africology might choose to study in the general field of history but use the functional paradigm. Or choose psychology and use the etymological paradigm. Of course, many combinations are possible and the student is limited only by her or his ability to properly conceptualize the topic for study in an Afrocentric manner. Since Africology is not history, political science, communication, literary analysis, or sociology, the student must be well grounded in the assumptions of the Afrocentric approach to human knowledge.

Scholars in our field have often been handicapped in their quest for clear and authoritative statements by a lack of methodological direction for collection and analyzing data, choosing and interpreting research themes, approaching and appreciating cultural artifacts, and isolating and evaluating facts. This has been the case although works by Larry Neal and Paul Carter Harrison in the literary theory field introduced us to the possibilities inherent in our own centered positions as early as the Sixties. However, as an increasingly self-conscious field African American studies, Africology, has begun to produce a variety of philosophical approaches to Afrocentric inquiry. These studies have served to underscore the need for solid methodological studies at the level of basic premises of the field and have become, in effect, pioneer works in a new perspective on phenomena.

The Afrocentric psychologists have led in the reconceptualization of the field of African personality theories. Among the leaders in this field have been people like Daudi Azibo of Temple, Wade Nobles of San Francisco State, Joseph Baldwin of Florida A and M, Linda James Myers of Ohio State, and Na'im Akbar of Florida State University. They have explored areas of human psychology which impinge on the African experience. Political Scientists qua political scientists such as Ronald Walter, Leonard Jeffries, Mack Jones, Manning Marable and James Turner have argued positions that may be called Afrocentric. Maulana Karenga, Patrick Bellegarde-Smith, from their original base in political science, have become Afrocentrists. The work of Houston Baker in the area of vernacular theory might be considered Afrocentric inasmuch as the source of his images are culturally centered. In addition, the works of several writers, such as Henry Louis Gates and Eleanor Traylor have elements of centered locations. The field of sociology, since the early days of the first departments in 1882 and 1884 at Chicago and Columbia respectively, has remained bogged down in social problems and paradigms that do not permit adequate assessment of African cultural data. A number of African American sociologists are attempting to break out of those quagmires. Robert Staples had been an early pioneer in this field and now the work of Bruce Hare at Syracuse is significant in this respect. Vivian Gordon has long been a major force in the Africana Womanist project in which sex and race are joined rather than separated as in the work of the Afrofemcentrists or the Black Feminists. Indeed, Gordon's work is joined with that of Clenora Hudson Weems and Brenda Verner to make the most Afrocentric statement on the woman question we have seen in Africology. They have found their models, like Dona Marimba Richards, in the ancient models of Auset-Ausar and Mawu-Lisa. In design and architecture scholars such as Bill Harris at the University of Virginia are exploring Afrocentric designs in housing. What would we have done without the porch as a daycare platform?

Africology is defined as the Afrocentric study of phenomena, events, ideas, and personalities related to Africa. The mere study of African phenomena is not Africology but some other intellectual enterprise. I make no judgment on those enterprises, I simply say that they are not Africological. Like other disciplines, more or less severe, our discipline is based upon certain assumptions, objectives, and constructions of language. Thus, the Temple Circle of Afrocentric scholars have tried to exorcise terms such as sub Saharan, Hottentot, Bushmen, pygmy, and minority. Such a massive project of redressing the de-centering of Africans will surely take us deep into the 21st century. The scholar who generates research questions based upon the centrality of Africa is engaged in a very different research inquiry than the one who imposes Western criteria on the phenomena. Afrocentric is the most important word in the definition, otherwise one might think that any study of African phenomena or people constitutes Africology. It is the commitment to perspective and method that distinguishes the discipline from others.

Geographical Scope

The geographical scope of the African world, and hence, the Africological enterprise, includes Africa, the Americas, the Caribbean, various regions of Asia and the Pacific. Wherever people declare themselves as African, despite the distance from the continent or the recency of their out-migration, they are accepted as part of the African world. Thus, the indigenous people of Australia and New Guinea are considered African and in a larger context subjects for Africologists who maintain a full analytical and theoretical discussion of African phenomena.

Although the major regions of the African culture are Africa, the Caribbean and the Americas, even within those regions there are varying degrees of cultural and technological affinity to an African world voice. Africology is concerned with Africans in any particular as well as all regions. Thus, Abdias do Nascimento, our visiting professor from Brazil at Temple this year, can remind us that Brazil is significant for understanding the African presence in the Americas. In Brazil, Zumbi, the greatest king of the Palmares Republic, Luisa Zahin, and Luiz Gama are principal figures in the making of history; in the Dominican Republic, Diego de Campo and Lemba provide the same historical and intellectual energy one finds in Venezuela with Oyocta, King Miguel, and King Bayano; and in Columbia there is Benkos Bioho; and in Mexico the great African American, Yanga.

Africology rejects the Africanist idea of the separation of African people on the continent from African people in the Diaspora as being intellectually shortsighted, analytically vapid, and philosophically unsound. One cannot study Africans in the United States or Brazil or Jamaica without some appreciation for the historical and cultural significance of Africa as source and origin. The reactionary position which sees African American Studies as African Slave Studies, that is the making and the un-making of the slave, is categorically rejected. Thus, if one studies Africans in a Northeast city in the United States, one must do it with the idea that one is studying African people, not made in America Negroes without historical depth. This has a direct bearing on data gathered for any analysis or study of African people. The researcher must examine everything possible to be able to make an adequate case. Actually the gathering of data must proceed on the basis that everything that can be used must be used. Therefore, it is impossible for a person to become an Africologist simply by using the historical method, or the critical method, or the experimental method, and so forth. In order to become the best type of Africologist one must use all the elements of data gathering in any particular area, for an adequate assessment. This means that I might have to use literary analysis and historical analysis in examining one theme or issue. Video records and oral records are as important as written records and must be seen as a part of the portfolio of documentation that is available to the Africologist.

The Temple Project

A final statement ought to be made about the classificatory aspects of Africology. These ideas are given within the framework of the creation of the doctoral program at Temple. Two fields, cultural aesthetics and social behavioral, exist in our department. They are the results of debate, discussion, consensus within the faculty. With twelve faculty members we have established a reputation for intellectual debate and dialogue that opens the discourse on discipline questions. Africology is a severe discipline. It became necessary for us to commit traditional discipline suicide in order to advance Africology within the structure of the university. The students we are training will not have that particular problem. They will start out being Africologists who have read everything in their concentrations, as well as the theoretical works in the discipline. Already we have seen our students expand the discourse in almost every field. Thus, we have proposed the following two areas of research and responsibility: 1) Creative inventive, artistic, literary: epistemic issues, ethics, politics, psychology, and modes of behavior; scientific issues, history, linguistics, economics, and methods of investigation; artistic issues, icon, art, motifs, symbols, and types of presentation. 2) Social, behavioral, action, historical: relationships, the living, the dead, the unborn cosmos, culture, race, class, gender; mythoforms, origins, struggles, victories; and recognitions, conduct, designs, signs.

These principal areas, cultural/aesthetic and social/behavioral, constitute the grounds upon which we must stand as we continue to build this discipline. I am certain that the scholars who will replace us will advance the relocating process in theory and practice as the generalship of the field improves in the give-and-take of critical debate. As it has been necessary in every aspect of the African's existence for the past five hundred years, it is also necessary in the area of human knowledge for us to struggle to enhance our perspective, recovering it from the distorted junk heap of Eurocentric hegemony. And as in the past, there will be those scholars of whatever cultural and racial background who will understand our interest in free and full inquiry from our own centered perspective and who will become the new Melville Herskovits and Robert Farris Thompsons. A field of study must be open to all who share its perspective and methodology; ours is no different.

The future of Africology will depend upon those who are committed to the principles of academic excellence and social responsibility. Those principles must be interpreted within the framework of an Afrocentric vision in order to maintain a space and location for Africology within the Academy. I have no doubt that this will be done by the scholars and students who are coming after us. They will find in their own time the energy and will to carry out their intellectual mission as we are trying to carry out ours in order to create new spaces for human discussion.

Hotep.

References

Asante, Molefi & Welsh-Asante, K. 1988. *African Culture: The Rhythms of Unity*. Trenton, NJ: Africa World Press.

Asante, M1olefi K. 1988. *Afrocentricity*. Trenton, NJ: Africa World Press.

Asante, Molefi. 1990. *Kemet, Afrocentricity, and Knowledge*. Trenton, NJ: Africa World Press.

Asante, Molefi. 1987. *The Afrocentric Idea*. Philadelphia, PA: Temple University Press.

Bellegarde-Smith, Patrick. 1990. *Haiti: The Breached Citadel*. Boulder, CO: Westview Press.

Bradley, Michael. 1980. *The Ice Man Inheritance*. Toronto: Dorset, 1980.

Diop, Cheikh Anta. 1974. *The African Origin of Civilization*. New York, N.Y.: Lawrence Hill.

Diop, Cheikh Anta. 1991. *Civilization of Barbarism*. New York, N.Y.: Lawrence Hill.

Diop, Cheikh Anta. 1976. *The Cultural Unity of Black Africa*. Chicago, IL: Third World Books.

Gould, Stephen. 1981. *The Mismeasure of Man*. New York. N.Y.: Norton.

Karenga, Maulana. 1987. *Introduction to Black Studies*. Los Angeles, CA: University of Sankore Press.

Keto, Tsehloane. 1988. *The Africa-centered Perspective of History*. Blackwood, N.J.: K & A Publishers.

Marable, Manning. 198?. *How Capitalism Underdeveloped Black America*. Boston, MA: South End Press.

Mosse, George. 1985. *A History of Racism in Europe: Toward the Final Solution*. Madison, WI: University of Wisconsin Press.

Nascimento, Elisa. 1979. *Pan Africanism and South America*. Buffalo, N.Y.: Afrodiaspora.

Obenga, Theophile. 1990. *The African Origin of Philosophy*. Paris: Presence Africaine.

Richards, Dona. 1991. *Let the Circle Be Unbroken*. Trenton, NJ: Africa World Press.

Rodney, Walter. 1980. *How Europe Underdeveloped Africa*. Washington, DC: Howard University Press.

2. AFROCENTRIC EPISTEMOLOGY, CONCEPTS, AND METHODOLOGY

A Philosophical Basis for an Afrocentric Orientation

Norman Harris

Background
By now, it is common knowledge that an Afrocentric orientation is one which places the interests and needs of African people at the center of any discussion. The awesome and ongoing intellectual contributions of Maulana Karenga; the works of several African American psychologists—particularly Wade Nobles, Asa Hilliard, Naim Akbar and Linda James Myers; and most certainly the work of Molefi Asante—all provide examples of how Afrocentric orientations structure ethical, psychological, socio-economic and cultural analyses. This paper proposes to indicate basic philosophical assumptions which seem to structure the application of all Afrocentric approaches. It does not critique the work of Afrocentric scholars-though such an essay would certainly be useful. Rather, the writer's assertions and observations about the philosophical underpinnings of Afrocentricity are a result of having for a number of years read, reflected and acted on the fundamental idea that the Afrocentric philosophy ought to structure any discussion of African people.

This essay has three related sections. The first indicates how Afrocentricity interacts with what the writer asserts to be fundamental motivations within African American life. The second section is an overview of Afrocentric ontological and epistemological orientations, and those are developed in terms of conceptions of time and logic. The third section illustrates that the way one thinks about time determines the role history plays in social change.

I.

Situated within the nucleus of the Afrocentric orientation is an assumption that a central motivation in African American life is the desire to achieve freedom and literacy.[1] Freedom is the ability to conceptualize the world in ways continuous with one's history. Literacy is the application of historical knowledge as the confluence between personality and situation dictates.

Freedom is an idealized conception derived from historical knowledge. This definition is one which turns analytical activity away from the quantification of gross changes in the socio-political and economic position of African Americans at any point in time (an end to chattel slavery, the passage of civil rights legislation, an end to various forms of discrimination, etc.) and towards a look at the way Africans in America define themselves and the extent to which they are able to implement their definitions of themselves. This definition of freedom therefore encourages research which seeks to distinguish between an appearance of change and the reality of change.

Historically, African Americans have been encouraged to confuse a rearrangement of reality with fundamental changes in reality. This phenomena is facilitated through the implementation of various modes of socialization which undercut or minimize African and African American humanity. These modes of socialization include everything from changes in law to the inclusion of African American images in the print and electronic media. To be sure, this process has never been entirely successful, and we are now living in an historical period characterized by increased attention to the role of Africa in shaping humanity.[2] In response to that attention, one might perceive an increased pathology in Eurocentric scholarship[3] as it seeks to displace and discount the African origins of humanity and the fundamental role of African peoples in shaping western civilization at its point of conception. The contention here is commonplace and it is that the fundamental antagonism of Whites toward Africans, be they on the continent or in the diaspora, has not altered over time. What has altered in this relationship is the form and appearance which While pathology might take at any given point in time. The definition of freedom used here provides a basis for the African American consciousness to merge with the best traditions in African and African American culture in order to more fully contribute to the forward flow of human history than the current ideas, definitions and subsequent attempts to attain freedom now allow.

Literacy is the practical dimension of freedom and is defined as noted above for two reasons: first, the definition acknowledges the subjective dimension of the human experience which makes one-to-one correlations between being exposed to or deprived of any given stimuli and having a specific response to that exposure or deprivation impossible to predict. To be sure, there is a range of predictable behavior among African Americans that non-African Americans rely on in creating and perfecting the methods they use to maintain the myriad systems of oppression. Alluded to here is the stubbornness of African humanity; its unwillingness to do as objective circumstances dictate—that is to succumb to any number of limiting phenomena. Secondly, literacy is materialist in its acknowledgement of differences over and within time relative to the situations people confront. More directly, the way literacy plays out in a given situation is in part function of what the opportunities and limitations of the material conditions under question dictate. The most sublime expression of literacy is of course rhythm. Here in *Roots of Soul*,[4] Pasteur and Toldson describe the phenomena:

> At the essence of man's basic nature, enveloping vital forces, rhythm is a critical factor in the organization or human behavior. It is required for the attainment and maintenance or momentary perfection in human performance, which is the platform for achieving happiness. To be in rhythm is popularly recognized as a form of human efficiency . . . At such moments, one does not move in an analytical, step-by-step progression, one is the spontaneous, rhythmic unfolding of the progression. One does not try to do, one happens to be an instrument of the doing. During such moments, nothing is difficult, there is no anxiety. (76-77)

Literacy seeks to attain the state described above, and its attainment is dependent on the application of historical understanding as the confluence between personality and situation dictates. This writer's assertion is that all African American ethical, psychological, socio-economic, political and cultural activity is an attempt to attain freedom and literacy.

Afrocentricity places the needs of African people at the center of all discussions. The quest to achieve freedom and literacy operates from that center.

II.

While not anti-materialistic, an Afrocentric orientation is one which asserts that consciousness determines being. Consciousness in this sense means the way an individual (or a people) thinks about relationships with self, others, with nature, and with some superior idea or Being. Certainly, the idea that consciousness determines being or the definition this writer gives to consciousness are not new. A variety of expressions drawn from classical and vernacular African and African American culture speak to this phenomena. For example, the ancient Egyptian assertion, "Man Know Thy Self," indicates that the way one sees (thinks about and conceptualizes) the world precedes and determines life chances more so than exposure to or deprivation from various material conditions. The popular refrain of the "Funkadelics": "Free your mind and your ass will follow," is an example from vernacular culture of the assumption that consciousness determines being. Put another way, changes in the material world are possible only after one is able to think freely about those changes. In like manner, one can understand Marcus Garvey's assertion that what man has done, man can do; or Maulana Karenga's assertion that the crisis in the African American community is a crisis of values; or Jesse Jackson's insistent refrain, "I am somebody." In each instance, the assertion is that new thought precedes new action.

The idea that consciousness determines being derives from an Afrocentric ontology and epistemology. The Afrocentric ontology is characterized by a communal notion of existence, and can be stated as follows: we are, therefore I exist. This communal orientation is in contrast to the Eurocentric orientation that is best characterized by Rene Descartes's assertion, "I think, therefore I am." The Afrocentric epistemology validates knowledge through a combination of historical understanding and intuition. What is known, what can be proven is demonstrated through the harmonization of the individual consciousness with the best traditions in the African past. Again, by way of contrast, the Eurocentric epistemology validates knowledge through a combination of objectivity and "scientific method" wherein it is assumed that similar results obtained through similar steps under similar conditions is an indication of reality. Carl Jung, not always known for forward thinking on matters of race,[5] says that "Scientific materialism has merely introduced a new hypostasis, and that is an intellectual sin. It has given another name to the supreme principle of reality and has assumed that this created a new thing and destroyed an old thing. Whether you call the principle of existence "God" matter, energy, or anything else you like, you have created nothing; you have simply changed a symbol" (xxxi).[6] Jung's observations humanize science by noting its arbitrariness, and, implicitly, its juvenile quality. More directly, unable to understand relationships among the various expressions of reality (an inability to attain the literacy that rhythm occasions), western science seeks to sub-divide reality into angry little parts that barely know how to converse with each other. One may understand current events as flowing from the disharmony of implemented Western science.

The significance of Afrocentric ontology and epistemology is profound. The way one constructs reality, one's place in it, and the way one validates[7] knowledge determine one's life chances. For example, the individualistic ontology into which we have all been socialized makes it all but impossible for many African Americans to conceptualize the idea of racial responsibility, particularly as it relates to racial empowerment. At worse, racial responsibility ends at the tip of one's nose, and at best, racial responsibility is merely a romantic concept, a passing stage in the individual's development before one reaches maturity.

The Eurocentric notion of individualism rests on the assumption that being determines consciousness, and it is this assumption which infuses materialism with a spirit it could never have. A new or better job, more income, a car, an outfit, etc. are all assumed to carry intrinsic meaning that will at the level of consciousness create a new person. As long as a Eurocentric ontology of individualism obtains in the African American community, one may expect casual and justified inhumanity. A Black brother might say, "After all, if it's good for me, it's good for me. So step off, chump." The gangster image of the individualistic African American just described is, if you will, the whiter side of an all-white philosophical phenomena that is not derived from the Black world experience. The eloquent stasis of neo-conservatives is but the other side. The writer has written elsewhere about their tendency to write as if history has no abiding force in the world; more directly, they assume that history has little if any contemporary and ongoing significance, particularly the history of enslavement, the various racist assumptions that sought its justification, and the continued phenomena of institutionalized racism. More will be said about the way one conceives time and the impact that it has on the role that history plays in social change in the next section. Suffice it here to say that those the writer labels as neo-conservatives conceptualize time in a linear fashion, have difficulty in seeing a contradiction between appearance and reality, and therefore assume that changes in appearance actually represent a change in reality.

To sum up, an Afrocentric ontology is one which is communal; therefore, individuals find their worth, and their most sublime expression of existence in relationship to a community, to nature, and in relationship to some supreme idea or being. The Afrocentric ontology seeks to use rhythm to harmonize with those forces which appear external to the individual, but are in point of fact, simply expressions of the individual's potential. Na'im Akbar makes this point in his essay "African American Consciousness and Kemet Spirituality, Symbolism and Duality,"[9] when he asserts that

> African people are concerned about the invisible more
> than they are about the visible. . . They are concerned about
> those forces that operate on a higher plane. . . That's the nature
> of the spiritual orientation of African people. African people
> are more concerned about the infinite than they are about the
> finite. (106)

The idea of the infinite is similar to what might be referred to as potential; both are without limit and cannot be known in the context developed here except in association with other positive forces in the African world. Thus we see again the holistic—indeed, the limitless— nature of humanity that is possible from an Afrocentric ontological stance.

The Eurocentric ontology is individualistic and in it, the individual finds his fullest expression of existence in isolation or in opposition to man, nature, or some supreme idea or being. In this model there is no transcendent order to which the individual can attach herself. Indeed, attachments are at best pragmatic, and at worse they are parasitic. Tragedy, outrage and imposition are the hallmarks of Eurocentric cultural achievement and these can be understood as flowing from a view of the world in which humanity knows no collective and nurturing tradition to which it can attach itself. Like a child in a tantrum, one must be amazed by the ferocity of its self-destruction, particularly when it is all so unnecessary. A comparison between the "creative" culture associated with an Afrocentric orientation and that associated with a Eurocentric orientation would yield exciting psychological data about the way the African and the non-African think about reality.

An Afrocentric epistemology validates reality (or what it claims to know) throughout a combination of historical knowledge and intuition. In this epistemology, history is key because when the individual appropriately submerges himself in the reservoir of African history, then that submersion

115

allows the individual to discover him or her self in the context of that history and thereby judge the reality of any given phenomenon. Wade Nobles[10] writes: "Unlike the 'stand for' connotation of the symbolic ulilized today, the symbolic of ancient African times, and the contemporary African as well, was a symbolism that went beyond the 'representational-sequential-analytic' mode to the 'transformation-synchronistic-analogic' mode" (100). The last mode about which Nobles writes derives from a holistic view of reality; it is an aspect of a communal ontology. From this perspective, knowing is both rational and supra-rational, for it incorporates both that which can be understood in terms of methods to measure the material world, and that which transcends the material. Implicit in what Nobles writes, and, indeed, in what one sees in the writings of a number of scholars who explore classical African civilizations[11] is that reality follows essence, and that if one really wishes to know, then one must go beyond what is possible by the measuring and cataloging of material reality.

In a remarkable, and perhaps overlooked essay, "Hunting is Not Those Heads on the Wall," [12] Leroi Jones makes the point that hunting, like art, is a process and what is left - a dead head hanging on the wall or the artifact—is not the reality; it is simply the artifact, the "leavings" of a process. So it is with reality as one has been taught to think about it: it is not the mere appearance of physical phenomena; rather, reality is the essence which connects the multiple expressions of appearances.

This discussion could continue along these lines in terms of defining a relationship between how one validates claims to knowing (epistemology) and one's notion of what reality is (a version of ontology). But the purpose here is to pose what the writer sees as a fundamental difference between an Afrocentric epistemology and a Eurocentric epistemology. The Afrocentric epistemology assumes transcendent order in the world, and the Eurocentric epistemology assumes that the only order in the world is that which it can "scientifically" demonstrate and that which it can impose. An Afrocentric epistemology attempts to validate claims to knowledge through immersion while the Eurocentric epistemology seeks distance from what it attempts to know and understand.

The differences between Afrocentric and Eurocentric epistemologies have pronounced effects on the way this society is organized and on the life chances of Africans in America. The more Afrocentric the epistemology of the African American[13] the more profound will be his contribution to humanity. The less Afrocentric the orientation, the more narrow will be the contribution. To be sure, for an African American to have a Eurocentric epistemology is consistent with the way many Blacks have been socialized. That African Americans have not marched entirely into the various slave holes constructed for them is remarkable testament to the transcendent nature of our humanity.[14]

To sum up here, the Afrocentric epistemology assumes transcendent order in the world. It seeks to verify its claims to knowing through a combination of historical understanding and intuition. Its methods are both empirical and supra-empirical.[15] An Afrocentric ontology and epistemology are necessary to advance the quest for freedom and literacy.

The following discussion relates how the Afrocentric ontology and epistemology structure the way one thinks about time, and, as a consequence, the way one thinks about the relationship of history to social change.

III.

The way one thinks about time determines the role that history plays in social change. If time is conceptualized in a cyclical fashion, then history plays a fundamental one might say, a definitional role in social change. If time is conceptualized in a linear fashion, then history has little if any role to play in social change.

Deriving from its ontology (view of the world), and epistemology (verifications of those views of the world), an Afrocentric orientation conceptualizes time in a cyclical fashion. It assumes that the appearance of phenomena always changes, but that the underlying essence of phenomena remains basically unchanged. Part of life's journey, part of the quest for freedom and literacy is to systematically discover meaning (connections) beneath the surface of appearance. One may say in this regard, that an Afrocentric conception of time is not impressed by progress, which, in the Euro-Western context, means the endless rearrangement of appearances for their own sake. No beauty here, no ethics, only the unending march of progress.

The Eurocentric orientation of time is linear, and it assumes, at least at the level of the way it organizes its various socializing agents, that there is a one-to-one correlation between appearance and reality. But, as Public Enemy says, "Can't Trust It,"[16] meaning of course that the mere appearance of change does not signify actual change—that is, a change in the power relationships between African Americans and non-African Americans.

A cyclical conception of time encourages immersion in history at a level and in a way that marries individuality or personality to precedent. As is the way of education in classical African Civilizations, the immersion is consistent with and necessary to self transformation, or, in another fashion, it is consistent with being born again.[17] This transformation must happen not only for the individual African in America, but for all African Americans.

To clarify: the social transformation is possible from an Afrocentric conception of time, and that notion of time is cyclical. The transformation itself simultaneously involves immersion and expansion in Black World history; only then can the individual discover herself or himself; only then can the race discover itself. As outlined here, self-discovery is freedom; the ability to conceptualize the world in ways continuous with one's history. This self discovery, this freedom, is again consistent with what the Ancients taught, "Man Know Thy Self." Finally, on this part of the discussion, there can be no social change with out freedom.

Literacy is the implementation of freedom and, as noted, is possible only when one thinks of time in a cyclical fashion. Social transformation is what is being struggled for. This is not an essay intended to list specific items or accomplishments that would signify social transformation. The Urban League and like organizations routinely publish these kinds of things. Rather, it would be more useful here to repeat and elaborate upon what has been said: literacy is the implementation of freedom, and the increasing ability of African Americans to implement freedom does signify social transformation.

IV.

This essay has sought to indicate the philosophical infrastructure on which Afrocentric scholarship rests. This will, the author thinks, provide others with a way of operationalizing the definition of Afrocentricity.

Endnotes and References

1. I have been working with and expanding these terms since I came across them a decade ago while writing my dissertation. My acquaintance with the concepts of freedom and literacy come from my reading of Robert Stepto's *From Behind the Veil,* and from a variety or things I have read by Northrop Frye. While African American literary analysis was the specific reason for my usage or these terms, further reading indicated that their philosophical basis rested in what Carl Jung calls the collective unconscious. Additional reading indicated that Jung's notion of a collective unconscious is consistent with Richard Wright's prosaic, yet profound observation of things unseen, and the more fundamental African orientation concerning death, ancestor veneration, and the role of the past (if indeed it is that) in structuring the present. In short, the idea that African American life is structured by predispositions that cannot be fully explained by reference to empirical data is the basis for what I am doing here. In effect, the desire to achieve freedom and literacy is a supra-rational desire that is consistent with the African philosophical assumption that consciousness determines being.

2. The systematic rescue of Nile Valley Civilizations by writers and scholars as diverse as Charles Fitch, Ivan van Sertima, Asa Hilliard, Larry Williams, W. Joyce Hardiman, Marlin Bernal, Jacob Carruthers, and organizations like the Association for the Study of Classical African Civilizations are indicators of this fact.

3. See Daudi Azibo's article in the Spring 1992 issue of *Word,* "Eurocentric Psychology and the Issue of Race."

4. Ivory Toldson and Alfred D. Pasteur. 1982. *Roots of Soul.* Garden City, New York, NY: Doubleday Anchor.

5. Naim Akbar notes in a speech that Jung asserts that the problem with America is that it is more or less infected by the African.

6. W. Y. Evans-Wentz. 1977. *The Tibetan Book of the Great Liberation.* Commentary by Carl Jung. New York, N.Y.: Oxford University Press.

7. I would include in this group those African Americans who are more concerned mashing what is unique in African and African American culture into existing paradigms than they are with indicating what is unique. See my essay, Who's zooming Who: The New Black Formalist, for a criticism of Louis Henry Gates, Jr., Robert Stepto and Houston Baker; see also my forthcoming book, *Signposts* for more discussions.

8. See my review of Shelby Steele's *The content of Our Character* in *Word* and also my review of *Reflections on An Affirmative Action Baby* in the Spring 1992 issue of *Word*.

9. This essay can be found in *Reconstructing Kemetic Culture, Papers, Perspectives, Projects*. 1990. Karenga, Maulana (ed.) Los Angeles, CA: Sankore University Press. 99-114.

10. Nobles, Wade. (Undated). Ancient African Thought and the Development of African (Black) Psychology. *Kemet and the African Worldview*, Karenga, Maulana & Carruthers, Jacob (eds).

11. See the works of Schwaller de Lubicz, Naim Akbar, Asa Hilliard, et al. For each, reality is essence, that which is at the center of physical phenomena and consequently that which does not change. One of the most remarkable elucidations of this is a speech that Louis Farrakhan gave on the Black Man (I heard on a colleague's tape machine and cannot give a specific reference) in which he discussed who and what the Black Man is in terms of what reality is.

12. See Leroi Jones, Hunting is Not Those Heads on the Wall, *Home Social Essays*; see also his essay Black Ethos, in *Raise Rays Raze*.

13. It should be noted that on one is necessarily born with a full-blown Afrocentric orientation, complete with an articulated ontology and epistemology. It should also be noted that people more directly of African descent (by whatever combination of scientific and cultural measures that seem appropriate) are more likely to be disposed to an Afrocentric direction than are those who are of European or Asian descent. Nonetheless, people who are of European descent -Count Volney, De Lubicz, Gerald Massey, Melville Herskovits, Martin Bernal, and others, are examples- can have an Afrocentric orientation. And this rather unremarkable observation achieves its strength based on the tendency of mainline scholarship to deny or denigrate the intellectual influences that Africa has exerted over its offspring in Europe and Asia.

14. It would be interesting here to explore as an historical continuum the Kemetic idea found in all of Africa that the purpose of all education is the definition of humanity. Could the stubbornness of this aspect of Classical African Civilization account for the transcendent nature of our humanity? This would be an intriguing question to explore.

15. To demonstrate this claim requires an elaboration on Nobles' discussion of the symbolic quoted earlier -specifically, the difference between "representational-sequential-analytic" mode and the "transformation-synchronic-analogic" mode. I would refer the reader to Nobles' article as a beginning discussion of the methods the ancients used to verify knowledge.

16. Their video of this song cuts between an enslaved African American whose female interest is raped by the White man, to a brother working in a factory whose female interest is harassed by a White man. The effect is to emphasize that the more things change the more they remain the same. "Can't Trust It!" What you cannot trust is the mere appearance of change. *Word*.

17. See Asa Hilliard's "Pedagogy in Ancient Kemet," this volume.

The Deep Structure of Culture: The Relevance of Traditional African Culture in Contemporary Life

Linda James Myers

Culture defined as the total way of life of a people, is somewhat indestructible. As long as there are people they will have a way of life. Culture determines quality of life in large measure. The importance of cultural identity to people of African descent has been emphasized repeatedly (Asante, 1983; Cruse, 1967; Karenga, 1983).

Part of what is being responded to is what Nobles (1976) describes as the "conceptual incarceration" of black people in a hegemonous European-American-oriented culture.

> The natural consciousness of black people is forced to relate to a reality defined by white consciousness. That is contemporary black people in the United States live in a psycho-social reality consistent with and supportive of white mental functioning. Such a situation is tantamount to black people living in [what for black people must be] white insanity.

It has been said that we must become "cultural scientists," learn the true nature of our African cultural heritage so that we might maximize its benefits in contemporary times (Asante, 1983). If we assume a single gene pool, accept the most current archaeological and anthropological evidence, and follow what has been shown to be true of dominant genes for color versus recessive, all people can be said to be of African descent depending on how far back they wish to go in tracing their ancestry. We owe it to ourselves to understand the nature of the conceptual system that yielded the first culture from which all other conceptual systems and cultures evolved (Ben-Jochannan, 1971; Diop, 1974; Van Sertima, 1983). If our premises are indeed true, having clearly identified the nature of this ancient system of thought, we should be able to distinguish the transmittal of its elements to all late cultures. This article will identify the deep structure of the African cultural heritage in terms of conceptual systems, discuss methods for reclaiming it, and the consequences of nonreclamation. In this instance, our discourse will be restricted to comparing and contrasting the ancient African and modern Euro-American cultural world views as the polar referents of the cultural continuum.

The Deep Structure of Culture

Culture has been defined as the total way of life of a people. A people's way of life may be examined at the level of sensory observation or surface structures, which are subject to relatively rapid change, constrained by time and space, and nongenerative in nature. Or another level of analysis may be the deep structure, which is archetypal, not bound to the specific group, and generative in nature. At the deep level of structural analysis evidence of a certain set of rules or system is sought that affords diagnosis of the features of empirical phenomena (Hammel, 1972).

Nobles (1980) identifies the deep structure of culture as the philosophical assumptions (e.g., ontology, epistemology, axiology, cosmology) underpinning and reflected in the culture's worldview, ethos, and ideology. The outward physical manifestations of culture and its artifacts (i.e., specific languages, specific knowledge of tribal origins, customs, and rituals, African socioeconomic organization, and so on) are amenable to change and/or destruction. However, the worldview yielded by a particular set of philosophical assumptions can be preserved in the conceptual system those assumptions structure. In terms of African/African-American culture, what persevered and developed were the essential qualities of the African worldview, a view concerned with metaphysical rather than purely physical interrelationships, such as that between music and poetry, religious functions and practice, man and nature (Walton, 1972).

Others have detailed the existence of a traditional African worldview, and certain cultural ethos seem continually to predominate (Asante, 1980; Balander and Maquet, 1974; Busia, 1963; Diop, 1978; Forde, 1954; Gerhart, 1978, Levine, 1977; Mbiti, 1970; Nobels, 1972; Parrinder, 1954; Sowande, 1974; Thompson, 1974; Williams, 1976; Zahan, 1979). Dixon (1976) and Nichols (1976) have been particularly clear in delineating and articulating the philosophical assumptions of the worldview. Ontologically, the nature of reality is believed to be at once spiritual and material (spiritual/ material, extrasensory as can be known through the five sense). Self-knowledge becomes the basis of all knowledge in Afrocentric epistemology and one knows through symbolic imagery and rhythm. In terms of axiology, highest value is placed on interpersonal relationships among people. Diunital (union of opposites) logic dominates this worldview and the process is ntuology (all sets are interrelated through human and spiritual networks).

The Afrocentric Conceptual System

Adherence to a cohesive set of philosophical assumptions, such as the one just described, creates a conceptual system, a pattern of beliefs and values that define a way of life and the world in which people act, judge, decide, and solve problems (Albert, 1970). It is this conceptual system that structures the worldview at the level of cultural deep structure to be reflected in surface structure across time/ space. For example, in analysis of the sacred and secular dynamics of the African American communication system, Daniel and Smitherman (1976) identify the traditional African worldview as significant for understanding patterns of black communication in the United States, and the call response pattern as exemplary of a "deep structure" cultural difference.

We can therefore speak reliably in terms of a European conceptual (definitional) system as well as an African conceptual system, each being distinctly different from the other in terms of basic survival thrust and fundamental character (Baldwin, 1980). Describing people of African descent, Asante (1980) acknowledges that they are a people who appreciate the continuum of spirit and matter, not distinguishing between them. Frye (1978) discusses, as the first construct of traditional African philosophical thought, the notion that there is an all-pervasive "energy" that is the source, sustainer, and essence of all phenomena. In contrast, the Western worldview is fragmented with its separation of spirit and matter (Capra, 1975). Rather than emphasize the dynamic unity of all things, such a system focuses on the segmentation of the phenomenal world (e.g., separating mind and body, persons against nature, self and other, and so on). Only within the last quarter century do we find an awareness of this spiritual/material paradigm gaining ground in Western science (Capra, 1975,1982; Gelwick, 1977; Jantsch, 1979; Pelletier, 1978). However, knowledge of the implications of the paradigm shift, for daily functioning still seems to elude Western culture.

The concept of self will be used to illustrate how the Afrocentric system functions. In order to make these ideas more fully comprehensible within a Eurocentric frame of reference, let us first entertain the nature of spirit and matter, the manifestations of spirit. Spirit is defined as that pervasive essence that is known in an extrasensory fashion (i.e., the fastest moving energy, consciousness, God). Think in terms of breaking down matter (the most outward manifestation of spirit). Chemistry has aided in this endeavor, with its periodic table we can identify all of the chemical elements known and their atomic (proton, neutron, electron) configurations. Subatomic physics then allows us to penetrate the nucleus of the atom and discover a particle world in which all particles of a given kind are completely identical. The constituents of particles are more elusive observationally. Strongly interacting particles (hadrons) are believed to be composed of elementary entities called quarks. Our technology does not allow us to "see" quarks or measure them. In modern physics, the question of consciousness has arisen in connection with the observation of these subatomic phenomena. Quantum theory has made it clear that these phenomena can be understood only as links in a chain of processes, the end of which lies in the consciousness of the human observer (Wigner 1970). Subsequently, we have simultaneous levels of existence ranging from the most inward, pervasive, fastest-moving energy, consciousness, to its most outward crystallized form, matter.

In ordinary life in American culture we are not always aware of the unity of all things, but divide the world into separate objects and events. Western culture assumes this division useful and necessary to cope with the everyday environment; however, it is not a fundamental feature of reality. It is an abstraction devised by our discriminating and categorizing intellectual orientation (Capra, 1975). In contrast, the African mind functions holistically, emphasizing the interrelatedness and interdependence of all things.

Africans of traditional culture apprehended a sense of self extended in time to include all of the ancestors, the yet unborn, all of nature, and the entire community (Nobles, 1976; Zahan, 1979). Thus they identified themselves at the level of permeating essence rather than specific outward manifestation (i.e., as consciousness or spirit, rather than individualized material form). According to Zahan (1979), from this point of view the individual does not constitute a closed system in opposition to the outside world in order to better secure her or his own substance and limitations. On the contrary, the individual enters into the surrounding environment, which in turn perpetuates her or him.

Identifying self in this way reflects the idea of holonomy, the whole being contained in each of its parts, which is so characteristic of nature (Bohm, 1980; Chew, 1964; Capra, 1982). The African is at once seeing herself or himself as one with Infinite Consciousness and yet individually, a unique part of that consciousness manifesting. Zahan (1979) speaks of the very widespread, if not universal, belief among Africans in the ability of the individual to "double" herself or himself at certain moments in her or his life. Within this frame of reference, the extended self, Infinite Consciousness, possesses a point of fission that assures man or woman an infinite range of possibilities.

The African extended self is God manifesting, the human being is one with God having structured consciousness through conceptual systems to be divine or supremely good. It is important to note, however, that within this worldview one is not automatically given the status of human being, nor does "dying" automatically make one an ancestor. Both statuses are accorded on the basis of one either evidencing the potential to manifest good consciousness (correct awareness according to the structure of the conceptual system) or in the case of the ancestor, having realized good consciousness in individual/group experience (self-actualized).

The African conceptual system with its spiritual/material ontology and subsequent notion of extended self assumes a self-organizing universe (Jantsch, 1980). The process of ntuology, all sets are interrelated through human and spiritual networks, assures that highest value must be placed on interpersonal relationships between individuals. Zahan (1979) notes that things and beings are not an obstacle to the knowledge of God, rather they constitute signifiers and indices that reveal divine being (i.e., one knows through symbolic imagery and rhythm in the expression of self-knowledge). Establishing the validity and reliability of the conceptual system is not the objective of this article per se (see Myers 1984), but the current paradigm shift of Western science, and Eastern philosophies (Buddhism, Hinduism, and Taoism), endorse the acceptance of such an holistic worldview. It is from the deep structure of traditional African culture that we can learn how to apply the height of this knowledge to everyday experience.

Reclaiming the Afrocentric Worldview

Our purpose in supporting the resurgence of the deep structures of African culture is not for the replication of ancient surface structure culture in modern times. Even if possible, that would be unnecessary, and likely, unbeneficial. For example, ancient Egyptians taught a deification process whereby man or woman could achieve everlasting peace and happiness, called the Egyptian Mystery System (James, 1954). We do not, however, need to go through the form and ritual of the Mystery System itself to benefit from its teachings. Indeed the conceptual system that we would be seeking to achieve would preclude that, because its basic premise is to allow the outward form to change freely while focusing on its source, inward spirit that is unchanging. Once that is accomplished we will have ensured that outward materiality will "take shape" consistent with underlying spirit in a manner far superior to anything a segmented conceptual system could fathom.

Given an Afrocentric conceptual system, life is meant to be carefree (free of worry, anxiety, fear, guilt, frustration, anger, hostility, and so on). The way the system is structured we are one with the source of all things good, and, as such, infinite beings. To the extent, however, we entertain the dominant Eurocentric conceptual system, at best, aspects of that truth will be fragmented in our experience. The choice of conceptual systems is ours; and at all times we can know that the law of mind is working so that whatever we are believing is, is for us at the moment of belief. Power is the ability to define reality.

Asante (1980) speaks of five levels of awareness in our souls. The fifth level, Afrocentricity, occurs "when the person becomes totally changed to a conscious level of involvement in the struggle for his or her own mind liberation." This level of awareness is of course requisite for adoption and maintenance of the Afrocentric conceptual system. The consciousness of the person is totally changed and empowered when he or she establishes the conceptual system of the African culture deep structure. I will now briefly discuss three approaches that will facilitate the reclamation process.

Methods of Reclamation

Young and Hardiman (1983) argue that the Afrocentric perspective can be taught in an academic setting and have devised a curricular approach consisting of five phases for the teaching of literature. I believe their approach is applicable to all disciplines. The first phase they identify is reclamation. This phase entails the documentation of evidence verifying the true African historical record. Phase two is emotional and intellectual identification in which students conduct their own investigations, raising questions and answering them in terms of research of personal relevance. Phase three is demystification in which emphasis is placed on defining and clarifying structural elements, form, content, and other devices of the discipline. In phase four, understanding, students focus on integrating, synthesizing, internalizing, and reflecting what they have learned through analysis of western orthodox work. The last phase, mastery, requires that students demonstrate their understanding by applying the information in a product of their own creation for future generations of humankind and thereby taking their place in the African legacy continuum.

Having analyzed the psychology of black expressiveness, Pasteur and Toldson (1982) provide the following suggestions for realizing and maintaining the Afrocentric identity of being one with nature, a prerequisite to healthy living: cultivate relationships with elements in the natural world; access knowledge of holistic medicine; resist formalizing and standardizing existence; guard against repetitive routines of the same old thing the same way; do some things when you feel like doing them and negotiate for freedom from time compulsion; be as frank, honest, and to the point as possible; move as naturally, relaxed, and rhythmically as possible; love life and self, wishing to see self multiply. In terms of general orientation, they advise asking the question, "It is natural?"

I have devised a psychotherapeutic approach called Belief Systems Analysis (Myers, 1981) for those who seek optimal well-being and wish to make a serious commitment to working at changing conceptual systems. Rooted in the Afrocentric conceptual systems itself, it cannot be called a preferential rational-emotive or cognitive behavioral therapy with complete accuracy, although the elements are there. The client's particular worldview or belief system is juxtaposed against the Afrocentric system we have identified. One system is identified and selected as preferable based upon the consequences it holds for the believer. Depending on the choices made, reality restructuring then takes place in terms of perceptions, cognitions, emotional responses, and behavior.

Because basic universal truths have been identified in the Afrocentric conceptual system, we can find aspects of these same truths in a wide variety of places. Consequently, do not be surprised to find them in Christianity, Islam, Buddhism, Hinduism, Taoism, Human Potential Movements in the West, and so on. Each path taken seems to lead us back to Africa when exhaustive research is done.

Consequences of Nonreclamation

The consequences of not recapturing the deep structure of our cultural heritage are clear, when one considers the options. Adhering to the Eurocentric conceptual system, with its material ontology as primary, inherently means destruction, because by definition materiality is finite and limited. A consciousness rooted in such a worldview will terminate itself (i.e., believe with full expectation it is going to die). We can see the long- and short-term consequences of Eurocentric functioning. Three long-term effects are an ecology thrown out of balance (acid rain, soil erosion, climate shifts, the greenhouse effect), a world on the brink of nuclear destruction, and a bankrupt economy based on totally imbalanced utilization of resources. We likely experience the short-term consequences very personally; they are stress, anxiety, insecurity, jealously, fear, hatred, anger, hostility, families torn apart, seeking peace and finding none.

Noted black psychologist Naim Akbar (1981) describes four categories of mental disorder among African-Americans based upon the consequences of being disenfranchised from our cultural deep structure and manifest in a false sense of self. The first category he identifies as an alien-self disorder. This group of individuals see themselves as material and evaluate their worth by the prevalence of material accoutrements. Assimilating into Euro-American society and denying those factors that have affected us historically and continue to shape us in contemporary society has succeeded in alienating these people from their very selves. Affectation best describes the demeanor of persons with this disorder and sexual problems and perversions are common.

The next category of disorder is the anti-self, which adds to the alien-self overt and covert hostility toward the group of one's origin and by implication toward oneself. According to Akbar, individuals with this disorder are motivated by a personal self-interest, using the approval of the dominant white group as the main influence on their behavior. They are likely models of mental health, according the standards of "democratic sanity" in this society. The apex of their self-rejection may sometimes be seen in the choice of a marriage partner from the dominant inferiorizing group. Fleeting glimpses of their isolation intensifies, in members of this group, their effort toward acceptability by the white dominant group and they become even more aggressive toward their group of origin. People with anti-self disorders are particularly susceptible to manipulation by the dominant group to aid in the suppression and control of progress in the African-American community.

The last category I will discuss here is the self-destructive disorder; people in this group are the most direct victims of oppression. Akbar states that these disorders represent self-defeating attempts to survive in a society that systematically frustrates normal efforts for natural human growth. Members of this category have usually found the doors to legitimate survival locked and out of the urgency for survival selected personally and socially destructive means to alleviate immediate wants. Included in this category would be pimps, prostitutes, substance abusers, and psychotics.

Conclusion

The issues raised in this article regarding the adoption of a conceptual system rooted in the African cultural deep structure are empirically verifiable and warrant further investigation. Autobiography comes as a most highly recommended methodology, simply because it is so purely consistent with the Afrocentric epistemology of self-knowledge as the basis of all knowledge. An open and honest encounter with yourself might be a first step in critical examination, particularly when dealing with the deepest levels of analysis. What are you assuming to be true? And having assumed it, how is it shaping your experience right now? How has it influenced your past? What better-informed choices might you want to make in the future?

The adoption of an Afrocentric conceptual system prompts us to reevaluate every aspect of our being, we begin to see an old world in a new way. As we begin our exploration, we might want to pay particular attention to folklore. Messages that folk are communicating in ordinary day-to-day situations may certainly prove as valuable a source of knowledge as much published information. For example, the ethnocentric histories dominant white culture had produced (Preiswerk and Perrot, 1978) serve primarily to reinforce the status quo rather than enlighten, as is the case with much so-called scholarship. Rather than elaborate on these issues further, suffice it to say that we can afford to be creative, no area of interest should be left untouched. The consequences for not liberating our minds will be ours to pay.

If you can control a person's thinking, you do not have to worry about the person's action. When you determine what a person shall think, you do not have to concern yourself about what the person will do. If you make a person feel that he or she is inferior, you do not have to compel him or her to accept an inferior status, for the person will seek it for himself or herself (Woodson, 1933).

References

Akbar, N. 1981. Mental disorder among African-Americans. *Black Books Bull.* 7(2).

Albert, J. 1970. Conceptual Systems in Africa . The African Experience, Padem, J. & Soja, E. (eds.) *The African Experience*, Vol. 1. Evanston, IL: Northwestern Univ. Press. 99-107.

Asante, M. 1980. *Afrocentricity: The Theory of Social Change.* Buffalo, N.Y.: Amulefi.

Asante, M. 1983. African Linguistics and Communication Continuities. Paper presented at the Fifteenth Annual Conference of the African Heritage Studies Association, New York, N.Y. April.

Balander, G. & Maquet, J. 1974. *Dictionary of Black African Civilization.* New York, N.Y.: Leon Amiel.

Baldwin, J. 1980. The Psychology of Oppression. *Contemporary Black Thought*, Asante, M. and Vandi, R. (eds.). Newbury Park, CA: Sage.

Ben Yochannon, Y. 1971. *Africa: Mother of Western Civilization.* New York, N.Y.: Alkebu-lan.

Bohm, D. 1980. *Wholeness and the Implicate Order.* London: Routledge & Kegan Paul.

Busia, K. A. 1963. The African World View. *African Heritage*, Dracher, J. (ed.). New York, N.Y.: Crowell-Collier.

Capra, F. 1975. *The Tao of Physics.* New York, N.Y.: Bantam.

Capra, F. 1982. *The Turning Point: Science, Society and the Rising Culture.* New York, N.Y. Simon & Schuster.

Chew, G. G., Gell-Mann, M., & Rosenfield, A.H. 1964. Strongly Interacting Particles. *Scientific American.* 210: 74-83.

Cruse, H. 1967. *The Crisis of the Negro Intellectual.* New York, N.Y.: William Morrow and Company, Inc.

Daniel, J. L. & Smitherman, G. 1976. How I got over: Communication Dynamics in the Black Community. *Q. J. of Speech.* 62(1): 239.

Diop, C. A. 1974. *The African Origin of Civilization: Myth or Reality.* New York, N.Y.: Lawrence Hill.

Diop, Cheikh Anta. 1978. *Cultural Unity of Black Africa: Matriarchy and Patriarchy in Antiquity.* Chicago, IL: Third World.

Dixon, V. 1976. World views and research methodology. *African Philosophy: Assumptions and Paradigm for Research on Black Persons,* L. King et al. (eds.). Los Angeles, CA: Fanon Center.

Forde, D. (ed.). 1954. *African Worlds: Studies in the Cosmological Ideas and Social Values of African Peoples.* New York, N.Y.: Oxford Univ. Press.

Frye, C. 1978. *Towards a Philosophy of Black Studies.* San Francisco, CA: R & E. Research Associates Inc.

Gelwick, R. 1977. *The Way of Discovery.* New York, N.Y.: Oxford University Press.

Gerhart, G. M. 1978. *Black Power in South Africa: The Evolution of an Ideology.* Berkeley, CA: University of California Press.

Hammel, E. A. 1972. The Myth of Structural Analysis: Levi-Straus and the three bears. *Addison-Wesley Module in Anthropology (Module xxv).* Reading, MA: Addison-Wesley.

James, G. 1954. *Stolen Legacy.* New York, N.Y.: Philosophical Library.

Iantsch, E. 1980. *The Self-Organizing Universe: Scientific and Human Implications or the Emerging Paradigm of Evolution.* New York, N.Y.: Pergamon.

Karenga, M. 1983. Nationalism: the Problematics of collective vocation. Paper presented at the Seventh Annual Conference of the National Council of Black Studies, Berkeley, April.

Levine, L. W. 1977. *Black Culture and Black Consciousness.* New York, N.Y.: Oxford University Press.

Mbiti, J. 1970. *African Religions and Philosophy.* Garden City, N.Y.: Doubleday.

Myers, G. J. 1980. Belief systems analysis: an African based cognitive therapy. Paper presented at the Thirteenth Annual National Convention of the Association of Black Psychologists, Cherry Hill, NJ, August.

Myers, L. J. (forthcoming) *Understanding an Afrocentric World View: Introduction to an Optimal Psychology.* Dubuque, IA: Kendall/ Hunt.

Myers, L. J. 1984. *The psychology of knowledge: the importance of world view. New England Journal of Black Studies.* 4: 1-12.

Nichols, E. 1976. *The philosophical aspects of cultural differences.* Paper presented at the meeting of the World Psychiatric Association, Ibadan, Nigeria, November.

Nobles, W. 1972. African philosophy: foundations for black psychology. *Black Psychology*, Jones, R. (ed.). New York, N.Y.: Harper & Row.

Nobles W. 1976. Black people in white insanity: an issue for Black community mental health. *Journal of Afro-American Issues.* 4: 21-27.

Nobles, W. 1980. Extended self: re-thinking the so-called Negro self concept. *Black Psychology*, Jones R. (ed.). New York, N.Y.: Harper & Row.

Parrinder, E. G. 1954. *African Tradition Religion.* London: Hutchinson.

Pasteur, A. B & Toldson, I. J. 1982. *Roots of Soul: The Psychology of Black Expressiveness.* Garden City, NY: Anchor/Doubleday.

Pelletier, K. R. 1978. *Towards a Science of Consciousness.* New York, N.Y.: Delacorte.

Preiswerk, P. & Perrot, D. 1978. *Ethnocentrism and History: Africa, Asia and Indian American in Western Textbooks.* New York, N.Y.: NOK.

Sowande, T. 1972. The quest of an African world view: the utilization of African discourse. *Black Communication: Dimensions of Research and Instruction*, Daniel J. (ed.). Washington, DC: National Endowment for the Humanities.

Thompson, R. T. 1974. *African art in Motion.* Los Angeles, CA: University of California Press.

Van Sertima, I. 1983. *Blacks in Science: Ancient and Modern.* New Brunswick, NJ: Transaction.

Walton, O. M. 1972. *Music: Black, White and Blue.* New York, N.Y.: William Morrow.

Wigner, E. P. 1970. *Symmetries and Reflections.* Cambridge, MA: MIT Press

Willams, C. 1976. *The Destruction of Black Civilization.* Chicago, IL. Third World.

Woodson, C. 1933. *The Mis-education of the Negro.* Washington, DC: Associated Publishers.

Young, A. F. & Hardiman, W. J. 1983. A curriculum approach to the teaching of literature from an Afro-centric perspective. Paper presented at the Seventh Annual Conference of the National Council of Black Studies, Berkeley, March.

Zahan, D. 1979. *The Religion, Spirituality, and Thought of Traditional Africa.* Chicago, IL: University of Chicago Press.

Africentric Social Sciences for Human Liberation

Na'im Akbar

Social science represents as much an expression of a people's ideology as it does a defense of that ideology (Asante, 1980). The extent to which that ideology contains elements of implicit oppression is the extent to which that particular social science is in fact an instrument of oppression. Nobles (1978a) discusses the fact that "Western Science, particularly social science, like the economic and political institutions has become an instrument designed to reflect the culture of the oppressor and to allow for the more efficient domination and oppression of African peoples." Consequently, the uncritical acceptance of the assumptions of Western science by African people is to participate in our own domination and oppression. Nobles, in the same discussion, goes on to justify the need for a social science system reflective of our cultural reality. Our objective in this discussion is to identify some characteristics of Western social science and to suggest some alternative assumptions for the establishment of an African social science.

African social scientists have failed to come to grips with the fact that the tools that they have acquired in the course of their training in the Western social science tradition have ill equipped them to deal with the fundamental task of liberating African people—socially, politically, economically, and psychologically. The apparent paradox of increasing numbers of Africans being trained in the social sciences paralleling exponential increases in African social problems is resolved when we understand the implicit character of the training that the African social scientists have received. Again, Nobles (1978a), in his insightful discussion, characterizes the African social scientist operating from this alien framework as being "conceptually incarcerated." He astutely observes:

> The worldview, normative assumptions, and referential frame upon which the paradigm is based, must, like the science they serve, be consistent with the culture and cultural substance of the people. When the paradigm is inconsistent with the cultural definition of the phenomena, the people who use it to assess and or evaluate that phenomena become essentially conceptually incarcerated.

Such an "incarceration" seriously handicaps the African social scientist in his or her objective of human liberation. The "conceptually incarcerated" social scientist has bought the assertion made by Western social scientists that science is an objective and consequently superior form of inquiry. Jacob Carruthers (1972) argues against the valuelessness of science in his masterful discussion of "Science and Oppression." This writer has argued elsewhere (Akbar, 1980) that the "objective" approach does not preclude values because objectivity is a value. When an observer chooses to suspend from his or her observations certain levels of reaction, then this is a value judgment. This is a critical value because it often involves dismissing certain important sources of information that could critically alter what is perceived as real. Ornstein (1981) offers support for this point of view in his observation:

> Science as a mode of knowing involves a limitation of inquiry. The essence of a good experiment is successful exclusion [italics mine]. One factor may be manipulated while a very few other processes are measured.... the method of psychology has itself become the goal; this confusion has led, in the last sixty years, to a 'radical underestimation' of the possibilities.

If such a methodology has resulted in a "radical underestimation" of the possibilities for the Westerners for whom the method was intended to benefit, one cannot fathom the extent of underestimation it has incurred for the people intended to be oppressed by such a perspective.

CHARACTERISTICS OF EURO-AMERICAN SOCIAL SCIENCE

The model that characterizes Euro-American social science can most succinctly be seen in its model of normality. Normality is established on a model of the middle-class, Caucasian male of European descent. The more that one approximates this model in appearance, values, and behavior, the more "normal" one is considered to be. The inevitable conclusion from such assumptions of normality is a brand of deviance for anyone unlike this model. In fact, the more distant or distinct one is from this model the more pathological one is considered to be. The obvious advantage for Euro-Americans is that such norms confirm their reality as the reality and flaunts statements of their superiority as scientifically based "fact." The history of Western social science is replete with evidence of this ethnocentric assumption of normality. Sociology has identified the "middle class" as the normative group. Anthropology has identified all non-Western peoples variously as savage, primitive, or uncivilized. The volumes of psychological literature over the last 100 years has been based on observations primarily on Europeans, exclusively Caucasian, predominantly male, and as Robert Guthrie (1976) has noted, "even the rat was white." The formulations of most of the notable scholars who have shaped the thought of Euro-American psychology such as Freud, Jung, G. Stanley Hall, William McDougall, and B. F. Skinner have all directly or indirectly asserted the superiority of European races over non European races.

Unaware of the ethnocentric assumptions of Western social science, many African scholars have become advocates of their own inferiority by utilizing these theories and their implicit norms. The research and scholarship of these African American social scientists have confirmed the negative assertions of their Euro-American counterparts. It has led to a preoccupation with deviance, deficiency, and an excessive involvement with "victim analysis." Native African scholars have often taken on the position of the neocolonialist scholar advocating the "improvement" of his or her people by the adoption of European personal traits and social patterns (see Fanon, 1967, 1968). African-American scholars have become the neo-slave master and neo-oppressor by advocating success by identification or integration with Euro-Americans as the only basis for success. Our position is not one of minimizing or denying the presence of rampant social and personal problems as a consequence of decades of colonialism and/or oppression and slavery. Such extreme human suffering is undeniable. The problem is that we are extremely limited in the capacity to alter any of these conditions because of the "conceptual incarceration" that Nobles has described and that we identify in this discussion as a kind of paradigmatic stagnation.

A similar difficulty is that of negative identification with the Euro-American social scientist. Such a perspective leads to rather extreme reactions against the Euro-American model. It advocates that whatever has been seen as positive in the European model must necessarily be viewed as negative in a Black model. Whatever has been viewed as negative about Blacks from the perspective of the White model is automatically assumed to be positive in the Black model. The point of this discussion, though it identifies real limitations with the Eurocentric approach, does not presume the Africentric approach to be the obverse. The Africentric model must be viewed as a perspective independent of the Eurocentric model; otherwise, it too will become merely reactive and therefore persistently dependent on the European model.

Models provide the definitions that give rise to methodologies. In fact, models or paradigms very clearly circumscribe not only the "askable" questions, but also the models of observation or methodologies. Ornstein (1981) observes:

> Any community of people holds in common certain assumptions about reality. Each scientific community of physicists, mathematicians, psychologists, or others, shares an additional set of implicit assumptions, called the paradigm.

The paradigm is the shared conceptions of what is possible, the boundaries of acceptable inquiry, the limiting cases.

Methodologies make sense, then, only in the light of models that breed them. In fact, Curtis Banks (1980) argues that methodologies are merely ways to confirm preexisting models. Therefore, understanding of the Eurocentric paradigm is essential for understanding its methodology. In addition to the model being normatively based on the Caucasian, middle-class male of European descent, it also has other characteristics. Among these additional characteristics of the Eurocentric model are that it is individualistic, rationalistic, and materialistic. We shall demonstrate briefly how each of these characteristics, particularly to the exclusion of others, renders a Eurocentric psychology essentially useless as an instrument of human liberation.

The individualistic focus of the model operates with the assumption that the human identity is essentially in the individual. His corporate identity is of secondary significance in conceptualizing the person. As a consequence, much of Western psychology has focused on individual differences as its major consideration. Even sociology deals with society's impact on the individual and history with a series of individual heroes. So fundamental is the assumption that the subject for primary consideration is the individual that most thinkers have difficulty conceiving of an alternative approach without sacrificing or violating the supreme illusion of an autonomous human existence and the sacred freedom of the illusionary being called an "individual." There is, in fact, a growing controversy among Euro-American psychologists as to whether or not there has been an over assertion of the role of independence as a desirable attribute of human beings. Psychological concepts of external fate control, dependence, and submissiveness are all viewed as negative personality characteristics. Such a negation is only a camouflaged assertion for the desirability of the American ideal of the rugged individualistic European immigrant who "single-handedly conquered this wilderness and settled this great country." The idea of the primacy of the individual and his unique motivations, and the nuclear family and its exclusiveness are fundamental concepts in Euro-American social science.

Another characteristic of this model that extends the notion of individualism is the desirability of competition. The fundamental American economic theory is one that glorifies competition as essential for social progress. The most efficiently functioning individuals are those who are most assertive and competitive. The "achievement orientation" is lauded as the prize of Western progress. Human beings are assumed axiomatically to be in conflict and human accomplishment is realized by the triumph of the weak over the strong. The classic McClelland (1961) book, *The Achieving Society*, concluded that a people could be accorded the status of being civilized (that is, industrialized) only if their motivations were characterized by a high need for achievement. Predictably his data showed non-Caucasian, non-European, non-male, non-middle class people to be at the lower end of this fundamental individual characteristic.

Oppressed humanity has failed to realize that in the garb of "science" the Western world has utilized a social and psychological paradigm that functions to legitimize the assertion of their racial and national superiority. What has been assumed to be an apolitical, objective system is, in fact, the essence of Euro-American, Caucasian politics.

To assert that Euro-American social science is rationalistic is to imply that a science should be irrational. Certainly, this is not our intention. It is clear that science as conceived in the Western tradition has some frequently unacknowledged limitations. Ornstein (1981) observes: "Science as a mode of knowing involves a limitation on inquiry." Because of its limitations, critical aspects of the human social process are often excluded from consideration. Ornstein continues:

> It is incomplete to hold that knowledge is exclusively rational. Even scientific inquiry, that most rational and logical of our pursuits, could not proceed without the presence of another type of knowledge.... Scientific investigators act on personal knowledge, biases, hunches, intuition. It is the genius of the scientific method that the arational thought becomes translated into the rational mode and made explicit, so that others can follow it.

Ornstein's designation of the alternative to a rational system as "arational" rather than irrational seems appropriate.

One of the limitations of this rationalistic component of the Euro-American social science model is its exclusion of feeling or affect. Emotion is considered irrelevant at worst and disruptive at best in the scientific endeavor. Great energy is expended to maintain objectivity and to exclude any affective component of the inquiry. The consequence is that such a scientist develops a passive insensitivity that permits and even condones an American slavery system, an Auschwitz, or even a neutron bomb—calmly described as capable of destroying all people, but leaving buildings and physical structures standing. The economist need not address the elements of his or her theory that define excessive opulence for the few to be based on the privation of the many. The observer who gives any demonstration of affective or emotional involvement in his or her subject matter is viewed as inappropriate, distracted, or just irrational and therefore deserves being discounted. Ornstein (1981) makes an observation pertinent to this point:

> We deemphasize and even devalue the arational, nonverbal modes of consciousness. Education consists predominantly of "reading," "ritin" and "rithmetic," and we are taught precious little about our emotions, our bodies, our intuitive capabilities.

Because of our "uneducated" emotional selves we usually remain emotional idiots and fail to obtain the benefits of knowledge that comes from that modality.

The final characteristic of this model, at least for the purposes of this discussion, is its materialistic focus. It is assumed that outer characteristics are essential characteristics. Whether these characteristics are designated as "behavioral data," or "class data," the assumption is that what is directly observable is the "most real." Therefore, what is knowable and what is relevant is restricted to some aspect of the material. Ornstein (1981) again makes a relevant observation to this issue. He states:

> A strict emphasis on verbal intellectual knowledge has screened out much of what is or could be legitimate for study in contemporary psychology — "esoteric" systems of meditation are much misunderstood; the existence of "nonordinary realities" is not studied because they do not fit into the dominant paradigm, and neither, of course, do phenomena named "paranormal. "

From the Western social science perspective, disparaging descriptions of non-Western peoples are made when inferences are made about the human being solely on the basis of material data. A dismissal of esoteric and nonmaterial information has resulted in the description of many intricate practices of non-Western people as "superstitious, pagan, or primitive." Such interpretations are a direct consequence of the Western social scientist's inability to grasp the esoteric. The tendency to fragment behavior from the broader context of the spiritual and esoteric dimensions of reality renders highly meaningful and significant human activities as meaningless and insignificant. It is not surprising that people with less opulent outer appearances are adjudged inferior, uncivilized, unintelligent, and barbaric, even when such people may far surpass the materially affluent in justice, charitableness, compassion, and peacefulness.

In summary, the Euro-American model or paradigm of social science views the characteristics of the Caucasian, middle-class male of European descent to be the paradigmatic norm for human beings. Individualism, rationalism, and materialism are other characteristics of this model that direct the perception and methodologies of Euro-American science. Although these components of any model of human functioning are critical, the limitation of the science ensues from the exclusive reliance on these modalities for observation. The premise of this discussion is that the exclusive reliance on these aspects of the model renders Western social science an effective instrument of human oppression and exploitation. The oppression is likely to be most evident among those least like the paradigmatic model that we have described above. The major objection is that all of these characteristics of Euro-American social science render it an ineffective instrument for human growth and liberation. It should not be surprising from this premise that Europe and America have the largest numbers of social scientists in the world and a greater number of social and human problems than any nation in the world. For example, child molestation, rape, bizarre sexual perversions, drug abuse, child abuse, and even racial conflict are virtually unknown occurrences in most parts of the world, but reach epidemic proportions as one approximates the characteristics of the Euro-American model. The importance of Euro-American social science in providing remedies to these problems is predictable as one evaluates this system as a model for human growth and liberation.

The methodologies emerging from this model are ones that reaffirm the basic assumptions of the model. The method is an "objective" one, the focus is on individual differences and the data is expressed through a count-and-measure system characteristic of material phenomena.

THE AFRICENTRIC MODEL OF SOCIAL SCIENCE

Our discussion of an Africentric model grows out of several assumptions. We do not argue that a model for human liberation should substitute the norm of a Black male of African descent for a Caucasian male of European descent. Such a concretization would merely substitute one limited model for another limited model. "Africentric" is utilized from the perspective that Africa constitutes the primordial context for human growth and liberation. African-Americans represent the most extreme examples of victims of human oppression and would be the most appropriate group on which to demonstrate a liberation psychology. Therefore, our focus is on the African ontological conception of man as a model of humanity in general since Africa represents probably the most "naturally human" concept. Though the model has specific relevance to the national liberation of all African people in the Diaspora, it is more generally applicable to the transformation of human beings in whatever national context.

One of the difficulties entailed in describing this model in a comparative context with the Eurocentric model is the implication that the Africentric model represents a contrast or reaction to the former. As we have noted above, this is definitely not the case in that the Africentric model actually antedates the Eurocentric one that is actually a conceptual devolution from its predecessor. For the sake of cohesion and greater clarity, we will focus on some aspects of this Africentric model that demonstrate its relative strength to the characteristics of Western social science, which we have described above.

AFRICENTRIC NORM

The norm of the Africentric model is nature. The normative characteristics of this social science are based upon the exquisite order of human nature. Vague though this may seem and certainly "unscientific" in the Western tradition, it is considerably more consistent with the philosophical, religious, and symbolic tradition of the most enduring human societies. Though concretely undemonstrable, "human nature" ascribes an order that is both universal and absolute. It is, in fact, metaphysical. Human adaptation and aberration is not to be confused with human potential. Arguments to this effect have been advanced by such Western notables as Maslow, May, Rogers, and many others of the humanistic tradition. Though lacking in the precision of the intricately specific language of the Western social scientist, it is more consistent with the holistic, multidimensional polydeterminism of being human. The oversimplification of Western social science, though impressively more manageable, is disastrously myopic in its exclusion of blatantly causal realities. Logical positivism and reductionism have tried to make men and women thoroughly rational and minute enough to fit a micro model of a unidimensional view of humanity. The Africentric model is comfortable with global conceptions and metaphysical conceptions, and offers a macro model that actually exceeds the manipulation of the observing observer whose object of observation is ultimately himself or herself.

The example of a concept drawn from this naturalistic model is the concept of survival. A consistent characteristic of the natural order is its tendency to preserve itself. Self-preservation has been identified as the "first law of nature." This "law" is derived from folk knowledge and not scientific fact, though it is the type of adage, intuitive or folk wisdom that guides even the structuring of Western science. The Africentric theorist takes such an assumption as an element of his or her paradigm and seeks to observe the consistency with which phenomena obey this "law." It then identifies a norm that is all-inclusive and holistic, which says that normality is any process that operates in consistency with the tendency of nature's self-preservative character. Such a conclusion is not dissimilar to the eminently profound assertion of the "Law of relativity" which maintains that matter can be neither created nor destroyed, that is, it is self-preservative, observing the first law of nature.

Theorists in African philosophy and African psychology, specifically Mbiti (1970) and Nobles (1980), have identified a principle of African social science that they identify as the principle of collective survival or "survival of the tribe." Observations, then, of human behavior can be understood as normal or abnormal to the degree that it adheres to this principle. Behaviors that maintain, enhance, or secure the "survival of the tribe" are normal. Behaviors that threaten the survival of the tribe are abnormal. Again, as Nobles has illustrated, the "normal" family is neither nuclear (that is, the Eurocentric family models) nor extended, as some rejoinders to Eurocentric victim analysis have asserted. The normal family is in fact flexible or "elastic" (Nobles, 1978b), capable of maximizing the fundamental natural objective of its survival. Such a family can be as effectively nuclear as extended, depending upon what kinds of circumstances affected the survival of the family (tribe). The same point is true of functions within the family. According to Nobles (1978b):

> Functionally, or the performance of its (family) functions, would be fluid or elastic. That is, the performance of a particular function does or can "expand" into many other functions.

Such a characterization of family functioning begins to hint of pragmatism. It is functional, but the pragmatism is restricted within the guidelines of natural orderliness. Family survival does require security from harm; it does not require domination in order to secure itself. Though there are barbaric instances of predator orientations that exist in various arenas of nature, because of certain "moral" capabilities of human beings, such qualities cannot be justified as the basis for human oppression. This balancing "moral" component will be discussed at greater length below.

CHARACTERISTICS OF AFRICENTRIC MODEL

The Africentric approach to social science conceptualizes self as a collective phenomenon. It does not deny "uniqueness," but it does deny the isolated notion of individualism, that is, that the person can be understood independent of other persons. The "other" is not just a mirror of the self in the Cooley sense but the "other" is an expression of self. The fundamental adage emerging from African philosophy that captures this collective experience of self is the proposition: "I am because we are and because we are, therefore I am."(Mbiti, 1970). This conception identifies the collective consciousness as the appropriate arena for human observation. Nobles (1980) refers to this as "experiential communality or the sharing of a particular experience by a group of people." The scientific question is not one of how do individuals differ, but in what ways are people fundamentally alike. Again, the holistic balance does not argue for a mass conforming national character, but a sharing of certain universal human values and goals and the degree to which a person's uniqueness facilitates those goals. For example, reproduction of effective human beings is a universal objective that is not violated by individual characteristics though individual freedom is circumscribed by the collective need to realize this objective. So, everyone does not have to reproduce, but everyone is accountable for the health of humanity's offspring.

Nobles (1980) maintains that the experiential communality is important in determining society's fundamental principles such as its belief about the nature of humanity and what kind of society humans should create for themselves. In other words, the work of the social scientist in describing, assessing, or even improving societies or human beings must be a collective rather than an individual phenomena. African social theory ascribes preeminence to the group, unlike the Western ascription of this status to the individual.

Another characteristic of the Africentric paradigm is that it identifies the essence of the human being as spiritual. Certainly a holistic model must include the full dimensions of the human make-up: physical, mental, and metaphysical. In Western dualistic thought, not only is mind and body (reason and emotion) considered to be independent phenomena, but there is a trinitarian tendency that views spirit as independent of both mind and body. Usually, however, spirituality is completely discounted in Western social science. Increasingly, with the growing emphasis on behavior in the social sciences, even the mental dimension or consciousness has been discounted as irrelevant to understanding human functioning. Relative to the Eurocentric approach, the Africentric social scientists take a "quantum leap" when they identify spirituality as a relevant dimension of the human experience.

The concept of humanity's essential spirituality merely suggests that when men and women are reduced to their lowest terms they are invisible and of a universal substance. Such an assumption implies that, ultimately, people are harmoniously alike and not dissimilar to the essence of all that is in nature. Oneness with nature is a natural extension of this point of view that precludes assumptions of inevitable conflict among men and women and with nature. Material, by its very nature, is fragmented and in conflict, obeying principles of polarity and tension. To the extent that the material dimension of human beings is viewed as their essence is the extent to which conflict is viewed as axiomatic to human existence.

The Africentric approach, viewing humanity as ultimately reducible to a universal substance that is harmonious with the entire cosmos, implies the fundamental goodness of humans— goodness being the tendency of life to enhance life in a constructive direction. Human relationships are considered potentially as compatible as are the relationships among all of the mutually facilitating components of nature. Consequently, morality is endemic to this conception of man. The Africentric social scientist does not shy away from articulating that that which is normal is also good. Morality and spirituality are inseparate, which is why both dimensions have been relegated to the domain of the theologian in the Eurocentric approach. However, the values that are made explicit in the Africentric approach are implicitly present in the Eurocentric approach. As we have noted above, objectivity is as much an implicit value as that attributed to the explicit values in a subjective system. There is a widely accepted myth of objectivity among Eurocentric social scientists. Since spirituality implies order, harmony, interdependence, and perfectibility then morality is a fundamental component of the human make-up. Morality, in the Africentric approach, is not in the form of the series of maxims found in the Eurocentric theological moral systems. Morality simply is an acknowledgement of a natural order and normality is man's harmony with that order.

Morality also constitutes a uniquely human trait. It represents the human being's capacity for self-mastery and self-direction. Unlike the lower animal species regulated by instinct, the human being has the unique capacity for self-regulation. This exonerates the human being from some of the more brutish components of the natural order. This moral form permits human beings to be in nature but not of nature in the sense of falling victim to some of its more destructive components. Morality becomes the instrumentation of balance and, in the Africentric model, it is an imperative of the human make-up and not an option.

However, the Africentric model does not deny the relevance of materiality. In fact, this model represents a balance between the extreme material and exoteric ontology represented in the Eurocentric model and the extreme spiritual and esoteric ontology represented in the Eastern models. This model will permit cross validation between subjective and objective experience. An example of this model is perhaps seen in the African traditional healer. Such healers are simultaneously herbalists (users of objective power) and griots (reciters of "self" or conjurers of subjective power). The traditional healer recognized the interdependence of moral order and material order. A violation in either impacts on all dimensions of the human make-up. Such an approach does not demand a denial of material mastery or technological advancement, but it demands a balanced development of the inner and outer worlds. In such a world, one does not construct huge skyscrapers as a precipice from which the deranged may throw themselves. Instead, one's skill in scaling the heights of gravity is paralleled by exploring the depths of the human make-up.

The final characteristic of an Africentric social science is its epistemological assumptions. As we have observed above, the rationalism of Eurocentric social science precludes the arational, consequently excluding much of the human experience. The Africentric approach assumes a universal knowledge rooted in knowledge of the make-up of the human beings themselves. The most direct experience of the self is through emotion or affect. Vernon Dixon (1976) observes:

> Homeland and overseas African persons know reality predominantly through the interaction of affect and symbolic imagery, that is, the synthesis of these two factors produce knowledge. In the "pure" Africanized worldview of the unity of man and the phenomenal world, there is no empty perceptual space between the self and phenomena. Affect refers to the feeling self, the emotive self engaged in experiencing phenomena holistically.

This approach of Africentricity admits both symbols and affect as legitimate determiners of human activity. Emotional reactions as a means of knowing and as a balance for rationality is legitimate within this model. Similarly, the significance of symbols in the Jungian tradition as an expression of certain collective archetypes is also an approach of value. Cultural symbols and rituals (such as naming ceremonies and puberty rites in traditional societies) are considered as important causative dimensions in human experience. Such symbols in Western science would have little validity as either independent or dependent variables, but in the Africentric paradigm they could be either. Dixon (1976) further characterizes this affect/ symbolic connection by observing:

> Affect, however, is not intuition, for the latter term means direct or immediate knowledge (instinctive knowledge) without recourse to inference from or reasoning about evidence. Affect does interact with evidence, evidence in the form of symbolic imagery.

Such holistic knowledge is critical in terms of both structuring the Africentric methodology as well as characterizing the appropriateness of certain observations. For example, rather than intelligence being defined as what is measured by an IQ test (that is, defining both a methodology and an arena of observation), intelligence would be defined by a person's adequacy in living and developing. Knowledge would be reflected in the degree to which a person is capable of maneuvering an environment offering obstacles to his or her development. So, intelligence would be reflected in the degree to which a person is capable of maneuvering an environment offering obstacles to his or her collective self's development. Consequently, intelligence would entail (1) knowledge of the collective reality of self, (2) knowledge of environmental obstacles to effective (collective) self-development, (3) actions initiated to remove or master such obstacles, and ultimately (4) knowledge of the Divine and universal laws that guide human development into knowledge of the

Creator. An adequate assessment of intelligence would require effectively tapping the full range of a people's symbolic imagery (such as, words, gestures, tones, rhythms, rituals). One could not evaluate a person's "knowledge" without knowing how effectively that person conducts his or her full being. Therefore, the possibility of a man or woman being assessed a genius on the basis of his or her external knowledge yet proving to be morally inept would not be conceivable from the Africentric approach. Similarly, a society with opulent technology but social and moral decadence could not be viewed as an advanced or model civilization.

CONCLUSION

Africentricity is the form of a new paradigm for the social sciences. It grows out of the increasing inadequacy of the Eurocentric model to address the escalating social problems of Western society adequately. Most importantly, the model seeks to correct the indirect oppressive function played by traditional Western science. Although the model is based upon the tenets of traditional African philosophy, it does not exclude in its fundamental assumptions the possibility for normative activity on the parts of people of other ethnic origins. The new paradigm in fact formalizes and provides a context for many of the issues that are increasingly being raised by Western social scientists themselves. Theorists such as Abraham Maslow, Rollo May, Alan Watts, and many others out of the existential and humanistic schools have addressed many of the same issues that are raised within the Africentric context and are resolved within the Africentric model.

The most important element offered by the Africentric paradigm is the opportunity for genuine human liberation through the social science model. An objective of Africentric social science is human liberation. Since it deals specifically with the humanly oppressive conditions experienced by African people throughout the Diaspora, it has an immediate objective of offering an instrument for the social, political, economic, and psychological liberation of our people. The holistic quality of the model offers direction not only for such social liberation but an avenue for human liberation in general.

The course of such liberation is through the vehicle of transformation. An individualistic, materialistic, and rationalistic model to the exclusion of other modalities seriously limits the possibility for human transformation. Human potential is limited according to this model and people can at best be modified, but not transformed. A collective, spiritual, and affect/symbolic system addresses a multidimensional being capable of vast potential and the capacity for transformation.

It is appropriate that this paradigm should be pioneered by African people. With our worldview completely denied in the Eurocentric paradigm, we became ready victims to the misrepresentation of their social science. It is within the humanistic tradition of Africans that we should evolve a system that not only retrieves our humanity but offers the opportunity of human advancement for all people.

References

Akbar, N. (1980) *The evolution of human psychology for African-Americans.* Published manuscript presented to SREB Student Conference, Atlanta.

Asante, Molefi K. (1980) *Afrocentricity: The Theory of Social Change.* Buffalo: Amulefi.

Banks, C. (1980) *Specifications for theories within Black Psychology.* Presented at 13th National Convention of the Association of Black Psychologists, Cherry Hill, NJ.

Carruthers, J. (1972) *Science and Oppression.* Chicago: Northeastern Illinois University Center for Inner City Studies.

Dixon, V. (1976) Worldviews and Research Methodology *African Philosophy: Paradigms for Research on Black Persons.* L. King et al. (eds.). Los Angeles, CA: Fanon Research and Development Center.

Fanon, F. (1968) *The Wretched of the Earth.* New York, N.Y.: Grove Press.

Fanon, F. (1967) *Black Skin, White Masks.* New York, N.Y.: Grove Press.

Guthrie, R. (1976) *Even the Rat was White: A Historical View of Psy*chology. New York, N.Y.: Harper & Row.

Mbiti, J. (1970) *African Religions and Philosophy.* Garden City, NY: Anchor Books (Doubleday).

McClelland, D. (1961) *The Achieving Society.* New York N.Y.: Van Nostrand.

Nobles, W. (1980) African Philosophy Foundations for Black Psychology. *Black Psychology* (2nd ed.). R. Jones (ed.). New York, NY: Harper & Row.

Nobles, W (1978a). *African Consciousness and Liberation Struggles: Implications for the Development and Construction of Scientific Paradigms.* Presented at Fanon Research and Development Conference, Port of Spain, Trinidad.

Nobles, W (1978b). The Black Family and its Children: The Survival of Humaness. *Black Books Bull.* 6, 2: 6-14.

Ornstein, R. (1981). *The Psychology of Consciousness.* New York, N.Y.: Penguin Books.

The Quest for a Method

Molefi Kete Asante

The most important finding of modern intellectual history is that all analysis flows from ideological assumptions. Whether one argues from a deconstructionist or Marxist point-of-view there are certain assumptions based on certain integrated assertions that could constitute a sociopolitical or cultural program.

An Afrocentric method, therefore, must be concerned with the liberation of oppressed people and is consequently engaged in discovering a frame of reference that will explain the speaking and writing of oppressed people. In the contemporary world, phenomenology, hermeneutics, structuralism, deconstruction, feminism and Marxism cannot be applied whole cloth to African themes and subjects without caveats. Based as they are on Eurocentric assumptions and objectives they fail to come to terms with fundamental cultural differences or more distant ideological assumptions. It is possible for example to mistake European agitation, manifested as rhetorical reaction to social and political repression, with African protest discourse that seeks the removal of oppression. One could make such an application in the case of the difference between the Palestinian's protest for total liberation and the German agitation for lower taxes. There is a major degree of difference in these two cases. I have always said that repression presumes that the persecuted have certain rights; oppression is the denial of these rights and humanity (Asante, 1998: 173).

The political, cultural, and economic condition of African people in the Americas, Caribbean, and Africa underscores the need for a method that will interrogate that condition. Since we are on a journey to regain freedom, then our method must be based on this predominant myth. We are not dibbling and dabbling around the edges of life in our quest for liberation; we are searching for ways to liberate ourselves and other human beings. I cannot think of a more fitting path for scholars to be on than this road to freedom. But first, we must challenge the universality of Eurocentric concepts. It is impossible to advance a particular cultural idea as universal without seeking to grasp territory, mental as well as real.

Perhaps the best approach to the problem of method is to examine the constituent elements in Afrocentric discourse to demonstrate how these constituents differ from others; and to suggest ways to turn Afrocentric theory toward a critical method for perfecting African American discourse as a liberating word against all oppressive words. What I have observed from the literature in various communication fields is that the perspective on discourse, whether critical or conciliatory, is essentially Eurocentric. While a Eurocentric vision is necessary perhaps for a person from a particular cultural and educational milieu, it cannot privilege itself as universal. I believe that as a particular viewpoint the Eurocentric stance should take its place alongside all other centric views. The categorical universal in theory, criticism, and practice is hopelessly flawed and cannot be recuperated.

As I read literary theory and communication theory in the modern and postmodern worlds it seems to me that the purposes of those disciplines have been to rescue the depravity of thought, the carnage of ruined dreams, and the death of vision engendered by the first and second great European wars. It is no wonder that since September 11, 2001, the same disciplines have rushed to examine the nature of terror in the world as if terror did not exist prior to the destruction of the World Trade Towers in New York. Two weeks after the tragedies, one great American university had sixty-five course proposals to study political violence and global terror.

Prior to September 11, 2001, Hitler was the most terrifying monster in European consciousness and consequently in the minds of African people as well. But Hitler had shattered Europe's vision of itself as morally superior although Europeans were quick to add that there was nothing wrong with the Aryan intellectual superiority as it was masked in the myths of German scientific heroics. Now we will see the real objective of the social sciences and liberal arts in the Western Academy as they pounce on this new terror, the Arab religious fanatic as morally inferior and inherently insane. Unfortunately, many other people will paint the Arab world and its people with the same broad brush as the juggernaut of Western self-righteousness moves along its path. Hitler's problem had been that he dared to enslave European people. Had he turned his wrath on Arabs or Africans instead of Europeans he would have become like Alexander, like King Leopold of Belgium, and like the German Kaiser Wilhelm, great heroes in the European style.

Thus, it was out of Europe's concern with its place in the world and what it saw as the potential for Western decline brought on by the first Great European War that Edmund Husserl's phenomenology and Martin Heidegger's hermeneutics, both inextricably absorbed in European culture, rose without apology or reservation to announce that Europe was not giving up intellectual leadership although it was morally bankrupt. Husserl's *The Crisis of European Sciences* drew from an ideological context where irrationalism flourished, and a bewildering array of sterile positivism appeared to scare the spirit out of European thought (Husserl, 1935). This was the time of Lester Thonssen, A. Craig Baird, Charles Lomas, Donald Bryant, and Carrol Arnold in the communication field. They felt the same intense desire and need to rationalize life in the midst of so much European irrationality. Another moment in the transformation of European thought was when the rage of Hitler caused scholars like Northrop Frye, Roman Jakobson, and Claude Levi-Strauss to hope for either the totalization of all literary genre or the seizure of a speech or text as an object in space, synchronically apart from any polluting social or political facts (Levi-Strauss, 1966). They hoped in vain. Sartre emerges also, post-War, to deal with the problem of analytical reason in his *Critique de la raison dialectique*. He was among the earliest Western writers to understand the complications of traditional Western analysis. He opposed dialectical to analytical reasons and claimed that the transcendental materialists, those who believed that dialectical reason was merely an extension of analytical reason, did not understand that dialectical reason was none other than the very movement of totalization (Sartre, 1960). This is close to the Mande conception of *woron* which means "to get to the essence" of anything. Thus, the Mande people seek to *yere-wolo*, that is, "to give birth to self." Sartre understood that dialectical knowledge came from the moment of totalization, not in a reflection of the moment but in the process itself. Inasmuch as he understood this idea that totalization goes on inside the moment he understood something of what Afrocentrists mean when we say that experiences must be reflective in the singularity of the moment. Sartre is challenged on this point by other Western writers. Levi-Strauss proceeding on the Marxist path argues a more traditional European idea when he says that the idea is not to constitute man but to dissolve man. In effect, studying humans for such "aesthetes" is not unlike studying ants, pigs, mice. In some respects, Levi-Strauss might be said to have foreshadowed Jacques Derrida and Foucault.

The fact that Sartre tries to escape the confusion he finds in traditional Western thought is to be applauded, but alas, I cannot accept Sartre's notion that freedom in an individual sense is the only meaningful expression of freedom when the direct, real, lived experiences of Africans say that freedom comes in community.

I cannot accept any ideological position that discusses Africans as the "other," whether capitalized or not. In fact, I believe that constructions such as "The Black Atlantic," "double consciousness," and the "Other" promote a Eurocentric supremacy and misstate the *agency*, that is, the evolving ownership and action of Africans' subject role. The Eurocentric writer, whether black or white, seeks to undermine African agency by artificially constructing, even in a postmodern way, the elements of Africanity. Alterity is an attack on centricity; it seeks to relocate the centeredness of the African away from Africa. Paul Gilroy's *The Black Atlantic: Modernity and Double Consciousness* in many ways continues the view on social death held by Orlando Patterson. Both Gilroy

147

and Patterson, located conceptually outside the African world, seemed not to have redressed in their own minds the conditions of intellectual oppression. For example, Patterson writes "the slave was someone who by choosing physical life had given up his freedom. Although he could, of course, have kept his freedom and died" (Patterson, 1982). He is thus making a judgment of moral failure by stating that the slave "lacked the courage to make such a choice" (Patterson). It is not correct to say that the African lacked courage to die. What the enslaved African demonstrated was the courage to choose life so that more abundant life might be possible the next day in the face of death. Indeed when death came it was welcomed, but suicide was not considered a sign of courage but a form of cowardice, escapism. We know from the historical records that Africans were not afraid to challenge the institution of enslavement. They did in every country where slavery existed from Brazil to the United States. Enslaved Africans did not shrank from death when they understood the possibility of life. It is only acting, when they did not have to, in the face of the certainty of death that was considered foolhardy.

Unfortunately, Gilroy takes a false turn in casting the African experience across the West African Ocean as disconnected from the continental African cultures. This is his most massive error. Such separation creates, *inter alia*, a multitude of problems with understanding the African as agent. Gilroy's fundamental mistake is to assume that there is some different order of hybridity in African cultures in the diaspora compared to African cultures on the continent. Indeed, all African cultures reflect, in either the recent or the remote past, evidence of hybridity, and to separate out the experience of Africans in the diaspora without appreciating the cultural roots in Africa is to construct "a mulatto consciousness" and impose it as an African consciousness.

Ways of Knowing: Afrocentricity does not reside in the glitches of the rationalism of European modernism or the aestheticism of European postmodernism. A symbol revolution which has attempted to show that the hallowed concepts of Western thought, rationality, objectivity, progress, are inadequate to explain all of the ways of knowing was initiated by the Civil Rights Movement. There were, of course, problems of focus. We were articulating a perspective about education that was radical even as we argued that Black Studies was not simply the study of African people but the Afrocentric study of African people. This movement was to inaugurate an entire system of thinking about social sciences and criticism and pointed to the inherent problems of Eurocentric theory when applied to the black literary and rhetorical movements. The intrinsic problems in Western discourse theory were revealed as systemic because even those who were sympathetic to civil rights often used a Eurocentric framework to speak of "agitative rhetoric," "protest literature," and so forth when we should never have forced ourselves to take that position. Thus, even in that situation the European center was assumed and the burden of proof rested with those called dissenters, dissidents, oppressed, or disturbers of myths.

As one of Western culture's chief ideals, objectivity has often protected social and literary theory from the scrutiny that would reveal how theory has often served the interests of the ruling classes. In this respect, it is like other disciplines that have been carved out of the arts and sciences. Although the 1960s and 1970s brought the Yale deconstructionists—Paul de Man, J. Hillis Miller, Geoffrey Hartman, and others—the whole intellectual enterprise could not be divorced from its internal framework. More damaging yet is the inability of European intellectuals to understand that human actions cannot be understood apart from the emotions, attitudes, and cultural definitions of a given context. The Afrocentric thinker understands the interrelationship of knowledge with cosmology, society, religion, medicine, and traditions stand alongside the interactive metaphors of discourse as principal means of achieving a measure of knowledge about experience.

Defining Afrocentric Discourse: I suggest three fundamental Afrocentric themes of transcendent discourse: (1) human relations, (2) human relationship to the supernatural; and (3) humans' relationships to their own being. I would propose the same areas for any culture and under any conceivable circumstances. To posit these three general areas is to try to diffuse some of the specific issues that occur as universals in contemporary analyses. Almost all knowledge has cultural relevance and must be examined for its particular focus. Cultural differences do exist and must be explained by perspective in any discussion of themes. Take the Ebonics example in language ("Got no money!"), or the fact that guilt and innocence elicit different responses in whites and blacks. We need more cultural data to develop something like an oratory or literary file or else Europe would even take African thinking as its own, so arrogant are those who believe that the only theorists are European.

Certain Afrocentric assumptions are necessary when we discuss African American discourse, both in its theory and its criticism. First, we assume that the objective of such discourse, on the whole, is the successful presentation of one of the three principal themes, often within the context of resistances to oppression, liberation from stereotypes, and action in anticipation of reaction. Secondly, we assume that that discourse conforms to certain elementary materials of our corpus of culture; this would suggest stylistic and argumentative features as well. Thirdly, we assume that the discourse is directed principally toward either a black, a nonblack, or a mixed audience. Furthermore, we assume that the discourse will make certain adjustments to each type of audience.

Since so much of African American discourse occurs within a Eurocentric context, it is necessary to isolate those aspects of a critical theory, derived from the conditions, that are applicable to discourse. The assumptions serve as emblematic stools upon which to rest the critical case. One cannot rightly call any African American discourse, merely because it is uttered by a black person, Afrocentric. In fact, donning the agbada of a critics, I believe that much so-called black discourse is essentially white discourse by black people. A black person's writing does not make the writing Afrocentric, no more than living in Africa makes a person Afrocentric.

A critical method applied to Afrocentric discourse presents a positive rather than a reactionary posture. When it is used to assess African American writers it would be considered a severe method because it would expose their lack of an

Afrocentric consciousness, much as Marxist methods would expose the class-based rhetoric of George Bush, Ronald Reagan, or Woodrow Wilson. While I do not castigate any other method, for all methods are valid within their contexts, I believe that analysis is culturally centered and flow from ideological commitments. To understand and appreciate the dilemma of African American writers and speakers trained in the West one has to study discourse from an Afrocentric perspective. This, therefore, is a continuation of a quest for the theoretical and critical equilibrium necessary for placing African American discourse in its proper place. What is true of discourse is also true of other forms of human activity.

References

Asante, Molefi. 1998. *The Afrocentric Idea*. Philadelphia, PA: Temple University Press.

Gilroy, Paul. 1993. *The Black Atlantic: Modernity and Double Consciousness*. Cambridge, MA: Harvard University Press.

Husserl, Edmund. 1935. *The Crisis of European Sciences*. Evanston, IL: Northwestern University Press.

Levi-Strauss, Claude. 1966. *The Savage Mind*. Chicago, IL: University of Chicago Press.

Patterson, Orlando. 1982. *Slavery and Social Death*. Cambridge, MA: Harvard University Press.

Sartre, Jean-Paul. 1960. *Critique de la raison dialectique*. Paris: Gallimard.

3. AFROCENTRIC THEORIES

Africana Womanism

Clenora Hudson-Weems

> Feminism. You know how we feel about that
> embarrassing Western philosophy? The destroyer of homes.
> Imported mainly from America to ruin nice African women.
>
> Ama Ata Aidoo, 1986.

Central to the spirit of Africanans (Continental Africans and Africans in the diaspora) regarding feminism in the African community is the above quotation by internationally acclaimed African novelist and critic, Ama Ata Aidoo. One of today's most controversial issues in both the academy and the broader community is the role of the Africana woman within the context of the modern feminist movement. Both men and women debating this issue, particularly as it relates to Africana women in their efforts to remain authentic in their existence, such as prioritizing their needs even if the needs are not of primary concern for the dominant culture. The ever-present question remains the same: what is the relationship between an Africana woman and her family, her community, and her career in today's society that emphasizes -in the midst of oppression, human suffering, and death- the empowerment of women and individualism over human dignity and rights?

While many academicians uncritically adopt feminism in its established theoretical concepts based on the notion that gender is primary in women's struggle in the patriarchal system, most Africana women in general do not identify with the concept in its entirety and thus cannot see themselves as feminists. Granted, the prioritizing of female empowerment and gender issues may be justified for those women who have not been plagued by powerlessness based on ethnic differences; however, that is certainly not the case for those who are Africana women. Those Africana women who do adopt some form of feminism do so because of feminism's theoretical and methodological legitimacy in the academic community. Moreover, they adopt feminism because of the absence of a suitable framework for their individual needs as Africana women today -in the academy and in the community- are reassessing the historical realities and the agenda for the modern feminist movement. These women are concluding that feminist terminology does not accurately reflect their reality or their struggle. Hence, feminism -even qualified as Black feminism, which relates to African-American women in particular- is extremely problematic as a label for the true Africana woman and invites much debate and controversy among today's scholars and women in general.

It should be noted here that there is another form of feminism that is closely identified with Africana women around the world. While African feminism is a bit less problematic for Africana women than is feminism in general, it is more closely akin to Africana womanism. According to African literary critic Rose Acholonu, in a paper she presented in July 1992 at the first international conference on women in Africa and the African Diaspora: Bridges across Activism and the Academy, Nsukka, Nigeria:

> The negative hues of the American and European radical
> feminism have succeeded in alienating even the fair-minded
> Africans from the concept. The sad result is that today [the]
> majority of Africans (including successful female writers)
> tend to disassociate themselves from it.

Hence, in spite of the accuracy of Filomina Chioma Steady in her astute assessment of the struggle and reality of Africana women (*The Black Woman Cross-Culturally*), the very terminology "African feminism" is problematic, as it inevitably suggests an alignment with feminism, a concepts that has been alien to the plight of Africana women from its inception. This is particularly the case in reference to racism and classism, which are prevailing obstacles in the lives of Africana people, a reality that the theorist herself recognizes. According to Steady (1981:23-4):

> Regardless of one's position, the implications of the
> feminist movement for the black woman are complex...
> Several factors set the black woman apart as having a different
> order of priorities. She is oppressed no simply because of her
> sex but ostensibly because of her race and, for the majority,
> essentially because of their class. Women belong to different
> socioeconomic groups and do not represent a universal
> category. Because the majority of black women are poor, there
> is likely to be some alienation from the middle-class aspect of
> the women's movement which perceives feminism as an
> attack on men rather than on a system which thrives on
> inequality.

In an essay, "African Feminism: A Worldwide Perspective" (Terborg-Penn et al., 1987), Steady asserts (1987:18-9) that

> For the majority of black women poverty is a way of life. For the majority of black women also racism has been the most important obstacles in the acquisition of the basic needs for survival. Through the manipulation of racism, the world economic institutions have produced a situation which negatively affects black people, particularly black women ... What we have, then, is not a simple issue of sex or class differences but a situation which, because of the racial factor, is castlike in character on both a national and global scale.

It becomes apparent, then, that neither the terms Black feminism nor African feminism are sufficient to label women of such complex realities as Africana women, particularly as both terms, through their very names, align themselves with feminism.

Why not feminism for African women? To begin with, the true history of feminism, its origin and its participants, reveals its blatant racist background, thereby establishing its incompatibility with Africana women. Feminism, earlier called the Woman's Suffrage Movement in the United States, started when a group of liberal, white women, whose concerns then were for abolition of slavery and equal rights for all people regardless of race, class, and sex, dominated the scene among women on the national level during the first half of the nineteenth century. At the time of the Civil War, such leaders as Susan B. Anthony and Elizabeth Cady Stanton held the universalist philosophy on the natural rights of women to full citizenship, which included the right to vote. However, in 1870 the Fifteenth Amendment to the Constitution of the United States ratified the voting rights of Africana men, leaving women, white women in particular, and their desire for the same rights, unaddressed. Middle-class white women were naturally disappointed, for they had assumed that their efforts toward securing full citizenship for Africana people would ultimately benefit them, too, in their desire for full citizenship as voting citizens. The result was a racist reaction to the Amendment and towards Africanans in particular. Thus, from the 1880s on, an organized movement among white women shifted the pendulum to a radically conservative posture on the part of white women in general.

In 1890 the National American Suffrage Association (NAWSA) was founded by northern white women, but "southern women were also vigorously courted by that group" (Giddings,1984:81), epitomizing the growing race chauvinism of the late nineteenth century. The organization, which brought together the National Woman Suffrage Association, departed form Susan B. Anthony's original women's suffrage posture. They asserted that the vote for women should be utilized chiefly by middle-class white women, who could aid their husbands in preserving the virtues of the Republic from the threat of unqualified and biological inferiors (Africana men) who, with the power of the vote, could gain a political foothold in the American system. For example,

155

staunch conservative suffragist leader Carrie Chapman Catt and other women of her persuasion insisted on strong Anglo-Saxon values and white supremacy. They were interested in banding with white men to secure the vote for pure whites, excluding not only Africanans but white immigrants as well. Historians Peter Carrol and David Nobles (1977: 296) quoted Catt in the *Free and the Unfree* as saying that "there is but one way to avert the danger. Cut off the vote of the slums and give it to [white] women." She continued (Carrol & Nobles, 1977: 296) that middle-class white men must recognize "the usefulness of woman suffrage as a counterbalance to the foreign vote, and as a means of legally preserving white supremacy in the South"). These suffragists felt that because Africana people (Africana men in particular, with their new status as voters) were members of an inferior race, they should not be granted the right to vote in advance of the female "half" of the dominant group. Thus, while the disappointment of being left out in the area of gaining full citizenship -i.e., voting rights- for white women was well-founded, their hostility and racist, antagonistic feelings toward Africanans in general cannot be dismissed lightly.

Feminism, a term conceptualized and adopted by white women, involves an agenda that was designed to meet the needs and demands of that particular group. For this reason, it is quite plausible for white women to identify with feminism and the feminist movement. Having said that, the fact remains that placing all women's history under white women's history, thereby giving the latter the definitive position, is problematic. In fact, it demonstrates the ultimate in racist arrogance and domination to suggest that authentic activity of women resides with white women. Hence, African women activists in America in particular, such as Sojourner Truth (militant abolitionist spokesperson and universal suffragist), Harriet Tubman (Underground Railroad conductor who spent her lifetime aiding African slaves, both male and female, in their escape to the North for freedom), and Ida B. Wells (anti-lynching crusader during the early twentieth century), can be considered *pre*feminists, despite the fact that the activities of these Africana women did not focus exclusively on women's issues. In view of the activities of early Africana women such as those mentioned above and countless other unsung Africana heroines, what white feminist have done in reality was to take the life-style and techniques of Africana women activists and use them as models or blueprints for the framework of their theory, and then name, define, and legitimize it as the only real substantive movement for women. Hence, when they define a feminist and feminist activity, they are, in fact, identifying with independent Africana women, women they both emulated and envied. Such women they have come in contact from the beginning of American slavery, all the way up to the modern Civil Rights Movement with such African women activists as Mamie Till Mobley, the mother of Emmie Louis Till, and Rosa Parks, the mother of the Modern Civil Rights Movement. Therefore, when Africana women come along and embrace feminism, they are in reality duplicating the duplicate.

Africana womanism is a term that I coined in 1987 after nearly two years of publicly debating the importance of self-naming for Africana women. Why the term *"Africana Womanism"*? Upon concluding that the term "Black

Womanism" was not quite the terminology to include the total meaning desired for this concepts, I decided that *"Africana Womanism,"* a natural evolution in naming, was the ideal terminology for two basic reasons. The first part of the coinage, *Africana,* identifies the ethnicity of the woman being considered, and this reference to her ethnicity, establishing her cultural identity, relates directly to her ancestry and land base: Africa. The second part of the term, *Womanism,* recalls Sojourner Truth's powerful impromptu speech "And Ain't I a Woman," one in which she battles with the dominant alienating forces in her life as a struggling Africana woman, questioning the accepted idea of womanhood. Without question, she is the flip side of the coin, the co-partner in the struggle for her people, one who, unlike the white woman, has received no special privileges in American society. But there is another crucial issue that accounts for the use of the term woman(ism). The term "woman," and by extension "womanism," is far more appropriate than "female" ("feminism") because of one major distinction -only a female of the human race can be a woman. "Female," on the other hand, can refer to a member of the animal or plant kingdom as well as to a member of the human race. Furthermore, in electronic and mechanical terminology, there is a female counterbalance to the male correlative. Hence, terminology derived from the word "woman" is more suitable and more specific when naming a group of the human race - in a word, more "human."

The Africana womanist is not to be confused with Alice Walker's "womanist" as presented in her collection of essays entitled *In Search of Our Mothers' Gardens.* According to Walker (1983: xii), a womanist is:

> A black feminist or feminist of color ... who loves other women, sexually and/or nonsexually. Appreciates and prefers women's culture ... [and who] sometimes loves individual men, sexually and/or nonsexually. Committed to survival and wholeness of entire people, male and female ... Womanist is to feminist as purple to lavender.

Clearly the interest here is almost in the woman: *her* sexuality and *her* culture. The culminating definition, "womanist is to feminism as purple is to lavender," firmly establishes the author's concept of the affinity between the womanist and the feminist. There is hardly any differentiation, only a slight shade of difference in color. The Africana womanist, on the other hand, is significantly different from the mainstream feminist, particularly in her perspective on and approach to issues in society. This is to be expected, for obviously their historical realities and present stance in society are not the same. African women and white women come from different segments of society and, thus, feminism as an ideology is not equally applicable to both.

Neither an outgrowth nor an addendum to feminism, *Africana womanism is not* black feminism, African feminism, or Walker's womanism that some Africana women have come to embrace. *Africana womanism* is an ideology created and designed for all women of African descent. It is grounded in *African* culture and, therefore, it necessarily focuses on the unique experiences, struggles, needs, and desires of Africana women. It critically addresses the dynamics of the conflict between the mainstream feminist, the black feminist, the African feminist, and Africana womanist. The conclusion is that Africana womanism and its agenda are unique and separate from both white feminism and Black feminism; moreover, to the extent of naming in particular, Africana womanism differs from African feminism.

Clearly there is a need for a separate and distinct identity for the Africana woman and her movement. Some white women acknowledge that the feminist movement was not designed with the Africana woman in mind. For example, white feminist Catherine Clinton asserts that "feminism primarily appealed to educated and middle-class white women, rather than black and white working-class women" (Clinton, 1987: 63). Steady (1987:3) admits that:

> Various schools of thought, perspectives, and ideological proclivities have influenced the study of feminism. Few studies have dealt with the issue of racism, since the dominant voice of the feminist movement has been that of the white female. The issue of racism can become threatening, for it identifies white feminists as possible participants in the oppression of blacks.

Africana men and women do not accept the idea of Africana women as feminists. There is a general consensus in the Africana community that the feminist movement, by and large, is the white woman's movement for two reasons. First, the Africana woman does not see the man as her primary enemy as does the white feminist, who is carrying an age-old battle with her white male counterpart for subjugating her as property. African men have never had the same institutionalized power to oppress Africana women as white men have had to oppress white women. According to the Africana sociologist, Clyde Franklin II, "Black men are relatively powerless in this country, and their attempts at domination, aggression, and the like, while sacrificing humanity, are ludicrous" (Franklin II, 1986: 112). Joyce Ladner (1972:277-8), another Africana sociologist, succinctly articulates the dynamics of the relationship between African men and women and does not view the former as the enemy of the latter:

> Black women do not perceive their enemy to be black men, but rather the enemy is considered to be oppressive forces in the larger society which subjugate black men, women and children."

Since African women never have been considered the property of their male counterparts, Africana women and men alike dismiss the primacy of gender issues in their reality, and thus dismiss the feminist movement as a viable framework for their chief concerns. Instead, they hold to the opinion that those Africa women who embrace the feminist movement are mere assimilationists or sellouts who, in the final analysis, have no true commitment to their culture or their people, particularly as it relates to the historical and current collective struggle of Africana men and women.

Second, Africana women reject the feminist movement because of their apprehension and distrust of white organizations. In fact, white organized groups in general, such as the Communist Party and the National Organization of for Women, have never been able to galvanize the majority of Africana people. On the whole, Africanans are grassroots people who depend on the support and confidence of their communities and who, based on historical instances of betrayal, are necessarily suspicious of organizations founded, operated, and controlled by whites. In general, Africanans focus on tangible things that can offer an amelioration of or an exit from oppression, which are of utmost importance for survival in the Africana community. Those Africana intellectuals who insist on identifying with organizations that offer them neither leadership no high visibility generally subordinate their blackness to the comfort of being accepted by white intellectuals. Unfortunately for those African intellectuals, philosophy and scholarship take precedence even over self-identity, and they seem to be satisfied with merely belonging to a white group.

Having established that the major problem with the African feminist is that of naming, what is the major problem with the black feminist? Briefly stated, the black feminist is an Africana woman who has adopted the agenda of the feminist movement to some degree in that she, like the white feminist, perceives gender issues to be most critical in her quest for empowerment and selfhood. On the outskirts of feminist activity, Black feminists possess neither power nor leadership in the movement. Black feminist bell hooks obviously realizes this, as she makes a call for Africana women to move "from margin to center" of the feminist movement in her book entitled *Feminist Theory: From Margin to Center* (1984). Receiving recognition as heralds of feminism by way of legitimating the movement through their identification with it, black feminists are frequently delegated by white feminists as the voice of Africana women. However, this peripheral promotion of black feminists is only transient, as they will never be afforded the same level of importance as white feminists enjoy. It is quite obvious, for example, that bell hooks will never be elevated to the same status as either Betty Friedan or Gloria Steinem. At best, she and her fellow black feminists are given only temporary recognition as representatives and spokespersons for Africana people in general and Africana women in particular. Black feminists advance an agenda that is in direct contravention to that in the Africana community, thereby demonstrating a certain lack of African-centered historical and contemporary perspective. Although white feminists contend that the movement is a panacea for the problems of Africana women, they have been unsuccessful in galvanizing the majority of Africana women to the extent of directing and dictating the latter's thought and action.

While Africana women do, in fact, have some legitimate concerns regarding Africana men, these concerns must be addressed within the context of African culture. Problems must not be resolved using an alien framework (e.g., feminism) but must be resolved from within an endemic theoretical construct - *Africana Womanism*. It appears that many Africana women who become black feminists (or are inclined more in that direction) base their decisions upon either naivete about the history and ramifications of feminism or on negative experiences with Africana men. For example, because there are some Africana women who pride themselves on being economically independent, (which was the way of life for African women long before the advent of feminism) and because one of the chief tenets of feminism in the larger society is that a woman is economically independent, many Africana women unthinkingly respond positively to the notion of being a feminist. To be sure, Africana women have always been, by necessity, independent and responsible co-workers and decision-makers. But while this naivete can easily be corrected, negative personal experiences cannot be rectified so readily.

True, one's personal experiences are valid ways of determining one's world view; however, the resulting generalization that many black feminists share -that all or most Africana men are less worthy than women- is based upon intellectual laziness, which requires effortless rationalization. By the same analysis, it is easy for some people to believe that all white people or all people of any race or sex form a homogeneous group, and it is difficult for them to treat people as individuals. This is important because, in reality, relationships are based on individual particularities rather than on an overriding group characteristic. For example, an Africana brother having had a bad experience with an African woman might conclude that all Africana women are undesirable, thus castigating this entire group of people. A classic example of gross exaggeration based not on facts but on polemics or limited personal experiences, is Michelle Wallace's book entitled *Black Macho and the Myth of the Super Woman* (1980). In this book, the author makes a serious attack on Africana men by categorizing them as super macho men who physically and mentally abuse Africana women. It is apparent that the author's personal negative experiences with Africana men, which she relates throughout the book, influenced her ideology. The tragedy is that her book, which was endorsed in different ways by the many feminists listed in the Acknowledgments, received such wide exposure that it consequently influenced the thoughts of an entire generation, thereby representing a watershed in the development of modern black feminist thought.

If one considers the collective plight of Africana people globally, it becomes clear that we cannot afford the luxury, if you will, of being consumed by gender issues. A supreme paradigm of the need for Africana women to prioritize the struggle for human dignity and parity is presented by South African woman activist, Ruth Mompati. In her heart-rending stories of unimaginable racial atrocities heaped upon innocent children, as well as upon men and women, Mompati (1982:112-3) asserts the following:

> The South African woman, faced with the above situation, finds the order of her priorities in her struggle for human dignity and her rights as a woman dictated by the general political struggle of her people as a whole. The national liberation of the black South African is a prerequisite to her own liberation and emancipation as a woman and a worker. The process of struggle for national liberation has been

accompanied by the politicizing of both men and women. This has kept the women's struggle from degenerating into a sexist struggle that would divorce women's position in society from the political, social, and economic development of the society as a whole. From the South African women who together with their men seek to liberate their country, come an appeal to friends and supporters to raise their voices on their behalf.

Overall, "human discrimination transcends sex discrimination ... the costs of human suffering are high when compared to a component, sex obstacle" (Mompati, 1982:6). Furthermore, according to Steady in *The Black Woman Cross-culturally* (1981:27-8):

> for the black woman in a racist society, racial factors, rather than sexual ones, operate more consistently in making her a target for discrimination and marginalization. This becomes apparent when the "family" is viewed as a unit of analysis. Regardless of differential access to resources by both men and women, white males and females, as members of family groups, share a proportionately higher quantity of the earth's resources than do black males and females. There is a great difference between discrimination by deprivation and exclusion.

Steady's assessment here speaks directly to the source of discrimination that Africana women suffer at the hands of a racist system. There is the oppression of the South African woman who must serve as maid and nurse to the white household with minimum wages earnings, the Caribbean woman in London who is the ignored secretary, and the Senegalese or African worker in France who is despised and unwanted. There is the Nigerian subsistence farmer, such as the Ibo woman in Enugu and Nsukka, who farms every day for minimum wages, and the female Brazilian factory worker who is the lowest on the totem pole. Clearly, the problems of these women are not inflicted upon them solely because they are black; they are further victimized because they are women living in a white-male dominated society.

The problems of Africana women, including physical brutality, sexual harassment, and female subjugation in general, perpetrated both within and outside the race, ultimately have to be solved on a collective basis *within African communities*. Africana people must *eliminate racist influences* in their lives first, with the realization that they can neither afford nor tolerate any form of female subjugation. Along those same lines, Ntiri (1982:5) summarizes Mompati's position that sexism "is basically a secondary problem which arises out of race, class and economic prejudices."

Because one of the main tensions between Africana men and women in the United States involves employment and economic opportunity, Africanans frequently fall into a short-sighted perception of things. For example, it is not a question of more jobs for Africana women versus more jobs for Africana men, a situation that too frequently promotes gender competition. Rather, it is a question of *more jobs for Africanans in general*. These jobs are generated primarily by white people, and most Africanans depend on sources other than those supplied by African people. *The real challenge for Africana men and women is how to create more economic opportunities within Africana communities*. Many people talk about the need for enhanced Africana economic empowerment. If our real goal in life is to be achieved -that is, the survival of our entire race as a primary concern for Africana women- it will have to come from Africana men *and* women working together. If Africana men and women are fighting within the community, they are ultimately defeating themselves on all fronts.

Perhaps because of all the indisputable problems and turmoil heaped upon the African community, much of which is racially grounded, Africanans frequently fail to *look closely at available options* to determine if those options are, in fact, sufficiently workable. Rather than *create other options* for themselves, Africanans ally with white privileged-class phenomena, such as feminism. On the other hand, when a group takes control over its struggle, tailoring it to meet its collective needs and demands, the group is almost always successful. When success in one's goals is realized, it makes for a more peaceful reality for all concerned, and one is more inclined to a wholesome and amicable relationship with others, knowing that the concerns of the people are respected and met. As Africana Womanism -rather than feminism, black feminism, African feminism, or "mere" womanism- is a conceivable alternative for the Africana woman in her collective struggle with the entire community, it enhances future possibilities for the dignity of Africana people and humanity of all. In short, the reclamation of Africana women via properly identifying our own collective struggle and acting upon it is a key toward human harmony and survival.

Notes

1. For many reasons, many white women as well as African women have become disenchanted with feminism.

2. Rose Acholonu presented a paper entitled "Love and the Feminist Utopia in the African Novel" at the first international conference on women in Africa and the African Diaspora: Bridges across Activism and the Academy, Nsukka, Nigeria, July 13-18, 1992.

3. Emmett Louis "Bobo" Till was the 14-year old Africana chicago youth who was lynched in 1955 in Money, Mississipi for whistling at a 21-year old white woman. For a detailed explanation of Till's importance to the Modern Civil Rights Movement, read Clenora Hudson (Hudson-Weems's) 1988 doctoral dissertation *entitled Emmet Till: The Impetus for the Modern Civil Rights Movement* and *Emmet Till: The Sacrificial Lamb of the Civil Rights Movement*.

Works Cited

Acholonu, Rose.1992. Love and the Feminist Utopia in the African Novel. Paper presented at the first international conference on women in Africa and the African Diaspora: Bridges across Activism and the Academy, Nsukka, Nigeria, July 13-18, 1992.

Aidoo, Ama Ata. 1989. Unwelcomed Pals and Decorative Slaves or Glimpses of women as Writers and Characters in Contemporary African Literatures. *Literature and Society: Selected Essays on African Literature,* Ernest Emenyonu. Oguta (ed.). Zim Pan African Publishers. 1-19.

Caroll, Peter N. & David W. Noble. 1977. *The Free and the Unfree: A New History of the United States.* New York, N.Y.: Penguin Books.

Clinton, Catherine. 1987. Women Break New Ground. *The Underside of American History.* Vol. 2, Thomas R. Frazier (ed.). New York, N.Y.: Harcourt Brace Jovanovich. 62-83.

Franlkin, Clyde, II. 1986. Black Male - Black Female Conflict: Individually Caused and Culturally Nurtured. *The Black Family: Essays and Studies,* Robert Staples (ed.). Belmont, CA: Wadsworth Press. 106-113.

Giddings, Paula. 1984. *When and Where I enter: The Impact of Black Women on Race and Sex in America.* New York, N.Y.: Bantam.

Hooks, bell. 1984. *Feminist Theory: From Margin to Center.* Boston, MA: Southend.

Hudson, Clenora. 1988. *Emmet Till: The Impetus for the Modern Civil Rights Movement.* Ph.D. Dissertation, University of Iowa.

Ladner, Joyce. 1972. *Tomorrow's tomorrow: The Black Woman.* Garden City, N.Y.: Anchor.

Mompati, Ruth. 1982. Women and Life under Appartheid. *One is Not a Woman, One Becomes: The African Woman in a Transitional Society,* Daphne Williams Ntiri (ed.).Troy, MI: Bedford Publishers. 108-113.

Daphne Williams Ntiri. 1982. *One is not a Woman, One Becomes: The African Woman in a Transitional Society.* Troy, MI: Bedford Publishers.

Steady, Filomina Chioma. 1981. *The Black Woman Cross-Culturally.* Cambridge, MA: Schenkman.

Steady, Filomina Chioma. 1981. The Black Woman Cross-Culturally: An Overview. *The Black Woman Cross-Culturally.* Cambridge, MA: Schenkman.

Steady, Filomina Chioma. 1987. "African Feminism: A Worldwide Perspective". *Women in Africa and the African Diaspora,* Rosalyn Terborg-Penn et al. (eds). Washington, D.C.: Howard University Press. 3-24.

Walker, Alice. 1983. *In Search of Our Mothers' Gardens.* San Diego, CA: Harcourt.

Wallace, Michelle. 1980. *Black Macho and the Myth of the Superwoman.* New York, N.Y.: Warner.

Defining African Womanist Theory

Nah Dove

Background

The results of my study of the life herstories of African mothers who send their children to culturally affirming schools forced me to go beyond the theoretical framework that I was working with. While my focus was on conceptualizing and defining the racialization of the world through European domination/white supremacy, it was impossible to ignore the specificity of the oppression of African women living in male-centered western society. Although my study comprised of only 21 herstories, a significant number of these mothers had experienced negative relationships with men who had played a critical role in their lives. These women neither hated nor separated themselves from men. They recognized their responsibilities to their sons, fearing for their son's survival and the safety of African men living under White supremacy. They wanted their sons to be fearless and to respect women. To be true to their feelings required that I not only use their words to tell their stories but develop culturally-based theory that could be sensitive to their experiences as African women. At the same time, it was important to use these mothers as examples of women who look to their re-Africanization[1] as the solution to challenging alien and inappropriate values and behaviors among African women and men.

Introduction

In order to bring clarity to the impact of European cultural oppression as a mental, spiritual, physical and material reality it has become no longer plausible to define ourselves solely as we have become known, as races -- Black, Brown, Yellow, Red and White. The White race, recognized as the most powerful, militarily and economically, essentially controls, directs and manages, through the structure of capitalism, the world's resources including the energies of the peoples. However, as a European institution structured to maintain the interests of western development it may also be defined as White supremacy. The use of a cultural analysis enables one to trace the social and ideological construction of race, gender and class structures to their European antecedents. At the same time it becomes evident that their exploitative characteristics demonstrate their centrality to the operation of Europeanized societies and the process of Europeanizing societies. While there is a recognition of the complex interplay among these unequal and unethical power relations, primacy is given to race as a social construct because racist oppression/White supremacy for African women, men and children takes precedence over and affects the natures of gender and class oppressions. It will be also argued that, European patriarchy underlies western social inequalities that effect African women and men in equally perverse ways.

A Clash of Cultural Interests

What was the relationship between European and African people prior to and during the invasion of Africa? What effect did the invasions of Africa have on African people? What were the contributing factors that aided Europeans in their attempt to conquer the world? These questions will be answered, in part at least. Underpinning the conceptual framework of this work is the belief that a clash of cultures between European and African people was instrumental in facilitating the European domination of Africa and her people. Importantly, while this focus is on the African experience there is the recognition that the European domination has altered and often destroyed cultural groups other than that of African people.

As Cheikh Anta Diop and others have shown Africa is the cradle of human civilization and therefore culture. Despite this fact, racist scholars have long since denied the connection between European and African civilization. On April 28, 1995, an article appeared in the *Washington Post* that claimed that early African tools, 90,000 years old, found in Zaire in Western Central Africa challenge the assumed advances of Europe and Asia compared to Africa. The new find "shows that humans in Africa had invented sophisticated technologies long before their European counterparts who have long been credited with initiating modern culture" (*Washington Post*, April 28, 1995:A[1]). While this knowledge may have shaken the foundations of White supremacist belief, it is not new to some Europeans and African-centered thinkers whose scientific research has focused upon Kemet (ancient Egypt) as a major center of African culture that grew out of central Africa and influenced the West[2]. Their discovery is that much of the knowledge of the technology, philosophy, writing, spirituality, health care, schooling and education from ancient Africa has influenced the development of what the West believes is its "modern" world. European cultural thought, however, has denied the relationship between Africa and Europe, and fabricated a belief that the "modern" world has no basis in the knowledge of the ancients. In this way, the prevention of access to benefits accrued within the "modern" world can be justified. While it may be true that the ancient African women and men could never have designed a global social order of this type (based on what we know or are learning of our ancestors' principled spiritual beliefs), nonetheless, African ideas have been imperialized to serve a European rationale.

For the purpose of understanding the significance of this condition, I use Diop's analysis of how these two major cultural groups, one an outgrowth of the other, manifest as antithetical entities. Diop (1959/1990) develops the concept of cultural unity in his examination of the genesis of African and Indo-Aryan or Indo-European culture. The idea that it is possible to trace similitude Africa-wide among institutional systems challenges contemporary Eurocentric arguments that claim that Africa is so diverse that cultural unity cannot be found as a social reality. Gyekye (1995), who argues that there is an African philosophical expressiveness that is grounded culturally in Africa, relates this European notion of African differentiation to an "exaggerated diversity" created by the European "invention of Africa" (1995:xxiv). From an Afrocentric perspective there is a recognition of the diversity among African ethnicities, however, diversity does not preclude sameness. In this light, one can only marvel at how European ethnicities were able to come together as a critical cultural mass to procure Africa from a people whom they claim today have few similarities. It is evident that the planning and executing the conquest of Africa and her people was undergirded by a general European belief that African people were very much alike. This belief was so prevalent that it manifested in well documented data that attempted to prove the cultural, genetic, psychological and mental inferiority of African people through scientific racism. Moreover, such ideas were supported by and fed into the academic world within fields like History, Biology, Sociology, Anthropology, Psychology and Education etc., (see Dove, 1990; 1993). At that time, it seemed politically expedient to support this idea in order to justify the subjection of African women, men and children to analogous forms of barbarian treatment under the auspices of European domination. Today, it is expedient to deny the earlier claim of cultural unity since this concept, retained in the minds of African people challenging academic racism and scholastic dishonesty, has taken on a new meaning. It poses a threat to the fundamental doctrine of White supremacy within the ivory tower.

Cultural unity is the bedrock of the more recent academic movement and development of African-centered and/or Afrocentric thinking (Asante, 1980) that reclaims and reconstructs an African world-view as central to the renovation of African values and beliefs and the restoration of Africa and her people (Shujaa, 1996). This assertion does not preclude the works of great thinkers or the ideas of activists prior to Diop who were aware of the role of Africa and her people before European conquest. Much free thinking about the greatness of Africa and her people has taken place outside the academic world (Dove, 1996). Importantly, cultural unity highlights the intergenerational transmission of values and beliefs that take place despite and regardless of an academic consciousness of Africanity. Awareness of this ongoing process may allow one to understand the link between the source of these ideas and the academic validation of them. The monumental research of Chancellor Williams (1987) adds credence to this concept. He found that all over Africa a single constitutional system existed as though African people regardless of differing social patterns, lived under one government. His study of continental-wide social and economic systems throughout history revealed "the same overall patterns of unity and sameness of all fundamental institutions" (1987:21). Furthermore, cultural unity enables one to understand how Europeans collaborated despite ethnic or national differences to enforce their supremacy over the world. At the same time one may understand how African people were able to survive that imposition and act continually to liberate themselves from it.

Diop's (1990) Cradle Theory argues that two distinct cradles of civilization the Southern cradle, Africa and the Northern cradle created modes of societal structures almost antithetical to each other. Africa, where humanity began, produced the matriarchal societies. Over time the migration of peoples to the colder climate produced patriarchal, male-centered societies. Diop challenges European evolutionist theories that claim that matriarchy is an inferior stage in human evolution and social organization. Quite simply he attributes matriarchy to an agrarian lifestyle in a climate of abundance and patriarchy to nomadic traditions arising from a harsh environment.

The concept of matriarchy highlights the complementarity aspect of female-male relationship or the nature of the feminine and masculine in all forms of life, which is understood as non-hierarchical. Both the woman and the man work together in all areas of social organization. The woman is revered in her role as the mother who is the bringer of life, the conduit for the spiritual regeneration of the ancestors, the bearer of culture and the center of social organization. Thus, according to Diop, to speak or behave inappropriately in front of a mother or to speak to a mother disrespectfully is tantamount to committing sacrilege. It is believed that such behavior will be known in the ancestors' realm and the repercussions will fall upon the families of the perpetrators. As a result of the mother's powerful role, and her wish to use this power wisely, she is often tolerant of her children and partner's behavior (Diop, 1990:70-71).

The role of motherhood or mothering is not confined to mothers or women even in the contemporary conditions. As Tedla (1995) explains, the concept of mother transcends gender and blood relations. A family member or friend who has been kind and caring can be said to be one's mother. It is an honor to have such a title bestowed upon one (1995:61). Values of this nature have been critical to the survival of African people during the protracted and continuing holocaust. Motherhood, thus, depicts the nature of the communal responsibilities involved in the raising of children and the caring of others. However, while the role of women and mothering in the process of reproduction is critical to the continuation of any society and culture, in a patriarchal society this role is not ascribed with the value that it bears in matriarchal society.

In the European context, as Diop explains, the woman is considered little more than "a burden that the man dragged behind him. Outside her function of child-bearing her role in nomadic society is nil...Having a smaller economic value, it is she who must leave her clan to join that of her husband, contrary to the matriarchal custom which demands the opposite" (1990:29). The differences that arise from these two cultural orientations are important. The debasement of women in one culture and respect for women in the other are distinctions that should not be ignored when analyzing the contemporary difficulties for African people, especially African women living in Western-oriented societies.

Stone's (1976) investigation into the devaluation and debasement of women in western society focuses on religion as an instrument of this oppression. She sought to discover how and why the ancient worship or rather reverence for the goddess and female deities became subjugated or even destroyed and replaced by the worship of god as a male. Although Stone does not refer to Diop's work, her research is illuminated by his Cradle Theory and his cultural unity concept. While the Southern and Northern cradles of civilization are given prominence in Diop's theoretical analysis of cultural distinctions, he also refers to a third cradle. This cradle is known as the zone of confluence, one such area includes what we now refer to as the Middle East. This zone once populated by African people is where the cradles met. It is the area where the migration of peoples from the Northern cradle arrived and stayed in the terrain of the Southern cradle. Over time, this essentially Indo-European invasion and conquest of African peoples resulted in the cultural and genetic amalgamation that produced the peoples to whom we refer, racially, as Semitic. Linguistically they constitute Arabic and Hebraic, while religiously they are Islamic, Judaic and Christian. It is through the imposition of these male-centered religions, according to Stone, that the earlier reverence for the female goddess was eventually destroyed.

Like Diop, Stone views the Indo-European conquest of the Middle East, particularly of ancient Palestine, as that of patriarchy over matriarchy or the process of male domination over female power. With reference to the Judaic-Christian "bible" story of creation, Stone notes how the debasement of the woman is mythologized through the story of Eve, the mother of creation. Eve is responsible for the fall of humanity from the grace of God and the garden of Eden. It is she who works against God and tempts the man Adam to eat of the forbidden fruit. In this way, humanity is borne into perpetual sin. According to Stone, this story is an integral part of the contemporary European belief system. As with Christianity, Islam in the attempt to destroy the reverence for the goddess, viewed this spiritual system as pagan. She quotes from the Koran, "Allah will not tolerate idolatry...the pagans pray to females" (1976: xviii). In this light, the domination of women by men may be seen as morally essential.

Stone's important findings uncover the matriarchal (African) roots of Semitic/middle eastern and African culture. Her intention is to link the contemporary status of women in Western society to the patriarchal conquest of women and the continuing subversion of women's power through religion. However, her analysis lacks a clear cultural or even racial analysis in that the conquest of matriarchy by patriarchy may also be viewed as the conquest of African women, children and men by Europeans. In addition Diop's definition of matriarchal culture and society as one based upon reciprocal, complementary and therefore non-hierarchical relationships does not suggest that women were at one time superior to men as Stone implies. Rather Diop (1990) states that: A matriarchal regime, far from being imposed on man by circumstances independent of his will is accepted and defended by him (1990:120). Thus, one may glean from these studies that patriarchy produces and perpetuates an imbalance in female-male relations that has had far reaching and negative consequences for the contemporary world.

Ani (1994) brings further clarity to this idea. She draws upon the story of creation of the Dogon people of Mali in West Africa to explain the female-male imbalance in the state of Western domination/White supremacy. Her intention is to lay a foundation for understanding the roots of the aggressive, violent nature of European or Western culture and its ideological role in rationalizing the carnage of humanity strewn in the path of its "progressive" and "modern" development. The character from her book *Yurugu* exemplifies this state of being for Ani. Yurugu is the Dogon name for the entity in their creation story who challenges the process of his own creation by the Creator Amma. As a result of his endeavor to influence his own creation, he does not fully develop. Instead, he becomes incomplete, devoid of his feminine self. In this incomplete stage he attempts to stand as a superior creator beyond that of the magnitude of the Creator Amma.

To summarize, the development of the distinctly different Northern and Southern cradles of civilization produced cultures almost antithetical to each other based largely upon differences encountered in surviving their terrains. These experiences were expressed through the differing beliefs about the roles and therefore the statuses of women and men. These ancient cultures, through the intergenerational transmission of values and beliefs, provided the cohesive forces from which the contemporary European/Western and African societies grew. On one hand, matriarchal, agrarian societies recognize(d) the importance of balance and reciprocity between the feminine and masculine elements in all forms of nature, spirituality and the communal nature of social relations. On the other hand, patriarchal, nomadic societies emphasize(d) hierarchy and the power of the masculine principle over the feminine principle an outcome of which is individualism. It may be said that the imbalance of power between the woman and the man is the basis for fundamental social inequalities that exist in patriarchal societies. After all, the woman and man create the smallest unit possible for the reproduction of family and society, it follows that this unequal, exploitative and unethical power relationship will be reflected throughout society on every level.

The conquests of Africa by Europeans from antiquity until the present may be viewed as conquests of matriarchy by patriarchy which was at the same time, the domination of African women, men and children by European women, men and children and the potential subjugation of African women by White men and women as well as African men. In this light, it is possible to understand how the imposition of Western values upon African people's more egalitarian female-male relations is so insidious especially when humanity is asked to view this condition as progressive, universal and natural.

The Roots of Racism

It is not possible to speak of the African his/herstorical experience without discussing the experience of racism. Racism may be defined as the practice of racist behavior in the construction and maintenance of a racialized social hierarchy that is grounded in a belief in race as the basis of human differentiation. The strength of this belief is a testament to the institutional ability of Europeans to impose their ideas. This ideological fabrication relegates women in each supposed racial group to a position inferior to that of their male counterparts. The role of European males in constructing this ideology has been effective. Not surprisingly, within these racialized definitions, White women like White men are considered the epitome of human evolution, mentally, psychologically, physiologically and culturally.

The belief in White superiority has been integral to building social hierarchies that place African people, particularly in the West, at the base in terms of access to proper employment, health care, schooling, education and other institutional facilities. In the Americas it would be an error to exclude the indigenous First Nations[3] women, men and children as victims of the ravages of this system. They compete statistically for placement at the base of the hierarchy. My focus on racism draws a link between European culture, the structure of European societies and the belief in the practice of racism against all peoples. While I have used the works of Diop, Stone and Ani to suggest that patriarchy is intrinsic to European culture, I do not subscribe to a White feminist perspective that most often fails to use a cultural analysis, and/or underscores the importance of racism and the role of European women in support of White supremacy. It is a fact that women and men work together within their cultural groups to reproduce culture. Thus, although it is clear that patriarchal power relations undermine women's power, the cultural unity of European women and men in the perpetuation of racist belief and practice has had deleterious effects upon cultural groups on a global scale.

Where does this racist ethos and behavior originate? With reference to the ancient roots of Indo-Aryan patriarchy, Diop (1990) importantly notes that a characteristic of Indo-Aryan culture was xenophobia[4] which he attributed to the harsh existence in the Northern environment. During the development of city states in Greece and Italy it was not considered a crime to kill a visiting stranger (1990:46). However, in the matriarchal society where xenophilia[5] was the accepted norm as it has been documented in Kemet during the twelfth dynasty (4,000 years ago) "Black, White and Yellow (wo)men had already been admitted to live as equal citizens" (1990:147).

By looking at the continuum of cultural transference and unity, it is possible to link xenophobia to the later development of racist behavior and ideology which can be viewed as the manifestation of a fear of foreigners or difference. The resulting concept of race has been the subject of discussion since its pseudo-scientific entry into the intellectual and academic world of European scholars and politicians from the 1700's (Bernal, 1987; Fryer, 1984; Gould, 1984; Stocking, 1982; Stepan, 1982). The concept is grounded in a belief that the "White race", including the psychology, religions, philosophies and social structures that materialize from that cultural group, is superior to all others. Given this rationale, superiority appears to be genetically determined and largely based on skin color. However, the roots of the ideological construction of race predate scientific attempts by Europeans to substantiate supposed genetic inequalities. Importantly, this assertion challenges Marxist ideas that racism rose out of capitalism. In reality, racism was fundamental to capitalism (Dove, 1995). Racist ideology defined the nature of the terms of global capitalistic development. An outcome of the belief in and possibly the fear of difference, manifest in the European practice of segregation between the so-called races imposed as law and social policy. It was and is in effect the attempt to maintain the dominion of the supposed White race. We see examples of forced segregation all over the world in the forms of townships, homelands, reservations and urban areas. Historically, there is evidence to show that the social construction of segregation and racialized power relations was developed in concert with European/Aryan control over traditional social structures which in some cases, I will argue, predated capitalism proper.

The psychological aberration, that is the belief in White superiority and the practice of White supremacy or racism, is mental illness (Hilliard, 1987; Cress Welsing, 1991; Wright, 1984/1994). Hilliard sees this type of sickness as a component of European culture. It enables Europeans to deny the reality of their historical role in the destruction and debasement of Africa and her people. He notes that, ironically, victims of racism may be "pro-racist" (identification with the aggressor) regardless of their genetic make-up. Thus, it is possible for people who look African to perpetuate Eurocentric ideals that are inconsistent with the well-being of African people. Cress Welsing attributes the depravity of racist behavior to the theory of caucasian[6] fear of genetic annihilation. In other words, Europeans believe that they will lose their power base, which is predicated upon their Whiteness, if they procreate with Black, Red, Brown or Yellow people. Thus, in order to sustain European power and control they must retain, through segregation, their supposed genetic superiority which is linked to a lack of melanin.

Ideas of racial superiority that crystallized in Europe in the seventeen hundreds were reflective of beliefs and behaviors that were apparent much earlier. Bradley's (1978) theory supports this idea. He uses the concept of race, rather than culture, as a basis for understanding the cultural and psychological distinctions between Europeans (caucasians) and the rest of the world. Using a sociobiological analysis, he traces the origin of the (White race) to an earlier human, the aggressive Neanderthal. Aggressive traits, Bradley argues, were retained genetically and culturally and transferred during Neanderthals' absorption into other migrating peoples who eventually became known as caucasoids. His analysis of caucasian behavior includes the propensity for male violence against females. He asserts that the physical differences between females and males led to their suspicion of each other. Thus, even procreation was an aggressive act given the male proclivity toward territorial assertion.

Not unlike Bradley, Welsing (1991) draws a correlation between sex and violence. Rape is, she believes, a symbol of White culture and an unjust, sick behavior where the genitals become a weapon. Sexual inadequacy is, she argues, the basis for the development of weaponry as a mode of European conquest or control in the development of White supremacy (1991:176- 178). Welsing connects the high level of rape within the African urban experience with the debasement of the African male under White supremacy (high levels of unemployment, underemployment, incarceration, police brutality, negative portrayal etc.), and his attempt to reduce what he perceives to be the higher status of African women, and her possible lack of respect for him, by debasing her. In this respect, the African male as a degraded human under White supremacy employs the cultural norm of Europeans to display his aggression.

Following the line of reasoning that White supremacy as a belief system and social structure is a manifestation of mental illness, Bobby Wright (1984/1994) makes a connection between the behavior of Europeans in the construction of White supremacy and psychopathic disorder. He points out that the psychopath is generally sexually inadequate. Wright suggests that historically psychopathic sexual inadequacies have translated into the construction of the belief in the oversexed Black person as the justification his/herstorically for the rape of the African woman and the castration of the African man (1994:7-8). Bradley roots the caucasian penchant for racism in the sexual aggression demonstrated towards females. Later this sexual aggression was transferred to challenge physical differences based on racial features. In effect, sexual aggression as racist aggression was played out against both the male and female of non caucasian, supposed, racial groups.

From a genetic perspective, Bradley's work supports the earlier discourse on the origins of European hostility, male-female inequality and the predisposition for racism. Bradley's perceptions, although critical of caucasian behavior, are subtly grounded in a belief in White superiority. Thus, while the construction of the world in the caucasian image has materialized through hostile behavior, for Bradley, the world holds possibilities that could not have arisen without caucasian aggression. Subtly, his ideas fit into the Western mold of rationalizing the rise of European or White supremacy as something positive, progressive and necessary. Thus the visions and aspirations of the Black, Red, Yellow and Brown persons of the world, no matter how humane and "compassionate", are marginalized along with their human status.

In summary, it is possible to suggest that the roots of racism may well originate from the earliest experiences of the humanity that came out of the Northern cradle culture after losing touch with their Southern cradle ancestors. From Diop's (1959/1990) analysis, xenophobia was a cultural tendency associated with the harshness of surviving in that environment, the lack of subsistence resources, and the need to control access to them, especially from strangers. In the same vein, Bradley's belief, that the aggressiveness of the caucasoid is both a genetic and cultural trait that can be traced to the severity of the ice-age, supports the idea that environmental conditions have an effect upon lifestyles and behaviors. Simultaneously, the psychological component in the construction of culture should not be ignored when referring to behavior or mental state.

As Welsing and Wright argue, the psychological aspect of White supremacist belief has had severe ramifications for African people in particular. Their analysis can be used to understand the impact of racialized hierarchies upon other oppressed groups as well as male and female relations within those groups. Although I do not support the sociobiological idea that race is the major determinant of human behavior and practice, I do believe that there is a significant relationship between cultural groups and the genetic similarities within these groups especially in relation to environmental factors.

Diop (1990) pointed out that culture, which influences our behavior, may be viewed as having evolved as a consequence of climatic conditions and the need to feed, clothe and shelter one's group. While it is possible to relate a people's genetic makeup to a cultural group, generally, it is culture that will determine the way that a people view themselves and, therefore, behave. Through a process of domination and deculturalization[7] it is possible to produce Europeanized people who look genetically African, but whose minds have been incarcerated by Eurocentric concepts, values and beliefs. Such women and men if they are unable to gain an understanding of who they are, will very likely believe in the European fabrication of the cultural and genetic inferiorization[8] of African people and become, as Frantz Fanon (1983) believed, alienated from their own humanity.

Rooting racist behavior, social structure and ideology, in the character of the European patriarchal experience, lays the groundwork for understanding its importance to the construction of White supremacy. The European way of perceiving the world is quite distinct from, and possibly antithetical to, the African perspective. An obvious example is the xenophobia of European culture and xenophilia of African culture which exhibit culturally conflicting ways of being. The ability to conquer the world (from the 15th century) and annihilate hundreds of millions of humans and then justify that conquest with the notion that some humanity is inferior and thus expendable, requires a particular cultural orientation, one that was quite outside the experience and practice of matriarchal Africa. In this sense the violently imposed racialization of the world may be seen as a European fabrication that is essentially patriarchal in origin.

Racist Ideology as an Aspect of European Culture

While racist behavior can be linked to European antecedents its manifestation as social hierarchy can be traced and documented at least to the Aryan influence on the Hindu spiritual system of India. The realization of Hinduism as a racialized social hierarchy is not much different from the more recent types created in places like the Americas, Europe, South Africa, Australia or New Zealand. The ideological justification for racist behavior has been critical to the erection of racialized social hierarchies. Ani (1994) views the ideological feature of culture as central in promoting group interests. Thus, in reference to ideological differences among peoples, she explains that in European culture, the outward ideological thrust, the aggressive stance, is developed more intensely than in any other culture. As we examine the culture, we find that its dominant modes of expression reveal an almost fanatically political or confrontational consciousness in which all cultural phenomena that are "other" or different are considered hostile to the group interest (1994:11). With this in mind it is possible to argue that race as ideology is reflective of the xenophobic behavior and may be viewed as a feature of European culture that facilitated the formation of White superiority and supremacy.

This belief has had a profound affect his/herstorically on the quality of life for the members of supposed races of people, the Black, the Red, the Brown and the Yellow. Ideas of this nature and their association with European logic are not new. They can be traced to at least 800 BCE (Rashidi, 1992) with the Aryan conquest of the Indus valley in Pakistan populated by Dravidians. This area is viewed in Diop's (1990) work as a zone of confluence, like the so-called Middle East, where the Northern cradle met the Southern cradle. In the same way, Northern patriarchy conquered Southern matriarchy.

This conquest began around 1900 BCE. The Dravidians, descendants of the Ethiopian or Cushite people, who populated Kemet (ancient Egypt), practiced their Hindu religion (Rashidi, 1988, 1992; Houston, 1926/1985), which was later transformed through Aryan domination into a caste system not based on labor but on skin color (Rashidi, 1992:87). The *Rig Veda*, the (Aryan) sacred text of the Hindu spiritual system, describes four castes that sprung from the God Brahma. Each caste is identified with a color. White is associated with the Brahmins, the priests (the Aryans). Red is affiliated with the administrators and military. Yellow, represents the color of the mercantile and agricultural caste while Black is distinguished by the lowest caste (Rashidi, 1989:216; 1992:87-88). Moreover, the life of the Sudras (Dravidians), the lowest caste, known as the untouchables was one of humiliation and degradation. It was believed that even their shadows polluted the earth(1992:90-92). The point in noting this racialized social hierarchy is that the present ideas about race are documented in a belief system created almost 3,000 years ago that can be traced to an Aryan ideology emanating from the Northern cradle. Once again, we can associate this barbaric racist logic with patriarchal beliefs. Stone (1976) notes the irony of the reference to women in the Rig Veda, which states that "[t]he mind of woman brooks not discipline. Her intellect has little weight" (1976:70).

Later we find traces of the idea of skin color and its association with behavior in the works of Aristotle (-389 to -332) the Greek philosopher. Considered one of Europe's greatest classical thinkers, Aristotle claimed that: those who are too black are cowards, like for instance the Egyptians and the Ethiopians. But those who are excessively white are also cowards as we can see from the example of women, the complexion of courage is between the two (Diop, 1991:17). This statement reveals the racist attitude towards African women and men and the sexist attitude towards Greek women and therefore all women. Ironically, Kemet (Egypt) was at that time the world center for knowledge. Visitors, especially the Greeks, traveled there freely as students to the universities to learn from their African tutors. Furthermore, for at least two thousand years prior to Aristotle's experience in Kemet, as Barbara Lesko's (1977) research shows, women had, enjoyed more legal rights and privileges than women have in many nations of the world today...there were certain features - such as the principle of matrilineal descent and matrimonial inheritance rights - which were basic to the Egyptian culture in antiquity (1977:i). Conversely, in Greece, even as late as the fifth century BCE the written observations of Herodotus state that Greek women even in Athens had few freedoms (Lesko, 1977:14).

In light of Aristotle's opinion, it is interesting that he was present when his pupil Alexander "the great?" began the process of conquest and colonization of Kemet (James, 1954/1989). Locating the genesis of the notion of racial ideology and its expression is important for understanding the contemporary racialized power relations. The Aryan conquest of the Dravidian people provides a perfect example of how a belief in superiority and inferiority based on skin color can become a religious faith, like Hinduism, not so much different from the Euro-Christian representation of White as good and Black as evil or the curse of Ham. At the same time, its expression in India's modern social hierarchy bears a resemblance to the contemporary conditions of African people living in the West under White supremacy (Rajshekar, 1987). It is possible to see how racist ideology may be culturally transferred to act as a cohesive force to bring together differing European ethnicity's and subdue their hostilities, under the auspices of White supremacy in the pursuance of the conquest and racialization of the world.

Patriarchal Aspects of a Developing White Supremacy

I have spoken earlier of the conquest of Africa by Europeans as the conquest of matriarchy by patriarchy. At the same time the zone of confluence in the area of today's middle east was also a parallel experience for the indigenous African people who populated that area prior to the Indo-Aryan conquest. The point I am making is that the matriarchal values that African people retained had a major impact on Europe during and after Kemet's destruction. Their influence spread throughout Europe inspiring women under the tyranny of patriarchal oppression to practice spiritual beliefs that invoked the feminine principles of the creator. As previously noted, African people had settled in Europe prior to the Moorish settlement from as early as 1000 BCE (Van Sertima, 1988:134-137). Moreover, the conquest of Kemet by the Greeks in 332 BCE and the Romans from 30 BCE until 323 ACE would certainly have had a major influence on Greek and Roman women. Diop's research reveals a European tradition of killing women, because of their support of matriarchal values, that can be traced to Greece and Rome when women who were forbidden from practicing the worship of Dionysus, an Egyptian (Kemetic) national god (Diop, 1990:175). Dionysus stood for the duality of the sexes and the development of humans, especially women. Diop says of him that "[h]e is the god whose teaching contains all the secret aspirations of the Aryan woman, so constrained and stifled by society" (1990:174). It seems that goddesses Diana and Isis were revered all over Europe from at least the fifth century. It is significant that both Diana[9] and Isis were African. Diana was Ethiopian (Diop, 1990:80) and Isis was from Kemet.

The Moorish presence in Europe would have done little to alleviate this problem. If the impact of African people in Europe inculcated a fear within Christianity of Moorish knowledge and its connection with Blackness it must also have transmitted a fear about the power and role of African women. For at that time the Islamic faith practiced by the African Moors in Spain still retained matriarchal influences as opposed to the patriarchy of the Catholic Christianity. Reynolds (1992) notes that the Moors "were known to have been ruled by female chiefs, holy women or queens even in the time of the Islamization of North Africa" (1992:111). This would account for both girls and boys attending school and the high status of women who were, for example, lawyers, doctors and professors in Moorish Spain (Jackson, 1992).

According to Mies (1986) millions of women were murdered as witches from the thirteenth century until the nineteenth century. She relates this holocaust to the protracted war carried out by European men against European women for control over female-centered institutions during the development of capitalism. This process of annihilation is defined as the "professionalization" of medical practice, religion and the law (1986:70). However, Sale (1991), Walker (1983) and Stone (1976) link the witch burnings to the Christianization of Europe. The sanctioning of these killings by the church, suggests Sale, was related to the fear of women because of their practice of other forms of worship like animism, goddess worship and paganism (1976:249). In other words the consolidation of Christianity in Europe may well have been a concerted attempt to wipe out matriarchal spiritual influences on European women.

Contemporaneously with the witch burnings, in order to facilitate the banishment of African people and their influence, the Inquisition was designed by the Catholic church to purge the land of non-Christians by burning so-called heretics. It is logical to suppose that heretics were in the main African women and men and their associates. Sale's research suggests that there was a relationship between the burning of heretics and the burning of witches. If this is the case, then who were the women murdered? In any case, we know that they were not Christian. Most likely, they were not all European as Mies and Sale imply. If what Mies postulates -- that the killing of witches was about the control of women's sexual reproduction -- is true, then given the xenophobic nature of Europeans, and their apparent fear of Blackness, we may surmise that many of these women must have been Black.

Any serious analysis of the cultural and racialized features underpinning the Christianization of Europe, must include the development of capitalism through European expansionism and the construction of White supremacy as a basis for the wholesale slaughter of African women, men and children, First Nations women, men and children and White women who practiced matriarchal values. It seems clear that the cultural forces that sprang from Northern patriarchy resulted in the deaths of millions of women whose cultural and possibly racial allegiance was put to the test.

Resistance to European Domination as Social Change

While it is important to define the oppressions that effect the lives of African women, men and children, for the purpose of developing liberationist theories and strategies, it is also necessary to understand that African people have a his/herstory rich in resistance to European forms of oppression. Acts of resistance must be placed within liberationist theory for they have laid the foundation for future strategies concerning the institutional development for self determination There has always been a belief within the cultural memory of another way of existing and being, and the retention of values that have sustained and maintained the lives of African people throughout the protracted holocaust (Hilliard, 1995; Nobles, 1985). Thus, the struggle for survival, the resistance of African people to the inhumanity involved in the capturing, enslavement and colonization process, has not only facilitated the humanization of western society but has provided the backbone of social change. The struggle for control over spirituality, psychology, minds, beliefs, values, integrity, dignity, herstory, history, knowledge, rights, lands and resources, has been long and bloody and countless of numbers have been lost on the way (Chinweizu, 1975; Rodney, 1972; Williams, 1987, Fryer, 1984; 1988; ben-Jochannan, 1972; Ani, 1994).

From antiquity, as spiritual, military and political leaders women's roles have been critical in the effort to control lands, resources and energies. Not surprisingly, few scholars have brought this to light. Early evidence of the role of women in defense of Africa comes out of the Kushite story of the Candaces who were women rulers. Following the Greek conquest of Kemet the Romans had taken over control by 30 BC. Their attempt to dominate Kush (Ethiopia) failed as a result of the Candace's (possibly Amanirenas) military and political skills. In fact, neither the Greeks nor the Romans succeeded in conquering Kush (Finch, 1990). This warriorship rose continuously from pre-enslavement to post-enslavement, for centuries on the continent, in the Caribbean, in North and South America and up until today.

Forms of resistance varied from individual heroism to mass uprisings. Asa Hilliard (1995) speaks of the need to rediscover and become inspired by the countless acts of bravery that should be resurrected from our cultural memory. The accumulation of these acts can be traced herstorically within the Black Nationalist and Pan Africanist movements. These movements can be viewed as having evolved from early violent European encounters with African people. In particular Maroon women and men have been attributed the greatest respect for their accomplishments in bravery and their success in gaining self-determination for their peoples during the enslavement period. Their origins have been traced from West Africa, in particular, Ghana (Hart, 1985). They set up their societies in the Caribbean and South America. In Brazil they built the first African republic, Palmares, in 1600 after escaping captivity from the Portuguese and the Dutch (Do Nascimento, 1992). Their story is rich in successful wars against the oppressors. They were involved in many of the hundreds of rebellions which in some cases included thousands of women, men and children.

From Africa came queen Nzinga (1581-1663) of Angola[7] a great military leader and Dona Beatrice (1682-1706) a political and religious leader from the Kongo. In Ghana, Yaa Asantewa (1840/60-1920) led a war against the British invasion in 1900 (Sweetman, 1984). From Jamaica, in the early 1700s, rose Nanny the great Maroon military leader and tactician (Hart, 1985:44). In the U.S., Harriet Tubman was the bravest of the freedom fighters on the Underground Railroad (James, 1985:23). There are countless stories of the bravery of African women and most have never been told. The reconstruction of herstory is important for understanding and defining African cultural identity outside the European paradigms constructed by White men and women.

These acts of defiance are some of the ways that women's bravery has fed into the genesis of the Pan Africanist and Black Nationalist movements. In the contemporary situation African women writers like Ifi Amadiume, Filomina Chioma Steady, Niara Sudarkasa, Rosalyn Terborg-Penn, and others highlight the critical roles that women across Africa from Mozambique, Angola, Namibia, South Africa, Nigeria and Kenya, for instance, have played in the struggles for independence from European domination. However, as a result of western patriarchy, men have been viewed and promoted as the major figureheads while women have been given less recognition or credit. Paula Giddings (1988) and Stella Dadzie (1990) provide herstories of prominent women who have been ignored in the annals of the African story.

Importantly, on all fronts, women as mothers have played the most critical role in the resistance movements. The love of the mother for her child, of necessity, challenges the European construction of her child's debased humanity. This love is in itself the seed of revolution because it is antithetical to the dominant belief in White superiority. How can the African mother believe that her child is inferior to the child of her oppressor? In reality, she does not. Mothers must be placed in the story of resistance so that girls and boys will learn of their potential roles as warriors in the African struggle and their centrality to social change.

While it is on the agenda of African thinkers and activists to reclaim the knowledge of our ancestors and reconstruct and practice values and beliefs that are conducive to our well-being, the impact of male-centered culture on the minds and behaviors of African women and men cannot be taken lightly. The reality is that African people are involved in a physical and mental war within which cultural allegiance is of the utmost importance. The ramifications of accepting a European determination of humanity as well as male female power relations are evident. From an Afrocentric perspective there is less herstorical evidence to show that the Europeanization of African people leads to improvement in the quality of life on a global scale than there is to show the opposite. Unfortunately, there are some who continue to assist in the process of deculturalization[7] as agents of oppression, either willingly or unknowingly. In light of this agenda of subjugation, Asa Hilliard (1995) states that the greatest fear of our oppressors is that we will become conscious, independent, and unified (1995:8).

Until this time, it is apparent that the physical and mental abuse of African women is condoned not only by European women and men but by African women and men. Some (African) Black women writers like Alice Walker, Masani Alexis DeVeaux, bell hooks, Toni Morrison and others, testify about our role in our own demise. My study of African mothers shows that the suffering of women in this context must be included in serious analyses of forms of oppression that African people withstand so that it is understood that struggle against the debasement of African women is both internal and external. In this way, the social reality of her oppression and her resistance to it will become a central part of developing theory concerned with the liberation of African people from European oppression:

> The degree of a civilization is measured by the relations
> between the man and the woman (Diop, 1991:175)

Thus, any future and continuing African liberationist theory and activism begins with the effort to recover, herstorically and culturally, the complementary relationship of the woman and the man as the basis for self determination.

Endnotes

1.   Re-Africanization is a term used by Amilcar Cabral in a speech called "National Liberation and Culture" delivered in 1970 which is defined as a process of reclamation that African people colonized by Europeans (Portuguese, in this case) of necessity must undergo in order to appreciate their cultural heritage. This process provides a basis for challenging the imposition of European cultural values that serve to debase Africa as an integral part of domination and conquest.

2.   See Browder, A. (1992) for a comprehensive list of scientists involved in research and studies on Kemet.

3.   First nations people refers to the indigenous and autochtonous people who inhabit what is known as the "Americas." This term originated in Canada and is used by the indigenous nations as a way of claiming their rights as original people in lands that are still being contested and fought over by invaders. Like African people, their collective interests have been subordinated to the interests of Europeans in the construction/destruction of what is called "America," North, South and Central.

4.   Xenophobia is the fear of foreigners.

5.   Xenophilia is the practice of making strangers welcome.

6.   Caucasian is a racial category created by Blumenbach in the 1700s, at the University of Gotthingham in Germany, to refer to White women and men. He placed this White race at the top of a hierarchy of supposed races of human kind (Fryer, 1987: 27-8).

7.   Deculturalization is an integral part of the European colonization process. It includes any or all of these things: the removal of people from their lands, the forbiddance of people to speak their languages and/or practice their cultural forms and the inculcation of alien values and practices either through forced or subtle means. It is, in this context, a dehumanizing,

violent and brutal process that includes denying people their humanity; taking control of or destroying traditional institutions; the violent removal of real leadership; the use of torture and abuse on children, women and men, physically, mentally, economically and spiritually to achieve control; the withdrawal of access to cultural knowledge and the imposition of ideas that are hostile to the cultural continuity of a people. These aspects of deculturalization are supported by a belief in the morality and righteousness of this process.

8. Inferiorization, to make inferior, is a concept used by Frances Cress Welsing in *The Isis Papers*.

9. See Barbara Walker (1983) *The Women's Encyclopedia of Myths and Secrets*, for information on Diana. She was considered the Queen of Heaven, Mother of Creatures and the Huntress. Diana's cult was so widespread in the pagan world that early Christians viewed her a their major rival, which is why she later became "Queen of Witches." The Gospels commanded total destruction of all temples of Diana, the Great Goddess worshipped by "Asia and all the world" (Act 19:27: 233).

Bibliography

Akoto, A. K. (1992) *Nationbuilding: Theory and Practice in Afrikan Centered Education*. Washington, D.C: Pan Afrikan World Institute.

Amadiume, I. (1987) *Male Daughters, Female Husbands*. London: Zed Books Ltd.

Ani, M. (1994). *Yurugu*. Trenton, NJ: Africa World Press.

Asante, M. K. (1980). *Afrocentricity*. Buffalo, New York N.Y.: Amulefi.

ben-Jochannan, Y. (1972). *Cultural Genocide*. Virginia: ECA Associates.

Bernal, M. (1987). *Black Athena*. London: Free Association Books.

Bradley, M. (1978). *The Iceman Inheritance*. New York, N.Y: Kayode Publications Ltd.

Cabral, A. (1973). *Return to the Source*. New York, London: Monthly Review Press.

Chandler, W. B. (1988). The Moor: Light of Europe's Dark Age. *African Presence in Early Europe*, I. Van Sertima (ed.). New Brunswick & Oxford: Transaction Publishers.

Chinweizu (1975). *The West and the Rest of Us*. U.S: Vintage Books.

Dadzie, S. (1992). Searching for the Invisible Woman: Slavery and Resistance in Jamaica. *Race and Class*. 327 (2).

Diop, C. A. (1991). Origins of the ancient Egyptians. *Egypt Revisited*, I. Van Sertima (ed.). New Brunswick & Oxford: Transaction Publishers.

Diop, C. A. (1990). *The Cultural Unity of Black Africa*. Chicago, IL: Third World Press. (Published originally in 1959 as *L'Unite Culturelle De L'Afrique Noire*).

Diop, C. A. (1974). *African Origins of Civilization: Myth or Reality?* New York, N.Y: L. Hill.

Do Nascimento, A. (1992). *Africans in Brazil*. Trenton, NJ: Africa World Press.

Dove, N. (1996). Understanding Education for Cultural Affirmation. *To Heal a People*, E. K. Addae (ed.). Baltimore, MD: Kujichagulia Press.

Dove, N. (1996). An African-Centered Critique of Marx's Logic. *The Western Journal of Black Studies*, 19, (4).

Fanon, F. (1983). *The Wretched of the Earth*. London: Pelican Books.

Finch, C. (1990). *The African Background to Medical Science*. London: Karnak House.

Fryer, P. (1984). *Staying Power*. London & Sydney: Pluto Press.

Fryer, P. (1988). *Black People in the British Empire*. London: Pluto Press.

Giddings, P. (1988). *When and Where I Enter*. New York, N.Y: Bantam Books.

Gould, S. J. (1984). *The Mismeasure of Man*. London: Pelican Books.

Gyekye, K. (1995). *African Philosophical Thought*. Philadelphia, PA: Temple University Press.

Hart, R. (1985). *Slaves who abolished slavery. Blacks in Rebellion*. Vol. 2. Jamaica: Institute of Social & Economic Research, University of the West Indies.

Hilliard, A. (1995). *The Maroon Within Us*. Baltimore, MD: Black Classic Press.

Hilliard, A. (1984). *Kemetic Concepts of Education*. London: Hackney Black Peoples' Association.

Hilliard, A. (1987). *Free Your Mind: Return to the Source*. Videograph. East Point, GA: Waset Educational Productions.

Holloway, J. E. (1991). *Africanisms in American Culture*. Bloomington & Indianapolis, IN: Indiana University Press.

Houston, P. D. (1985). *Wonderful Ethiopians of the Ancient Cushite Empire*. Baltimore, MD: Black Classic Press. (First published in 1926).

Jackson, J. (1992). The Empire of the Moors. *Golden Age of the Moor*, I. Van Sertima (ed.). New Brunswick, U.S: Oxford, U.K: Transaction Books.

James, G. (1989). *Stolen Legacy*. New York, N.Y.: United Brothers Communications Systems.

James, C. L. R. (1985). *A History of Negro Revolt*. London: Race Today Publications.

Lesko, B. (1977). *The Remarkable Women of Ancient Egypt*. Berkeley, CA: University of California, Berkeley.

Mies, M. (1987). *Patriarchy and Accumulation on a World Scale*. London: Zed Books.

Nobles, W. (1985). *Africanity and the Black Family*. Oakland, CA: A Black Family Institute.

Rajshekar, V. T. (1987). *Dalit: The Black Untouchables of India*. Atlanta, Ottawa: Clarity Press.

Rashidi, R. (1992). *Introduction to the Study of Classical African Civilizations*. London: Karnak House.

Rashidi, R. (1988). Africans in Early Asian Civilizations. In, *African Presence in Early Asia*, I. Van Sertima & Rashidi, R. (eds.). New Brunswick, U.S., Oxford, U.K: Transaction Publishers.

Robinson, C. (1983). *Black Marxism*. London: Zed Press.

Rodney, W. (1972). *How Europe Underdeveloped Africa*. London: Bogle L'Overture Publications.

Sale, K. (1991). *The Conquest of Paradise*. New York, N.Y: Alfred A. Knopf.

Steady, F. C. (1987). African Feminism: A Worldwide Perspective. *Women in Africa and the African Diaspora, R.* Terborg-Penn (ed.). Washington, D.C: Howard University Press.

Stepan, N. (1982). *The Idea of Race in Science*. New York, N.Y.: MacMillan Press Ltd.

Stocking, G. (1982). *Race, Culture and Evolution*. Chicago, IL: University of Chicago Press.

Stone, M. (1976). *When God was a Woman*. San Diego, New York, London: A Harvest/HBJ Book.

Shujaa, M. (1996). Afrocentric Education. Reading, U.K: *African Peoples Review*. Vol., 5. (2).

Sudarkasa, N. (1987). "The Status of Women" in Indigenous African Societies. *Women in Africa and the African Diaspora*, Terborg-Penn, R. (ed.). Washington, D.C: Howard University Press.

Sweetman, D. (1984). *Women Leaders in African History*. London, Ibadan, Nairobi: Heinemann.

Tedla, E. (1995). *Sankofa: African Thought and Education*. Washington, Baltimore, San Francisco, Berlin, Bern, Frankfurt, Maine, Vienna, Paris: Peter Lang.

Terborg-Penn, R. (1987). *Women in Africa and the African Diaspora*. Washington, D.C: Howard University Press.

Van Sertima, I. (1992). *Golden Age of the Moor*. New Brunswick & Oxford: Transaction Publishers.

Van Sertima, I. (1988). *African Presence in Early Europe*. New Brunswick & Oxford: Transaction Publishers.

Walker, B. G (1983). *The Woman's Encyclopedia of Myths and Secrets*. N.Y: Harper Collins Publishers Inc.

Welsing, F. C. (1991). *The Isis Papers*. Chicago, IL: Third World Press.

Williams, C. (1987). *The Destruction of Black Civilization*. Chicago, IL: Third World Press.

Williams, E. (1966). *Capitalism and Slavery*. New York, N.Y: Capricorn Books.

Wilson, A. (1993). *The Falsification of Afrikan Consciousness*. New York, N.Y: Afrikan World Systems.

Wright, B. (1994). *The Psychopathic Racial Personality*. Chicago, IL: Third World Press.

Zaslavsky, C. (1985). The Yoruba Number System. *Blacks in Science*, I. Van Sertima (ed.). New Brunswick & Oxford: Transaction Books.

Afrocentricity: An Emerging Paradigm in Social Work Practice

Jerome H. Schiele

Although several models of social work practice that can better assist people of color have emerged, the cultural values of this population generally have not been used as a theoretical base to develop new practice models. This situation not only prevents a truly diversified theoretical base in social work but also reinforces the hegemony of Eurocentric concepts for explaining and solving human and societal problems. Recently the concept "Afrocentricity" has been used to describe the cultural values of people of African descent. This article presents the values and describes the philosophical concepts of Afrocentricity as a social science paradigm on which social work practice can be conceived and built and explains the reasons for the emergence of an Afrocentric social science perspective. Social workers are encouraged to embrace the Afrocentric paradigm because of its emphasis on eliminating oppression and spiritual alienation.

Key words: Afrocentricity; cultural diversity; oppression; social work practice

Although considerable attention in social work practice has been aimed at addressing the concerns of people of color, the general thrust in what is called ethnic-sensitive (or "minority") (Devore & Schlesinger, 181; Lum, 1992) or cross-cultural (Greene & Ephross, 1991) social work practice is to adapt existing practice models to serve people of color, with special attention given to racism (Pinderhughes, 1989). Although this strategy is a step in the right direction toward cultural sensitivity and political consciousness, it de-emphasizes the legitimacy of using the cultural values of people of color as a theoretical base to develop new practice models. Moreover, the failure to use the cultural values of people of color in developing new models can be viewed as an implicit expression of Western ethnocentrism, or the belief that Eurocentric values are the only values that can explain behavior and should be the basis for solving people's problems. Consequently, the theoretical foundations of many established social work practice models do not mirror the diversity of cultural values and worldviews found in the broader U.S. society, which includes people of color. In addition, because people of color, especially African Americans and Hispanics, experience greater poverty and have fewer material resources than the general population (U.S. Bureau of the Census, 1994), it is important that practice models reflect the cultural values and worldviews of these most likely social work clients.

Social workers and social scientists from oppressed groups, especially African Americans, have begun to affirm and integrate their cultural values and worldviews into their scholarship and professional practice (see, for example, Abramovitz, 1988; Chau, 1992; Hill-Collins, 1989; Manoleas & Carrillo, 1991). As a consequence of slavery, African Americans have been particularly victimized by cultural denigration, which has been manifested in all areas of life, including the social sciences. African American social scientists and practitioners have responded by developing theoretical and practice models that reflect and affirm the values and worldviews of African Americans (see, for example, Akbar, 1984; Asante, 1988; Brisbane & Womble, 1991; Burgest, 1982; Daly, Jennings, Beckett, & Leashore, 1995; Everett, Chipungu, & Leashore, 1991; Jackson, 1976; Kambon, 1992; Phillips, 1990; Schiele, 1994).

This article describes and explains the Afrocentric paradigm that has been used in social work practice. It describes the reasons for and the theoretical assumptions of Afrocentricity; it describes the way Afrocentricity conceives social work practice and social problems. Although some people prefer the term "Africentric" see Akbar, 1984; Daly et al., 1995; Everett et al., 1991), I prefer the term "Afrocentric," primarily because of its prevalence. There appears to be no political difference between Afrocentric and Africentric, and they are often used interchangeably. Some members of the African American community (Ani, 1994; Kambon, 1992) have begun to use what they refer to as a more politically and culturally correct label, which is Africancentric or African centered. I use Afrocentric to mean African centered.

Afrocentric Paradigm - Origins and Reasons

The Afrocentric paradigm is a social science paradigm predicated on the philosophical concepts of contemporary African America and traditional Africa. The origins of this worldview, however, are found in traditional Africa before the advent of European and Arab influences (Carruthers 1981; Williams, 1987).

Although the colonization of Africa by Europeans and Arabs modified traditional Africa somewhat (Serequeberhan, 1991), several writers maintain that the philosophical integrity of traditional Africa has survived among continental Africans (Mazrui, 1986; Mbiti, 1970; Zahan, 1979) and among people of the African Diaspora (Akbar, 1979; Asante, 1988; Dixon, 1976; Kambon, 1992). These writers imply that slavery and the denial of African culture did not destroy all of the cultural vestiges of Africa in African Americans.

Several writers believe that the social isolation of African Americans created by slavery and racial segregation, in addition to sustaining the desire to maintain tradition, helped preserve traditional African philosophical assumptions among African Americans (Franklin, 1980; Herskovitz, 1941; Martin & Martin, 1985; Nobles, 1980; Sudarkasa, 1988). The social scientists who have advanced the Afrocentric paradigm in the United States accept the veracity of these assumptions.

Although they acknowledge that African Americans vary in their internalization of traditional African values, Afrocentrists contend that traditional Africa has survived enough to render African Americans a distinct cultural and ethnic group. Furthermore, these writers maintain that the application of Eurocentric theories of human behavior to explain the behavior and ethos of African Americans is inappropriate (to varying degrees) (Akbar, 1979,1984; Baldwin & Hopkins, 1990; Bell, Bouie, & Baldwin, 1990; Kambon, 1992).

Eurocentric theories of human behavior reflect concepts of human behavior developed in European and Anglo-American culture. The practice of using Eurocentric theories to explain the behavior and ethos of African Americans can be inappropriate because a major assumption of the Afrocentric paradigm is that social science theories are derived from the specific experiences and cultural perspectives of the theorist. Unlike the predominant Eurocentric ideal, the theorist, from an Afrocentric standpoint, is not viewed as an objective, detached observer but as an observer shaped by a particular cultural, autobiographical, and political standpoint. Therefore, Afrocentrists do not believe in social science universalism—that one theory or paradigm can be used to explain social phenomena among all people and in all cultures. Afrocentrists, who desire cultural pluralism without political hierarchy, recognize that there are similarities between and among people of various cultural and ethnic groups. However, they view differences, especially cultural differences, as important and feel that these differences should not be minimized. Afrocentrists believe that these differences speak to a cultural and ethnic group's ethos, which is and should be revealed in social work and social sciences. Moreover, Afrocentrists believe that an emphasis on difference does not necessarily lead to an emphasis on negativity or hostility. The Afrocentric perspective fosters the belief that there can be social unity among people sharing a particular time and space but that cultural uniformity is not essential (Asante, 1992).

Eurocentric Knowledge Hegemony. Afrocentrists also contend that the application and imposition of Eurocentric theories of human behavior, especially to explain the behavior and ethos of African Americans, are implicitly oppressive. Most of the theories of human behavior to which social workers and social scientists in the United States are exposed have sprung from a Eurocentric perspective because of the political and economic hegemony that European Americans exercise over U.S. social institutions.

European political and economic hegemony, Afrocentrists say, has led to a hegemony of knowledge production and knowledge validation (especially apparent in academia) that omits or marginalizes the indigenous worldviews of people of color (Akbar, 1984; Ani, 1994; Asante, 1990). It is interesting to note that several feminists make a similar observation, although from a gender hegemonic perspective (Abramovitz, 1988; Gilligan, 1989; Harding & Hintikka, 1983).

Eurocentric Basis for Racism. Eurocentric theories of human behavior and society have historically vilified people of African descent and other people of color (Akbar, 1984; Ani, 1994; Asante, 1990). This vilification can be discerned in Hegel's (1837, 1956) *The Philosophy of History*, Terman's (1916) *The Measurement of Intelligence*, and the works of other writers who explicitly or implicitly have claimed that people of African descent were inferior or pathological in their personality, social, or moral development. The origins of this denigration can be found in the European slave trade; slave investors, traders, and owners were pressed to justify the enslavement of Africans (Ani, 1994; McIntyre, 1993). The first justification came from theology and was especially noticeable in the "Hamitic myth," which contends that Africans are the descendants of Ham, who in Genesis were cursed by Noah into servitude (see McIntyre, 1993).

After the European Enlightenment of the 17th and 18th centuries, the slave investors, traders, and owners turned to the emerging social sciences in Europe and America for justification of slavery. This justification was conspicuously noticeable in scientific theories of intelligence, family organization, and crime. The fallout of this historic scientific racism is the portrayal of the culture of people of African descent as "uncivilized" and the projection of the belief that people of African ancestry have contributed nothing to world development and human history, thus creating the perception that it was impossible for them to have developed a credible philosophy on which to base a social science (Ani, 1994; Asante, 1990).

Although explicit scientific racism is difficult— but possible—to find in social science theories today, what increasingly is found is subtle or symbolic scientific racism (Rothenberg, 1990), which involves the use of superficially race-neutral codes that carry racist connotations (that is, dysfunctional family values, affirmative action, urban crime and violence, youth violence, welfare cheats or frauds, and drug addicts).

Objectives of the Paradigm

Because of these historical factors and other factors discussed later in this article, Afrocentricity has three objectives: (1) It seeks to promote an alternative social science paradigm more reflective of the cultural and political reality of

African Americans; (2) it seeks to dispel the negative distortions about people of African ancestry by legitimizing and disseminating a worldview that goes back thousands of years and that exists in the hearts and minds of many people of African descent today (Carruthers, 1981; Diop, 1978); and (3) it seeks to promote a worldview that will facilitate human and societal transformation toward spiritual, moral, and humanistic ends and that will persuade people of different cultural and ethnic groups that they share a mutual interest in this regard. As Karenga (1993) stated, Afrocentricity is both particularistic and universalistic; it speaks to the specific liberation needs of people of African descent and to the spiritual and moral development of the world.

Afrocentric Assumptions about Human Beings

The Afrocentric paradigm asserts three major assumptions about human beings: (1) human identity is a collective identity; (2) the spiritual or nonmaterial component of human beings is just as important and valid as the material component; and (3) the affective approach to knowledge is epistemologically valid (Akbar, 1984; Asante, 1988; Bell et al., 1990; Boykin & Toms, 1985; Dixon, 1976; Everett et al.7 1991; Harris, 1992; Kambon, 199; Myers, 1988; Nobles, 1980; Schiele, 1990).

Individual Identity as Collective Identity. Considerable emphasis in the Afrocentric paradigm is placed on a collective conceptualization of human beings and on collective survival; individual identity is conceived as a collective identity (Akbar, 1984; Harris, 1992; Kambon, 1992; Myers, 1988; Nobles, 1980). The paradigm does not reject individual uniqueness (Akbar, 1984; Boykin & Toms, 1985), but it does reject the idea that the individual can be understood separately from others in his or her social group (Akbar, 1984; Nobles, 1980). Afrocentricity's disavowal of an isolated, detached identity is based on the belief that there is no perceptual separation between the individual and other people (Dixon, 1976). Mbiti (1970:III) used the African adage "I am because we are, and because we are, therefore, I am" to capture the essence of this value. Thus, the Afrocentric paradigm conceives of individual identity as a fluid and interconnected way of uniquely expressing a collective or group ethos. In addition, the focus on collectivity in the Afrocentric paradigm also encourages an emphasis on sharing, cooperation, and social responsibility (Daly et al., 1995; Kambon, 1992; Martin & Martin, 1985) .

Spiritual Nature of Human Beings. The Afrocentric paradigm also acknowledges and underscores the importance of *spirituality* or non-material aspects of human beings. Spirituality, from an Afrocentric perspective, can be defined as that invisible universal substance that connects all human beings to each other and to a Creator or a Supreme Being (Schiele, 1994). In traditional African philosophy God, or the generative spirit, is thought to be reflected in all elements of the universe and is thus seen as the connective link between humanity and the universe (see Mbiti, 1970; Zahan, 1979). In the Afrocentric paradigm, the soul, which is the amorphous part of the human being that transcends time and space, is considered just as much a legitimate source of study as the mind and the body. In addition, soul, mind, and body are considered interdependent and interrelated phenomena (Mbiti, 1970; Nobles, 1980; Schiele, 1994). Furthermore, unlike many Eurocentric social science theories (with the exception of the existentialist, humanistic, and transpersonal schools of thought), the Afrocentric paradigm considers the soul a vital part of social science inquiry. The Afrocentric paradigm does not limit its concept of science to directly observable or quantifiable phenomena and does not impose distinct boundaries among science, philosophy, and theology.

Affective Knowledge. In the Afrocentric paradigm, affect (feelings or emotions) is viewed as a valid source of knowing. The scientist's or practitioner's life experiences, as expressed through emotion, are considered essential for furthering knowledge. A major tenet of Afrocentricity is that emotions are the most direct experience of self (Akbar, 1984). The focus on affect in the Afrocentric paradigm does not preclude recognition of the rational. Rather, rationality and emotionality are two transparent and penetrable sides of the same coin, that coin being the ways people experience life. In this paradigm, reasoning or thoughts do not occur in a vacuum but are filtered through the maze of people's emotions and values. Thus, thoughts do not occur independently of feelings, and feelings do not occur independently of thoughts. Thoughts are no more superior to emotions than emotions are to thoughts. Unlike the dichotomous logic characteristic of European American culture, the Afrocentric paradigm relies more on a holistic or diunital (that is union of opposites) way of making sense of the world (Bell, 1994; Dixon, 1976; Nichols, 1987).

The emphasis on feelings as a source of knowledge is akin to social work's tradition of emphasizing feelings in practice. Many social work practitioners believe that for transformation to occur in practice, feelings must be shared between the helper and the client. The concept of practice wisdom, which recognizes the importance of the practitioner's feelings and life experiences, is another demonstration of how the profession places emphasis on emotions or feelings as a means of knowing. Furthermore, many concerns that social workers have about inequality and injustice arise not only from rationality but also from the emotional experience of the pain of injustice, either directly or vicariously. Despite this emphasis, however, the extent to which traditional social work has fully integrated concepts and assumptions of the Afrocentric paradigm is questionable.

Afrocentric Sources of Human Problems

From an Afrocentric perspective, the major sources of human problems in the United States are oppression and alienation. *Oppression* is defined as a systematic and deliberate strategy to suppress the power and potentiality of people by legitimizing and institutionalizing inhumanistic and person-delimiting values such as materialism, fragmentation, individualism and inordinate competition. These values together under gird a society that teaches people to see themselves primarily as material, physical beings seeking immediate pleasure for their material, physical, or sexual desires. In this social context, values such as spirituality, collectivity, mutual aid, and cooperation are de-emphasized and underdeveloped (Myers, 1988). This situation leads to a kind of alienation from the spiritual and the moral. In this alienation, an individual's worth and sense of self become fragile and diminished, because the emphasis on materialism fosters a belief that human worth is equivalent to physical appearance, wealth, possessions, education, and so forth (Myers, 1988). This orientation leads to a lack of spiritual and moral development that prevents people from tapping into the spirit of the Creator and from viewing themselves as intimately connected to all people and world elements.

European Worldview. The Afrocentric paradigm posits that there is a reciprocal relationship between the values of materialism and individualism and the political and economic systems and social institutions that oppress people. For many Afrocentrists, these values are a result of a world view that they argue has its origins in the geohistorical, political, economic, and philosophical traditions of Europe (especially Anglo-Germanic culture) (Ani, 1994; Asante, lg90; Diop, 1978; Kambon, 1992; Myers, 1988). Afrocentrists contend that this worldview emanated from Europe and sprang from several factors unique to Europe. They maintain that because of 500 years of political and economic domination, European nations were able to successfully disseminate and impose their worldviews onto the non-European nations that they colonized or conquered and to suppress and devalue the worldviews of these countries (Ani, 1994; Diop, 1978; Kambon, 1992). Thus, from an Afrocentric perspective, a major problem of the current era is the increased and pervasive Europeanization of human consciousness and culture (Karenga, 1993).

Spiritual Alienation. The Afrocentric paradigm maintains that although the Eurocentric worldview has been especially devastating to people of color throughout the world, it also has been detrimental to people of European descent. This worldview encourages individual alienation from spiritual and moral development for all. It also has led to global enslavement and imperialism, inordinate conflict between nations and ethnic groups, and unequal consumption of global resources (Akbar, 1984; Kambon, 1992; Karenga, 1993). It has fostered a nation like the United States that spends over 50 percent of its budget on a worldwide military-industrial complex but only 4 percent on social welfare programs (U.S. House of Representatives, Committee on Ways and Means, 1993). The Eurocentric worldview supports ludicrous debates by U.S. politicians that question the rights of people to equal opportunities for education and training, affordable housing and health care, and higher wages. Moreover, it supports the practice of denigrating groups and people based solely on their gender, skin color, weight, age, and other exterior characteristics and then uses this denigration as justification for excluding people from meaningful participation in major sectors of society (Myers, 1988; Schiele, 1994).

The Afrocentric Paradigm and Social Problems

How does the Afrocentric paradigm in social work explain specific problems that social workers deal with daily, and what recommendations for social work practice would it have? Street violence by youths and substance abuse are two social problems that have received considerable attention recently, not only in the social work literature but also in popular literature. These

191

problems have had grave consequences for society and are in need of Afrocentric analysis if social work is to diversify and strengthen its arsenal against them. It is important to underscore that in explaining these problems, the Afrocentric paradigm does not claim universality; its explanations may not be appropriate for all youths who commit violence or all substance abusers.

Violent Crimes by Youths

Although violent crimes overall have decreased in the United States since 1991, violent crimes committed by youths have increased (U.S. Bureau of the Census, 1994). For youths who commit violent crimes, the Afrocentric paradigm maintains that oppression and spiritual alienation are the fundamental causes of the commission of these violent acts. It is my perception that youths commit violent acts because they live in a society that institutionalizes impediments to their economic mobility and livelihood and legitimizes the disconnection of people from nonmaterial and morally affirming values about human self-worth and social relationships.

Because much of youth street violence is related to participation in activities that are illegal (Myers & Drescher. 1994), the Afrocentric paradigm underscores the need to examine the effects of the U.S. political economy. From an Afrocentric standpoint, youths turn to violence because of the limited options and choices they have to advance themselves economically. The U.S. system of capitalism and labor exploitation causes many people, especially those at lower income levels, to develop a sense of hopelessness about succeeding in the legitimate labor market (Myers & Drescher, 1994).

Faced with minimum wages, layoffs, lack of opportunities for training or education, and more competition for existing jobs, many at the lower or moderate income levels consciously decide to participate in lifestyles that place them at risk of committing violent street crimes, even though these decisions may seem to lack grounding in reason by not considering adverse consequences of a life of street crime, such as being murdered or incarcerated (Cloward & Ohlin, 1960). An Afrocentric analysis contends that these decisions reflect the youths' political maturity and understanding that the United States clearly does not support the positive potentiality of all its citizens. These youths see a life of street crime as a logical means to cope with, and protest against, a society that practices pervasive employment discrimination (Lemelle, 1991). Moreover, these youths mentally calculate that they can make just as much, if not more, money from a life of street crime than from going through the prolonged experience of attending college and graduate school or from attempting the long shot of starting a legitimate business with very little start-up capital (Lemelle, 1991).

Victims in a hostile Situation. Afrocentricity's focus on the role of political and economic oppression supports the view that in spite of their destructive behaviors, violent youth offenders are victims of U.S. exploitation and hypocrisy (Oliver 1989). Social workers, therefore, are urged to adopt a "victim-in-hostile-situation" perspective: at-risk youths in the United States facing hostile practices of exploitation and hypocrisy. From this viewpoint, interventions should encourage and bring into existence socially caring policies and patterns of social behavior that economically and politically advance all people and enhance their positive potential. Instead of focusing intervention strategies more on individual adaptation or ego deficits, the Afrocentric paradigm advocates that more attention be placed on systems-accommodation and systems-replacement models of intervention. To this extent, the worker should take on the roles of policy practitioner (Jansson, 1994) and community organizer.

Violence and Spiritual Alienation. Spiritual alienation also can provide some explanation of youth street violence in the United States. Spiritual alienation is the disconnection of nonmaterial and morally affirming values from concepts of human self-worth and from the character of social relationships. The key concept here is disconnection, the disconnection that allows people to take on an insular, detached identity of self—individualism—and to view themselves primarily, if not exclusively, as material beings. 1 believe that the detached and materialistic identities of self cause youths to lack a spiritual connection to others, the sort of connection that allows them to see themselves and others as part of an interdependent web held together by the acknowledgment of the sacredness of, and the Creator's presence in, all human life.

The lack of awareness of this sacredness and spiritual interconnectedness provides a justification for exploiting and intentionally harming people, because people are seen as mere things or objects. In this objectification of human beings, people suspend—if only momentarily—caring or loving emotions toward others.

In my view, youth violence is a process of reciprocal objectification of human beings wherein physical aggression becomes the primary mode of expression that can be overcome only through an Afrocentric perspective. The reciprocal objectification of human beings that leads to violence is reinforced by ideas of human beings as inherently evil, aggressive, and selfish. Supported by the Judeo-Christian ethic and prominent Eurocentric theories of human behavior, these ideas, when internalized by young people, may lead to the false belief that humans lack the inherent capacity to be peaceful, caring, and morally affirming. Youths who commit violent acts often say, "I had to get him before he got me." Such statements reveal the internalization of the pessimistic vision of human behavior that is too often perpetuated by the values, philosophy, and social sciences of Western, Eurocentric societies (Akbar, 1984; Schiele, 1994).

Promoting Holistic Thinking. An Afrocentric analysis contends that this pessimistic, aggressive viewpoint is nurtured by the cruel effects of oppression, which too frequently engenders communities in which violence becomes a way of life (Oliver, 1989). The goal of the Afrocentric social worker is to try to eliminate spiritual alienation in young people and to begin to replace it with values that affirm a more holistic, spiritual, and optimistic viewpoint of human beings. This can be achieved by promoting and teaching holistic reasoning among youths as opposed to fragmented or analytic reasoning, which some say lays the foundation for the objectification and ultimately the exploitation of human beings (Ani, 1994; Burgest, 1981; Schiele, 1994).

Holistic reasoning or logic is thinking predicated on at least two concepts: union of feeling and thought (Ani, 1994; Bell, 1994) and the spiritual oneness of human beings. Acknowledging the interconnectedness of feelings and thought allows young people to make decisions that more completely tap the multidimensional makeup of their being. This acknowledgment allows them to get in touch with latent aspects of themselves that can serve as new avenues through which to achieve a greater capacity for positive potentiality and change.

The Afrocentric perception of human beings is based on the belief that at the core of the human being there is a spiritual essence that releases vast capabilities for interconnectedness or what Nobles (1980) called "spiritual oneness." Bringing young people into spiritual oneness helps them to understand that they are spiritually and socially connected to others, to acknowledge the sacredness of all human life, and to appreciate the many shades and variations of human beings and human experiences.

This transformation from materialistic-individualistic thinking to spiritual-holistic thinking among those who seek professional help can be brought about by a therapeutic process known as belief systems analysis (Myers, 1988). Although this helping process can be conducted through direct, one-on-one practice, the Afrocentric paradigm in social work practice invariably views the Eurocentric worldview as the primary target or change.

Substance Abuse

Most societies in history have sanctioned the use of some form of mood-altering substance, if for nothing more than ceremonial occasions (Goodman, Lovejoy, & Sherratt, 1995). Thus, the Afrocentric view is that the use of mood-altering substances is not deemed inherently deleterious (Christmon, 1995). What is damaging is the abuse or overuse of these sub stances and the reasons people use them in the first place. For this reason, the Afrocentric paradigm of social work acknowledges that substance abuse, like most other problems, must be viewed within the sociocultural and political-economic context in which it occurs (Oliver, 1989).

Sociocultural and Political-Economic Context. It is my perception that the Afrocentric paradigm in social work asserts that the political-economic and sociocultural attributes of the United States are the bases for the existence of substance abuse in this country. Specifically, substance abuse is a function of two phenomena: (1) Addictive substances are part of a broader arsenal used to dominate people more efficiently by rendering them politically passive and indifferent, and substance abuse is a response to spiritual alienation. I believe that Afrocentric social work perceives the dominant group in the United States as having a vested interest in keeping the majority of citizens politically passive and indifferent. The idea is to contain people by any means necessary or appropriate so that power can remain in the domain of a few. Because insurgency and dissipation of their power base is always of concern to the dominant group, the Afrocentric paradigm contends that this group will not stop at nothing to ensure and maximize its power. The broad availability of drugs in the United States, which contributes to the existence and increase in substance abuse, possibly helps the dominant group maintain its control and privilege over others as well as the material universe (Lusane, 1991).

Substance abusers are predictably politically passive; in the case of those in the worst socioeconomic conditions, such as African Americans, they too often participate in violent acts that destroy members of their own oppressed or exploited communities, thereby unconsciously capitulating to the political interests of the "white power elite" (Wilson, 1990).

Social workers working within the Afrocentric paradigm endeavor to expose the social contradictions, inequalities, and consequences of policies about drug trafficking, distribution, and control. For example, social workers could fight against the disproportionate location of liquor stores in urban communities of color. Social workers could also serve as educators to raise the political consciousness of those who abuse substances—especially those from lower socioeconomic groups and communities of people of color—by pointing out the relationship between substance abuse and the political oppression of affected communities. Finally, social workers could help organize boycotts of activities and organizations that are sponsored by the alcohol industry or that are known to be heavily financed by the illicit drug trade.

Substance Abuse and Spiritual Alienation. Substance abuse in the United States can also be viewed as a response to spiritual alienation. The effects of spiritual alienation have deep psychological consequences that the abuse of substances may help ease. The Afrocentric paradigm posits that humans at peace with themselves have the best chance of drawing on their vast potential when they acknowledge that the core of their being is spiritual. When people fail to admit this or when a society dissuades them from this belief, a limited view of life content and happiness emerges. Within this starved notion of human existence, happiness and human self-worth gets translated into how much and what one owns, how one looks, and how fast or much one's career advances (Myers, 1988).

Furthermore, time, especially the future, is thought to be an enemy to compete against, because, in this worldview, all phenomena are regarded as things or objects the individual must compete against or overcome. This perspective places undue stress on the individual to succeed or to win, and the stress related to "winning" these material battles becomes even more pronounced for the oppressed. Thus, the Afrocentric paradigm should view substance abuse as a mode through which individuals attempt to compensate for their perceived failure to overcome life's material obstacles.

The role of the Afrocentric social worker whose specialty is substance abuse is to help bring into existence a new society in which relations between and among people and between people and the physical world are not based on conflict or antagonism. In doing this, the Afrocentric substance abuse worker explores and helps reinterpret experiences that abusers perceive occurred because of their failure to successfully overcome obstacles. Thus, eliminating spiritual alienation in abusers' lives becomes a primary goal of intervention. The Afrocentric substance abuse worker augments the examination of the detrimental corollaries of spiritual alienation on abusers and their families and integrates this knowledge in training seminars, schools of social work, and organizations that serve substance abusers. Social workers from an Afrocentric framework view spiritual alienation as a major public health problem. I believe such a view allows Afrocentric social workers to advocate a more complete definition of health that incorporates unobservable and too often untapped dimensions of human functioning and potential.

Afrocentric Essentials in the Helping Process

The Afrocentric paradigm maintains that the personalization of the professional relationship and reciprocity within professional relationships are essential components of the helping or healing process (Brisbane Womble, 1991; Jackson, 1976; Myers, 1988; Phillips, 1990).

Personalization of the Helping Relationship

Personalizing the professional relationship involves downplaying aloofness and emotional distance between the helper and the client. Professionalism is not associated with objectivity because objectivity, within the Afrocentric paradigm, is viewed as a false attribute of human beings.

For Afrocentric social work, emotional distance is seen as unproductive because it prevents the complete development of a trusting, authentic helping relationship. The demonstration of positive feelings by the helper cues the person being helped that the helper does indeed care about his or her life. This perception of caring provides the foundation for the relationship to be viewed and practiced as a sacred and special one—a unique point where people meet to advance human transformation. It leads to the formation of a shared consciousness between the helper and helped, and the helping relationship becomes an avenue through which both the helped and helper tune into an aspect of life that has implications for both their lives (Phillips, 1990).

Although the problem of the client is the focal point of the relationship, the helper understands that the problem is a human one that can and does have direct or indirect implications for his or her own life. Afrocentricity realizes that the worldview to which all are exposed can have detrimental consequences for all. Thus, "feeling" the client's problem (that is, personalizing the problem and understanding that it directly or indirectly affects the helper's life too) is an essential skill in Afrocentric social work.

Reciprocity in the Helping Relationship

The Afrocentric paradigm also emphasizes reciprocity in the helping relationship. Reciprocity not only implies the identification of problems mutually important to the client and helper but also means that the helper can learn and be assisted by the helped. Both the helper and helped can be the sources and recipients of information and assistance (Brisbane & Womble, 1991).

From an Afrocentric viewpoint, all human beings have the potential to help others; all human beings have experiences and knowledge that can be used to enlighten the thinking and enhance the lives of others. To this extent, the

Afrocentric paradigm is not elitist; it does not view the worker as the only expert in the helping relationship. To do so is to de-emphasize and devalue the experiences and knowledge of the client in a way that is dehumanizing and oppressive. As Pinderhughes (1989) and Saleebey (1992) noted, practitioners must be willing to give up power to empower the client and be able to identify strengths of the client that can and should be integrated in the helping process. Afrocentricity agrees strongly with this observation and encourages a social work practice predicated on equality.

Conclusion

Afrocentricity is an emerging social work paradigm with particularistic and universalistic characteristics that can be used to uplift oppressed groups and advance spiritual and moral development in the world. Its call for spiritual and moral growth and the liberation of historically oppressed groups is in keeping with social work's mission of equality and justice for all. With its focus on the interaction between macro and micro problems, Afrocentricity fits well within social work's person-in-environment perspective. Probably Afrocentricity's most significant contribution to social work is its application of traditional African philosophical concepts as a foundation for a new social work practice model. By codifying the cultural values of people of African descent into a paradigm for explaining human behavior and solving societal problems social work's knowledge base can be expanded and become more inclusive of the plurality of values found in a multiethnic and multicultural society and world.

References

Abramovitz, M. 1988. *Regulating the lives of women: Social welfare policy from colonial times to the present.* Boston, MA: South End Press.

Akbar, N. 1979. African roots of black personality. *Reflections on black psychology,* W. D. Smith, H. Kathleen, M. H. Surlew, & W. M. Whitney (eds.). Washington, DC: University Press of America. 79-87.

Akbar, N. 1984. Africentric social sciences for human liberation. *Journal of Black Studies.* 14: 395-414.

Ani, M. 1994. *Yurugu: An African-centered critique of European cultural thought and behavior.* Trenton, NJ: Africa World Press.

Asante, M. K. 1988. *Afrocentricity.* Trenton, NJ: Africa World Press.

Asante, M. K. 1990. *Kemet, Afrocentricity, and Knowledge.* Trenton, NJ: Africa World Press.

Asante, M. K. 1992. "The Painful Demise of Eurocentrism." *World.* 1: 305-317.

Baldwin, J., & Hopkins, R. 1990. African-American and European-American Cultural Differences as Assessed by the Worldviews Paradigm: An Empirical Analysis. *Western Journal of Black Studies.* 14: 38-52.

Bell, Y. R. 1994. A Culturally Sensitive Analysis of Black Learning Style. *Journal of Black Psychology.* 20(1): 471.

Bell, Y. R., Bouie, C. L., & Baldwin, J. A. 1990. Afrocentric Cultural Consciousness and African American Male-Female Relationships. *Journal of Black Studies*. 21: 162-189.

Boykin, W., & Toms, F. 1985. Black Child Socialization: A Conceptual Framework. *Black Children*, H. P. McAdoo (ed.). Beverly Hills, CA: Sage Publications. 35-51.

Brisbane, F. L., & Womble, M. 1991. *Working with African Americans: The professional's Handbook.* Chicago, IL: HRDI International Press.

Burgest, D. R. 1981. Theory on White Supremacy and Black Oppression. *Black Books Bulletin.* 7(2): 230.

Burgest, D. R. 1982. Worldviews: Implications for social theory and third world people. *Social work practice with minorities*, Burgest, D. R. (ed.) Metuchen, NJ: Scarecrow Press. 45-56.

Carruthers, J. H. 1981. Reflections on the history of the Afrocentric worldview. *Black Books Bulletin.* 7(1): 4-7.

Chau, K. L. 1992. Educating for effective group work practice in multicultural environments of the 1990s. *Journal of Multicultural Social Work.* 1(4): 1-15.

Christmon, K. 1995. Historical overview of alcoholism in the African American community. *Journal of Black Studies.* 25: 318-330.

Cloward, R. A., & Ohlin, L. E. 1960. *Delinquency and opportunity.* New York, N.Y: Free Press.

Daly, A., Jennings, J., Beckett, J., & Leashore, B. 1995. Effective coping strategies of African Americans. *Social Work.* 40: 240-248.

Devore, W., & Schlesinger, E. 1981. *Ethnic-sensitive social work practice.* St. Louis, MS: C.V. Mosby.

Diop, C. A. 1978. *The Cultural Unity of Black Africa.* Chicago, IL: Third World Press.

Dixon, V. 1976. World views and research methodology. *African philosophy: Assumptions and paradigms for research on black persons*, King, L., Dixon, V. & W. Nobles (eds.). Los Angeles, CA: Fanon Center Publications. 51-93.

Everett, J. E., Chipungu, S. S., & Leashore, B. R. (eds.). (1991). *Child welfare: An Africentric perspective.* New Brunswick, NJ: Rutgers University Press.

Franklin, I. H. 1980. *From slavery to freedom: A history of Negro Americans.* New York, N.Y.: Alfred A. Knopf.

Gilligan, C. 1989. Woman's place in man's life cycle. *Feminist frontiers II: Rethinking sex, gender, and society*, L. Richardson & V. Taylor (eds.). New York N.Y.: McGraw-Hill. 31-42.

Goodman, I., Lovejoy, P. E., & Sherratt. A. (eds.). 1995. *Consuming habits. Drugs in history and anthropology.* New York, N.Y.: Routledge & Kegan Paul.

Greene, R. R., & Ephross, P. H. 1991. *Human behavior theory and social work practice.* New York, N.Y.: Aldine de Gruyter.

Harding, S., & Hintikka, M. 1983. Introduction. *Discovering reality: Feminist perspectives on epistemology, metaphysics, methodology, and philosophy of science*, Harding, S. & Hintikka, M. (eds.). Boston MA: D. Reidel. ix-xix.

Harris, N. (1992) . A philosophical basis for an Afrocentric orientation. *Western Journal of Black Studies*. 16: 151-59.

Hegel, G.W.F. (1837) 1956. *The philosophy of history*. New York, N.Y.: Dover Publications.

Herskovitz, M. J. 1941. *The myth of the Negro past*. New York, N.Y.: Harper & Row.

Hill-Collins, P. 1989. The social construction of black feminist thought. *Signs*. 14:745-773.

Jackson, G. G. 1976. The African genesis of the black perspective in helping. *Professional Psychology*. 7: 292-308.

Jansson, B. S. 1994. *Social policy: From theory to policy practice*. Pacific Grove, CA: Brooks/Cole.

Kambon, K. 1992. *The African personality in America: An African-centered framework*. Tallahassee, FL: Nubian Nation Publications.

Karenga, M. 1993. *Introduction to Black Studies*. Los Angeles, CA: University of Sankore Press.

Lemelle, A. J. 1991. Betcha cain't reason with 'em: Bad black boys in America. *Black male adolescents: Parenting and education in community context*, Bowser B. P. (ed.). Lanham, MD: University Press of America. 91-128.

Lum, D. 1992. *Social work practice and people of color: A process-stage approach*. Pacific Grove, CA: Brooks/Cole.

Lusane, C. 1991. *Pipe dream blues: Racism and the war on drugs*. Boston, MA: South End Press.

Manoleas, P., & Carillo, E. 1991. A culturally syntonic approach to the field education of Latino students. *Journal of Social Work Education*. 27: 135-144.

Martin, J. M., & Martin, E. P. 1985. *The helping tradition in the black family and community*. Silver Spring, MD- National Association of Social Workers.

Mazrui, A. 1986. *The Africans: A reader*. New York, N.Y.: Greenwood Press.

Mbiti, J. 1970. *African religions and philosophy*. Garden City, N.Y.: Anchor Books.

McIntyre, C. 1993. *Criminalizing a race: Free blacks during slavery*. New York, N.Y.: Kayode Publications.

Myers, L. 1988. *Understanding an Afrocentric worldview: Introduction to an optimal psychology*. Dubuque, IA: Kendall/Hunt.

Myers, S. L., & Drescher, P. J. 1994. The economics of violent crime. Paper presented at the annual Black Family Conference, Hampton University, Hampton, VA.

Nichols, E. 1987. Counseling perspectives for a multiethnic and pluralistic workforce. Paper presented at the annual meeting of the National Association of Social Workers, New Orleans.

Nobles, W. W. 1980. African philosophy- Foundations for black psychology. *Black psychology.* Jones R. (ed.). New York, N.Y.: Harper & Row. 23-35.

Oliver, W. 1989. Black males and social problems: Prevention through Africentric socialization. *Journal of Black Studies.* 20: 15-39.

Phillips, F. B. 1990. NTU psychotherapy- An Afrocentric approach. *Journal of Black Psychology.* 17(1): 5-74.

Pinderhughes, E. 1989. *Understanding race, ethnicity and power.* New York, N.Y.: Free Press.

Rothenberg, P. 1990. The construction, deconstruction, and reconstruction of difference. *Hypatia,* 5(1): 42-57.

Saleebey, D. (ed.). 1992. *The strengths perspective in social work practice.* New York, N.Y.: Longman.

Schiele, J. H. 1990. Organizational theory from an Afrocentric perspective. *Journal of Black Studies.* 21: 145-161.

Schiele, J. H. 1994. Afrocentricity as an alternative worldview for equality. *Journal of Progressive Human Services.* 5(1): 5-25.

Serequeberhan, T. (ed.). 1991. *African philosophy: the essential readings.* New York, N.Y.: Paragon House.

Sudarkasa, N. 1988. Interpreting the African heritage in Afro-American family organization. *Black families.* McAdoo, P. (ed.). Beverly Hills, CA: Sage Publications. 273.

Terman, L. M. 1916. *The measurement of intelligence.* Boston, MA: Houghton Mifflin.

U.S. Bureau of the Census. 1994. *Statistical abstract of the United States.* Washington, DC: U.S. Government Printing Office.

U.S. House of Representatives, Committee on Ways and Means. 1993. *Annual budget report, fiscal year 1992.* Washington, DC: U.S. Government Printing Office.

Williams, C. 1987. *The destruction of black civilization: Great issues of a race from 4500 B.C to 2000 A.D.* Chicago, IL: Third World Press.

Wilson, A. 1990. *Black-on-black violence: The psycho-dynamics of black self-annihilation in the service of white domination.* New York, N.Y.: Afrikan World Infosystems.

Zahan, D. 1979. *The religion, spirituality, and thought of traditional Africa.* Chicago, IL: University of Chicago Press.

An Afrocentric Approach
to Language Planning

Ama Mazama

Afrocentrism, as an ideology committed to the liberation of African people from the destructive grips of the West, involves the displacement of the European mode of thinking and being, and its replacement by concepts, attitudes, and behaviors in tune with African values and the ultimate interest of African people. Asante (1990), who deals more specifically with Africology, the implications of Afrocentrism for research on African people, suggests that it is necessary to "abandon ethnocentric and racist systems of logic and, therefore, to place the *undiscussed* in the center of discourse" (1990: 140; italics added).

The present article seeks to contribute to the Afrocentric debate by raising some usually unaddressed but nonetheless critical issues for African people within the particular academic discipline of linguistics. I will deal more specifically with language planning, a subfield of sociolinguistics. My focus on that particular field is dictated in great part by the relationship between language planning studies and the so-called Third World. Indeed, language planning studies developed in the 1960s as a result of the emergence of new states in Africa and elsewhere. Its aims were to address what was seen as the "language problems" of "developing nations" (Fishman, Ferguson, & Das Gupta, 1968).[1]

Language planning itself, however, was simply the more recent application to the domain of language of techniques and practices of social control intricately linked to the rise of Western modernity (Escobar, 1992:132). Two of the major assumptions of such activities are that human beings and nature are tools that can be manipulated, and that through appropriate manipulation and planning "social change can be engineered and directed, produced at will" (Escobar, 1992:132).

Furthermore, planning was not simply seen as an option but became a necessity as the West engaged wholeheartedly in "progress," its "spiritual foundation" (Sbert, 1992) since European Enlightenment. Progress meant, among other things, that through increased knowledge (acquired through reason, i.e., "scientific" knowledge) appropriately applied (resulting in efficient techniques), human beings would reach unprecedented levels of happiness. Planning, therefore, was to ensure that humankind would embark on the proper path toward felicity, toward progress. Obstacles, mainly in the form of inappropriate behaviors and irrational attitudes, had to be overcome through adequate training and intelligent planning. One major effect of planning in the West has undoubtedly been the homogenization and standardization of life, "which in turn entails injustice and the erasure of difference and diversity" (Escobar, 1992:134). As for the promise of endless happiness, it has become unmistakably and painfully clear that progress "may in the end mean simply avoiding the worst, i.e., the destruction of the planet" (Sbert, 1992: 202).

As far as "the rest of us" (Chinweizu, 1978) are concerned, "The idea of progress, after its birth in the West, was carried to the Third World in the baggage trains of imperial conquest beginning in the fifteenth century" (Young, 1982:87). Thus progress presented itself under various forms. In the 19th and early 20th centuries it was civilization. Since 1949 it has been development. Although there may have been some disagreement at the time of independence over the quickest way to achieve it (e.g., socialism vs. capitalism), development as the ultimate goal was rarely questioned. Few in the so-called Third World doubted the necessity of turning to modern science and technology as the solution to their supposedly major problem, underdevelopment. In a similar fashion, few seriously wondered whether the nation-state was the best political organization for them. They rather rapidly embarked on "nation building."

Underlying all this was and is, of course, the deep-rooted belief that the European experience could and should provide a model for the rest of humankind to follow as well as the standards by which to measure humanity. This in turn stems from the conviction that Europe was and is in a position to lead the world because it has supposedly reached the highest levels of achievement yet. Mudimbe (1988) has been very successful, in my view, in exposing the double mechanism of reduction and conversion through which Westerners have occupied the mental space of those they wanted to colonize, that is, the whole world. Defined by them as inferior, we had no choice but to imitate them to remedy our newly invented deficiencies. We had to move from a state of savagery to one of civilization, from primitiveness to modernity, and more recently, from underdevelopment to development.

Thus one must recognize that development, and its necessary corollary of planning activities, has been a major form of pro Western propaganda, as well as having facilitated the Westernization of the world (Alvares, 1992). This I will illustrate by looking more specifically at language planning and its key component, "language development."

Languages, language planners tell us, are tools that can be transformed into precious resources and managed by states through the elaboration of language policies to be carried out through language planning. Linguists commonly distinguish between status planning and corpus planning. Status planning essentially involves the allocation of particular languages to given function, official and national. Although the national language stands as a symbol for the uniqueness of the nation, the official language remains the key to power. It is, in effect, the language of formal public transactions such as education and the workplace. Corpus planning, on the other hand, concerns itself with developing the language(s) targeted. More specifically, language development involves a threefold process: "graphization" (the elaboration or modification of a script), "modernization" (lexical expansion, in particular, to meet the demands of industrialization, and other aspects of modern life), and finally, "standardization" (the selection or elaboration of a norm among many competing dialects).

Language Planning as Pro-Western Propaganda

The very concept of language development is problematic for many reasons. To begin with, from a linguistic point of view, languages change, they do not develop. The notion of development seems to imply that some languages are not as perfect as others, and therefore need some remedial assistance. This conception is oddly reminiscent of the position held by 19th-century European historical linguists, who argued that languages progress from an isolating imperfect state, through agglutination, to the "perfection" of inflected languages, which were, of course, mostly Indo-European languages (Bernal, 1987; Mopurgo Davies, 1986).

In considering the criteria set for language development in the 20th century, one has every reason to suspect that the same racist idea may simply be replicated under another form. One need simply look at the rather disturbing typology elaborated by Kloss (1968), a linguist instrumental in the development of language planning studies who is cited as a model in Eastman's (1983) textbook on the subject. Kloss, in effect, recommends the classification of languages in six categories, ordered along a continuum. At the very bottom of the continuum one finds "preliterate languages," followed by "unstandardized alphabetized languages," "young standard languages," "archaic standard languages," "fully developed small group standard languages," and finally, at the top, "mature standard languages" (Kloss, 1968:82). Needless to say, most Western European languages, the so-called world languages, be long to the last category.

Thus, for a language to become part of the mature standard languages club, it must undergo development, the first step of which being, as indicated, the elaboration of an appropriate script, preferably one using the Roman alphabetic conventions. I would argue, however, that the underlying and fundamental assumption guiding the elaboration of a script is that people must learn to read and write, that is, become literate. In fact, the language must be developed so that its speakers themselves can become developed via literacy. This was certainly the idea behind the push for "functional literacy" in the 1960s and later.

The analysis of the notion and function of language development must, therefore, go beyond language per se. It must become part of the analysis of the value placed on literacy, as well as of the definition of development itself.

Literacy   Literacy has been the locus of incredible and extravagant speculation in the West, leading to what Graff (1987) has called a Western "literacy myth," which I will briefly review here. The main articulation of that myth is that literacy has extremely powerful liberating effects. According to many, literacy indeed plays a key role in cognitive, group, and social mobility.

Literacy and Cognitive Mobility   A common theme is that literacy allows one to move from concrete thinking to abstract thinking. According to Olson, for example, anyone unable to write seems condemned to remain locked in the Piagetian concrete operational stage (Olson, 1977: 278). As a result, we are told that "oral" language "is an instrument of limited power for exploring ideas" (Olson, 1977: 278) . This view is fully espoused by Ong (1986:23), for whom "writing is a technology that restructures thought"; "exploratory thinking," he argues, is "relatively rare" among oral people who keep their "thinking close to the human life world, personalizing things and issues, and storing knowledge in stories" (1986: 25). Ong states his case most strongly and clearly when he asserts:

> We know that philosophy depends on writing because all elaborate, linear, so-called "logical" explanation depends on writing. Oral persons can be wise, as wise as anyone, and they can of course, give some explanation for things. But the elaborate, intricate, seemingly endless but exact cause-effect sequences required by what we call philosophy and by extended scientific thinking are unknown among oral peoples, including the early Greeks before their development of the first vocalic alphabet. (1986: 43)

The unique role in triggering mental abilities accorded the script used in Greece, the alphabet, is not new. This task was carried out most thoroughly by scholars such as Havelock (1963; 1976), and Goody and Watt (1977). Goody (1983:85), in particular, believed that the alphabet was the "perfect" script, responsible for the Greek "intellectual revolution," which he and Watt characterized as "a change from mythical to logico-empirical modes of thoughts" (Goody & Watt, 1977: 43).[2] Their analysis, Goody and Watt admitted, owes much to Levy-Bruhl' s antithetical primitive and modern categories. And indeed, many scholars have not failed to notice the fundamental similarities between the now unacceptable (or is it?) dichotomy between primitive and civilized, and the present-day one between illiterate and literate (Finnegan,

1973; Street, 1984). The link, in fact, was made rather clear by the racist sociologist Parsons (1966), who saw writing as nothing less than the "fateful development out of primitiveness" (1966:26), and by Olson (1977), who declared rather pompously that "speech makes us human and literacy makes us civilized" (1977:258).

Group Mobility The most dramatic effect of the introduction of writing into a particular community, according to the literacy myth, is that only through writing can a community become part of history: In other words, history starts with writing (Goody & Watt, 1977; Parsons, 1966; Stubbs, 1980). Any event taking place prior to the use of writing by a particular group is dismissed as "prehistorical" (Prieswerk and Perrot, 1978: xxi). The criterion of transmission of knowledge through the written medium has certainly been used to disqualify Africa as a place where any meaningful history could have occurred, as pointed out by Keita (1977:141):

> Until quite recently it was generally believed that the concept of history was alien to African societies. Barring unsubstantiated stereotypical views about African society in general, evidence of the argument that African peoples were traditionally ahistorical was produced by pointing to the fact that there was no tradition of written history in Africa.

Another alleged significant impact of the introduction of writing is that it makes possible the accumulation of knowledge and subsequent collective development of wisdom and science (Stubbs, 1980:103). It is believed that oral people cannot store and pass on significant information through the ages. Instead, each generation is said to start from scratch, an idea consistent, of course, with the alleged ahistoricalness of oral societies. Accordingly, a cyclical conception of time is a sign of "primitiveness," and a linear one is a sign of "intellectual maturity" (Stubbs, 1980:103-4). Another alleged consequence of the intellectual resources unleashed by literacy is economic take-off. Some have argued that for a nation to do well economically a certain percentage (40%) of its population must be literate (Graff, 1987:64; Street, 1984: 2).

Literacy and Social Mobility With the preceding claims in mind, it will come as little surprise that literacy is also said to be indispensable to upward social mobility. If literacy does indeed have powerful effects on the intellect, then anyone blessed with literacy should be in a highly favorable position to improve her or his social condition.

A major problem with all these grandiose claims (and with others not mentioned here for lack of space) about the consequences of literacy, is that they have never been convincingly argued. Instead, one generally finds a succession of strong and ridiculous statements, such as those quoted above, either without any proof to validate them or with very weak or confused justifications.[3] The main reason, for instance, why literacy is supposed to play a key role in the development of critical attitudes and logic, is that, as Ong (1986) put it, "writing separates the known from the knower" (1986:37). The written text is "objective," with a built-in, given, and immutable truth, "whereas oral cultures tend to merge interpretation with data" (1986:38). In fact, whereas written language is geared toward the communication of information, oral language has a strong phatic function. Of course, such crude positivism can and has been easily debunked. Poststructuralism, in particular, has seriously undermined the myth of meaning as stable and predetermined. There is no such thing as an objective text (Sarup, 1989:3).[4] Given that the reasons given to support the superiority of writing over orality are particularly shaky, individuals who are truly committed to scholarship (rather than pro-Western propaganda) should denounce the weakness of those arguments, and consequently, the groundlessness of any claim to (writing) superiority or (oral) inferiority based on these arguments.

As for the correlation between national literacy rates and economic take-off, that too has never been clearly demonstrated. Graff (1987:65) pointed out that,

> Productivity and wealth do not necessarily follow from mass literacy, as the histories of Sweden and Scotland demonstrate. Both achieved near universal literacy before the 19th century, but both remained desperately poor.

Finally, with regard to the allegedly unique effects of the alphabet on the mind, it is, in my view, an additional attempt at the a posteriori justification of the belief in the superior achievements of the Greeks, i.e., of Whites. Greek civilization was definitely not as original and innovative as some would have us believe, for, as shown by James (1954) and more recently Bernal (1987), it owed much to the African civilization that had developed in Kemet.[5] Moreover, there is little historical evidence to support the correlation between the introduction of the alphabet in Greece and sub sequent intellectual developments there (Street,1984:52). Ironically, prior to the great wave of racism that overtook Europe in the 19th century, Europeans themselves, far from glorifying the alphabet, recognized the Egyptian and the Chinese writing systems as superior to their own. The hieroglyphs in particular were praised for their deep, rich symbolism and meaning (Bernal, 1987:152, 164).

There are other problems with the very notion of literacy. Indeed, it has proved quite elusive and difficult to define (Berggren & Berggren, 1975:22; Venezki, 1990:304), thereby rendering dubious and suspect any absolute literate/illiterate dichotomy (Brodkey, 1991:163) .

More significantly, literacy cannot be reduced to the mere acquisition of technical skills (writing and reading), for it is also a social practice. Street (1984), in particular, has argued against what he calls the "autonomous" model of literacy, as opposed to an "ideological" one. He rightly insisted that the act of reading and/or writing always takes place in a particular context, which ultimately determines its form, function, and significance. In other words, people always read or write something in a particular context and for a particular purpose. Street also pointed out that most essays dealing with writing, instead of taking into consideration the full range of literacy practices, arbitrarily and implicitly reduce written language to academic prose, which is only one type of literacy practice. Historically, in fact, writing appeared to serve business and religious purposes rather than "intellectual" ones (Berggren & Berggren, 1975).

The effects of literacy must be considered within the particular context in which the act of writing and reading occurs. Although it is indeed possible that reading and writing may in some cases raise critical consciousness, a recommendation that made Paulo Freire famous, in most cases literacy, and language development associated with it, has been used to domesticate rather than liberate. It has, for instance, become well established (Collins, 1991; Graff, 1987, 1991) that the major motivation underlying the spread of mass literacy in Europe or North America in the 19th century, was directly correlated with the need to impose new patterns of thought and behavior compatible with industrial life upon the working masses. As Graff (1987:66) stated:

> To "educate" the workers was the problem. It was not an education in reading and writing, but rather it was the need to train them to a new work discipline, permeated with the middle class obsession with character and morality.

In other words, literacy was used, and is still being used, to facilitate the imposition of a bourgeois social order, antithetical with the well-being of those subjugated to it.

This points up the necessity of looking at the fundamental philosophical assumptions and political aims of any language policy that claims to develop a language, so as to assess its potential and actual effects on the speakers of the language in question. This is, however, rendered difficult by the concept of language problems, which obfuscates the eminently political nature of the issues at stake in language policies. As a matter of common sense it might be necessary to remember that languages are not autonomous, living organisms and cannot, therefore, be said to have problems per se. People have problems, which manifest themselves, in addition to many other areas, in language. Language conflicts are simply the manifestation of human conflicts resulting from race, ethnicity, class, and so forth. Tollefson (1991) has rightly criticized the widespread (neoclassical) language problems approach for its conservative ideological base. He argues instead (1991:32) for a (admittedly strongly Marxist oriented) "structural-historical" approach, one within which

> language policy is viewed as one mechanism by which the interests of dominant sociopolitical groups are maintained and the seeds of transformation are developed. The major goal of policy research is to examine the historical basis of policies and to make explicit the mechanisms by which policy decisions serve or undermine particular political and economic interests.

Such a perspective forces us to reconsider the concept of language development and the discourse on the virtues of literacy, as well as the

Europeans' use of literacy as a tool in the reproduction and subsequent entrenchment of their hegemony.

Language Planning as Westernization

Starting. in the 19th century and continuing throughout the present era, many African languages have been developed. However, sweeping generalizations should be avoided. African indigenous scripts were obviously created prior to, or concurrent with, the European invasion of Africa. But it would be difficult to retain the illusion that the development of African languages was based on a true appreciation and respect of the African culture and experience. Given the colonial and neocolonial context of such development, it must rather be seen as part of a process of pacification and alienation.

Let us consider as examples of such development two major agencies, the Christian church and UNESCO.

As far as the church is concerned, its goal was to spread Christianity among Africans. The church deemed it wise to resort to the native language of those it sought to convert, and consequently devoted tremendous effort to the study and writing of African languages (Mehnert, 1973:387). It undertook not just the inculcation of Christianity but of values and attitudes beneficial to colonialism. The ultimate goal was full acquiescence and total submission to a White god and to those who look like it.

Franck Laubach, a Christian missionary who became known as the "father of literacy" in the 20th century for his relentless elaboration of alphabets for previously undeveloped languages through out the world (Jeffries, 1967), explained rather clearly that what was at stake, by means of literacy and the elaboration of scripts for African languages, was the protection of "international peace," in other words, the existence of a context favorable to the thriving of monopoly capitalism. Laubach (1960:14) stated, for example, that

> It will be wonderful or terrifying, depending upon whether these vast multitudes awaken with their hearts full of Christ's love or with their hearts full of hate. They will bless or blast the world. That is why the church must step to the front and take a leading share in the mighty upsurge of the sunken half. We must not only help them rise but we must also put the right kind of reading in their hands [italics added]; and that is the staggering task.

On many occasions, Laubach (1960:14-5), carried away by his European "mission," described it in quite grandiose and revealing terms:

> For ages Asia and Africa, with 300 million more people than all the rest of the world together, have been sunk in apathy and stagnation. They followed in the footsteps of their ancestors, ignoring the rest of the world. They believed it was wrong to break with any of the customs of the past. But with our imperialism, our business invasions, our missions, our

radios, our airplanes, our armies, we have stabbed these peoples awake, and now the passion for progress burns like fire in their veins. They make more changes now in ten years than they used to make in a thousand years. [6]

In addition to the activities of individual church agents, there were those of the influential and hyperactive Summer Institute of Linguistics (SIL), an American-based Christian organization, which was specifically created in 1934 to deal scientifically with the development of undeveloped languages. It has made no mystery of its philosophy (Laitin, 1992"98-9):

It describes itself as conservative, evangelical, and fundamentalist. Most of its missionaries are whites from the Midwest and South. Their ideology suggests that Satan and Communism are one, and that God, whites, and Americans are on the other side. [7]

Today the SIL operates in 29 countries, many of which are in Africa: Ghana, Cameroon, Togo, Ivory Coast, Burkina Faso, Ethiopia, Sudan, Kenya, and Chad (Laitin, 1992; 99).

UNESCO, on the other hand, is well-known for launching the notion of functional literacy at the Teheran Conference in 1965. This idea was to focus on specific and limited literacy skills, those most likely to be necessary in the workplace. According to Berggren and Berggren (1975:14), the emergence of the concept of functional literacy must be seen within the context of a shift toward the precepts of the "Economics of Human Resources" school of thought. The latter emphasizes human beings as capital to be maximized. Berggren and Berggren (1975:29) concluded that:

Functional literacy is a multi-national concern conducted through the auspices of UNESCO with financing from the United Nations. It is a method that has gained support from private business enterprises throughout the world.

In fact, through the pretext of being taught to read and write, Africans, among others, have been trained how to be modern[8], a pattern quite similar to the one during the industrial revolution in Europe and America in the 19th century.[9]

The notion of lexical modernization is equally suspect. What this modernization process seeks is not so much the creation of new words—for after all, new words are born to languages every day, all over the world as part of a natural process of change and adaptation—but rather the imposition of Western concepts on our minds as an effective way of violating the boundaries of our mental privacy while forcing us further into a Eurocentric mold. Indeed, beneath the apparently innocent and necessary creation of indigenous terms for computer, technology, bank account, development, progress, planning, democracy, capitalism, revolution, birth control, accumulation of capital, stock exchanges, sexual freedom, human rights, women's rights, children's rights, self-expression, and a multitude of others, what is forced upon us is a particular worldview that is European and alien to us.

As a first step toward the recovery of our mental integrity, I would recommend that the African involved in language planning studies discard the phrases "language development" and "lexical modernization," for they are misnomers laden with racism. Many may also consider it necessary to replace European languages with African ones, so as to undermine the foundations of Western imperialism (Diop, 1979, 1987).[10]

However, the most important issue remains the ultimate relevance of language planning to Africology and the African world view as a whole. Indeed, the definition of language as a tool, which is implicit in language planning, presupposes a utilitarian, materialistic approach to life, one that divorces people from their language, in other words, from themselves (Ngugi, 1986) and eventually enables language to become a source of division and alienation. Similarly, language standardization (the selection or elaboration of a norm) establishes a hierarchy in the midst of diversity and transforms differences into marks of inferiority. Instead of appreciating and celebrating the richness and diversity of life, this point of view prescribes annihilating forms of life in order to control people, supposedly for their own good, as Europeans have done. If African languages are to participate in a positive manner in the African reconstruction, this will have to be on truly African terms, not on borrowed European ones.

Notes

1. Ferguson (1968), also an influential American sociolinguist, provides further illustration of ethnocentric bias in linguistics. Although he admitted that "there is no simple scale of superiority in structure and no simple line along which known linguistic structures could be placed" (1968:28), Ferguson nonetheless went on to ask "If judgements of backwardness or limited development cannot be made on the basis of linguistic structure, how can they be made?"(1968:28). In other words, because of his apriori, and probably unconscious, assumption that some languages are indeed superior to others, Ferguson persisted in asking (and answering) a question that he knew did not make much scientific sense.

2. In that same vein, Ong (1986: 41) declared that "All formal logic in the world, down to that used for computer, stems from the ancient Greeks."

3. Graff (1991: 3) could not refrain from an ironic comment about the pathetic gap between such confusion and the alleged superior effects of writing on the intellect. In fact, in the end such statements tell us more about the ideological position of their author than about the nature of literacy. In their analysis of ethnocentrism, Preiswerk and Perrot (1978:97) have denounced this position as "alphabetism," the "attitude which gives preference to writing as a means of social communication".

4. A point illustrated by Prieswerk and Perrot (1978:43), in particular, who cite the numerous interpretations of the French Revolution.

5. Bernal (1987:102) even suggests that the very word "philosophy" is of Egyptian origin.

6. In other passages Laubach (1960) describes the Africans as "trembling with hope," "hysterical," or "beaming like angels," at the thought of learning to read and write, and, in any case, as saved from "stark-nakedness" and "cannibalism" by literacy.

7. Newmeyer (1986:60-1) confirms that "The political orientation of SIL is staunchly conservative (the identification of Communism with Satan is a consistent theme in its writings) and charges abound that it has, on numerous occasions, acted on behalf of one or another national government, particularly when that government's immediate interests have coincided with American foreign policy designs. Indeed, there are charges that SIL has gone so far as to put its resources at the disposal of US-based multinational corporations and the CIA."

8. Inkeles and Horton (1974) suggest some of the following attributes of the "modern man": openness to new experience, punctuality and a linear conception of time, sense of control over the environment, literacy, and even the ability to locate Washington and Moscow! Many of these so-called modern attributes are simply the European experience idealized and erected as the norm, whereas others correspond to the needs of an effective division of international labor. As a matter of fact, the authors argue that the typical modern man is found in the factory, "the epitome of the institutional pattern of modernization"(1974:5).

9. Meanwhile, European colonial languages were reserved the crucial position of official language. The official language, it must be remembered, is the key to power, for it is the language whose mastery is required for upward social mobility. It is no mystery that European languages, as well as European formal education, have played and continue to play a major role in the selection and formation of an African elite who are often deeply involved in the maintenance and entrenchment of imperialism in Africa. At the end of his recent survey of the language situation in Africa today, Laitin (1992) foresees, sadly enough, no substantial challenge to the hegemonic position of European languages in Africa, "in large part because postcolonial bureaucratic elites have invested heavily in European languages and do not want to lose the benefits of that investment" (1992:104).

10. However, to recommend a greater official use of African languages cannot be lauded until one clarifies the intended goals of such action. The past and present use of literacy in African languages to subjugate the African mind does not allow taking for granted that the promotion of African languages will automatically serve the interests of Africa. A good example of how ambiguous such a recommendation can actually be is provided by Djite (1990) in his treatment of language planning in Ivory Coast, where French plays the role of official and national language. Recognizing the racist roots of the francophonic movement, Djite recommends that African languages be allotted a greater role in Ivory Coast public life. One of the clear benefits of such a policy, we are told, would be to fill the increasing gap between the elite and the masses. This, Djite (1990:97) says, is in the interest of the elite, for it would prevent social

discontent. In other words, African languages, here too, should be used in order to protect the established capitalist and neocolonialist social order, although this order is unfair as it is based on the shameless exploitation and oppression of African people.

References

Alvares, C. (1992). *Science, Development and Violence*. Delhi: Oxford University Press.

Asante, M. K. (1988). *Afrocentricity*. Trenton, NJ: Africa World Press

Asante, M. K. (1990). *Kemet, Afrocentricity and Knowledge*. Trenton, NJ: Africa World Press.

Bauman, G. (1986). Introduction. *Modes of Thought: Essays on Thinking and Non-Western societies*, R. Horton & R. Finnegan (Eds.). London: Faber & Faber. 1-22.

Berggren, C., & Berggren, L. (1975). *The Literacy Process: A Practice in Domestication or Liberation?* New York N.Y.: Writers and Readers Publishers Cooperative.

Bernal, M. (1987). *Black Athena* (Vol. 1). New Brunswick, NJ: Rutgers University Press.

Brodkey, L. (1991).Tropics of literacy. Rewriting literacy and the discourse of the other, C. Mitchell & K. Weiler (eds.). New York, N.Y.: Bergin & Garvey. 161-168.

Chinweizu (1978). *The West and the Rest of Us, Black Slavers and the African Elite*. London: NOK.

Collins, J. (1991). Hegemonic practice: Literacy and standard language in public education. *Rewriting literacy and the Discourse of the Other*, C. Mitchell & K. Weiler (eds.). New York, N.Y.: Begin & Garvey. 229-254.

Diop, C. A. (1979). *Nations Negres et Culture* (Vol. 2). Paris: Presence Africaine.

Diop, C. A. (1987). *Black Africa: The Economic and Cultural Basis for a Federated State* (Harold Salemson, trans.). Westport, CA: Africa World.

Djite, P. (1990). The Place of African Languages in the Revival of the Francophone Movement. *International Journal of the Sociology of Language*. 86: 87-102.

Eastman, C.(1983). *Language Planning: An introduction*. San Francisco, CA: Chandler & Sharp.

Escobar, A. (1992). Planning. *The Development Dictionary, a Guide to Knowledge as Power*, W. Sachs (ed.). London: Zed Books. 132-45.

Ferguson, C. (1968). Language development. Language problems of developing nations, J. Fishman, C. Ferguson, & J. Das Gupta (eds.). New York, N.Y.: Wiley. 27-35.

Finnegan, R. (1973). Literacy versus non-literacy: The great divide? Some comments on the significance of literature in non-literate cultures. *Modes of thought: Essays on Thinking and non-Western Societies*, R. Horton & R. Finnegan (eds.). London: Faber & Faber. 112-144.

Fishman, J., Ferguson, C., & Das Gupta, J. (1968). *Language problems of developing nations.* New York, N.Y.: Wiley.

Goody, J. (1983). Literacy and achievement in the ancient world. *Writing in focus,* F. Coulmas & K. Ehlich (eds.), Berlin: Mouton. 83-97.

Goody, J., & Watt, I. (1977). The Consequences of Literacy. *Literacy in Traditional Societies,* J. Goody (ed.). Cambridge: Cambridge University Press. 27-68.

Graff, H. (1987). *The Labyrinths of Literacy: Reflections on Literacy Past and Present.* London: Falmer.

Graff, H. (1991). *The Literacy Myth: Cultural Integration and Social Structure in the Nineteenth Century.* New Brunswick, NJ: Transaction.

Havelock, E. (1963). *Preface to Plato.* Cambridge: Harvard University Press.

Havelock, E. (1976). *The Origins of Western Literacy.* Toronto: Ontario Institute for Studies in Education

Inkeles, A., & Horton, D. (1974). *Becoming Modem: Individual change in six Developing Countries.* Cambridge MA: Harvard University Press.

James, G. (1954). *Stolen Legacy: Greek Philosophy is Stolen Egyptian Philosophy.* Trenton, NJ: Africa World Press.

Jeffries, C. (1967). *Illiteracy: A world problem.* London: Pall Mall.

Keita, L. (1977). Two philosophies of African history: Hegel and Diop. *Presence Africaine.* 91: 41-49.

Kloss, H. (1968). Notes concerning a language-nation typology. *Language Problems of Developing Nations,* J. Fishman, C. Ferguson, & J. Das Gupta (Eds.). New York, N.Y.: Wiley. 69-85.

Laitin, D. (1992). *Language Repertoires and State Construction in Africa.* Cambridge MA: Cambridge University Press.

Laubach, F. (1960). *Thirty years with the Silent Billion: Adventuring in Literacy.* Westwood: Fleming Revel.

Mehnert, W. (1973). The language question in the colonial policy of German imperialism. *African Studies,* T. Buttner & G. Brehmen (eds.). Berlin: Akademie Verlag. 383-397.

Mopurgo Davies, A . (1986). Forms of writing in the ancient Mediterranean world. *The Written Word: Literacy in Transition,* G. Bauman (ed.). Oxford: Clarendon. 51-77.

Mudimbe, V. (1988). *The Invention of Africa.* Bloomington: Indiana University Press.

Newmeyer, F. (1986). *The Politics of Linguistics.* Chicago, IL: Chicago University Press.

Ngugi wa Thiong'o. (1986). *Decolonising the Mind: The politics of Language in African Literature.* London: James Currey.

Olson, D. (1977). From utterance to text: The bias of language in speech and writing. *Harvard Educational Review.* 47: 257-281.

Ong, W. (1986). Writing is a technology that restructures thought. *The written word: Literacy in transition,* G. Bauman (ed.). Oxford: Clarendon. 23-50.

Parsons, T. (1966). *Societies: Evolutionary and Comparative Perspectives.* Englewood Cliffs, NJ: Prentice-Hall.

Prieswerk, R., & Perrot, D. (1978). *Ethnocentrism and History: Africa, Asia and Indian America in Western textbooks.* New York, N.Y.: NOK.

Sarup, M. (1989). *An Introductory guide to Post-structuralism and Postmodemism.* Athens. GA: University of Georgia Press.

Sbert, J. M. (1992). Progress. *The Development Dictionary: A guide to Knowledge as Power,* W. Sachs (ed.). London: Zed Books. 192-205.

Street, B. (1984). *Literacy in Theory and Practice.* Cambridge: Cambridge University Press.

Stubbs, M. (1980). *Language and Literacy: The Sociolinguistics of Reading and Writing.* London: Routledge & Kegan Paul.

Tollefson, J. (1991). *Planning Language, Planning Inequality: Language Policy in the Community.* New York, N.Y.: Longman.

Venezki, R. (1990). Definitions of literacy. *Towards Defining Literacy,* R. Venezki, D. Wagner, & B. Cliberti (eds.). Newark, N.J.: International Reading Association. 2-16.

Young, C. (1982). Ideas of progress in the Third World. *Progress and its Discontents,* G. Amond, M. Chodorow, & R. Pearce (eds.). Berkeley, CA: University of California Press. 83-105.

The Aesthetic Conceptualization of Nzuri

Kariamu Welsh-Asante

Theories of African aesthetics are specific or general. The specific theories focus on one ethnic group or nation. The general or Pan African aesthetic aims at individualizing the common characteristics that occur in the African aesthetic. It is not my goal to describe a fixed aesthetic that is Afrocentric but rather to determine what the issues and characteristic terms of an Afrocentric aesthetic might be. There are literally thousands of African centered aesthetics that exist in the world. In addition, in the Diaspora there are aesthetics born out of deep structure shaped by surface structure that are also decidedly African. That these aesthetics exist does not necessarily imply conscious will. Certainly in the African Diaspora the presence of the aesthetic is part of the survivalist tradition that has provided the African in America with strength, continuity and, albeit synthetic, culture. My deliberate use and mix of Kiswahili, Shona and other African language terms demonstrate precisely my theory of an Afrocentric aesthetic that is Pan African in focus and perspective. Perhaps it is only the diasporan African who can conceptualize and contextualize different traditions under one rubric. It is the diasporan African's privilege and position that allows her to see Africa as a concept as well as a diverse and multicultural continent. This conscious vision and perspective of the African in America has guided, informed and inspired the African to reclaim Africa politically as well as historically and aesthetically. An understanding of the African aesthetic(s) facilitates any paradigm or blueprint for artistic, literary and philosophical criticism and scholarship.

There have been numerous and vigorous arguments over the existence of aesthetics in Africa. I shall side step those arguments respectively with this caveat. The science of perception has always existed in Africa. If you define aesthetics as a science of perception then a discussion about aesthetics and African art can begin. A working definition of art needs to be employed for our purposes here. I like Edman's definition, "Wherever materials are given form, wherever movement has direction, wherever life has, as it were, line and composition, there we have intelligence and then we have that transformation of a given chaos into a desired and desirable order."[1] Again if you use Edman's definitions of the arts then art exists in traditional Africa. The context for both the aesthetic and art will be the thrust here. Scholars have begun to address the concept of aesthetics in Africa.[2] Robert Farris Thompson defines the African aesthetic as "an intellectual mode of energy that is only operative when used."[3] Functionality is normative in traditional African aesthetics and contemporary African and African American aesthetics tend to involve some aspect of functionality. Philosophically traditional Africa refers to values that reflect a specific world-view. I will focus on one approach in examining a Pan African aesthetic, that is an aesthetic that transcends geographical and ethnic boundaries and functions on certain commonalities that I shall put forward here.

A universal aesthetic that is applicable to all of the arts is valid only within the context of a particular culture based on criteria derived from history and mythology. Barbara and Carlton Molette discuss the application of the concept:

> The myth of objectivity has an interdependent relationship with the myth of universality . . . members of a privileged class of white men may claim that that which is not observable by them is not real. That is the myth of objectivity. But the myth of objectivity alone would allow the rest of us to recognize that their failure to perceive something that the rest of us perceive is their problem. Hence, the need for the accompanying myth of universality, which enables this elite group to convince most of the rest of us that what they observe is observed by all who know how to observe well.[4]

In effect, the cultural dynamics of a people create a specific aesthetic complexion. An aesthetic which reflects the images and symbols of a culture exists in harmony with the cosmology of that society, thus facilitating the highest creative expression and innovation.

The nature and complexion of an aesthetic will differ from one culture to another, depending on its history and mythology which almost always involve religion. Church and State were often divided during the European Middle Ages and the aesthetics of the various European nations evolved freed of moral and papal pressures although reflecting religious themes. In the Middle East, Islam and the State have often existed as a union, thereby creating an aesthetic that reflects the dictates of Islam. In pre-colonial Africa, the concept of State was intertwined and interdependent with the traditional religions. The aesthetic reflects the union of government and traditional religion. An artist "in the tradition" worked for the community and his or her task was considered part of a divine order. An artist in African society does not view society as an impartial observer in order to create, rather society actively gives vision and perspective from which to express oneself. It is a structured vision and perspective with parameters that permit individual expression but simultaneously support the collective artistic expression. Distinctions between society and artist and between spectators and performers are not linear and so rigidly separate. In traditional African society, the spectators and the artists are one. According to Fabre this is also true of African American aesthetics. "African American dance is still a spectacle but one that blurs the distinction between spectators and participants."[5] Individual creativity emerges from the expressive tradition of the communal canon instead of in response to the reactions of an audience, adoration or wealth. It is from this context that an artist is appreciated, acclaimed and affirmed.

The twentieth century phenomena of discipline amalgamation and integration makes it necessary to define what the aesthetics are and how they function for both the African and African American. Numerous writers have expounded on the historical and cultural bond between continental and diasporan Africans. It is not based solely on color, but the bond exists because of a common African heritage that dates back to predynastic Egypt (Ancient Kemet).[6] Within the general African aesthetic there will exist a multitude of national and what I call family aesthetics. Family aesthetics are related by specific common characteristics while maintaining individual ethnic aesthetic identities. Thus the Sabaar dance of the Wolof people of Senegal is unquestionably Wolof; at the same time it shares common aesthetic traits with the Gure dance of the Chopi people of Mozambique. As in the case of the Sabaar whose meaning, language and context are decidedly Wolof, the Gure is decidedly Chopi. Both dances can be understood and appreciated in the more general context and that is predicated on the aesthetic characteristics that link these two dances and numerous others.

I focus here on the similarities in the general African aesthetics. What I attempt to underscore is the commonalities linking many African cultures. A viable aesthetic facilitates expression, icons, myths and symbols that come out of the people's senses even as they inter-react with the aesthetic of technology. "Because technology introduces machines that reduce mystery, it also reduces the possibility of the transcendence of the spirit."[8] The humanizing African aesthetic is conflicted by its inevitable but contrary relationship with the technological Western aesthetic which is linear, finite and efficient. Any art form that celebrates the features and history of the people is corresponding with the highest expression of the aesthetic. A viable aesthetic becomes a significant cultural barometer with a responsibility to the entire community both living and dead. When discussing an African aesthetic one must make mention of the

African's relationship with time and space, the concept of community, rhythm and myth (symbolic representation of mythical forces),

Key to Aesthetic

Molefi K. Asante states that for him "form, feeling and time (rhythm) are the key criteria in discussing the aesthetic for black people. The form, feeling, and rhythm must come out of our cultural consciousness or memory. Black people internationally can draw upon a collective bank that houses images, symbols, references and resources based upon history and mythology."[9] Alfred Pasteur and Ivory Toldson explicate Asante's thesis by stating: "The readiness of the African mind to comprehend and express reality in Aesthetic forms, giving credence to its artistic nature, is the result of fluid contact with the area of consciousness that is responsible for our experience of imaginative imagistic sensations and impulse signals, the right side of the brain."[10]

Africans manifest rhythm's symbolism in both the artistic products and religious institutions. Participation in the cosmic forces which brings about a cosmic rhythmic reasoning that is supra-rational, extra sensory and inter-perspective. Often times, one's inability to understand, reach or connect with an African person is based upon this complex rhythmic reasoning.[11] This fluidity of rhythm that Pasteur and Toldson describe operates at the preliminal, liminal and post-liminal stages manifested in complex and structured artistic compositions as well as the rhythms of everyday living. Africans distinguish and discern by rhythmic flux in addition and sometimes in opposition to material changes.

Spirit, rhythm and creativity are the key criteria in discussing any aesthetic for African people. Spirit, rhythm and creativity derive from epic memory (Welsh-Asante, 1985) or sense of ancestorism (Thompson, 1975) or race memory (Larry Neal, 1972).[12] African people can draw upon a collective aesthetic bank that houses images, symbols and rhythms based upon history and subsequent mythology. The court dances of every ethnic group in Africa embody certain behavior on the part of the royalty and the masses. These dances become part of the epic memory and serve as resources for artistic expression today. Much like the contemporary ballets of Europe and the much lauded court dances and attitudes of Louis XIV, they secure the foundation for the European aesthetic. The aesthetic bank of Africa provides a useful and usable canon for creativity and emulation.

Benedetto Croce once wrote, "art is expression of impressions, not expression of expression."[13] In the case of Africans, art is the conscious expression of the impression and experience, individual or collective, whether it is by memory or activity. In fact, the expression of impression becomes a dynamic tradition that acts like a two-way mirror reflecting the community and the person within the community (beholder). This tradition perceives, molds and responds in a metaphorical ululation.

Richard Wright insists that "tradition is no longer a guide" in determining a black aesthetic.[14] Wright misunderstands the power and flexibility of tradition. Tradition is history with its customs and rituals. Tradition changes; it is not static but serves as both foundation and continuity of a society as progression occurs. This progression is cyclical and values the past as much as it anticipates the future. Tradition serves as a necessary link between an individual and his/her mode of expression as well as his/her means of expression as well as a link between the person within the community and the community.

Aesthetics as Reflective History

When the historian and philosopher deal with the question of aesthetics, they represent a particular frame of reference. The aesthetic establishment always reflects the will of the dominant culture, thereby insuring the hegemony of a particular frame. For example, the idea of "art for the sake of art" has firm roots in European culture. Africans, traditionally for the most part, did not believe in the concept of "art for art's sake" or art that is self referential.[15] The life force is the motivating factor in the expression and the product of art.[16] Museums created to house and preserve art are necessities in the West but exist outside of the traditional African milieu. African art and artists have been criticized for lack of authorship, documentation and preservation. In the Western context the issue of documentation and preservation is warranted but in the context of traditional African societies it was not a concern, intention or value. Process and function serve as organic institutions and consequently provide a temporal permanence.

There are some fundamental differences between the European aesthetic and the African aesthetic. Both Europe and Africa are entities with many different cultures though possessing cross-cultural universals. The European aesthetic derived from a Greco-Roman foundation is set in a profile, posture and position mindset. The "line" constitutes an ideal in all of the disciplines of Western art. The line of a dancer is developed, exalted, admired and applauded, sometimes at the expense of expression itself. The profile is another example of what African scholars call a *linear mentality*.[17] Posture is the antithesis of stance; both represent the body as icon but posture embodies a freezing of position and an attitude that only belongs to the dance itself, stance represented in the dance is a reflection of the values of the society itself.

Artists go to great lengths to correct an obscene, vulgar or irregular profile as if life or the quality of life was contained within the profile. The European aesthetic has affected the entire world, partially because of the number of years of imperialism and because of the domination of technology which adheres to a linear structure. The European aesthetic is viable and beautiful within a Eurocentric context, and yet excludes and precludes as if by necessity or mandate three fourths of the world's people.

In order to understand a specific art form of Africans and African Americans, one must look at certain particulars within the aesthetic. Clearly, an aesthetic that puts a great emphasis on straight hair is going to present a problem for people with curly hair. An aesthetic that glorifies blond hair and blue eyes consequently promotes blond hair and blue eyes. A people who are naturally dark should not even have to hope for such a transformation. And therein lies the problem. An aesthetic defines and establishes culturally consistent elements and then enthrones standards based on the best historical and artistic examples.

If the aesthetic claims universality by virtue of use or imposition, then it must accommodate various cultures into its aesthetic frame in order to function as a relevant aesthetic. Failure to do so creates an elitist limited panorama of a particular ethnic group.

Radical transformation based on physical appearances should not be a criterion for an aesthetic. Examples of Africans or Asians modifying their physical features to appear more European suggest a distorted view of an aesthetic function. Actually an aesthetic provides ground for cultural inclusion not ground for cultural exclusion. Indeed there are numerous aesthetic examples of individuals intraculturally transforming or altering certain features to more closely approximate the ideal. But it is the ideals of their own particular aesthetic based on the history, mythology and symbolism of that society. Kikuyu women aid the process of the spacing of the teeth by pushing a stick between the front two teeth; or Mende girls are taught how to walk to ensure that their thighs and legs will close as that is a desirable trait in Mende culture.[18] The Eurocentric aesthetic can no longer serve as a catch-all for Africans and Asians; it is essentially a limited perspective.

An aesthetic draws upon the history, mythology, motif and creative ethos of a group of people by virtue of its reflection of the images and symbols of its own group. The African aesthetic is responsible for an art that resembles, mirrors and echoes the creative ethos of a specific or general African people. An aesthetic that manifests history, mythology and values will transcend time, geography and boundaries, and evidence itself in both surface and deep structure realities. The need to define an Afrocentric aesthetic is in direct response to the continuous dislocation of Africans from their own particular and collective centers.[19] Understanding the African aesthetic will permit us to interpret the re-centering process in our human history. A North Philadelphia native once explained that "culture is what you do or what you don't do. How you dress or how you don't dress. How you poet or how you don't poet. How you be or how you don't be." The concept of culture as a way of life is a universal one. Indeed, culture is life, and the aesthetic that is derived from one's history and mythology is reflected in an ever transforming process of life. Too often, Africans have received images and symbols of Europe as representative of Africa. The essays in this volume speak to the need for Africa to look within to create express symbols and images that allow Africans an immediate route to properly communicate to future generations. Indeed the lack of a pronounced viable aesthetic means participation in a distorted one even when it has been carefully designed to resemble the African aesthetic.

Africans often experience ambiguity and ambivalence toward a conscious recognition of an African aesthetic. The historical acknowledgment of aesthetic traditions and motifs lends itself to what is called consciousness of victory.[20] It is the consciousness of victory that produces in a cyclical fashion an aesthetic will. The consciousness of victory involves reclamation, redefinition, and reconstruction and eliminates the need for reactionary art forms or what I call substitution art forms. Substitution art forms are those forms that insert a black face, scene, play, dance while adhering to the structure, format and development of a cultural aesthetic that comes out of a completely different tradition. While the artistic product of such a combination may work, it essentially supports a Eurocentric artistic tradition while demonstrating empathic sensitivity.

The Eurocentric aesthetic has become imperialistic and consequently subverts and subjects all other aesthetics. It is not uncommon to see Eurocentric African art. Redefinition and reconstruction require research, commitment and a fundamental understanding of the creative processes, historical factors and cultural legacies of Africa. Inspiration springs from a substantive foundation and in order for inspiration to be optimally employed the foundation must be culturally centered. The consciousness of victory reiterates the will of the collective consciousness and the aesthetic helps to underscore that fact. A victorious consciousness is instructed by pain and struggle, thus becoming a world-view that organizes perspective, minimizes defeat, and encourages an Afrocentric aesthetic imperative. Witness the recent phenomena of young people all around the world wearing medallions with Nelson Mandela and the outline of Africa on them. In the face of great adversity (Apartheid) people have manifested aesthetically a political reality and spiritual eventuality (Mandela's release) by wearing popular inexpensive amulets that have become icons.

Culture and Myth

Sir Edward Tylor's classical determination of the terms of culture - knowledge, belief, law, morals, custom - applies to African culture as well.[21] Rather than existential entities independent of one another, these forces operate in tandem and constitute the world-view of the culture. This world-view structures and extends the aesthetic by determining and establishing symbols, codes, motifs, themes, in both sensory and abstract styles. The aesthetic organizes values in an artistic material form. Soba, the Senegalese rites of passage dance for young women, conceptualizes through movements the values of that society (Wolof) and stylizes those ideals in a manner that is aesthetically pleasing but also provides communal reinforcement and perpetuation.

Mircea Eliade defines myth as "a narration of sacred history; it relates an event that took place in primordial time, the fabled time of the beginnings." In other words, myth tells how, through the deed of supernatural beings, a reality came into existence, be it the whole of reality, the cosmos, or only a fragment of reality-an island, a species of plants, a particular kind of human behavior, an institution. Myth then is always on account of a "creation," it relates how something that was produced began to be.[22] Eliade's definition of myth is compatible with K.C. Anyanwu's description of myth. Anyanwu states that: "Myths about the origin of things, man, society, universe, social institutions abound in African communities. In spite of their variations all have common characteristics. They speak about God-creator or organizer of the world. His ministers or divinities, spirits and ancestors, man and animals etc. All these myths express and sustain human attitudes towards extra human forces, life forces, believed to permeate the whole universe. In these myths, we find a correspondence between social organization and the world order even up to hunting, farming, betrothal and child-birth."[23] Myth, then, is employed as a structure, a framework for continuity and perpetuation of certain iconic cultural values. It can be epic myth, institutional myth or improvisational myth. All perform the same function but extend themselves by different means.

Epic myths are myths that are historically thematic and axiological. They are generational and there is continuity with characters, locale and structure. *Institutional myths* are myths that are more loosely structured in terms of rhythm, situation and locale but adhere rigidly to the characters, values and themes. *Improvisational myths* are myths that perform the functions of myths but are more individual, flexible in synthesis of characters, themes and locale, and topically current. "Myth," according to Molefi Asante and myself, "in its Afrocentric reinterpretation may be used to elevate and sustain African Americans in the challenges ahead. A communicative experience, deriving from our own symbology will add to the human capacity . . . Thus, we have presented this Ogunic stab into the creative flesh of history in an attempt to render our African American myths meaningful for the artistic frame of mind."[24]

Descriptive Aesthetics

African aesthetics can be expected to utilize and highlight *Kente, Adinkra and Adire* rather than Scottish plaid and herring-bone designs. The significance of the symbols and images one uses when creating cannot be understated because it reflects the aesthetic perspective. Aesthetics can be descriptive in the context of history even within this techni-cultural society. A Black woman describing herself as cashew colored is speaking from her history. There is a need to speak of classics and universals that render names like Coltrane, Soyinka, Gwendolyn Brooks and Katherine Dunham, W.E.B. Dubois and Harriet Tubman. Classics and universals can be identified based on the canons of truth and value evolved from an Afrocentric perspective. There is a rich tradition of images, symbols and myths both specific and general from which to draw. Only through a vigilant effort at insuring continuity can the creative motifs of this aesthetic be focused and developed.

Reality is tragic but art as the intimate expression of the two forces, the natural and the supernatural, in African thought is sometimes indistinguishable and always inseparable. Reality can promote the aesthetic but illusion and myth inspire the art form.

Aesthetics as Symbol

Aesthetics is the branch of philosophy that deals with beauty or the beautiful, especially in art, and with taste and standards of value in judging art. Addison Gayle states that the Eurocentric aesthetic was established during biblical lime.[25] It focused on beauty in terms of light and dark as good and evil, which established the dichotomy of essential characteristics of white and black aesthetic and the concept of superior versus inferior beauty.

The Eurocentric aesthetic is based on Plato's concept which separates the mind from the body and places the mind above feelings. In Gayle's discussion of Plato's use of symbols, he mentions natural symbols as those that correspond to absolute beauty as created by God and proscriptive symbols as those proscribed by humans. Symbols became part of an aesthetic hierarchy that established European art as high and other artistic traditions as low.

According to Silvano Arieti, "a symbol is a representative of something else, even when that 'something else' is completely absent."[26] Symbols that are associative require organization and interpretation in order to create new energies, both individual and collective, that can sustain and manifest artistic renditions. For more than twenty years I have been engaged in the *Umfundalai*, which has come to mean artistic school of thought. When I developed *Umfundalai*, which means literally "the essential" in Kiswahili, I saw it as an Afrocentric discipline manifesting itself in all of the art forms-literature, dance, poetry and the plastic arts-allowing for individual and collective expression. The poetry form of *Umfundalai* verse is a set of rhythms that run five syllables and seven syllables in alternation for seven lines (5,7,5,7,5,7,5). This verse reflects the polyrhythmic and multi-layered ethos of the African aesthetic. *Umfundalai*, an African dance technique structured in a series of five and seven movements, supports and exposes the unique physicality, mythology and ethos of African people. Rituals and ceremonies deconstruct to become resources for classical and contemporary literature, art and music. Indeed, Katherine Dunham was able to establish a primary dance technique based on the Haitian folklore and religion "Voodoo." The technique draws from the movements and expressions of the religion even though the technique itself is not a component of Voodoo.

The African performing and visual arts are disciplines that require critical and analytical skills from an Afrocentric perspective. A black face in a painting is recognizable but the painting is not automatically Afrocentric. What are the symbols? What ethnic groups are represented? African Americans are a separate ethnic group, one of thousands of ethnic groups that trace their origins to Africa. There are basic fundamentals about Africa that can help the understanding and perceptions of the art forms. While emotions can be perceived on a universal and multi-national level, it becomes impossible to evaluate, appreciate and perpetuate the art form without knowledge of symbols, history, geography, language and conceptual actions such as time, space and elements.

Criteria for Constructing an Aesthetic

Nzuri is the conceptualization of a Pan African aesthetic. It extracts the axiological premise of the aesthetic which is that beauty and good are not only synonymous but they are interchangeable, and that the opposite of beauty is ugly but that is not synonymous with bad.

There are seven aspects to the *Nzuri* model each drawing from three concentric sources that are ontologically ordered. Method, form, meaning, ethos, function, mode and motif are the essential aspects. *Spirit*, *rhythm* and *creativity* are the essential cyclical entities upon which all of the aspects converge. *Spirit*, *rhythm* and *creativity* provide the axiological premise of the Nzuri model and offer a solid foundation for the aspects of the model to actualize and concretize as artistic manifestation. The *Nzuri* model focuses on process even in its analyses on product. Process in the African aesthetic is a dynamic tradition that consumes the event as well as consecrates the finale or end. According to Dona

Richards, "process can be determined as vision of reality that are made manifest . . . ideas that become life-waves . . . it makes concrete those things in which we believe."[27]

The *Nzuri* model is comprised of seven aspects, three sources, the "*Ashe*," "*Ehe*" and Oral principles. *Nzuri* is a theoretical concept that contextualizes the function of beauty, good, and pleasure in society. The *Ashe*, *Ehe* and Oral Principles are concepts that interact within the *Nzuri* model. The *Ashe* principle is an affirmation of societal symbols, myths and other cultural traditions. The *Ehe* principle manifests itself as a response to creativity discovery and renewal.

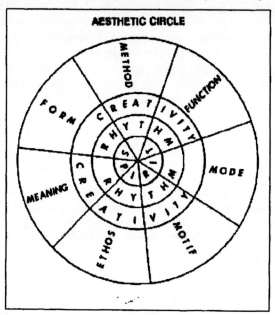

FIGURE 1.1

The Welsh-Asante Nzuri Model
AESTHETIC CIRCLE

MEANING:	SIGNIFICANCE OF EXPRESSION IN RELATION-SHIP TO INDIVIDUAL AND COMMUNITY.
ETHOS:	QUALITY OF EXPRESSION THAT EXUDES SPIRIT, EMOTION AND ENERGY.
MOTIF:	INCORPORATION AND USE OF SYMBOLS IN ARTISTIC PRODUCT THAT REFLECT A SPECIFIC CULTURE AND HERITAGE. MODE
MODE:	MANNER IN WHICH ARTISTIC PRODUCT IS EXPRESSED.
FUNCTION:	OPERATIVE RELATIONSHIP OF ARTISTIC PRODUCT TO INDIVIDUAL AND COMMUNITY.
METHOD/TECHNIQUE:	PRACTICAL, PHYSICAL AND MATERIAL MEANS OF REALIZING ARTISTIC PRODUCT.

FORM: STATUS OF ARTISTIC PRODUCT IN TERMS OF STRUCTURE, SHAPE AND COMPOSITION.

NZURI MODEL

Nzuri is a theory that regards perception and values as complimentary entities. It is the belief that good and beauty are interchangeable.

SOURCES

Sources are ntuonic (that is, each source is a unit of Ntu, the Life Force or vital energy) units that establish the inner core of the Nzuri model. This unit is infused with Ntu-the life force, the infinite cosmological energy that permeates all beings and all things. Ntu joins everything and flows through everything. Each unit has a specific character and a unique manifestation of Ntu. The three units are Spirit, Rhythm and Creativity.

Spirit-first manifestation of Ntu as it is most closely linked to Kra or the soul. According to Dona Richards, spirit cannot die, it cannot be measured, quantified or seen.[28] Richards also states that "spirit is a bonding agent and that it is a prerequisite for creativity."[29] Indeed, spirit is the metaphysical experience of humans and as such it provides an ethereal extension to both the super world of deities and the inner world of ideas, thoughts and emotions.

Rhythm- ntuonic energy and life force that permeates and guides all acts of creations and the material results of artistic thought.

Alfred Toldson and Ivory Pasteur make this salient commentary on the concept of "vital rhythm": [30]

> Many things contribute to the value base of African culture - priority of group identity (inherent in collective and communal participation) over individual identity: respect for elders who are closer to that which is divine or spiritual in the universe; acceptance of unseen forces as real, visible elements in the organization of one's own behavior. Respect for fertility and procreativeness as manifested in praise for generative powers. The ability to bring the vital spiritual force into being-all combine to create the fabric of African culture and frame African behavior under the commandership of vital rhythm.[31]

It is the sense of rhythm that gels human reality. Rhythm is paramount in the African self-image as defined in her philosophical conception of the world. Rhythm is integral to the life force of every African. Rhythm is omnipresent; it permeates the existence of all beings and is expressed in Muntu, humanbeingness, *Hantu*, time and place, and *Kintu*, things. The relationship between Africans and rhythm is not only constant but it is essential. It is not a question of having rhythm or not having rhythm but how well does one negotiate rhythm in life and in the artistic expressions of life. On time or off time is a simplistic result of a very basic relationship with rhythm. The complexity of rhythm generates multi-layered, multi-leveled, multi existence so that it is possible for people to respond to different layers, levels and planes and still be in harmony with the framework of the rhythms and with each other.

The relationship to rhythm is key not only in dance and music but in visual arts, architecture, theater, literature and film.

Creativity-the creative element has been the most identifiable and attainable, yet the most intangible. We have had little problem in creating, but what has been created and who evaluates what has been created is just as important as the creation. Silvano Arieti makes this point about creativity:

> A creative work cannot be considered in itself only; it must also be considered in reference to man. It establishes an additional bond between the world and human existence . . . Creative work thus may be seen to have a dual role, at the same time as it enlarges the universe by adding or uncovering new dimensions, it also enriches and expands man, who will be able to experience these new dimensions inwardly. It is committed not just to the visible but in many cases, to the invisible as well. Indeed, it is the perennial (and almost always unverbalized) premise of creativity, to show that the tangible, visible, and audible universe is infinitesimal in comparison to the one that awaits discovery through exploration of the external world and of the human psyche. Thus any creative product has to be considered from two points of view: that is, as a unit in itself; and as part of a culture - either a specific culture or the general cultural patrimony [sic] of mankind.

The "dual role" that Arieti speaks of works in several ways in speaking of creativity as a source in the *Nzuri* model. First, it is indeed an expansive concept, one that enlarges and envisions the world as a specific society as well as the artist him/herself. Secondly it is one of the material manifestations of spirit and rhythm, the two preceding sources. Thirdly, creativity is both communal and individual consequently affirming and serving both. Finally, creativity is the metatext for creation itself and through man's and society's creative expressions, clarity and purpose is shed on the Supreme Being's master plan.

ASPECTS

Aspects are pyramidal entities that are used in the production of an artistic manifestation (see figure). Meaning, motif, ethos, mode, function, method, form.

Umfundalai-Essential-the technique used to devise or create a specific character or persona in an artistic product.

PRINCIPLES

Principles are models in the Nzuri model that transmit, affirm and respond to the artistic product. These modes emanate out of the sources and generate a support system for the Nzuri model aspects.

- **Oral principle**- (not to be confused with Nommo) *Transmission* of traditional art forms including storytelling, music, dance and literature.

- **Ashe principle**-affirmation of one's tradition through re-inforcement, reliance, enhancement and retrieval in the artistic product.
- **Ehe principle** - integral to the creative response. It places a value on expression that comes from an individual that is new but is a creative voice that is contained and continued within the value parameters of society. It acknowledges the existence of the activity and inherent in that acknowledgement is a critical response. Essentially, the Ehe principle is discovery and renewal.
- **Nommo Spiritual mode**-the manifestation of energy in all of its varied forms both spoken and unspoken, movement and gesticulation.

Critical Evaluation

Robert Farris Thompson makes two statements about criticism in Africa that are relevant to my discussion. One is that "Artistic criticism is deemed so important in this African civilization [Dan] that the process of judging music and dance can become a performance in its own right, entertaining and informing the inhabitants of an entire village."[34] Implicit in this passage is the idea of the audience being informed. Participation means not only affirmation of the performance process but acknowledgement of skill, meaning and history. These traditional values of criticism are especially relevant to any Afrocentric critical treatises of performance. The second statement by Thompson is that "African traditions of artistic criticism, in some important instances at least, tend to favor discretion." "The comments of the local observers were never so technical as to destroy the flavor of the motion as a work of art."[35] A sensibility and sensitivity is required in order to protect the artistic and consequently the aesthetic tradition. The goal of criticism is not to destroy but to improve, affirm, expand and recommit. Clearly, both the artist and society are enhanced in this manner. In addition, the model of performance is an inclusive one and not an exclusive one. One so that as Paul Carter Harrison says, "no one is left outside the mode; we become the mode itself which accounts for the unpredictability of the overwhelming potency of the event."[36] This "unpredictability" that Harrison describes is in fact spontaneity and an essential ingredient in the creative process and product.

The aesthetic must allow for critical analysis and review within the cultural context of art forms. Some of these areas have been dealt with individually, all with separate criteria. Africans have a universal aesthetic that would sanction and glorify those masters that best exemplify the ideals and standards of a collective Afrocentric aesthetic. This would allow for categories that reflect traditional, neo-traditional, classical, abstract and avant garde arts. Inevitably, the language itself must change to effectively accommodate descriptions and definitions within the aesthetic. There can be no distinction between Egyptian Art and African Art. Egyptian Art is African Art, and African Art encompasses Egyptian Art. It is historically and culturally accurate to include Egypt in Africa. The African aesthetic in order to be centered must use as its foundation the geography, timetable and historical events of cultures of Africa. Once definition, codification and classification are complete, artists of the Afrocentric aesthetic

227

and the community will benefit. All aesthetics are universal in that they collectively express the memories of a people while acknowledging certain truths, values and histories. Universalities exist in many forms and places. An Afrocentric aesthetic that is universal will take its place alongside other universal aesthetics including other Afrocentric ones. The imposition of fixed, inflexible truths is just as destructive if forced on a society that does not recognize, know or honor those truths. By necessity, an aesthetic reflects and that reflection bears witness to the normative values of that particular society. These values delineate not only what is contained but what is kept out. By implication and example, any Afrocentric aesthetic teaches that the patronization, criticism and collection of African art must be directly linked to history and mythology. Indulgence must not be given to someone's romantic image of African people that they are somehow creative without artistic and technical expertise, that is, without any formalized concept of space, design or form. Africans have a highly developed spatial, kinesthetic and design sensibility. The idea of just creating for the pleasure of an individual is considered to be an aberration outside of society. Works of art must be created based on tradition, heritage and reason. The Afrocentric aesthetic dictates and defines what is "good," "beautiful" and "valid." This is not to say one cannot be influenced or inspired by other cultures; we know historically that transmutation and synthesis do occur. Transmutation and synthesis according to Larry Neal involve change and a bringing together of forces that are harmonious with that society.[37] One does not create to disrupt, destroy or insult existing traditions, values and beliefs. Vigilance is required in the maintenance of classical African and African diasporan art forms. This maintenance can only be insured by informed interpretation of African cultures and other cultures in context and that context must be related to the history, activity and mythology of African peoples.

The issue of an Afrocentric aesthetic must be examined from several points of view: the artist, the critic and the patron (patron or audience depending on the discipline). The artist is the teacher innovator and mythology maker. The critic evaluates the artist in terms of aesthetic, form, structure, artistic content and context. The patron or audience responds by supporting the artist and hopefully promoting understanding and appreciation. These people must have a common ground on which to relate to each other. There has to be a common denominator so that the aesthetic is expanded, documented and preserved. There are many questions, but even questioning must have as its focus the knowledge of the particular worldview. Then, Is this work symbolic, literal, abstract, *Umfundalai*, etc. becomes a question that is in context and not out of it. The quality or level of performance and execution is evaluated on the basis of technical and creative skills and in the context of an Afrocentric technique. The priority is always to be centered. The discussion, evaluation or documentation of artistic products must come out of an Afrocentric context.

Literature both written and oral can serve many functions that will support, identify and explain the culture. Technique is a means, significant and integral, but nevertheless a means that cannot contribute to an aesthetic without a sound cultural foundation that includes the philosophical underpinnings of that society.

Documentation of works must include the prerequisite videotapes, books, catalogues, broadsides, journals and monographs. The exchange and continuity are paramount to insure longevity. Artists must document their works regardless of their medium. The important thing is continuity of the cultural and artistic legacy. Artists must support one another and be able to comment freely on influences and styles of other African artists. The Afrocentric aesthetic will have many forms, structures, perspectives and foundations.

The aesthetic is organic and flexible, incorporating time, space and values. An Afrocentric philosophy will project the aesthetic into the future with a solid foundation, capable of supporting the tradition of thousands of cultures and encouraging new and innovative ideas at the same time. The African aesthetic as keeper of the traditions will be able to absorb influences, progress and cultures as long as it is located and its development, including influences and amalgamation, is on its own terms. The universe of discourse realizes itself in a holistic paradigm that functions through separate artistic vehicles canonized as one unit. The integration of music, dance, and theater has been simplistically understood as just that. However, it is more than integration; it is the complementarian synthesis that combines yet distinguishes. "This interaction of opposites is known as complementarity. This masculine feminine interaction is the vary nature of the universe."[38]

Aesthetics reflects and expresses cosmology, sometimes explicitly as in the headdress of the *Gelede* (Nigeria) and sometimes only by implication. Explicit in the cosmology are symbols that permit us to follow the patterns that connect and tie it to the general aesthetic. *Lindjen* the Wolof (Senegal) dance and *Mbakumba* the Karanga (Zimbabwe) dance both use the "break" (a movement and rhythmic response initiated and manipulated by the drummer) even though they represent specific cultural aesthetics. They are linked by a general or Pan-African aesthetic. Because the aesthetic is the virtual creation, production and reproduction of aural, visual, kinetic languages, an Afrocentric aesthetic must be contextualized as self-reflective as opposed to self-referential. It must be proactive instead of reactive reaching for the symbols and expressions that exist and rise out of the many African cultures. Aesthetics reflected in the cosmology by implication usually occurs in non-institutional artistic forms and in the secularization of the artistic disciplines.

Reward of Recognition

Contextualization of an Afrocentric aesthetic requires the incorporation of a *Reward of Recognition* so that the beholder, the participant and the creator are recognized. Each act then is recognized and serves as a positive expression of affirmation or *Ashe* of each other and their community. The *Reward of Recognition* essentially affirms. Affirmation then is the requisite reward. In traditional and contemporary African societies it is a given. When the community of the Shangaan watches the Shangara, the Zimbabwean male dance, they participate, witness and receive the *Reward of Recognition*. They know, they bear witness, they remember and they empathize. This empathetic association is crucial in the viability of an aesthetic. Symbols, motifs, myths and icons combine to create images that affirm the society or dislocate the society. The *Reward of Recognition* through the affirmation process allows for criticism and creativity but there continues to be a reflection that resembles. As long as there is that resemblance and recognition, the aesthetic is functional.

Conclusion

The axiological mode of an African centered aesthetic embodies those specific principles of a culture that gird, fortify, magnify and enhance the artistic products that symbolize the aesthetic ideals.

Nzuri as a conceptualization of an African centered aesthetic represents a panoply of different aesthetics that emanate from a central core, no matter how removed, how distant, how filtered, the link to the core (Africa) is there. The popular African American social dance "The Running Man" has at its core the key ingredients of an African dance sans meaning as does the Tsoi Tsoi the South African running dance which symbolizes mobilization of the masses in a more concrete way also employs the classic characteristics of the African dance. These connections cross continentally, cross culturally, cross linguistically, and cross disciplines share a deep structure, epic memory that restores, reclaims and re-establishes that aesthetic which is fundamental yet myriad in its guises, complexions and manifestations. The process of perception in an African centered worldview combines the sacred and profane, mind and body, the natural and the supernatural as organic dynamic entities, able to manifest themselves in all sorts of combinations and disciplines. The hierarchical paradigm that equates European art with classical must be dismantled. A paradigm of multicultural aesthetics must be instituted that doesn't engage in tautological structuring, but rather in depth analysis and criticism. One's ability to see the colors of *Shango* and *Obatala* should not have to be linearly placed above or below the colors of *Jesus Christ* or *Mary*. Seeing and perceiving will always be in someone's context, both personally and socially. The violent overlapping of aesthetics that seek to destroy the foundation of the original, or cultural or natural aesthetic must be seen for what it is: an imperialistic, aggressive philosophy that insists on its life as the only life. And when forced to deal with any "other" they are relegated to inferior, peripheral and *dislocated* places that negatively affect and effectively distort, ignore and devalue the aesthetic of "others."

Reconceptualization of Afrocentric aesthetics requires transmutation and synthesis. Traditions of the past will become history and traditions of today will become edicts. Reconceptualization does not mean Westernization even when the Afrocentric and Eurocentric aesthetic converge at the core of their humanity. Conceivably, the many Afrocentric aesthetics will expand and enlarge not only their community but the community of others. What the world could learn from the role that dance plays in all African societies. Dance facilitates all phenomena and provides a link to both the ancestral world and the Divine world. Witness the transformation and transcendence of the *Mbira* dance of the *Shona* and we learn not only about the aesthetic of the Shona dance but we learn something about metaphysics. In the *Mbira* dance as with so many African dances, the earth is sacred and so the feet not only carve designs on it but most importantly in the African dance aesthetic, send sound through the earth, so the sounds travel and become infinite and eternal to reenter the cosmic order.

Reconceptualization acknowledges change and influence but insists on regarding the African centered perspective as the only one which would be totally harmonious and ontological. Change and influence then from whatever direction must be reconceptualized as well. The "shape of content" is not the same as the "shape of context." Appearances may on the surface resemble each other but it is the shape of context that will ultimately inspire, direct and infuse the shape of content. The shaping of context must come from within even as it absorbs from without. Core dynamics in the *Nzuri* model are centrifugal and extend themselves outwards as well as cyclically. As context, the *Nzuri* model locates; as content, the *Nzuri* model defines. Both are part of the dual unity that has come to characterize the most essential qualities of an Afrocentric aesthetic.

Endnotes

1. Edman, 1967.
2. Asante, 1980. The author (82-84) discusses briefly the idea of an Afrocentric aesthetic.
3. Thompson, 1974.
4. Molette, B. & Molette C, 1986.
5. Fabre, 1983, 232..
6. Asante, 1987..
7. Welsh-Asante, 1985. 71-82.
8. Asante & Welsh, 1981.
9. Asante, 1980. 83-84.
10. Pasteur & Toldson, 1982. 17.
11. Pasteur & Toldson, 1982. 69-71.
12. Welsh-Asante's seven senses in *African Culture: Rhythms of Unity* (79-80); see Larry Neal in *The Black Aesthetic*, 1972, 12-15; see Thompson's ten canons of the African aesthetic, *African Art in Motion*, 35.
13. Croce, 1978. 13.
14. Wright, Undated. 315-26.
15. Richards, 1985. 229.
16. Barrett, 1974. 82.
17. Harrison, 1972. 208, 231.
18. Boone, 1986. 119.
19. See Asante's "Location Theory."
20. Asante, 1980. 50-2.
21. Tylor, 1871, 1.
22. Eliade, 1963.
23. Anyanwu, 1981. 271.

24. Asante & Welsh , 1981. 395.
25. Gayle, 1972. 39.
26. Arieti, 1976. 38.
27. Richards, Lecture Given at "First World," New York, NY, April 1990.
28. Richards, 1985. 208.
29. Richards, "Spirituality in African American Studies," Lecture Given at Temple University, Philadelphia, PA, March 16, 1990.
30. Pasteur & Toldson, 1982. 71.
31. Ibid., 71.
32. Janheinz , 1961. 99-104.
33. Arieti, 1976. 5.
34. Thompson, 1974. 2.
35. Ibid., 3.
36. Harrison, 1972. 197-98.
37. Neal, 1972. 12-15.
38. Barrett, 1974. 19.

References

Arieti, Silvano. 1976. *Creativity The Magic Synthesis*. New York, N.Y.: Basic Books.

Asante, K& Asante, M (eds). 1985. *African Culture: Rhythms of Unity*. Trenton, NJ: Africa World Press.

Barrett, Leonard. 1974. *Soul Force*. Garden City, N.Y.: Doubleday.

Boone, Sylvia. 1986. *Radiance from the Waters*. New Haven, Conn.: Yale University.

Chernorf, John. 1979. *African Rhythm and African Sensibility*. Chicago, IL: University of Chicago Press.

Croce, Benedetto.1978. *Aesthetic As Science of Expression and General Linguistic*. Boston, MA: Nonpareil Books.

Deurden, Dennis. 1977. *African Art and Literature: The Invisible Present*. London: Heineman Educational Books.

Dickie, George. 1982. *Aesthetics: An Introduction*. Indianapolis, IN: Bobbs, Merrill Publishing Co.

Edman, Irwin. 1967. *Arts and the Man*. New York, N.Y.: W. W. Norton & Co.

Eliade, Mircea. 1963. *Myth and Reality*. New York, N.Y.: Harper and Row.

Fabre, Genevieve. 1983. *Drumbeats, Masks and Metaphor*. Cambridge, MA: Harvard University Press.

Gayle, Addison.1972. *The Black Aesthetic*. New York, N.Y.: Anchor Books

Harrison, Paul Carter. 1972. *The Drama of Nommo*. New York, N.Y.: Grove Press.

Haydon, Geoffrey & Marks, Dennis (eds). 1985. *Repercussion: A Celebration of African-American Music*. London: Century Publishing, 1985.

Hurston, Zora Neale. 1981. *The Sanctified Church*. Berkeley, CA: Turtle Island Press.

Jahn, Janheinz. 1961. *Muntu: The New African Culture*. New York, N.Y.: Grove Press.

Mbiti, John. 1975. *Introduction to African Religion*. Portsmouth, NH: Heinemann Educational Books.

Molette, Carlton W. & Barbara J. 1986. *Black Theater: Premise and Presentation*. Bristol, IN: Wyndham Hall Press.

Neal, Larry. 1972. The Black Aesthetic. *The Black Aesthetic*, Addison, Gayle (ed.). New York, N.Y.: Anchor Books.

Pasteur, Alfred & Toldson. 1982. *Ivory. Roots of Soul*. Garden City, N.Y.: Doubleday.

Richards, Dona M. 1989. *Let the Circle Be Unbroken*. New York, N.Y.: Privately printed.

Ruch, E. A& Anyanwu, K. C.1981. *African Philosophy*. Rome: Catholic Book Agency.

Shahn, Ben. 1957. *The Shape of Context*. Cambridge, MA: Harvard University Press.

Thompson, Robert Farris. 1974. African Art in Motion. Los Angeles, CA: UCLA Press.

Tylor, Edward. 1958. *Primitive Culture*. New York, N.Y.: Harper & Row.

Williams, Denis. 1974. *Icon and Image: A Study of Sacred and Secular Forms of African Classical Art*. New York, N.Y.: New York University Press.

Locating a Text: Implications of Afrocentric Theory

Molefi Kete Asante

We have fully arrived at a cultural junction where several critical avenues present themselves to the serious textual reader. Any fair estimate of the road that got us to this point must conclude that it has been a difficult one, filled with intellectual potholes and myopic cultural roadblocks, but at last there is an Afrocentric viewpoint on texts. There seems to be a growing number of writers who have abandoned or are attempting to abandon the staid domains of an encapsulated theory.

Afrocentric theory as advanced in numerous works, including my own, establishes two fundamental realities in situating a text: "location" and "dislocation." The serious textual reader is able to locate a text by certain symbolic boundaries and iconic signposts offered from within the text itself. However, much like any traveler the reader's location is also important in order to determine the exact location of the text.

An inordinate number of African American scholars have become lost souls trying to negotiate the Eurocentric pathways of mono-culturalism and mono-historicalism. An equal number of non-African scholars have floated around ethereally when it came to locating an African American text. Both sets of readers have been victims of a breach in good highway manners. They have ignored all of the signs of Afrocentric literacy in favor of blind alleys based in a mono-cultural reality. What I hope to demonstrate is that multi-cultural literacy can lead to a critical transformation in the way we approach any discourse.

However, multi-cultural literacy does not exist apart from the substantive knowledge of specific cultural communities. There is no multi-cultural literacy apart from cultural bases. It is the ability to use and integrate these cultural bases that allows us to speak of multi-cultural literacy. An examination of an African American writer such as Henry Dumas provides an example of the range and vision of Afrocentric theory.

AN ORIENTATION TO MOTIF

Charles Fuller, a colleague in my department who won the Pullitzer Prize for drama in 1982 for his work *A Soldier's Play*, claims that many of the dramatic characters for his plays come from people he knew on Broad Street in North Philadelphia. Not knowing what Fuller knows and not seeing what he sees in the faces of people on Broad Street might create difficulty in understanding the nuances of his drama. While there are certain readily understandable guideposts in good literature, accessible to the least literate of us, to truly capture the setting of Charles Fuller's drama one must have more than a passing appreciation of African American culture. Indeed the good critic and serious reader of African American literature should have been exposed to a variety of cultural information, for example, the Dozens, folk tales, Ebonics, barber shops or beauty parlors, Baptist churches, Hoodoo and Root rituals, Ebony Magazine, Jet, and numerous authors and musicians. All of this information may not be useful on every trip through the literary territory in the African American world, but it is surely advantageous on most occasions for the critic and reader. This means that critics must take courses in African American culture and history as they take courses in Euro-American history and culture. In fact, they must search the ancient foundations of the African's cultural response to reality and environment much as one looks to Greece or Rome for analogues in the Euro-American writers and authors. The only reason, it seems to me, that this is not done in the first place is the abiding bias against African culture that continues to disorient most critics.[1]

An explosion of interest in multi-cultural issues, diversity in the classroom, and centered visions in curricula has contributed to a critical transformation in literature. Like Thuthmosis IV, who in the third year of his reign asked his scribes to take a retrospective of all that had gone before, we must take a critical look at what has happened in the last few years in multi-cultural literacy. The king's intentions were to re-establish the foundations of the kingdom, to examine the preparations for the future, and to re-assert the unity of the Two Lands. Our aim in a retrospective is simply to be able to navigate the cultural highways of a multi-cultural society.

A NEW HISTORIOGRAPHY

The critical spirit that has served to temper the received position on certain texts is the result of a multi-cultural consciousness brought about by a new historiography. Based on the idea that ancient Kemet and Nubia are to the rest of Africa as Greece and Rome are to the rest of Europe, this new historiography has insinuated itself into contemporary thinking in education, anthropology,

236

sociology, history, and literature.[2] Pioneered by African American scholars such as George James, Chancellor Williams, Leo Hansberry, Cheikh Anta Diop, and Theophile Obenga, this critical historiography influences the most elementary discussions of texts by bringing the gift of new information. Unfortunately, as Martin Bernal has said in his monumental re-assessment of the European classical tradition, *Black Athena*, most white scholars have ignored the writings of such scholars (1987: 434-437). Bernal believes that in the last five centuries racism has been the source of the mono-ethnic and mono-cultural portrayal of the production and acquisition of knowledge.

In his book *The African Origin of Civilization: Myth or Reality?*, Cheikh Anta Diop laid a revolutionary foundation for the new pathways of critical knowledge in the field of human creativity. He argued a position that was radical only because five hundred years the Western world had denied Africa's role in human history. Diop contended that western scholars have tried to take ancient Egypt out of Africa and Africans out of Egypt. The context for this attack on Africa was the rise and promotion of the European slave trade. So massive was this vulgar trade in human beings that it colored every relationship in the European and African worlds. Nothing was untouched by the anti-African attitudes developed in the fifteenth century. Art, literature, dance, music, theology, and philosophy were adjusted to deal with the Great Enslavement and domination of Africans. Defamation of Africans and African intellectual gifts was sanctioned at the highest levels of western literature and government; subjugation of Africa was confirmed ultimately in the way writers wrote about the encounter between the two peoples.

In the *Mismeasure of Man*, Stephen Jay Gould reports that some of the key leaders of the West recorded their anti-African attitudes in clear and straightforward terms. For example, Thomas Jefferson wrote, "I advance it, therefore, as a suspicion only, that the blacks whether originally a distinct race or made distinct by time and circumstance, are inferior to the whites in the endowments of both body and mind" (1981:32). Indeed Gould demonstrates that the British philosopher David Hume held negative attitudes about the contributions of Africans to human society. David Hume asserted "I am apt to suspect the Negroes and in general all the other species of men to be naturally inferior to the whites. There never was a civilized nation of any other complexion than white, or even any individual eminent either in action or speculation, no ingenious manufacturers among them, no art, no sciences" (1981:41). Indeed Louis Agassiz wrote of Africa, "there has never been a regulated society of black men developed on the continent" (1981:47). Arnold Toynbee, one the Western world's leading historians said, "When we classify mankind by color, the only one of the primary races, given by this classification, which has not made a creative contribution to any of our twenty-one civilizations is the black race" (1981:41). The famous German philosopher Georg Wilhelm Friedrich Hegel wrote of Africa, "This is the land where men are children, a land lying beyond the daylight of self-conscious history, and enveloped in the lack color of night. At this point, let us forget Africa not to mention it again. African is no historical part of the world ..." (Davidson,

1984:64). These attitudes often find a place in the most contemporary views of western thinkers. The publication of the *Great Books of the Western World* in 1990 under the editorship of Mortimer J. Adler continues the Eurocentric idea that Africans have made no contribution to the West. A typical collection of white male writes (there are only four women writers out of the total of 130 writers) the *Great Books of the Western World* serves as an instrument to block the road to multi-culturalism. With no African Americans and only four women included in the list of writers, the collection is certain to be without much enduring credibility. Any group of "Great Books" that does not include writings from Frederick Douglass, W.E.B. DuBois, Edward Blyden, Richard Wright, Martin Luther King, Jr., Zora Neale Hurston, Langston Hughes, James Baldwin, Ralph Ellison, Alice Walker, or Toni Morrison is surely a pretense to inclusiveness.

LOCATING A TEXT

There are several elements that help to locate an African American text or any text: language, attitude, and direction. These elements might be used alone or in combination. I shall examine each of these elements as they relate to African American writers and critics. However, a word should be written about the nature of the creative production derived from authors engaged in the communicative process with readers. Writers are fundamentally committed to the principle of expression; one cannot express one's self without leaving some insignia. From the writer's own textual expression the Afrocentric critic is able to ascertain the cultural and intellectual address of the author.

THE PLACE

Among the complications in the location process for critics of African American texts is the devastating extent to which African American authors have been removed from general cultural terms. There are two types of texts produced by individuals who have been removed or have removed themselves from terms of blackness: the decapitated text and the lynched text. A text that is decapitated exists without cultural presence in the historical experiences of the creator; a lynched text is one that has been strung up with the tropes and figures of the dominating culture. African American authors who have tried to "shed their race" have been known to produce both types of texts.

The decapitated text is the contribution of the author who writes with no discernible African cultural element, whose aim appears to be to distance herself or himself from the African cultural self. Among the best practitioners of this genre is the author Frank Yerby. His contributions to literature have been made as a part of the European and white experience in the West. Although he responded to criticism long enough to produce the Dahomeans, he remained fundamentally committed to a style of writing that placed him outside of his own historical experiences. Thus his African voice remains essentially silent. Yerby is the kind of author one reads and says, "If you do not know that, this must be a white writer." Even my white students are surprised to discover that the author of some of the finest Southern plantation novels is an African

American. While he became relatively successful in a commercial sense in this vein of writing, Frank Yerby has no clear literary tradition and adds to no new school of aesthetics. He produces decapitated texts with no guiding heads and sense of soul.

The lynched text is more easily produced by African American authors who have literary skills but little cultural or historical knowledge. Images tend to be thoroughly Eurocentric, producing lines such as "the warlike natives" in a historical novel or "the Valhallian quest of the black hero" in poetry. An African writer who uses such language may be rewarded by the Eurocentric establishment for demonstrating a mastery over or expertise in handling European themes, but it does not mean that the writer is placed in his or her own center. Since the literary establishment often reinforces Africans the more removed we are from our cultural terms, there is social pressure on the writer to "write what whites write." One can perhaps see why James Baldwin, Richard Wright, Toni Morrison, John A. Killens, and John Edgar Wideman are not given greater prominence in the literary curricula of this nation. Neither attempted to shed blackness; in fact, some tried to re-accumulate what they had lost through education.

ELEMENTS OF LOCATION

Language

Normally we say that language is a regularized code that has been agreed upon by a community of users. There is nothing particularly wrong with this general definition of language. However, language can be said to involve grammatical rules, nuances, words, and deep structures. In that case, if we concentrate on one aspect of language, words, for instance, we can obtain a fairly good assessment of where a writer is located.

Words have function, meaning, and etymology; my concern in this discussion is primarily with meaning. An African American author or any author, for that matter, who writes of "Hottentots," "bushmen," and "pigmies" has already told the Afrocentric critic something about where she or he is located. Of course, the same observation can be made by any critic of any author. Location is determined by signposts. In any situation where the author is trapped in the language of a racist society that provides pejorative terms, the critic is seeking to see how the particular writer handles the situation. What turn of phrases, what lacunae and nuances, what unique rendering makes this particular writer succeed. Language is the most important element because it is the most easily manifest in the text. One sees words on paper. If one sees a reference to Africans as primitive or to Native Americans as "a bunch of wild Indians" or Latinos as "greasy," then one knows the cultural address of the author. While it is true that authors might use irony, sarcasm, and other techniques of language to deliver a certain point or perspective, the Afrocentric critic is sensitive to the persistent and uniform use of pejoratives as demonstrating the author's location. When an author uses pejoratives unknowingly to refer to Africans, the critic often is being confronted with an unconscious writer, one who is oblivious to the social and cultural milieu.

Attitude

Attitude refers to a predisposition to respond in a characteristic manner to some situation, value, idea, object, person, or group of persons. The writer signals his or her location by attitude toward certain ideas, persons, or objects. Thus, the critic in pursuit of the precise location of the author can determine from the writer's characteristic or persistent response to certain things where the writer is located. The attitude is not the motive; attitudes are more numerous and varied than motives. Consequently, the attempt to locate a writer by referring to "motivating attitudes" may be useful in some situations. The common adage, "I cannot hear what you say because what you are shouts so loudly in my ear" is a remarkable example of how our attitudes influence our appraisal of those around us. This is the same for writers. Once a critic has read certain portions of a text to "get the drift" of what it is the writer is getting at, he or she can usually locate the author.

Direction

The line along which the author's sentiments, themes, and interest lie with reference to the point at which they are aimed I refer to as direction. It is the tendency or inclination present in the literary work with regard to the author's objective. One is able to identify this tendency by the symbols that occur in the text. For example, a writer who uses Ebonics, African American language, in his or her works demonstrates a tendency along the lines of Afrocentric space. The reader is capable of digesting some of the arguments, the poetic allusions, and situations because of the tendency identified in the writing.

Therefore, a text must be seen in the light of language, attitude, and direction when the serious reader wants to locate it. Each text carries if own signature, a stamp, if you will, of the place to which it belongs or to where it is going. In any case, the reader will be able to adequately locate the text in order to make judgments about the author's creative abilities as well as the author's philosophical underpinning. Ultimately a text must fit within a multiplicity of places, each one defined by the dynamic interplay of culture and purpose.

AN EXAMPLE FROM HISTORY

One of the greatest (in my judgement) African American writers was born on July 29, 1924 and killed in New York on May 23, 1968. His name was Henry Dumas and his death at the age of thirty four cut short the brilliant career of a poet and short story writer who gave meaning to the Afrocentric term, *located.*

Henry Dumas's work, *Ark of Bones and Other Stories and Poetry for My People*, was published posthumously. However, he had been engaged in teaching at the Experiment in Higher Education at Southern Illinois University and served as a member of the editorial staff of the Hiram Poetry Review and through these activities had made many friends and acquaintances who knew his creative power. Hale Chatfield and Eugene Redmond ably brought Henry Dumas to life again in the editing of his works. Few African American writers have been so successful as Henry Dumas in demonstrating the opposite perspective of the race shedders. Dumas was pre-eminently an Afrocentric writer in every aspect of the term.

For the reader seeking to possess the literacy necessary to understand the stories or the poetry of Dumas, it suffices to say that one must pay attention to every nuance of the African American culture. That is to say, one must understand the "bop" and the "do." Furthermore, the reader must be able to see how nicknames locate a person in the text as well as the author's ability to write culturally, that is, out of the culture. For example, Henry Dumas gives his characters names like Blue, Fish, Tate, and Grease. These are important names in the context of Dumas's stories. Actually, each of the names carries definite meanings. Blue, for example, relates to a person's being so black he looks blue. Fish is the nickname for a person who swims very well. Tate is the nickname of a smooth-talking individual. There are several reasons why these names are significant in Dumas's cultural understanding and our appreciation of his art. In the first place, nicknames are means for placement, location, identity. They are often more descriptive and defining than the European names given to African American children. Since many people did not have access to African names, the practice of nicknaming became a major avenue for the maintenance of African culture and expression. Names could still mean something, much like names had meant among the Yoruba, Ibo, Fanti, Asante, and Congo. Dumas understands the relevance of the nickname and appropriates its use to the functions of his art. Another reason Dumas's use of these names is important comes from the creation of atmosphere in his works. He seeks always to expand the boundaries, to move against the tide, and to raise the difficult questions. There is no better way to create atmosphere than to allow the traditions to blossom, particularly in reference to what people call things, that is, the words given to identify persons and objects.

The richness of Dumas's language, the clarity of his symbolic attitude, and the rhythm of his trajectory cannot be over-estimated. He impressed himself as well as others with the tremendously accurate portrayal of the African American language. Indeed, Eugene Redmond wrote in his introduction to *Ark Bones and Other Stories*, "Dumas – a brilliant, creative linguist- contracts and expands English, Black Language and various African tribal [sic] sounds to come up with what is perhaps a 'found' utterance" (xiv). Redmond's introduction to the stories of Henry Dumas is a penetrating look at the style of the artist. What Redmond observes in the language of Dumas is what places him squarely within an Afrocentric location. When Redmond says "Dumas is also the first among black writers to re-acculturate," he is speaking to Dumas' love of his language (xv). There is no caricature of the African in his use of African language; no self-conscious concentration on loss exists in the mind of Henry Dumas. He finds the African American language richly endowed, as he found the people.

In the powerful story "Ark of Bones," Dumas brings together all of the experiences of his young life to produce a text richly contoured with cultural artifacts of language. Headeye, one of the character, had a *mojo bone* in his hand. But we learn that "Headeye, he ain't got no devil in him." His only problem was that he had "this *notion* in his head about me *hoggin* the luck."

Dumas knows the close community language as well as the religious allusions, but his knowledge of this language is a gift of his sensitivity to the voices he has heard. The reader knows precisely where Dumas is at all times, even though as you read him you know that he is aware of everything he is doing in the text. There is no stream of words here floating endlessly on with no point; this is a master writer whose point is made in every sentence. "Headeye acted like he was *iggin* me" is about as precise as you can get with language. To understand *iggin* is to penetrate right in the center of the culture; however, it is an understanding that comes from experience or from study. One of the most insidious forms of critical hierarchy is the criticism of Afrocentric writers by those who have neither studied nor lived the culture. The assumption that one can imply make critical judgement and commentary about the text, perhaps to locate the writer, without serious study of the culture is an arrogant and false assumption. As one who does not know white American culture cannot truly understand it without some background, neither can Afrocentric writers be understood without some background. Normally, the student of American literature gains the knowledge of the nuances of white American literature and can adequately place the writers. But Afrocentric literature is much like Old English Literature in the sense that it must be studied seriously or else the reader will usually miss the point. I am not speaking about knowing the meaning of words or understanding the structure of Ebonics – that is a starting point. More fundamentally, the reader must know from what center of experience the writer writes. An African American writing from an Eurocentric basis will produce texts that may have some references to the cultural materials of the African American people but will remain essentially a white writer with a black skin. Such a writer is not much different from a white writer who writes knowledgeably about certain cultural icons of the African American community. But to really come from an African centered perspective in literature, the writer must immerse herself or himself in the culture of the people. The value of this immersion is that one becomes more authentically a voice of the culture, speaking much like Henry Dumas the language of the African American heritage with all of its universal implications in similar experiences of other people. To deny Afrocentric writers this possibility, either through criticism or creation, is to assume that the special language of the African American is somehow different from other languages, such as Spanish, Yoruba, Gikuyu, or Polish.

Dumas understood the nobility of the culture from which he had come and so when he wrote that Headeye's daddy "hauled off and smacked him side the head," he recognized that the perfection of action could only be told with two verbs. Rather than say, as might be said in English, that his daddy "smacked him side the head," Dumas goes into the culture and brings to bear the full meaning of this action. To truly complete the act the daddy had to have "hauled off and smacked him." This construction is like the one I often heard in Georgia as a child when someone had become a member of the local church. People would say, "Child, she got converted and joined the church." Another such construction of language is the command "Turn loose and jump down from there" to a child who is climbing a tree (Asante, 1990: 233-252).

In his stories as in his poetry Dumas gives his readers all of the signposts of his location. He is not a writer without a place in his own culture; he is firmly planted in the midst of ancestors, ghosts, haints, and spirits of the past as well as the generative power of the present condition of African Americans. Among the expression and terms that he employs are Glory Boat, Afro-horn, Aba, Heyboy, Sippi, catcher-clouds, and Saa saa aba saa saa. While his corpus is limited because of his early death, he remains one of the most centered of African American authors. Language, attitude, and direction are clearly demarcated in his works. When we read Dumas we are reading a profoundly honest writer who tells his and his people's special truth to the world. Contained in the language, the attitude, and direction of his work is the symbolism of strength, mystery, energy, dynamism, intelligence, wisdom, and trust. A compact exists between Dumas and the characters of his stories that allows him to use their language to tell the truth. He "ain't give on to what he know," but the reader knows that Dumas found the center of his cultural being intact and never left it. Why should he have left? What other writers would be required to leave? How silly of a writer to think that he or she must leave the source of power in order to be universal; true universalism in literature adheres in the ability of a writer to capture the special story or stories of his or her own culture in ways that make those stories impact on others, regardless of the first language. In the end, the serious reader of writers must work to re-affirm the centrality of cultural experience as the place to begin to create a dynamic multi-cultural literacy because without rootedness in our own cultural territory, we have no authentic story to tell.

References

Asante, Molefi Kete. 1990. The African essence in African American language. *African Culture: The Rhythms of Unity*. Trenton, NJ: Africa World Press. 233-252.

Bernal, Martin. 1987. *Black Athena*. New Brunswick, NJ: Rutgers University Press.

Davidson, Basil. 1984. *The Lost Cities of Africa*. New York, NY: Little, Brown and Company.

Diop, Cheikh Anta. 1974. *The African Origin of Civilization: Myth or Reality?* New York, NY: Lawrence Hill.

Dumas, Henry. 1970. Ark of Bones and Other Stories. *Ark of Bones and Other Stories*. Hale Chatfield & Eugene Redmond (eds). Carbondale, IL: Southern Illinois University Press.

Gould, Stephen Jay. 1981. *The Mismeasure of Man*. New York, NY: W.W. Norton.

Redmond, Eugene. 1970. Introduction. *Ark of Bones and Other Stories*. Hale Chatfield & Eugene Redmond (eds). Carbondale, IL: Southern Illinois University Press. 1-15.

[1] The controversy over the "Great Books" that ensued in 1990 is a case in point. The fact that Mortimer Adler and others who organized and published the works considered "great" did not include one book by a writer of African descent demonstrates the point made by numerous authors that mono-culturalism remains the dominant ideology of the literary establishment in the West.

[2] Among the works in this vein are Molefi Asante, 1987, *The Afrocentric Idea*, Philadelphia, PA: Temple University Press; Molefi Kete Asante, 1990, *Kemet, Afrocentricity, and Knowledge*, Trenton, NJ: Africa World Press; Cheikh Anta Diop, 1974, *The African Origin of Civilization*, New York, NY: Lawrence Hill; Martin Bernal, 1987, *Black Athena*, New Brunswick, NJ: Rutgers University Press.

Education and Schooling: You Can Have One Without the Other [1]

Mwalimu J. Shujaa

In the folk language of African-descended people in the United States the phrases "going to school" and "getting an education" are typically used in ways that imply that "schooling" and "education" are overlapping processes. It is not uncommon to hear people say, for example, "I am going to finish school and get a good education." The implied expectation is, of course, that "education" will be an outcome of "schooling."

However, our folk language also contains expressions to signify that "going to school" is not always thought to be consistent with "getting an education." Anyone growing up in a community of African-descended people in the U.S. has more than likely heard the rhyming verse:

> bought you books and sent you to school,
> but you still ain't nothing but an educated fool!

This is obviously an insult intended for someone for whom "schooling" has not overlapped with "education." This type of signifying is often reserved for college-trained persons who are perceived to look condescendingly on the common folk in the community because they consider them uneducated. Folk expressions are instructive because they reflect reality as it is experienced and interpreted in cultural communities.[3] They bring to light the fact that African-descended people in the U.S. have long understood that schooling can both serve as well as betray their interests.

In this chapter I argue that a strategic differentiation between "education" and "schooling" is fundamental to the transmission, maintenance, and development of an African-centered cultural orientation and identity. I contend that "education" and "schooling" are different processes and that, while it is possible for them to overlap, it is also probable that most people of African-descent in the U.S. receive more schooling than education. Using the United States as a social context, I present a conceptual model that links the process of schooling to the perpetuation of existing relations of power within the society. To support the model, I use examples taken from interview data collected during my involvement in an earlier study of participation among people of African descent in independent schools created specifically to serve their communities.[4]

Conceptual Background

The failure to take into account differing cultural orientations and unequal power relations among groups that share membership in a society is a major problem in conceptualizations that equate schooling and education. Cultural orientations "involve cognitive, affective, and directive processes in people's strategies to solve problems. . . . They are tenacious, persistent, superorganic principles that resist pressures for change brought about by the institutional transformation of society."[5] However, cultural orientations must be understood to exist in the context of group historical experience.[6] African-descended people's cultural identities have been and continue to be influenced by the U.S. social context, but it is essential to note that their cultural orientations also represent an experiential context. Thus, while African-descended people exist within the U.S. social context, they also exist within an African historical cultural continuum that predates that social context and would continue to exist even if the nation-state and its societal arrangements were to transform or demise.

Schooling is a process *intended* to perpetuate and maintain the society's existing power relations and the institutional structures that support those arrangements. All societies must provide a means for their members to learn, develop, and maintain adequate motivation throughout their life cycles for participation in socially valued and controlled patterns of action.[7] However, what is crucial to understand for this discussion is that when multiple cultural orientations exist within a nation-state, it is the leadership among the adherents to the politically dominant cultural orientation that exercise the most influence on the "concepts, values, and skills" that schools transmit. Such is the case with White Anglo Saxon Protestants in the United States It is the leadership within this cultural group whose world view largely determines what is socially valued and controls patterns of action within the society.

Education, in contrast to schooling, is our means of providing for the inter-generational transmission of values, beliefs, traditions, customs, rituals and sensibilities along with the knowledge of why these things must be sustained. Through education we learn how to determine what is in our interests, distinguish our interests from those of others, and recognize when our interests are consistent and inconsistent with those of others. Education prepares us to accept the staff of cultural leadership from the generation that preceded ours, build upon our inheritance and make ready the generation that will follow us. Education transmits knowledge all things that give our particular cultural orientation its uniqueness. Every cultural group must provide for this transmission process or it will cease to exist.

Education and schooling processes are not mutually exclusive -- they can and do overlap. There are aspects of schooling that can serve the common interests of all members of a society, regardless of their particular cultural orientations. Carol D. Lee, Kofi Lomotey and myself list three such areas of overlap.[8] We believe that public schools in the United States can and should:

1. Foster the development of adequate skills in literacy, numeracy, the humanities, and technologies that are necessary to negotiate economic self-sufficiency in the society;

2. Instill citizenship skills based on a realistic and thorough understanding of the political system, and support such citizenship skills by promoting questioning and critical thinking skills and teaching democratic values;[9]

3. Provide historical overviews of the nation, the continent and the world which accurately represent the contributions of all ethnic groups to the storehouse of human knowledge.[10]

The attainment of goals such as these would constitute a significant step toward providing all citizens of the nation-state with the kinds of skills needed for full and equal participation in the society.

While the broad dissemination of these skills would, no doubt, be of benefit to the society, it would do little to enable individuals who lack adequate knowledge about their own cultural history to put such skills to use for the uplift of their cultural communities. We acknowledge this limitation of schooling and conclude, ultimately, that it is an inappropriate interpretation of public schooling's societal role to expect that it will provide for

> ...the achievement of ethnic pride, self-sufficiency, equity, wealth, and power for Africans in America.... These goals will require a collective (although not monolithic) cultural and political worldview. [11]

The worldview we speak of can only be transmitted through a process of education strategically guided by an African cultural orientation and an understanding of how societal power relations are maintained. Moreover, it is the responsibility of each adult generation of African-descended people in the United States or wherever in the world they may be to ensure that the educational infrastructure for transmitting this knowledge to their progeny exists.

The first step in fulfilling our responsibilities to our culture is to develop collective practices for determining what cultural knowledge is to be transmitted. This could begin among groups of families, within organizations, and eventually include entire communities. The next step is to assess the extent to which our cultural knowledge is being transmitted in schools, churches, early childhood programs, and other settings where organized and guided learning takes place. The third step is to create new resources to satisfy any aspects of the cultural knowledge base that are not addressed by existing facilities.

In this infrastructure model, independent African-centered schools represent institutions fully committed to collectively determining what aspects of cultural knowledge are to be transmitted. This process is reflected in the schools' curricula and the means by which the curricula are developed. In the current reality, however, relatively few of our children attend such institutions. The majority of our children are in European-centered public, private, and religious schools. The process of assessing the extent to which our cultural knowledge is taught must include an examination of what is happening to our children who attend these schools. The inherent shortcomings must be met with demands for culture affirming curricula. However, while these struggles are being waged, resources must be created to provide for the transmission of cultural knowledge among students who attend European-centered schools. Here, the Black supplementary school movement in the United Kingdom offers a useful model.[12] The supplementary schools operate on weekends and evenings to provide a culture affirming environment for students who would otherwise be at the mercy of Britain's state run schools. In the United States, Saturday academics, after school programs, rites-of-passage organizations and study groups have been developed to facilitate the transmission of cultural knowledge.

Our ability to meet our cultural responsibilities is facilitated by our understanding of the linkages that exist between the process of schooling and the oppression of people of African descent. In the next section I analyze factors that influence our understanding of these linkages and suggest the conditions that are necessary for making critical distinctions between schooling and education.

The Strategic Differentiation of Education and Schooling: A Conceptual Model

Figure 1 is a conceptual model that represents decision making about schooling and education as a flowing process that bifurcates at four critical points. The model shows how decisions are influenced by the interplay between a society's structural conditions and its members' achievement expectations and perceptions about the quality of their lives (achieved outcomes). Structural conditions are the "institutionalized arrangements of human life."[13] The influence of a society's structural conditions on an individual's achievement expectations is cumulative. Schooling exerts an influence on members' achievement expectations through policies (e.g., tracking and testing), reward systems (e.g., grading and awarding credentials), and patterns of human interaction (e.g., social inclusion and exclusion) that reinforce and are reinforced by the society's structural conditions.

Bifurcation #1 represents any point in a person's life at which s/he evaluates the quality of his/her life. An individual will probably do this several times in the course of a life span. The individual will either conclude that the quality of his/her life is consistent with his/her achievement expectations or that it is not.

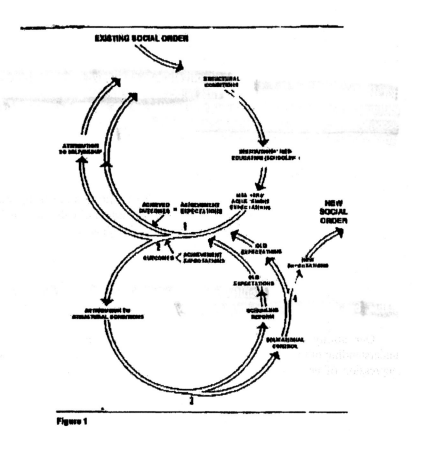

Figure 1

Fig. 1.2

The upper branch at Bifurcation #1 represents congruence between achievement expectations and outcomes. This situation exists when a person's perceptions about the quality of his/her life are consistent with his/her expectations. A person who expects to achieve prosperity and is, in fact, prosperous is likely to be highly motivated to support the social arrangements that are believed to be conducive to his/her prosperity. Therefore, in the model, the path branches back toward the existing social order to symbolize the perpetuation of the prevailing structural conditions.

If the existing structural conditions contribute to expectations of poverty for an individual and s/he is, in fact, poor, s/he may fatalistically accept his/her condition. Believing that things cannot be changed, such individuals are unlikely to challenge the social order. Fatalistic attributions can occur among African-descended people in America because, as a group, we have experienced generations of oppression in the United States. When individuals believe that their subordinate condition is inherent in the order of the society, they may withdraw from what they consider to be a useless pursuit of social mobility.

Thus, in either case, prosperity or poverty, if the existing social order and its structural conditions are not challenged, the social order and its power relations are perpetuated. Consequently, the motivation to challenge the social order does not develop for two reasons. The first is because of the congruence between the individual's social expectations and the quality of life s/he is experiencing. The second is because of the individual's belief that the existing social order and its structural conditions should not or cannot be changed.

The lower branch from Bifurcation #1 represents an individual's unmet achievement expectations. These are attributed either to self or group characteristics or to the society's structural conditions. Bifurcation #2 illustrates these possibilities. The upward flowing branch symbolizes unmet achievement expectations that are attributed to self (individual) or group characteristics. The downward branch represents an attribution to the society's structural conditions. I will discuss the upper branch first.

The maintenance of the social order depends upon the development of this pattern of thinking among some of the society's members. It is one of schooling's functions to facilitate the "selection" of individuals to occupy low-status, but necessary, roles in the society. What better way to accomplish this selection process than to imbue some members with the idea that they (or their group) are unworthy or unprepared for the quality of life they see enjoyed by others? The adoption of this kind of thinking has often led African-descended people in America to support all kinds of programs and projects intended to "fix" the things that are "wrong" with us. Individuals pursue these courses of action when they internalize explanations for unmet achievement expectations that focus on self/group deficits rather than explanations that de-legitimize the social order. This is as much a part of the selection process as pushing some members of the society toward high-status roles by enmeshing their thinking with the idea that they (or their group) can accomplish anything. When we attribute unmet achievement expectations to our own group characteristics, we see the realization of racism's ultimate impact as a strategy for maintaining and perpetuating social domination. Its most overt manifestation is the internalization of the racial inferiority ideology. The most insidious manifestation is the adoption of the "minority" perspective. In the former instance "Whiteness" is perceived as superior. In the latter case there is the perception that White people will always be in power because they are the majority. The internalization by African-Americans of White supremacist ideologies is painful to discuss (and many of us do not discuss it); but it can and does occur. Frazier illustrates this problem through a statement from an interview with a 20-year-old African American high school graduate.

> Our chances aren't as good by any means as the White man's and never will be unless the White man's attitude changes and Blacks make adjustments in their training and study. It's a situation like that which makes fellows like me not want to waste years studying to do what? I know there's

> no difference between the White man and me, *but I can't help*
> *feeling he is better than I am when he is trained to do his work*
> *and then has all the chance of doing it.*[14] (emphasis mine)

This excerpt provides an indication of the weight that racist treatment has placed upon this young man. He has to struggle with himself to avoid feeling that he, and not the structural conditions of his society, are responsible for the incongruence between his social expectations and the quality of his life. To the extent that he attributes his condition to himself, there will be no stress placed upon the society's structural conditions to change.

The overall concern here has to do with schooling's role in perpetuating this kind of attribution. Woodson opened the *Mis-education of the Negro* with these words:

> The "educated Negroes" have the attitude of contempt
> toward their own people because in their own as well as in
> their mixed schools Negroes are taught to admire the Hebrew,
> the Greek, the Latin and the Teuton and to despise the
> African.[15]

Woodson's reasoning has been further developed by contemporary African-descended writers, particularly in the field of psychology such as Wilson,[16] Akbar,[17] and White & Parham.[18] The critical issue is that the leadership within the politically dominant culture in the U.S. utilizes schooling to inculcate its world view as universal. The effects of exclusion that Woodson describes continue to be problematic because the nature of our schooling in U.S. society is unchanged. Essentially, this means taking the position that the support given the schooling of African-descended people by government and "philanthropy" is and has historically been intended to serve the interests of the politically dominant members of U.S. society.[19]

The lower branch from Bifurcation #2 represents courses of action that can occur when unmet achievement expectations are attributed to the structural conditions of society. Individual attention is focused on countering the society's structural conditions to make achievement expectations obtainable. This degree of consciousness is the basic prerequisite for social activism in education and other areas of social life. There is, of course, a long history of activism that has coalesced African-descended constituencies to work toward achieving some measure of change in the structural conditions of U.S. society. The civil rights movement is a prime example. However, any reasonable analysis of the civil rights movement would indicate that not every person of African descent who opposed Jim Crow shared the same vision of the course of action that would best serve the interests of African-descended people in a post-Jim Crow society.[20]

Marable argues that in the 1990s the belief that racial equality had been achieved is a post-Jim Crow spectre that haunts African Americans.[21] He explains why this belief has emerged and persists

> The number of Black elected officials exceeds 6,600;
> many Black entrepreneurs have achieved substantial gains

within the capitalist economic system in the late 1980s, thousands of Black managers and administrators appear to be moving forward within the hierarchies of the Private and Public sector.[22]

Marable continues with an explanation of why he considers racial equality to be an illusion

The true test of any social thesis is the amount of reality it explains, or obscures. And from the vantage point of the inner cities and homeless shelters, from the unemployment lines and closed factories, a different reality emerges. We find that racism has not declined in significance, if racism is defined correctly as the systematic exploitation of Blacks' labor power and the domination and subordination of our cultural, political, educational and social rights as human beings.[23]

The significance of Marable's argument for this discussion is that it helps to illuminate the fact that people of African descent view their relationship to the social order in different ways. A key factor influencing such views is the tension between individualistic and group orientations. Some African-descendants view themselves, as being essentially individuals competing with other individuals to achieve the best the society has to offer them. Others take the view that individual achievement has no significance outside the quality of life experienced by African-descendants as a group. An individual's perceptions about the legitimacy of the schooling options available to African-descendants will reflect the extent to which s/he has adopted an individualistic or a group orientation. Accordingly, not all African-descendants who attribute their unmet achievement expectations to society's structural conditions, reflect the same view of reality in their analyses of what needs to be done about schooling.

Bifurcation #3 symbolizes how differing interpretations of one's relationship to the social order are evident in choosing between public school reform (the upper branch) and the rejection of public schooling (the lower branch). In my conceptual model schooling reform is an avenue leading to the attainment of achievement expectations that reinforce the existing social order. My reasoning is that our notions about quality of life are relative. Achievement expectations are constructed within the societal context and shaped by its institutions and hierarchies. Schooling reforms are not intended to produce fundamental changes in the role schooling plays in reproducing both the value system of the politically dominant culture and the social ordering that serves its elite. For example, in a capitalist society like the United States the accumulation of personal wealth is held up as a standard for measuring success. Thus, many symbols of success take on meaning in relationship to the perceived styles of the wealthy. Many schooling reforms gain public support because they imply changes that will make these symbols of personal or individual success accessible to more people.

Beyer discusses this fallacy of schooling reform in a critique of *A Nation at Risk*.[24] He describes the rationale for the schooling reforms supported in that document as ...

> a pretext that justifies current social practices and institutions, a way of covertly supporting the status quo, a way of diverting attention away from basic social, political, and economic disparities and forms of oppression, and resultant forms of inequality. . . . By recasting the frustration, impatience, and anxiety that typify American social life in terms that safeguard those social institutions that support current inequalities, this report provides a "sleight of hand" that is at once ideologically ingenious and socially injurious.[25]

Beyer's description illustrates how reforms can address changes in schooling's packaging and methods of delivery while reinforcing the individualistic and materialistic value orientations that serve the interests of those in power.

Fundamental change in schooling can only be accomplished within the framework of fundamental change in the society's power relations. While there are many who would cast schooling reforms as vehicles that can facilitate the attainment of unmet achievement expectations, I believe this is possible only when such expectations are not contradictory to the existing power relations. Reforms do not challenge schooling's role in the maintenance of status quo power relations in society. Therefore, in my conceptual model, schooling reform is placed on a path that perpetually leads back to decision making about whether or not the quality of an individual's life is consistent with his/her achievement expectations in the existing social order (see Bifurcation #1).

The lower branch at Bifurcation #3 represents the decision to seek a better quality of life by controlling the schooling process. This is accomplished by utilizing options outside public schools such as home schooling and independent schools. The rate at which African-descendants are enrolling in independent schools has increased steadily since the late 1960s.[26] The Institute for Independent Education reports that more than 330,000 students of African descent are enrolled in independent schools.[27] The schools these students attend represent a wide range of types. Most 226,590 students are in Catholic schools. The next highest category is independent neighborhood schools (52,744). Students of African descent predominate in many of these schools' enrollments. The remaining students African-descent are spread among schools associated with the National Association of Independent Schools and various denominationally affiliated Christian schools.

Ratteray and myself reported that independent neighborhood schools deal with cultural and religious orientations in a variety of ways.[28] In particular, we found that there were very definite differences in both the quality and quantity of the attention given to maintaining and developing African-centered cultural orientations among their students. All of the parents who were interviewed at these schools indicated that they had decided against public school, however, they expressed different expectations regarding the extent to which an African-centered cultural orientation was important to them in choosing their children's schools. Some parents' choices were influenced by concerns that a particular school might be "too Black" and others had consciously chosen schools that would help their children develop African-centered cultural orientations. [29] Thus, these schools can be viewed as vehicles that are used by parents to pursue very different achievement expectations.

These varied expectations are symbolized at Bifurcation #4. In discussing these expectations I will use segments from interviews conducted with parents of students who attend independent schools owned and operated by people of African descent to illustrate how schooling and education are differentiated in their thinking. The left branch from the bifurcation point symbolizes decisions based on achievement expectations that reinforce the existing social order. Here, independent schools are used as alternative pathways to achieving goals that reinforce existing power relations and value orientations of the society's politically dominant culture.

One mother we interviewed in Baltimore believes that it is important for her children to believe in themselves. She wants the school to help her children develop enough self-confidence and motivation to work as hard as necessary to overcome any feelings of personal shortcoming relative to someone else. In addition to academic needs, the parent describes the school's contribution in terms that relate to the development of a positive self-image:

> [school name] instills in the children a better self-image as far as living up to your full potential and trying harder, you know basically what you can do, and not having no one say that because you may be a little slower than the next child that if you don't work just a little bit harder, you can come up to the level of the child that you think you are a little slower than.... I think they instill . . . a better self-image in the children and give them a better motivation as to want to try harder. [1.002-94]

This mother is making a comparison that is based on what she feels happens to children in public schools and what she expects her children to gain from the independent school they attend. She believes that success for children of African-descent is determined by the resolve that they have to overcome personal shortcomings. She favors the independent school because she feels its teachers have the skill and dedication to develop this attribute in her children. This viewpoint implies a belief that individuals vary in their abilities and that relative shortcomings can be overcome through hard work, and an optimism about meeting achievement expectations. One does not get a sense that this mother enrolled her children in an independent school because of a sense of contradiction between personal goals and mainstream notions of personal success. The independent school is viewed as a way of offsetting barriers to achieving personal success. The barriers, however, are perceived in terms of personal attributes and not in the context of the structural conditions of the society. My interpretation is that this parent is not making a critical distinction between schooling and education. She is not challenging the social order, but attempting to offer her children an alternate means of access to its rewards.

Another parent we interviewed also sees the development of personal attributes as the most important contribution the independent school can make. In this instance the personal attribute is described as "the ability to adapt." The adaptation is to being "a minority." What the parent wants is for her son to learn how to compete in U.S. society as a "minority." She is concerned that her child's enrollment in the independent African American school, because its students are all of African-descent may result in a "lack of exposure" to minority status.

> Exposure to and the ability to cope with and adapt to being a minority, for lack of a better term, in the world is something that has to be developed.... In a black environment or a black school you can be under-exposed so that you develop a sense of complacency.... Or, that you don't develop your abilities to adapt. [1 .003-338]

According to her perception of "minority" status, this mother believes that her son will always be competing with Whites for social rewards. Unless he learns to compete, she feels, he will not be successful in meeting his achievement expectations. Again, the independent school is viewed as a means to overcoming barriers to achieving success in the context of the society's existing structural conditions. There is no challenge to the social order implied here.

The right branch from the bifurcation point symbolizes the strategic differentiation of education from schooling. This process is motivated by achievement expectations that are based on new values and the realization that the power to educate is conditioned upon freeing the process from the controlling influences of the politically dominant culture. Education becomes part of the infrastructure needed to preserve progress made toward the emergence of a new social order.

A mother in Washington, D.C. indicated that her son had negative experiences in public school even though he was enrolled in classes for the academically gifted. His inquisitiveness was stifled and often interpreted as insolence. This mother was raised "on the picket lines" and has always involved her children in community issues. She is deeply concerned that her children develop a commitment to uplifting African-American people. Several times during our interview she stressed that "each one must teach one" is a principle that she lives by and attempts to instill in her children. She also indicated that she wants her children to learn self-assuredness because she believes they would need it in order to overcome White racism. While we were discussing her feelings about her children's enrollment in a school where all the students were of African descent she made this comment about her expectations of the schooling process:

> In the first place, most public schools in the District are Black. So, I mean, there's no difference really here as far as that is concerned. The other thing is that nurturing and the positive imagery that takes place here is so necessary, I think, to making people who are well adjusted strong and creative who then can go out into the work force and say, you know I respect you. You *will* respect me... Because that is what I tell them, they don't have to like you and don't think that they will. You get along as well as you can. You succeed as well as you can.... The whole thing is that while you're in the learning process, you need to learn from your own, with your own and that type of thing. [1.004-809]

She went on to describe what she perceives to be the role of the independent school in providing education that will help her children to achieve what she expects them to as adults

> ...I want the children to be taught not that you get educated and you learn as much as you can so you can work for someone else. But that we, you know, you get educated, you develop your own. They could even go so far as to have the junior achievement programs here, that type of thing. [1.004-926]

Evident in these statements is the mother's concern that her children be agents for change. She sees the independent school and the home as extensions of each other in fostering the achievement of this goal. Thus, for her, involvement in the independent school is a part of parenting:

> These children are so awesome. You know? I mean, we have just heavy discussions at my household and I want them to be politically aware and economically sound.... They need to learn economics and these kids with these minds that are going out like this need to learn to manage money and that kind of thing. They could have a bank, a school store, anything in here. Those are some of the things I'd like to see develop and I'm on the curriculum committee. I'm going to try and work at that. [1.004-1048]

This mother is one who has made a strategic distinction between schooling and education. She acknowledges the importance of being prepared to earn a living amid the social conditions that exist. Beyond that, however, is the emphasis she places on helping her children appreciate the significance of contributing to the uplift of people of African descent.

When African-American parents strategically differentiate education from schooling the decisions they make about where to enroll their children are based on their perceptions of the social and cultural realities that influence their lives. These decisions involve careful consideration of other schooling options, most often public systems that are well integrated into the societal infrastructure.

They include assessments about the relationship of schooling to the social order and schooling's role in the attainment of individual achievement expectations. Most significantly, these decisions entail taking stock of both one's individual and group relationship to the existing social order and determining how to provide one's children with the best preparation for assuming their responsibilities in the maintenance and perpetuation of an African cultural orientation.

Overcoming Schooling: A Cultural Imperative

My conceptual framework emphasizes the exigencies of our African cultural orientation over those of the nation-state (U.S.). Consequently, I treat schooling and education as differentiated processes. Schooling ties me to the social order framed by the nation-state. Education informs and locates my thinking within an African historical-cultural context.

Cultural orientation makes a difference in the way one critiques society. This can be illustrated through contrasting examples taken from the writings of John Dewey and W. E. B. DuBois. These men were social contemporaries, however the ideas expressed in the samplings from their writings presented below indicate that they saw U.S. society in very different ways. First, consider Dewey's discussion of the function of education in a democratic society. In the following statement, he explains the criteria needed to evaluate education's role in a society:

> Since education is a social process ... a criterion for education criticism and construction implies a particular social ideal The two points selected by which to measure the worth of a form of social life are the extent to which the interests of a group are shared by all its members, and the fullness with which it interacts with other groups.

Of course, the social ideal that concerns Dewey is democracy. He regards a democratic society as one which

> . . .makes provision for participation in its good of all members on equal terms and which secures flexible readjustment of its institutions through interaction of the different forms of associated life is in so far democratic.[31]

He then describes the role of education in democratic society:

> [It] gives individuals a personal interest in social relationships and control, and the habits of mind which secure social changes with out introducing disorder.[32]

Dewey's notion that a particular kind of education can bring about change "without introducing disorder" is problematic. Although, by his own words, Dewey understood that the United States is "composed of a combination of different groups with different traditional customs,"[33] he, nonetheless, ignores the dialectics of domination and resistance associated with these cultural differences. There is no mention of how the power over institutionalized education held by the politically dominant members of the society is used to maintain the order he wants to preserve. He also avoids the issue of oppressed peoples' challenge to that power. For Dewey, social change is to be determined by the rational thinking of the politically dominant members of the society.

DuBois and Dewey shared membership in the same society but related to different primary cultural groups. Dewey's cultural orientation was European and American; DuBois' was African and American. DuBois presents a quite different analysis of education's role than Dewey. To begin with, DuBois focuses on the cultural conflict in the United States and its impact on cultural identity. He saw the legislation of equal rights in voting and education as the ". . . beginning of even more difficult problems of race and culture." He also reckons with the question of what would become of the cultural identity of people of African descent in a United States where equality was supposedly the law of the land

> . . . what we must now ask ourselves is when we become equal American citizens what will be our aims and ideals and what will we have to do with selecting these aims and ideals. Are we to assume that we will simply adopt the ideals of Americans and become what they are or want to be and that we will have in this process no ideals of our own? . . . We would take on the culture of white Americans doing as they do and thinking as they think.[34]

DuBois considered the cultural assimilation of African-descendant people into the politically dominant culture in the United States to be unacceptable. He saw a clear dilemma -- refuse to go to school or go to school and run the risk of becoming alienated from the African-American cultural community:

> Here for instance, is the boy who says simply he is not going to school. His treatment in the white schools . . . is such that it does not attract him. Moreover, the boy who does enter the white school and gets on reasonably well does not always become a useful member of our group. Negro children . . . often know nothing of Negro history.... Some are ashamed of themselves and their folk.[35]

The dialectics of power do not escape DuBois' analysis, as they do Dewey's. The exigencies of culture, not society, establish imperatives for DuBois. He is unwilling to accept social arrangements that restrict the ability of the person of African-descent to understand and appreciate his/her relationship to the African historical-cultural continuum.

Freire gives an indication of having reached conclusions similar to DuBois' regarding the importance of culture.[36] He points out that an attack on a people's culture is the first step in any process of domination:

> Cultural identity is the first point the dominative people, or class, or nation, or individual [attempts] to destroy in the

dominated people. In other words, there is no oppression, no domination with out the attempt . . . to destroy the cultural identity of the invaded.

There is much to suggest that one of the functions of schooling in the United States has been to effect a gradual destruction of the cultural identity of people of African-descent. This process has been justified as being consistent with the promulgation of a common American culture.

The common culture concept is inherently one-sided in favor of the politically dominant culture. It is put forth typically by people who already believe that their cultural orientation is "the" common culture. Consequently, they feel justified in demanding the acquiescence of others. They assign little or no significance to the different cultural orientations of the people with whom they share societal membership nor are they concerned with the fact that other people attach importance to their own cultural identities. An illustration of how the cultural diversity in U.S. society is downplayed is found in Hirsch's discussion of his concept of cultural literacy.

> By accident of history, American cultural literacy has a bias toward English literate tradition. Short of revolutionary political upheaval, there is absolutely nothing that can be done about this.... We have kept and still need to keep English culture as the dominant part of our national vocabulary for purely functional reasons.[37]

Hirsch's is the particularistic view of an individual who is privileged and empowered by the politically dominant culture in the United States. He is essentially arguing that the political dominance of the White Anglo Saxon Protestant is incontestable and all who live within its influence are compelled to accept it, if for no other reason than in the interests of national unity. Hirsch's argument rests on a conception of social history that is in reality the history of the society's politically dominant culture. And therein lies the problem with "common culture." The United States is, as Asante[38] and others have argued, a hegemonic society, in which the relatively powerful members trace to the cultures of Western Europe their ways of thinking, their philosophical foundations, and their canons of knowledge. Over the generations, these people have used societal institutions and resources to glorify their Western European cultural heritage while, at the same time, devaluing through processes of omission, distortion, and misrepresentation knowledge centered in the cultures of others in the same society. African-descended people are among these "other" groups that are systematically oppressed through institutionalized relations of power and resource distribution based on race. "Whiteness" has served as the biological symbol of Western European cultural descendence. Hare points out that immigrants who left Europe as Poles, Italians, Germans, or Russians, became "Whites" when they reached the shores of the United States.[39] They became part of an institutionalized set of social relations that offered them inclusion into the family of "Whiteness." Schooling facilitated this process for them because it

259

was through schooling that they learned to aspire to a place in the U.S. social order and its "common culture." "Blackness," then, becomes the criterion on which "non-Whites" are assigned to a caste status of perpetual subordination to "Whites."[40]

Education, and not schooling, is, indeed, a cultural imperative for people of African descent who live under Western cultural hegemony. Men and women of African descent in the United States and in the Caribbean have maintained a long tradition of cultural resistance based on the recognition that their abilities to preserve and perpetuate their own cultures have been consistently under attack. This thinking is evident among the published works of David Walker,[41] Edward Wilmot Blyden,[42] Drusilla Dunjee Houston,[43] Carter G. Woodson,[44] and W. E. B. DuBois,[45] to name just a few.

Woodson proposed that African-descended people establish a new program of education for themselves to undo the mis-education inculcated by schooling in the United States. He supports his reasoning in the following manner:

> The so-called modern education, with all its defects, however, does others so much more good than it does the Negro, because it has been worked out in conformity to the needs of those who have enslaved and oppressed weaker peoples. For example, the philosophy and ethics resulting from our educational system have justified slavery, peonage, segregation, and lynching. The oppressor has the right to exploit, to handicap, and to kill the oppressed. Negroes daily educated in the tenets of such a religion of the strong have accepted the status of the weak as divinely ordained [46]

To Woodson, it clearly makes no sense to expect a system of schooling controlled by the politically dominant culture for its own interests to provide education for African-descended people. Yet, for the most part, this is what we have done.

I foresee no change in this situation that does not involve African-descended people taking control of our own education. When education is strategically differentiated from schooling, there is no reason this cannot be done. It means empowering ourselves to ensure that African-centered cultural knowledge is systematically transmitted to our children. In many cities, African-centered independent schools are providing a means for acquiring educational control. Where such schools do not exist or are not accessible, families, groups of parents, community-based organizations, churches, and rites-of-passage organizations can and have become networks for passing on cultural knowledge. This is our cultural imperative.

Conclusion

In concluding I want to share a personal recollection that focuses much of what I have said in this essay. In 1957, when I was a second grader at Frederick Douglass School in Parsons, Kansas, my teacher, Miss Lacy Clark, taught a lesson that illustrates how African descended people who understand the importance of doing so have always had to make strategic distinctions between education and schooling. One morning Miss Clark asked us to stop what we were doing and put everything on our desks away. She then distributed to each of us a copy of a drawing that looked as if it had come from a coloring book. The drawing showed an autumn scene in which a group of children were playing among piles of raked leaves. There were oak trees in the drawing with leaves tumbling from their branches. The children were dressed warmly in caps, jackets, and scarves.

Miss Clark's instructions were simple. We were to use our crayons to color in the picture. Although it was not necessary, she added an incentive prize would be given to the student who did the best job coloring the picture. Miss Clark collected our drawings when the bell for recess rang. When we returned after recess and took our seats, Miss Clark announced the winner of the prize. It turned out to be a boy who had colored the faces of the children in the picture brown to match his own. He was the only student among this class of 25 African-descended children to do so. The rest of us had colored in every detail of that picture except the faces of the children.

Because 1957 was the last year of Douglass School's existence Miss Clark was doing what she could to prepare us for that inevitable day when our teachers and most of our classmates would be White. She knew that we would have to fight for our cultural identities in the formerly all-White schools. Miss Clark intended to prepare us to participate in and contribute to both the larger society and to our own cultural community. At times, her teaching emphasized knowledge specific to the ancestral cultural identity she shared with her students: at other times the focus was on the second grade curriculum prescribed by the all-White school board.

As a teacher, Miss Clark was strategically differentiating between education and schooling. What she did for my classmates and me is done by many, but unfortunately not all, teachers and administrators of African descent everyday. The actions of individuals like Miss Clark and the teachers and administrators described by Foster[47] and Lomotey[48] provide indications that human agency can and often does intervene in the reproduction of politically dominant ideology. The critical task confronting us is to broaden our understanding of the role that the strategic differentiation of education from schooling can play. This differentiation is vital to the success of African people's resistance to political and cultural domination and in guiding the development of our cultural nation in a new world order where egalitarian relationships between cultures replace exploitative hierarchies.

Notes and References

1. This is a slightly revised version of a chapter by this author which bears the same name in his edited book *Too Much Schooling, Too Little Education: A Paradox of Black Life in White Societies* (Africa World Press, 1994)

2. V Gadsden. 1993. Literacy, Education, and Identity among African Americans: The Communal Nature of Learning. *Urban Education. 27 (4): 352-369.*

3. Ogbu, J. 1974. *The Next Generation: An Ethnography of Education in an Urban Neighborhood.* New York, N.Y.: Academic Press. 16.

4. Ratteray, J. D. & Shujaa, M. J. 1987. *Dare to Choose: Parental Choice at Independent Neighborhood Schools.* Washington, DC: Institute for Independent Education.

5. Shimahara, N. K. 1979. *Adaptation and Education in Japan.* New York, N.Y.: Praeger. 2.

6. Akoto, A. Undated. *Nationbuilding: Theory and Practice in Afrikan-Centered Education.* Washington, DC: Pan Afrikan World Institute.

7. Parsons, T. 1966. *Societies: Evolutionary and Comparative Perspectives.* Englewood Cliffs, NJ: Prentice Hall. 5-18.

8. Lee, C. D.; Lomotey, K. & Shujaa, M. J. 1990. How Shall We Sing Our Sacred Song in a Strange Land? The Dilemma of Double Consciousness and the Complexities of an African-Centered Pedagogy. *Journal of Education.* 172: 45-61.

9. Gutmann, A. 1987. *Democratic Education.* Princeton: Princeton University Press; McNeil, L. 1988. *Contradictions of Control: School Structure and School Knowledge.* New York: Routledge & Kegan Paul.

10. Lee, C. D.; Lomotey, K. & Shujaa, M. J. 1990. How Shall We Sing Our Sacred Song in a Strange Land? The Dilemma of Double Consciousness and the Complexities of an African-Centered Pedagogy. *Journal of Education.* 172: 49.

11. Lee, C. D.; Lomotey, K. & Shujaa, M. J. 1990. How Shall We Sing Our Sacred Song in a Strange Land? The Dilemma of Double Consciousness and the Complexities of an African-Centered Pedagogy. *Journal of Education.* 172: 49.

12. Dove, N. 1993. The Emergence of Black Supplementary Schools: Resistance to Racism in the United Kingdom. *Urban Education.* 27 (4): 430-447.

13. Shimahara, N.K. 1972. *Adaptation and Education in Japan.* New York, N.Y.: Praeger.

14. Frazier, E. F. 1940. *Negro Youth at the Crossways: Their Personality Development in the Middle States.* Washington, D.C.: American Council on Education. 136-137.

15. Woodson, C. G. (1933) 1969. *Mis-Education of the Negro.* Washington, D.C.: Associated Publishers.

16. Wilson, A. 1978. *The Developmental Psychology of the Black Child.* New York, N.Y.: Africana Research.

17. Akbar, N. 1984. *Chains and Images of Psychological Slavery.* Jersey City, NJ: New Mind Productions.

18. White, J. L. & Parham, T. A. 1990. *The Psychology of Blacks: An African American Perspective.* Englewood Cliffs, NJ: Prentice Hall.

19. Anderson, J.D.1980. *The Education of Blacks in the South,* 1860-1935. Chapel Hill, NC: University of North Carolina; Butchart, R. E. 1988. Outthinking and Outflanking the Owners of the World: A Historiography of the African-American Struggle for Education. *History of Education Quarterly.* 28:333-366.

20. Stuckey, S. 1987. *Slave Culture Nationalist Theory and the Foundations of Black America* (New York, N.Y./Oxford: Oxford University Press; Clarke, J. H. 1991. *African World Revolution: Africans at the Crossroads.* Trenton, NJ: Africa World Press.

21. Marable, M.1990. Toward Black American Empowerment: Violence and Resistance in the African-American Community in the 1990s. *African Commentary.* 2:16-21.

22. Marable, M.1990. Toward Black American Empowerment: Violence and Resistance in the African-American Community in the 1990s. *African Commentary.* 2:16.

23. Marable, M.1990. Toward Black American Empowerment: Violence and Resistance in the African-American Community in the 1990s. *African Commentary.* 2:16.

24. Beyer. L. E. 1985. Educational Reform: The Political Roots of National Risk. *Curriculum Inquiry.* 15: 37-56.

25. Beyer, L. E. 1985. Educational Reform: The Political Roots of National Risk. *Curriculum Inquiry.* 15: 48.

26. P. L. Benson. 1991. Private Schools in the United States: A Statistical Profile, with Comparisons to Public Schools. Washington, DC: Department of Education; Institute for Independent Education African-American Enrollment in Independent Schools (Research Notes on Education). Washington, DC: Author, 1990; Ratteray, J. D. & Shujaa, M. J. 1987. *Dare to Choose: Parental Choice at Independent Neighborhood Schools.* Washington, DC: Institute for Independent Education.

27. Institute for Independent Education African-American Enrollment in Independent Schools (Research Notes on Education).Washington, DC: Author, 1990.

28. Ratteray, J. D. & Shujaa, M. J. 1987. *Dare to Choose: Parental Choice at Independent Neighborhood Schools.* Washington, DC: Institute for Independent Education.

29. Shujaa, M. J. 1988. *Parental Choice of an Afrocentric Independent School: Developing an Explanatory Theory.* Sankofa. 2: 22-25.

30. Dewey, J. (1916) 1944. *Democracy and Education.* New York, N.Y.: The Free Press, 99.

31. Dewey, J. (1916) 1944. *Democracy and Education.* New York, N.Y.: The Free Press, 99.

32. Dewey, J. (1916) 1944. *Democracy and Education*. New York, N.Y.: The Free Press, 99.

33. Dewey, J. (1916) 1944. *Democracy and Education*. New York, N.Y.: The Free Press, 99.

34. DuBois, W.E.B. 1973. *Whither Now and Why. The Education of Black People. Ten Critiques*, 1906-1960 by W. E. B. DuBois, Aptheker, H. New York, N.Y.: Monthly Review Press. 149.

35. DuBois, W.E.B. 1973. *Whither Now and Why. The Education of Black People. Ten Critiques*, 1906-1960 by W. E. B. DuBois, Aptheker, H. New York, N.Y.: Monthly Review Press. 149.

36. Freire, P. 1991. *The People's Education and Participant Research*, Cassette recording no. RA-1-35.15. Washington, DC: American Educational Research Association.

37. Hirsch, E. D. Jr. 1987. *Cultural Literacy: What Every American Needs to Know*. Boston, MA: Houghton Mifflin. 106- 107.

38. Asante, M. K. 1991. Multiculturalism: An Exchange. *American Scholar*. 60:267-276.

39. Hare, B. R. 1991. *The Effectiveness of Desegregation as a Strategy for Improving the Quality of African-American Education*. Keynote address at the Beyond Desegregation: Perspectives from the 1990s. Conference held at the State University of New York at Buffalo, November.

40. Wynter, S. 1992. *Do Not Call Us Negroes: How "Multicultural" Textbooks Perpetuate Racism*. San Jose, CA: Aspire Books. 9-10.

41. Walker, D.(1829) 1965. *Walker's Appeal in Four Articles, together with a Preamble to the Coloured Citizens of the World, but in particular, and very expressly, to those of the United States of America*, Wiltse, C. M. New York, N.Y.: Hill and Wang, 1965).

42. Blyden, E. W. 1895. Black Spokesman. Lynch, H. R. London: Frank Cass and Co.

43. Houston, D. D. (1926) 1985. *Wonderful Ethiopians of the Ancient Cushite Empire*. Baltimore, MD: Black Classics Press.

44. Woodson, C. G. (1933) 1969. *Mis-Education of the Negro*. Washington, D.C.: Associated Publishers.

45. DuBois, W.E.B. 1973. *Whither Now and Why. The Education of Black People. Ten Critiques*, 1906-1960 by W. E. B. DuBois, Aptheker, H (ed). New York, N.Y.: Monthly Review Press. 149.

46. Woodson, C. G. (1933) 1969. *Mis-Education of the Negro*. Washington, D.C.: Associated Publishers. Xxxii.

47. Foster, M. 1992. Educating for Competence in Community and Culture: Exploring the Views of Exemplary African-American Teachers. *Urban Education*. 27: 370-394

48. Lomotey, K. 1992. African-American Principals: Bureaucrats /Administrators and Ethno-Humanists. *Urban Education*. 27: 395-412.

Pedagogy in Ancient Kemet

Asa Hilliard

The surface has been hardly scratched in the study of history of Africa and its people. The rough outlines of that history are beginning to emerge as well-prepared African and African American historians have begun the painstakingly detailed work of documenting the African experience in antiquity. It is hard enough to trace the broad general outlines of the African experience, such as pedagogy, with any degree of clarity. And yet there is the need for us to do precisely that.

Our concern with the connection to our African past is really future oriented. It is not merely for sentimental or aesthetic reasons that we return. While it is true that no one can or should live in the past, it is equally true that all futures are created out of some past. Ancient Africans not only existed, they developed a way of life, the remnants of which continue to influence world development. As we view competing designs for human institutions and competing philosophies, it is incumbent upon us to come to that process as fully disciplined, and especially as creative participants. A review of our past will reveal that no people has a better place from which to start.

The intent of this essay is to draw the best possible picture of one small aspect of a total development process of ancient Africans in the Nile Valley region and in the Great Lakes region. Simply put, how did the ancient Africans design and carry out the educational process? What were the aims, the methods, and the contents of ancient African education? The best preserved records of cultural activity are to be found in Kemet (Ancient Egypt). As a result, a great deal of our attention must be focused on that point. However, it is always important to keep in mind the fact that ancient Egypt was, as Gerald Massey said, "merely the mouthpiece for a more deeply rooted Africa birthplace."

Anyone who is familiar with the material on ancient Egypt is well aware of the fact that there exist few if any books on the educational system of Egypt. Consequently, the reconstruction of what must have been a highly developed and vast system of education necessarily requires an approach that is highly inferential. Nonetheless, the inferences are not without empirical grounding. For example, the evidence that gives information about the educational system can be found in paintings, monuments, architecture, technology and, above all, in the hieroglyphic and demonic writings, which include stories, rituals, songs and so forth. In addition, the skilled eye can detect in the widespread African diaspora an extensive variety of cultural forms whose antecedents are clear matches to those of the Egyptian and earlier ancient cultural forms. And so we are not short of evidence for the fact that educational systems existed. Rather the task is to sift through a plethora of data in order to reconstruct a picture of the past.

It is important at this point that a few words be said about the general orientation that I consider to be essential to any understanding of the raw data or summarized interpretation of data about ancient Egyptian education. First, in doing our analysis we must always keep in mind the "antiquity" of African culture. Second, and just as important, we must always keep in mind what Cheikh Diop has referred to as the "unity" of African culture. In order to explain the culture, and particularly the educational system of Egypt, we must appeal not only to data in Egypt but to data about education from the cultural antecedents of Egypt. We must also appeal to manifestations of the core African culture, not only in the Egyptian part of the diaspora, but in the rest of the continental diaspora and later in the intercontinental diaspora as well.[1]

History

Briefly, let me summarize some of the main points of ancient African history with which most of us are now quite familiar. It is now clear from the archaeological record that the whole body of data supports an African origin for mankind. What is equally important is that the earliest record of what we call civilization developed first in the same areas where the earliest fossil remains of humans are found. That is to say, long before Egypt began, it was Black people in Africa along the southern Nile River valley, close to its source, who produced the first stirrings of "civilization," that can be documented.

Albert Churchward is merely echoed by Richard Leakey when he says that the first paleolithic man was a pigmy. This pigmy evolved in central Africa at the sources of the Nile River and valley. Churchward says that from there all others originated and migrated throughout the world. Churchward says that the sources of the Nile in the equatorial provinces, where the great lakes and the papyrus swamp were located, were regarded by the ancient Kemetic people as their "Ta-Nuter," in other words their holy land. It was called the land of the spirits of the gods.

It was Henri Frankfort, among other students of Egyptian history and culture, who recognized from the evidence that Egypt's historical and cultural antecedents were to be found "south" of Egypt, deeper in the Nile Valley. Frankfort tells us that the roots of Egyptian unity go all the way back to the distant past. He says that the population of the Nile Valley was homogeneous physically and culturally, as much as any large group can ever be. He used the evidence from fauna and flint tools that suggest that the inhabitants descended in early neolithic times from surrounding desert plateaus, and argues that the physique of the inhabitants of the valley from the delta deep down into Nubia remains the same from predynastic to late historical time. These Africans shared a common material culture in predynastic times. There are indications that the material culture extended even into Libya and reached the Red Sea in the east. The features of their language and their ethnological resemblances connect the ancient Egyptians firmly with the Hamitic speaking peoples of east Africa, according to Frankfort. It seems that the Pharaonic civilizations arose on this northeast African Hamitic substratum. So for Frankfurt, the prehistorical inhabitants of the Nile Valley possessed a common spiritual culture as a correlate of the homogenous physical and archaeological remains.

Of course, we are all familiar with the fact that the very first unification of the two lands was initiated from the south. John Jackson has said that Egypt's first golden age was actually started by an invasion from Ethiopia. He quotes Flinders Petrie as saying that a conqueror from Sudan founded the Third Dynasty, and many entirely new ideas entered Kemet (Egypt) at this time. This new movement culminated in the vast schemes of Khufu, who was a dominating personality and builder of the first true pyramid. According to Jackson, with Khufu the lines of Egyptian growth were established and the course of events became the subject of written records.

And it is Yosef ben-Jochannan who often cites the records from the Papyrus of Hunefer where the Egyptians themselves announced that their home was to the south at the "source" of the Nile near the foothills of the "Mountains of the Moon" (or Mt. Kilimanjaro).

Clearly what we are getting is the picture of highly developed civilized behavior long before Egypt began to the south of Egypt. For example, hieroglyphic writing existed long before the First Dynasty in Egypt. Further, the hard evidence from such great monuments as the great "Sphinx" of Giza (or as Africans called it, Hor-Em-Aket), indicates that it was much older than the pyramids and probably much older than Egypt as a nation.

According to John Jackson, the Egyptians made their first appearance on the stage of history, somewhere between 8,000 and 10,000 years before Christ. He felt that this date should not be considered excessive, and cites as evidence the fact that the ancient statue now called the Great Sphinx was estimated by another French Egyptologist, Professor Pierre Hippolyte Boussac, to be at least 10,000 years old. Jackson cites the evidence from an inscription of the Pharaoh Khufu, who built the Great Pyramid, who tells how a temple adjoining the Sphinx, which had been buried under the sand for generations, was actually discovered by chance in his reign. The inscription that Jackson referred to was in the Boulak Museum in Cairo, and says that the Sphinx was much older than the

Great Pyramid, and that the giant statue actually required repairs during the reign of Khufu.

John Jackson tells us that the Edfu texts is an important document On the early history of the Nile Valley. This text was found in the temple of Horus at Edfu and gives an account of the origins of the ancient Egyptian civilization According to that account, civilization was brought to the north of Egypt from the south by a band of invaders under the leadership of a king named Horus, who was later deified and ultimately became the Egyptian Christ. The followers of this king Horus were called Blacksmiths because they had iron implements. According to Jackson, this early culture had been traced back to Somaliland, although it may have originated in the Great Lakes region of central Africa. In Somaliland, Jackson says, there are ruins of buildings constructed with dressed stones showing the close resemblance of the architecture of Somaliland to that of early Egypt. And then Jackson cites Professor Arthur G. Brodeur who speculated that the ancestors of the southern Egyptians came originally from that region, and that they entered the Nile Valley through Nubia and brought with them a well-developed civilization. That migration had occurred somewhere in the distant past before 5,000 BC.[6]

Looking again to evidence for a southern origin of Egyptian civilization, we must note the recent evaluation of material from archaeological digs taken just before the waters behind the Aswan Dam flooded Nubia. Margaret Drower points out that south of Abu-Simbel there were some conical mounds at Ballana, and on the opposite bank of Qostol. Excavations were made, and more mounds were examined, all with similar results. Eventually the actual graves of the kings were found, and they were described by Drower as "tall men, with Negroid features."[7]

And so it is very recently that establishment Egyptologists such as Bruce Williams at the University of Chicago, have begun to say that Egyptian civilization had a parent, perhaps more than one, and that the most likely candidate for direct parenthood is the Nubian civilization of Ta-Seti to the south of Egypt.[8]

Barbara Mertz has said that as far as she knew there was never a blond queen of Egypt. She mentions that one woman was believed to be blond or red-headed, but later evidence showed that she was actually wearing a yellow headcloth. There were never any other candidates for that description. What emerges clearly from the evidence is that "indigenous Black Africans" developed the whole Nile Valley, including Egyptian civilization.[9]

Culture

Cheikh Diop's concept of cultural unity is very important to us. It is a powerful explanatory construct, and it helps to guide empirical investigation. The concept of cultural unity helps us to link Egypt (East Africa) with the rest of Africa and the intercontinental diaspora. It cannot be emphasized too strongly that we are not limited to mere speculation on these points, as Diop's book on the cultural unity of Black Africa has demonstrated. There is abundant evidence for the cultural unity, both in antiquity and in the present.[13]

In West Africa, according to DeGramont, ethnologists who studied the Bozos say that the tiny island of fisherman actually came from Egypt 5,000 years ago and settled in the Niger bin. They have not moved or changed their ways since that time. These ways seem to be derived from the river people of the Nile, under the early dynasties, as is the language of the Bozos. The Bozos have maintained their spiritual independence from Islam and Christianity, and have kept alive traditions that originated before the fall of the city of Memphis in ancient Egypt. According to DeGramont, watching a Bozo ceremony with the dancers' heads covered with animal masks is like watching living hieroglyphics.[11]

I must emphasize that it was the "empirical" evidence that led DeGramont to such a conclusion. Similarly, the study of voodoo religion in West Africa reveals its similarity to ancient Egyptian religion, and to its offspring, European religion.

Maya Deren has said that the role of the mysteries named Legba correspond to those of the Egyptian Hermes, celebrated in Hellenistic culture. Since so many of their symbols are identical, the analogy can hardly be dismissed either as incidental or as a consequence of what anthropologists call "convergence." According to Deren, the similarities comprise a total image of the god and are furthermore symbolically consistent, even when rendered in the rites and myths, and as interpreted by "qualified Houngans." "In any case, no matter what the explanation may be, the parallel between the myth and cult in contemporary Haiti, and those not only of 17th century Africa but over antiquity are undeniable and abundant."[12]

We can look at another culture in West Africa. DeGramont in his book, *The Strong Brown God*, was fascinated by the ancient West African city of Djenne, a companion city to Timbuktu in Mali, which he called an "African Venice."

He says that when the river was high, it could only be reached by boat, protected by water. Djenne was said to have resisted 99 sieges in the course of its history. According to DeGramont, if Pharaoh woke up in Djenne, he would think he was in ancient Egypt. They have clay houses and decorated facades with trapezoidal porticos and pointed glens and columns in low relief. The mosque that he saw was as large as a gothic cathedral, and was inspiring in its use of "primitive materials on a monumental scale." The people of Djenne are fishermen and traders, attached to their city and seldom leaving it, said DeGramont.[13]

It is amazing how often scholars who wish to understand ancient Egyptian culture, especially its religion, are driven to the study of other Black African populations who are descendants of ancient Egyptians or who descended from a common source as the ancient Egyptians. This was expressed explicitly by E. A. Wallace Budge and also by Henri Frankfort in his book, *Kingship and the Gods*, as he states that there are two ways to penetrate behind the words of the text. First there were alive at the time in Africa subgroups of people who, according to Frankfort, were the survivors of that great east African substratum out of which Egyptian culture arose. Among other things that Frankfort sought to study was how deeply the divine nature of kings affects both the ruler and his subjects.

Once again, the essential point to be made here is there is an overwhelming abundance of "empirical" data to show both the historical and contemporary cultural connection between East Africa, including Egypt, and its continental and intercontinental diaspora. [14]

We need the linguistic terms from Noam Chomsky of "surface structure" and "deep structure" to explain the apparent diversity that exists throughout the African continent and, indeed throughout the diaspora. Foreign explorers have been fascinated by what they considered to be significant differences among Africans, differences in the physiognomy of peoples, in ways of worship, etc. However, they have been attracted to the surface structural manifestations. Clearly, an impartial investigation based upon empirical facts will demonstrate, as Cheikh Anta Diop and others such as Robert Thompson and Janheinz Jahn have done, that cultural unity is far more significant than is superficial diversity.[15]

If time permitted, it would be instructive to examine the records of African neighbors in what we now call the Middle East, in Asia, and in Europe. In doing this, we would see that during the early part of development of civilization the source of civil ideas was almost completely African. Three thousand years of unbroken development along the Nile Valley positioned Africans to have a major influence on the world, an influence that still continues.

Education
This brings me to my major task, which is to attempt to sharpen our picture of Egyptian education. We are hampered in our attempt to learn about ancient Egyptian education not only by the widespread loss of documentary materials, the destruction of social institutions and civilizations, including their library records, and years of prejudice and neglect; but also by the fact that some of the most important parts of the educational process were conducted in "secret." Much of the tradition was passed on orally to the prepared initiate.

We are indebted to such writers as George G. M. James, R.A. Schwaller DeLubicz, Robert Thompson, Albert Churchward, and others for helping to unveil some of this "secret" tradition. George James studied the reports of the establishment historians and collected fragments of accepted information, placing them in a new perspective. R. A. Schwaller DeLubicz studied the ruins of the Temple at Luxor and Egyptian symbolic writing and thought. Thompson studied cultural patterns of existing Bantu groups, especially their religious practices. Churchward studied the evolution of the use of symbols from their source in the Great Lakes region and Nile Valley to the dispersion of the use of those symbols through the world. What I'm trying to show once again is that there is an empirical base for emerging descriptions of an ancient Egyptian educational system. [16]

As we look at the ancient Egyptian cultural patterns, we see that there was not only a cultural unity among apparently diverse groups of people. There was also an essential unity within the culture that was reflected in the intimate and harmonious ties between and among education, politics, economics, religion, and so forth. It would make no sense whatsoever to consider the educational process apart from a deep study of the worldview and religion of ancient Egypt. Ancient Egyptians lived close to nature, basically as a sedentary population under highly favorable environmental conditions. They were in a position to make repeated observations of natural processes over thousands of years. As clearly as anywhere else in the world, it can be seen in the Nile Valley that nature has regular processes of birth, growth, aging, death, decay, and rebirth. All nature seems to tell the same story. The behavior of the Mother Nile was cyclical. Within general limits, this behavior could be predicted. Indeed, the successful predictions of its rise and fall determined the degree to which its bountiful resources could be exploited.

The skies were almost always clear, providing an unparalleled opportunity for long-term systematic observation of the behavior of heavenly bodies. The enduring repetitive cycles obviously made a profound impression upon the ancient dwellers on the Nile. The Nile River in Egypt is but a thin ribbon in a vast land with a full population. From its beginning, Egypt was crowded and provided the basis for easy transportation up and down the smooth Nile River. Transportation on the Nile was assisted by the winds that blow from the north to the south, enabling travelers to take a current downstream to the north and to return to the south aided by the light breezes.

The ancient Egyptians observed movement, change, and life itself. What seems to have impressed them most was the degree to which a grand design appeared to be evident throughout the universe, enabling one who studied any part of the universe to understand the rest of it through the play of analogies. For example, the Nile was a river on the earth and the Milky Way was a "river in the sky." The observations of plant and animal life provided the opportunity to reflect on human life as well as with cycles of birth, growth, death, decay, and rebirth.

A major technology arose in the northern end of the Nile Valley. That technology is reflected in thousands of temples, tombs, pyramids and in writings and scientific developments and discoveries. The observational technology that produced the first zodiac such as that seen in the Temple of Dendera or in the Tomb of Seti I in the Valley of the Kings at Waset (Luxor to the Arabs and Thebes to the Greeks), gives evidence of a long line of development. The construction of the Great Pyramid at Giza, attributed to Pharaoh Khufu, with its 2.2 million limestone rocks averaging two tons each, some weighing as much as forty tons, giving ample evidence of a high level of technical development. This is especially true when we realize that until the present time, no one appears to have been able to repeat the feat.

But given these and many other examples of high level technical developments in Egypt, what is important is not so much the level of technical development as the "philosophical orientation of the users of the technology." The purpose of technology is to develop a greater understanding of man's relationship to nature and mankind's place in nature. This is in stark contrast to some contemporary expressions of technology. Today, we seem to seek technical developments for the sole purpose of "exploiting" the environment for personal gains in wealth and power. Sometimes the goal of technology is

271

expressed merely as one of helping people or nations to know, but toward "what end?"

At this point we need to return to George G. M. James who has given an excellent summary description of the Egyptian Mystery System. The ultimate aim of education in Egypt was for a person to become "one with God" or to "become like God." The path to the development of godlike qualities was through the development of virtue. A person was seen as being essentially spiritual whose essence was housed in a finite body. It was the spirit that had an eternal existence. The capacity of a person to become godlike was determined by the degree to which the person was able to overcome certain natural impediments of the body. These were character flaws, and virtue was the antidote to character flaws. But virtue could be achieved only through special study and effort. According to James, the following 10 virtues were sought by students in the ancient Egyptian Mystery System:

1. Control of thought
2. Control of action
3. Steadfastness of purpose
4. Identity with the spiritual life
5. Evidence of having a mission in life
6. Evidence of a call to spiritual orders
7. Freedom from resentment under persecution and wrong
8. Confidence in the power of the master as teacher
9. Confidence in one's own ability to learn
10. Readiness or preparedness for initiation 17

Even a brief study of this list of 10 virtues reveals just how different it is in character from typical educational objectives with which most of us are familiar. In *Stolen Legacy*, James goes into great detail to explain and to interpret the meaning of these 10 virtues.

George G. M. James also tells us that the center of the higher education system in ancient Egypt was located at the ancient Egyptian city of Waset, which means "the septer," after the town or name of province from which this small city developed. It was sometimes referred to as the city of Amun, which was the name of the great god. Apparently, Waset was so important that it was sometimes simply referred to as "The City." Waset was later given the name Thebes by European invaders, and after that, the name Luxor, by the Arab invaders. Various sections of the city of Waset had their own names. One section of the city was called Ipet Isut the translation, "most select of places." Later populations would refer to it as Karnak where a great temple now stands. Another part of Waset was called the Southern Ipet or sanctuary. Later, populations would refer to this section as Luxor, the name by which the whole city is now called.

It was at Waset (Thebes or Luxor) where the oldest records of a university headquarters existed. We may think of this as the main branch. Speculation places the age of this headquarters as far back as 3,000 BC. There was another "grand lodge" in lower or northern Egypt dedicated to God in the name of Osiris. It was called the Osiriaca. This lodge had branches in other parts of the Egyptian sphere of influence. According to George James, several were located as follows: the Ionian Temple at Dydma, Euclid's Lodge at Megara, Pythagora's Lodge at Cortona, and the Orphic Temple at Delphi.

We begin to get some inkling of the high level of esteem for the Egyptian civilization and all that the Greeks and Romans felt for it by a review of the activities of the Europeans when confronted with African civilization. It is hard to account for the behavior of European conquerors of Kemet except to note that they must have felt themselves to be in the presence of a superior civilization. They tried to imitate it.

Jill Kamil remarks that Ptolemaic rule was noted for its architectural activity, and that the Greeks tried in every way to add to the splendor of national buildings after one of the Egyptian priests had told Alexander that he was the son of the god Amon, and that he should revere him. The Romans also repaired ruins and built temples in the traditional style, but it was a losing battle, since the past could not be recaptured. Thebes, according to Kamil, could hardly hide its well-worn wrinkles; a time-weathered quality lay over the metropolis.

Not only were buildings copied, European kings and people joined the African religions in Africa and in Europe. It was this "African religion" of Isis, Osiris, Horus, and Amen (Amon or Amun) that remained one of the major religions of Europe until the national government of Rome installed Christianity as the state religion, after the Council of Nicea, nearly three hundred years after the death of Christ.

Parenthetically, we can illustrate at this point the close connection between education and religion. We can also show some antecedents of western religion. In doing this, we take our material directly from the remains of the monuments themselves, in this case, the Temple of Luxor.

As Kamil states, the temple contains a birth room, and in that birth room on the left-hand wall in three rows is the story of the conception and birth of Amenhotep. In one row, the god Khnum, is making the baby Amenhotep and his guardian spirit on a potter's wheel while the goddess Isis sits in the presence of Amon. In the middle row, the ibis-headed god, Jehuti, God of Wisdom, leads Amon to the queen's bedchamber. Here, Amon approaches her in order to beget the child whom Khnum has already molded. After the delivery, Amon will stand with the child in his arms in the presence of the goddesses Hathor and Mut. Shown in the top row are the infant king being suckled, the infant king's guardian spirits, and his presentation to the god Amon by Horus. Horus promises him "millions of years like Ra." [18]

Here we have then -in the Eighteenth Dynasty- a visual record of the virgin birth of Amen-Hotep. We find the same scene portrayed in the mortuary temple of Hatshepsut. Once again, it is in the birth colonnade of that temple.

The birth colonnade corresponds to the Punt Colonnade. It was constructed to allay concern about the legitimacy of Queen Hatshepsut's claim to the throne. Here we see the theory of her divine origin: the ram-headed Khnum is shaping

Hatshepsut and her Ka on the potter's wheel, while being instructed by Amon; it is Amon who has impregnated the queen's mother, Ahmose, with Hatshep Sut.

The careful listener may wonder why we skipped a period in the Twelfth Dynasty over as far as the Eighteenth Dynasty. It must be noted there that during this period of time, the government of Egypt was in the hands of invading kings, the Hyksos from Asia. However, their reign is less important than it might be for a very simple reason. They seem to have had little to offer to Kemet.

As Elizabeth Riefstahl has observed, the Hyksos had very little culture of their own, and as a result they readily adopted the Egyptian arts and customs and to some extent even the religion of the Egyptians. The new Hyksos rulers took over the titles of the Egyptian kings, and like those kings referred to themselves as "sons of Re," the ancient Egyptian solar god from whom all pharaohs claimed descent. Riefstahl also mentions that some scant remains show that the Hyksos added to and embellished some Egyptian temples, while they destroyed others. Through what little survives from the Hyksos period in the way of art and architecture, we see a decline in skill. What papyri from that period remain, however, show that learning in the temples continued undiminished.[19]

Certain authors have looked at the initiation system that still exists in West Africa. It is good to do this because that system is a direct outgrowth of the more ancient initiation system that was utilized in the Nile Valley. Contemporary information and historical study of the initiation in West Africa reveals that the process operated in the following way. According to Pierre Erny in his book, *Childhood and Cosmos*, the following things were included in the initiation process:

1. The initiates were physically segregated from the regular activity of daily life.
2. They retreated from their familiar environment to an environment that enabled them to get more directly in touch with nature. This symbolized a move from the infantile situation into a situation that would allow for more maturity.
3. The initiates joined with other initiates of the same age and shared their lives in common, since the common living experience was also a common learning experience.
4. The initiates were separated from their parents in addition to being separated from the large community.
5. The initiates had to renounce all that recalls the past.
6. The initiates were then taught by the old men and old women of the village or town.
7. The initiates frequently went nude or wore clothes made of grass to symbolize the clothes of the first men or women.
8. The initiates underwent purification baths.
9. During the course of initiation, a number of tests of audacity, courage, fasting, flogging, hazing, mutations, scarifications were conducted. (The purpose of the test was to give the opportunity for the initiates to demonstrate a refusal to take life as it is given as a way of opening the mind to beauty, joy and ecstasy).

10. Initiates learned a new and secret language.
11. Initiates were given new names.
12. The initiation processes symbolize a rebirth. The initiation process included a number of exercises and things to be learned such as physical and military training, songs, dances, how to handle sacred things such as math and tools.[20]

Dadisi Sonyika summarizes the initiation process into seven steps. [21]

1. Separation
2. Location in a sacred place
3. Symbolic death and burial
4. Testing or revelation
5. Testing
6. Resurrection (symbolic)
7. Reintroduction of the initiate into the larger community

It can be seen from the study of Isha DeLubicz's work, *Her-Bak*, that the West African initiation process, as described by Sonyika and Erny, is quite congruent with the initiations that are described by DeLubicz, based upon the study of documents, carvings, and paintings from ancient Egypt. At its base, initiation is a comprehensive education system. In addition to the narrowly vocational aims one can discern in the ancient Egyptian and ancient African educational system, the goals were the following:

* Unity of the person, unity of the tribe, and unity with nature

- The development of social responsibility
- The development of character
- The development of spiritual power [22]

It was these higher aims that drove the educational process. Vocational skill training was merely a small part of the whole process.

In the ancient Egyptian educational system, little thought seems to have been given to the question of the "inept intellectual capacity" of a person. Much more attention was given to the character as an impediment or as a facilitator of educational development. While learning was obviously done by individuals, the picture that we get of the method used is that it was a collective rather than an individual effort. The educational process was designed in such a way that it seemed to be a true rebirth that occurs through successive series of personal and social transformations.

Initiates were deeply immersed in a comprehensive process. It was an interactive process. There were interactions among students and interactions between student and teacher. The process was full including much time for stories, examination of signs, symbols, the use of proverbs, the use of songs, dances, and so forth -all combined to convey values and to convey a special view of the world. Teachers or "masters" modeled the behavior that they expected the initiates to learn. The masters were alert and in a position to react to and to nurture the direct experience of students in order that they could learn higher-level lessons.

At its base the educational process was a religious process in the broadest sense of that word. The entire living environment was organized and constructed to the smallest detail as a teaching environment. The architecture was symbolic to the smallest detail. Even the layout of buildings within a city carried symbolic meaning. Clothing that was worn, names that were given, everything had multilevels of meaning. This indicated a full-time commitment to the goal of personal transformation through education.

The best single description of education in ancient Egypt is given by Isha Schwaller DeLubic. In two books, she presents her findings through the use of an initiate, *Her-Bak*. DeLubicz and her husband, R. A. Schwaller DeLubicz, spent nearly [15] years on a detailed study of the Temple of Luxor- and its environs. R. A. Schwaller DeLubicz has written numbers of important books on that work. In *The Temple in Man* and, *Symbol and the Symbolic*, DeLubiczs tried to "enter into the mentality of the Egyptians" by an in-depth study of their records, both written and archaeological. In Isha Schwaller DeLubicz's books, almost all narrative is supported by illustrations of temple carvings, drawings, relief carvings, and building configurations, primarily at Luxor and Karnak Temples in Waset.

It must be kept in mind that both Luxor Temple and Karnak Temple are built on the site of older temples! For example, the "White Chapel," the oldest part of the Eighteenth Dynasty temple at Karnak, is a reconstruction from fragments that were made by crushing the old chapel. The small places were then used as "seeds" from which the new Temple of Amon would grow. The fragments were found in the third Pylon of the Temple of Amom. The older temple, the White Chapel, was built by Sesostris during the Twelfth Dynasty (1950 BC.) as an offering to the great Black God Min. Both represent extensions of religious and educational practices that were known from the beginnings of Egyptian civilization.[23]

While no one can be certain of all the details of ancient Egyptian culture, one must respect writers such as the DeLubiczs who do not stray far from primary sources, as best they can be understood.

The Aims of Egyptian Education

We must keep in mind that the Egyptians made no separation between "church and state," or for that matter, between religion and life. They lived a totally religious life, just as is the case with traditional African religions today. Therefore, education was religious at its base.

The lower education system, no matter how unstructured, allowed for a natural progress along a path that reached certain choice points. Having started along a path of advanced education, a student could reach the major choice of his or her life, according to Isha Schwaller DeLubicz, the "choice between leadership and high positions or knowledge and wisdom." The student who chose ambition also chose limits. It was said that "ambition does to intuition what weevils do to wheat." On the other hand, for one who was able to sacrifice personal ambition, the act of sacrifice was said to "defend consciousness against the deadly effect of the search for satisfaction." For that person, the path leading to wisdom was open. The initiate could reach the outer Temple or "Peristyle" where "utilitarian" knowledge was mastered. However, once admitted to the Inner Temple, the initiate learned about symbols and came to know him or herself. Undoubtedly, as George G. M. James, has so clearly shown, Greek students of the African "mysteries" came to respect this goal, "man know thyself," which has been falsely attributed to Socrates, the Greek latecomer of dynastic times. The highest aim of Egyptian education was for one to become godlike through the revision of one's own "Neter," of how God is revealed in the person.[24]

Methodology in Egyptian Pedagogy

Serious education began by putting the initiate on the path of observation of nature. Usually the initiate would be assigned to a master as an apprentice. But the purpose of the apprenticeship was for the student to learn the laws of matter (materials). It was the knowledge of these laws that separated the master craftsman from a mere worker. So the "observation" of nature was really a participatory observation. Revealed in any craft were nature's laws. During the apprenticeship, the initiate was confronted with problems of conscience. This would allow for the development of a sense of responsibility and judgment. At the end of a successful apprenticeship, the initiate was offered the chance to choose between the two paths, "political power" and "wisdom."

Heavy use was made of proverbs, songs, and stories. Direct or symbolic lessons were taught through these. It was the fundamental belief in the unity or interconnectedness of all things that made the use of analogies such a powerful pedagogical tool "for above is exalted by below." The use of proverbs and analogies permeates African and African diasporan culture today.[25]

Parenthetically, it is interesting that racist psychologists claim that Black people are not capable of "Level II thinking," the kind of abstract thinking that is reflected in proverbs and analogies. To the contrary, this is our strong suit. It is the mismatch in experiential content between such psychologists and African Americans that causes them to miss the extensive use of proverbs and analogies among us.

The African reader of ancient Egyptian writings will find familiar methodology in the use of such things as the sayings of Ptahotep, Fifth Dynasty, (circa 2350 BC.)

> Do not be arrogant because of your knowledge, but confer
> with the ignorant man as with the learned, for the limit of skill
> has not been attained, and there is no craftsman who has
> [fully] acquired his mastery. Good speech is more hidden than
> malachite, yet is found in the possession of women slaves at
> the milestones.[26]

Then there are the teachings of Kagemni that are contained along with the teachings of Ptahotep in the "Prisse Papyrus." The teachings of Ptahotep say such things as the following:

...The submissive man prospers, the moderate man is praised, the tent is open for the silent man, and the place of the contented man is wide. Do not talk [freely], for the flint knives are sharpened against the one who strays from the road; there is no hastening, except in deed against his misdeed.[27]

The instructions of Amenomope are estimated to have been written during the Eighteenth Dynasty just before the Amarna period, possibly during the reign of Amen Hotep III. These sayings have close parallels to later Hebrew Scriptures in the book of Proverbs.

The hot-headed man in the temple is like a tree grown indoors; only for a moment does it put forth roots. It reaches its end in the carpentry shop, it is floated away from its place, or fire is its funeral pyre. The truly temperate man sets himself apart. He is like a tree grown in a sunlit field. But it flourishes, it doubles its yield, it stands before its owner; its fruit is something sweet, its shade is pleasant; and it reaches its end as a statue. [28]

When we look at the "Memphite Theology," writings that are estimated to have been composed at the beginning of the pyramid age, we see something remarkably similar to the method of Karl Marx, the dialectic, complete with the use of contradictions. In the Memphite Theology, writings on stone at Memphis in Egypt, we find the doctrine of the four elements and the four qualities. This "law of opposites" (the relationship between pairs of elements) sets up the conditions under which creativity occurs. The Pyramid texts also use the principle of opposites in the description of the African "pantheon," or place of "the Gods." Like the later Greek and Roman copies, there was an Ennead -a pantheon of nine Gods, or more correctly, a diagram of nine aspects of the one Great Neter (God).[29]

Egyptian Aspects of God

Atum	Shu (Air)	Tefnut (Moisture)
Geb (Earth)		Nut (Sky)
Osirus	Isis Seth	Nephthys

In early times the Sun-God had his own family of gods that was also the supreme council of the gods. This group, which had its chief center at the Temple of the Sun at Heliopolis, was the Ennead, "the Nine," consisting of four interrelated couples surmounted by one common ancestor. This Ennead or "Nine" may be placed in contrast to the "Eight," for "Eight" comprised elements of cosmic disorder, whereas the "Nine" contained only progressive steps of cosmic order: air and moisture, earth and sky, the beginnings on earth.

The Content of Egyptian Pedagogy

I have already referred to George G. M. James' list of curriculum content. Those courses -grammar, rhetoric, logic, arithmetic, astronomy, geometry and music - were the liberating or liberal arts. They supported the quest of the initiate for the highest form of self-knowledge. The initiate would study for "form," "name," "place," and "symbol" of things. Having done that, it was believed that the "function" of things would be revealed.

The important thing to remember is that "nature itself," the environment or the person, was the basic content for study. In addition, the study of nature was facilitated by the study of symbols, stories, proverbs, songs, puzzles, rhythm, and the sacred writings of the Mdw Ntr (hieroglyphics). These studies also gave insight into human nature, which was as shown before, merely the study of one aspect of nature.

In the final analysis, the ancient Egyptian sought MAAT (truth, justice, and order). To be more correct, I should say that they sought to become one with MAAT, the cosmic order.

The window to what was a well-developed education system is through ancient Kemet. Even though the best records in antiquity are found in Kemet, the picture is not yet complete. Suffice it to say that ancient Kemet was an African culture and it shared then, and shares now, in the greater cultural unity of the African continent and in the diaspora of ancient African people.

A careful study and reconstruction of this aspect of our African past can guide the reconstruction and development of educational aims, methods, and content appropriate to the children of the sun. As Gerald Massey has said, "Truth is all powerful with its silent power/if only whispered and never heard aloud/But working secretly almost unseen, except in some excommunicated book/Truth is like lightning with its errand done before you hear the thunder."[30]

Endnotes

1. Diop, 1978.
2. Churchward, 1978.
3. Frankfort, 1969.
4. Jackson, 1974.
5. Ben-Jochannan, 1988.
6. Jackson, 1974.
7. Drower, 1970.
8. Williams, 1980.
9. Mertz, 1978.
10. Diop, 1978.
11. DeGramont, 1977.
12. Deren, 1951.
13. DeGramont, 1977.
14. Frankfort, 1969.
15. Diop, 1978; Thompson, 1981; Jahn, 1961.
16. James, 1976; de Lubicz, 1977; Thompson, 1981.
17. James, 1976.
18. Kamil, 1976.
19. Riefstahl, 1964.

20. Erny, 1968.
21. Sonyinka, 1984.
22. Stierlin, 1978.
23. Ibid.
24. James, 1976.
25. Reed, 1978.
26. Simpson, 1972.
27. Ibid.
28. Wilson, 1956.
29. Lichteim, 1975; James, 1976.
30. Massey, 1994.

References

ben-Jochannan, Yosef. [1971] 1988. *Africa: Mother of Western Civilization.* Baltimore, MD: Black Classic Press.

Churchward, Albert. (1913) 1978. *Signs and Symbols of Primordial Man.* Westport, CN: Greenwood Press.

DeGramont, Sanche. 1977. *The Strong Brown God: The Story of the Niger River.* Boston, MA: Houghton Mifflin.

De Lubicz, R. A. Schwaller. 1977. *The Temple in Man.* Brooline, Mass.: Autumn Press.

Deren, Maya. 1951. *Divine Horsemen: The Voodoo Gods of Haiti.* New York, N.Y.: Delta.

Diop, Cheikh Anta. 1978. *The Cultural Unity of Africa.* Chicago, IL: Third World Press.

Drower, Margaret. 1970. *Nubia: A Drowning Land.* New York, N.Y.: Atheneum.

Erny, Pierre. 1968. *Childhood and Cosmos.* New York, N.Y.: Black Orpheus Press.

Frankfort, Henri. 1969. *Kinship and the Gods: A Study of Ancient Near Eastern Religion as the Integration of Society and Nature.* Chicago, IL: University of Chicago Press.

Jackson, John. 1974. *Introduction to African Civilizations.* Secaucus, NJ: Citadel Press.

James, George G. M. (1954) 1976. *Stolen Legacy.* San Francisco, CA: Julian Richardson Associates.

Janhn, Janheiz. 1961. *Muntu: The New African Culture.* New York, N.Y.: Grove Press.

Kamil, Jill. 1976. *Luxor: A Guide to Ancient Thebes.* New York, N.Y.: Longman.

Lichteim, Miriam. 1975. *Ancient Egyptian Literature.* Berkeley, CA: University of California Press.

Massey, Gerald. (1881) 1994. *Books of the Beginnings.* 2 vols. Baltimore, MD: Black Classic Press.

Mertz, Barbara. 1978. *Redland, Blackland: Daily Life in ancient Kemet.* New York, N.Y.: Dodd, Mead & Co.

Thompson, Robert & Cornet, J. 1981. *Four Moments of the Sun: Kongo Art in Two Worlds.* Washington, D.C.: National Gallery of Art.

Reed, Bika. 1978. *Rebel in the soul.* New York, N.Y.: Inner Traditions International, Ltd.

Riefstahl, Elizabeth. 1964. *Thebes in the Time of Amunhotep III.* Norman, OK: University of Oklahoma Press.

Simpson, William. 1972. *The Literature of Ancient Egypt.* New Haven, CT: Yale University Press.

Sonyinka, Dadisi. 1984. Initiation. Paper presented at the first Annual Egyptian Studies Conference in Los Angeles, on African Education Systems.

Stierlin, Henri. 1978. *The World of the Pharaohs.* New York, N.Y.: Sunflower.

Williams, Robert & Mitchell, H. (1980). The Testing Game. *Black Psychology.* Jones, R. (ed.). New York, N.Y.: Harper & Row.

Wilson, John. 1956. *The culture of Ancient Egypt.* Chicago, IL: University of Chicago Press.

INDEX

213, 223, 233, 234, 271
Thompson, R. 42, 52, 120, 128, 214, 216, 225, 229, 230, 231, 268, 277, 279
Thonssen, L. 145
Thuthmosis IV 236
Till, E. 154, 160, 161
Till Mobley, M. 154
Time
    linear 117, 211, 219
    cyclical 117, 205, 219
Toldson, I. J. 111, 116, 124, 128, 216, 223, 229, 230, 231
Tollefson, J. 205, 212
Toms, F. 187, 196
Towa, Marcien 17, 34
Toynbee, A. 235
traditional Africa, 57, 120, 121, 123, 140, 184, 185, 187, 195, 198, 214, 215, 217, 274
Traylor, E. 103
triumphalism, 50
Tubman, H. 154, 177, 220
Turner, B. 10
Turner, J. 82, 105
Two Lands, The 234
Tylor, E. 219, 229, 231

U
UCLA, 50, 97, 231
UCLA-SNCC 99
Umfundalai, 221, 224, 226
Underground Railroad, 154, 177
UNESCO, 206, 207
Urban League, 115

V
Van Horne, W. 49
Van Sertima, I. 119, 128, 174, 179, 180, 181
Vandi, A. 52, 126
Venezki, R. 204, 212
Verner, B. 103
Voodoo (see loa) 51, 221, 278

W
Walker, A. 157, 163, 180, 238
Walker, B. 181, 183
Walker, D. 9, 260, 264
Wallace, M. 96, 158, 161, 267
Walter, R. 103, 106
Walton, O. M. 120, 128
Watt, I. 202, 203, 211
Weisborg, R. 34
Wells, I. B. 154
Welsh-Asante, K. iii, 29, 106, 213, 216, 222, 229
Welsing, F. 170, 172, 179, 181
Wesley, C. 95, 127
West, C. 40, 41, 45, 52, 92
West African Ocean, 146
Western
    social science, 129, 130, 131, 134, 135, 137
    thought, 145, 146
White
    Anglo-Saxon Protestants 156, 187
    people, 250
    race, 163, 169, 170, 178
    racism 255
    supremacy 99, 165-167, 170-177
White, J. L. 262
Whiteness 13, 29, 172, 260
Wideman, J. 237
Wigner, E. P. 121, 128
Williams, B. 268
Williams, C. 168, 183, 200, 237
Williams, D. 233
Williams, E. 183
Williams Ntiri, D. 161
Williams, R. 281
Wills, G. 96
Wilson, A. 67, 183, 200, 262
Wilson, J. 281
Wilson, W. 150
Womanism, 27, 154
Womanist, iii, 27, 103, 155, 163
Womble, M. 184, 194, 196
Woodson, C. 74, 92, 95, 126, 128,